CARTIER

1900 · 1939

JUDY RUDOE

HARRY N. ABRAMS, INC., PUBLISHERS
THE METROPOLITAN MUSEUM OF ART

This book is published in conjunction with the exhibition 'Cartier 1900–1939', held at The Metropolitan Museum of Art, New York, from April 2, 1997, through August 3, 1997, and at the British Museum, London, from October 3, 1997, through February 1, 1998. The exhibition is organised jointly by the two museums.

Library of Congress Cataloging-in-Publication Data
Rudoe, Judy.
    Cartier : 1900–1939 / Judy Rudoe.
      p.   cm.
    Catalog of an exhibition held at the British Museum, London and the Metropolitan Museum of Art, New York.
    Includes bibliographical references and index.
    ISBN 0–8109–4047–7 (clothbound) / ISBN 0–87099–780–7 (mus. pbk.)
    1. Cartier (Firm)—Exhibitions. 2. Jewelry—France—History—20th century—Exhibitions. I. Cartier (Firm) II. British Museum.
III. Metropolitan Museum of Art (New York, N.Y.) IV. Title.
NK7398.C37A4 1997
739.27'092'2—dc21   96–47813

Published in 1997 by Harry N. Abrams, Incorporated, New York, a Times Mirror Company, and The Metropolitan Museum of Art, New York

Designed by Harry Green

Printed and bound in Italy

HALF-TITLE PAGE Gem-set plaque with Chinese-style objects on a tray, set into a cigarette case in agate and enamelled gold, 1929 (see cat. 129).

TITLE PAGE Alfred Cartier and his three sons (see fig. 1).

OPPOSITE Emerald and pearl tassel necklace, 1925 (cat. 101).

CONTENTS

FOREWORD

The firm of Cartier is widely recognised as one of the world's greatest designers and manufacturers of jewellery and *objets d'art*. This exhibition is timed to coincide with the 150th anniversary of the founding of the company in Paris in 1847. In the early years of this century Cartier opened branches in London and New York, and the exhibition focuses on the first four decades, when these three historic branches were each run by one of three brothers, grandsons of the founder.

This exhibition, 'Cartier 1900-1939', will be shown at the Metropolitan Museum of Art from April to August 1997 and at the British Museum from October 1997 to February 1998. The exhibition was organised and selected jointly by staff of the two institutions, but the catalogue and the photography of the Cartier collection is the sole work of the British Museum.

The core of the exhibition is Cartier's own historic collection, assembled over the last two decades. To this has been added loan material from both public and private collections. On behalf of both institutions I wish to thank the Musée des Arts Décoratifs in Paris and the Hillwood Museum in Washington, Mr and Mrs George L. Lindemann and those private lenders who wish to remain anonymous.

Our warmest thanks must go to Cartier for lending the greater part of the exhibition and for their generous sponsorship, which made the entire project possible. This exhibition would not have taken place without the support of:

Alain Dominique Perrin, President of Cartier International

Franco Cologni, Vice-President of Cartier International

Eric Nussbaum, Director of the Cartier historic collection

Pierre Rainero, Director of International Communication

Simon Critchell, President and CEO, Cartier Inc.

Ralph Destino, Chairman of Cartier Inc.

Arnaud Bamberger, Managing Director of Cartier Ltd.

DR ROBERT G. W. ANDERSON
Director
British Museum

PREFACE

Previous exhibitions devoted to Cartier have encompassed the entire period of the firm's history, from 1847 to the present. The aim of this exhibition is to take a fresh look at a more closely defined period, from around 1900, when the firm's distinctive style becomes identifiable, to the end of the 1930s, which saw a dramatic change of style that led to a quite different aesthetic. The selection of material for the exhibition has been made jointly by myself and by J. Stewart Johnson, Consultant for Design and Architecture, Department of 20th Century Art, at the Metropolitan Museum of Art and co-curator of the exhibition. His astute eye for juxtapositions has enhanced enormously the visual excitement of the various groupings, as well as bringing clarity to the exhibition concept as a whole, and I am much indebted to him.

Confining the selection to a limited period has enabled us to concentrate on some of Cartier's most original design, making it possible to assemble significant groups of material illustrating characteristic features such as the highly acclaimed colour combinations of the 1920s and the lesser-known and surprisingly avant-garde pieces made before the First World War. In addition to fine jewellery we have included the accessories for which Cartier is justly famous - the cigarette and vanity cases, which display both mastery of surface ornament and consummate skill in construction - as well as a group of objects in the Russian style, executed in enamelled gold or carved hardstones. These objects were intended for the same clientele as those made by Fabergé; indeed, when Fabergé closed his London shop in 1917 many of his clients, who were often clients of Cartier as well, continued to buy similar items from Cartier.

The restricted period covered has also made it possible to focus in greater detail on those aspects of Cartier's production that have particular relevance to the collections of the British Museum and the Metropolitan Museum of Art. Thus, several sections of the exhibition, including both objects and designs, demonstrate the genius with which motifs from ancient Egypt, Persia, India, China and Japan were adapted by Cartier to suit contemporary taste. These objects are, for the most part, no mere essays in antiquarianism but a reworking of ancient designs in a modern idiom.

There is much that we have omitted, and we do not claim to have made a fully representative selection of the whole range of Cartier's production. Our criterion throughout was visual interest: having identified our themes, we selected objects to illustrate and elucidate them. Thus, for example, Cartier's celebrated mystery clocks will be found as examples of the Chinese or Japanese style, while their tiny baguette watches appear as examples of diamond jewellery between the wars.

The design drawings in the final section, on the other hand, have been selected to add a further dimension by documenting pieces that were not available for a variety of reasons - either because they were later broken up (for example, the stunning creations made for the 1925 Paris Exhibition) or because they were never actually made. This section has benefited greatly from the inclusion of a group of working designs by Charles Jacqueau,

Cartier's outstanding designer in Paris from the 1910s onwards, many of which have never been shown before. The study of this group, which has a direct provenance from Jacqueau, has enabled the attribution to him of many other designs as well as objects, in the Cartier collection and elsewhere.

This exhibition would not have been possible without the co-operation of many people at Cartier. Our greatest debt is to Eric Nussbaum, Director of the Cartier historic collection, and to the archivists in each of the three original branches of the firm - in Paris, Betty Jais; in London, Teresa Buxton and her successor, Dorothy Bosomworth; and in New York, Anne Holbach. Eric Nussbaum has been responsible for building up the Cartier collection since the early 1980s: his achievement is a remarkable one and he has guided us through the collection, offering advice and support at all stages of the project. Cartier's private archive has exceptionally been opened to us for this project and we are immensely privileged to have been given access to material from all three archives that has not been exhibited or published before. Because the Paris archive is the most extensive, Betty Jais has inevitably had the lion's share of the work, but all four archivists have given unstintingly of their time and expertise.

Many other members of Cartier staff have made our lives easier. In Paris, Pierre Rainero, Director of International Communication for Cartier International, has ensured that everything ran smoothly. In Geneva, Arlette Dahan, Rafiqul Islam, Pascal Milhaud and Bernard Berger helped to make the collection available to us over long hours so that we could plan the exhibition in the limited time that we had, and answered countless questions with infinite kindness and patience. In London, we wish also to thank Terry Davidson, Director of High Jewellery, and Pilar Boxford, Communication Director, Caroline Perry and Clare Crawford; and in New York, Bonnie Selfe, Director for High Jewellery, and Gail Winston, Assistant Vice President Corporate Communication, Cartier Inc.

We would also like to thank the other lenders to this exhibition: Mr and Mrs George L. Lindemann; Evelyne Possémé at the Musée des Arts Décoratifs; Anne Odom and Liana Paredes-Arend at the Hillwood Museum in Washington; and others who wish to remain anonymous but all of whom have been unfailingly helpful.

The exhibition has been installed in each of the two institutions by their own design teams, and we wish to thank the design staff of the Metropolitan Museum of Art and the British Museum.

The preparation of the catalogue text could not have been completed in such a short time without the assistance of all those mentioned above and many others. The major source of information has been the Cartier archive. Eric Nussbaum read and commented on the entire catalogue. Betty Jais, Dorothy Bosomworth, Bonnie Selfe and Anne Holbach read and commented on the sections relating to material in their care and supplied huge quantities of information. I am deeply grateful to all of them for the time and trouble they took with such an onerous task: it is a much better book as a result.

Within each entry an attempt has been made to uncover the sources of inspiration, where relevant. This has involved the help of many colleagues and other scholars working in different fields from my own. Robert Skelton, Michael Spink and Benjamin Zucker have all provided information about carved Indian emeralds and Indian sources in general. I also wish to thank Susan Stronge, Anthony North and Richard Edgcumbe at the Victoria & Albert Museum. At the British Museum, Carol Andrews has supplied information on Egyptian sources; Richard Blurton, Sheila Canby, Victor Harris, Jessica Harrison-Hall, Carol Michaelson, Rachel Ward and Michael Willis have given information on Indian, Islamic, Chinese and Japanese sources, and Christopher Spring on African sources. David Thompson has answered many horological queries.

Many others have given advice and information. I wish to thank Jane Adlin, Clare Le

Corbeiller and Jared Goss at the Metropolitan Museum of Art; also Ralph Esmerian, Harry Fane, Marie-Noël de Gary, Henry Ginsburg, Marie-Rose Grollier-Jacqueau, Fanny Jacqueau Deshayes, Nigel Israel, Geoffrey Munn, Penny Proddow, Katharine Purcell, Alexandra Rhodes and James Robinson.

Special thanks must go to Charlotte Gere, who provided many of the contemporary quotes from memoirs and biographies cited in the catalogue; to Imogen Loke, who assisted with the preliminary research and documentation for the project and spent much time at the British Library Newspaper Library to find many of the fashion plates and portraits reproduced here; and to Daniel Davies, who assisted with the preparation of the text for publication, corrected proofs and assembled much biographical information on Cartier clients.

The photography of the Cartier collection pieces, and thus the greater part of the photography in this catalogue, was undertaken by David Gowers and John Williams of the British Museum, who worked extremely hard in Geneva and London to produce stunning results. Photographs of comparative material have come from a great variety of sources, and I wish to thank John Fasal for allowing me to use the photograph of Sir Yadavindra Singh, Maharajah of Patiala; Véronique Sacuto at Cartier International; Ann Gunter and Scott Thompson at the Freer Gallery of Art; John Rhatigan at the British Library Newspaper Library, and Paul Jenkins. In the British Museum I wish also to thank Geoffrey House, Head of Public Services, and Paul Gardner, Head of Photography.

At British Museum Press the catalogue has been expertly edited and produced by Teresa Francis and Julie Young. Thanks must also go to Emma Way, Head of Publishing, Alasdair Macleod, Marketing Manager, Catherine Wood and Katherine West. The designer, Harry Green, has worked miracles in a very short space of time.

JUDY RUDOE
Department of Medieval and Later Antiquities
British Museum

1

A BRIEF
HISTORY OF
CARTIER

Cartier today is a large international firm with shops in many countries and cities around the world. This is a development which has occurred only in the past twenty-five years, however; during the years 1900–39, with which this catalogue is concerned, Cartier was divided into three branches – in Paris, London and New York – which were both retailing and manufacturing operations. For almost all this period each branch was managed by one of three Cartier brothers (fig. 1). This is the origin of perhaps the most striking aspect of Cartier at this time: although closely connected, each branch was run independently and had its own designers and workshops, resulting in a great sensitivity to both international and local tastes.

The firm was founded in 1847 by Louis-François Cartier (1819–1904). His first premises were at 29 Rue Montorgueil, where he took over the business of Adolphe Picard, his former employer. In 1852 he set up his own shop at 5 Rue Neuve-des-Petits-Champs in the fashionable area near the Palais Royal, transferring in 1859 to larger premises at 9 Boulevard des Italiens, a busy shopping district. At this time, and until the end of the century, the shop was primarily a retailer of jewellery and *objets d'art* bought in from a range of manufacturers. Louis-François must have been a successful salesman, as from early days he attracted prominent clients such as the wife of the Count of Nieuwekerke, the most powerful figure in the French art world under Napoleon III.

In 1874 Louis-François' son, Alfred (1841–1925), took over management of the shop with a success equal to his father's. The number of important customers steadily expanded, as did the range of suppliers. Among the latter were such outstanding firms as Fossin, Froment-Meurice, Gueyton, Falize and Boucheron. Demands from clients must have gradually led Cartier first into repairing and improving jewels and then into designing and manufacturing them. The key event that prompted this transition was the move in 1899 to a new address at 13 Rue de la Paix, in the heart of the high jewellery and couturier quarter of Paris (see fig. 2). Near neighbours were the jewellers Mellerio, Vever and Aucoc. These are still Cartier's main premises in Paris.

In 1898 Alfred had taken his eldest son Louis (1875–1942) into partnership. In the same year Louis married Andrée Worth, granddaughter of the founder of the famous

FIG. 2. Cartier's Paris shop at 13 Rue de la Paix,
c. 1910. Cartier archive, Paris.

fashion house. By this stage the firm was already supplying many of the leading families of Europe. The coronation of Edward VII in 1902 was something of a landmark. So many orders were received from London for the event that Alfred sent his second son, Pierre (1878–1965), and his salesman Alfred Buisson to London to deal with them. Legend in the firm holds that it was Edward VII himself who suggested that Cartier should open a branch in London. Such connections were the spur to the international expansion of the following years.

The London branch was opened that same year, 1902, though transactions with clients in London are recorded prior to this. It was first at 4 New Burlington Street, and then moved in 1909 to 175–6 New Bond Street (see fig. 3), where it remains today. In 1906 the youngest son, Jacques (1884–1942), was sent to take charge, and remained as director in London for the rest of his life.

Seven years later, in 1909, a branch was opened in New York to deal with the American millionaires who, from the very beginning, formed a large part of Cartier's clientele. In charge of this was Pierre Cartier, who had married an American, Elma Rumsey, in 1909. Initially the branch occupied premises on the fourth floor of 712 Fifth Avenue; in 1917 it moved to 653 Fifth Avenue, a converted town house in the Renaissance style which had belonged to Morton Plant (see fig. 4). Cartier acquired the house in exchange for a two-row oriental pearl necklace which Plant's wife coveted.

In the years before the First World War, however, the range of Cartier's business stretched far beyond these three cities. In 1904–5 Pierre Cartier made a long trip to St

FIG. 3. Cartier's London shop at 175–6 New Bond Street: photograph taken in the 1920s. Cartier archive, London.

FIG. 4. Cartier's New York shop at 653 Fifth Avenue, c. 1922. Cartier archive, New York.

Petersburg and Moscow. His purpose was twofold: to sell Cartier jewellery to the Russians, and to buy enamels and hardstone carvings in which Russian workshops specialised. These were much in demand in the West thanks to the international success of Fabergé. Following this visit, Cartier held a series of regular exhibitions in St Petersburg until the outbreak of war.

Cartier had a number of Indian clients in Paris and London, and in 1909 all aspects of this business were handed over to London. In 1911 Jacques himself went to India to deal with the orders linked with the Delhi Durbar for the coronation of George V. Later, in the years between the wars, this was to become a very large part of Cartier's trade, both in jewellery sold to wealthy Indian princes and in stones and pearls imported from India. These were either sold as delivered or were incorporated into Cartier's own designs.

From the turn of the century Cartier had been designing and manufacturing on its own account. Initially it did not have its own workshops and the manufacturing was carried out by other firms, some of them working exclusively for Cartier. The first branch to set up its own workshop was New York, around 1917, although the precise date is not certain. London had set up its own workshop by 1922, and Paris followed in 1929 (see below, pp. 41–4). Most of the workmen in London were English; those in New York were mostly French. The designers were probably French in the early years, but after the First

World War English designers were employed in London. New York continued to employ a number of French designers.

In the years right up to the 1960s, the three branches were all part of a single firm but operated independently. They would collaborate whenever the need arose. For example, Americans in Paris or London would often have designs drawn up to their taste, based on objects seen in Cartier's stock. But since unmounted stones, as opposed to finished pieces, were not subject to import duty, they often had Cartier New York make them up, using their own stones or stones supplied by the New York branch (for examples, see cat. 292, 294 and 297).

The firm's participation in each of the great exhibitions of the inter-war years seems to have been handled by one of the three branches acting independently. The display at the Exposition Internationale des Arts Décoratifs et Industriels Modernes held in Paris in 1925 was entirely the work of Cartier Paris, who used it to present a spectacular array of specially made pieces (see section 9). In 1929 followed the Exposition Française at Cairo, which was the responsibility of Jacques Cartier in London. The 1937 Exposition Internationale des Arts et Techniques dans la Vie Moderne in Paris again fell to the Paris branch, while the New York World's Fair of 1939 was organised by Cartier New York.

In 1942 both Louis and Jacques Cartier died, and this, rather than the Second World War, marks the end of an epoch in the history of the firm. In 1945 Pierre returned to Paris to take over management of the Paris branch, while Jacques' son, Jean-Jacques, took over the London branch. Pierre retired to Geneva in 1947, and Louis' son Claude took over in New York in 1948. The New York branch was sold by Claude Cartier in 1962. After Pierre's death in 1965, his daughter sold the Paris branch. The firm was only reunited as Cartier Monde in 1979.

2

THE YEARS
1900–1939

The first four decades of the century were a period of tremendous originality and interest both in design and technique and in the invention of new types of object.

The use of ancient fragments

The creation of objects in various historic styles is one of the most fascinating aspects of Cartier's work, and a particular effort has been made to uncover the sources of inspiration for each piece. One of the more original aspects of this work was the incorporation of ancient Egyptian faience into entirely new creations (see section 4). There was an immensely fertile imagination behind some of these pieces. With a fragmentary scarab body or wings, it might seem obvious to complete the missing parts in gemstones (cat. 82), but other ideas are without precedent, for example the vanity case (cat. 86) incorporating an Egyptian carved calcite plaque on each side. The plaques are in fact from a single amulet which has been split down the middle. It is inconceivable that the plaques were acquired by Cartier in this form; the idea of splitting the stone in this way must have been Cartier's. The lipstick case (cat. 137) is another unique instance. In its present state, which dates from 1929, the body is decorated with a geometric pattern inlaid in turquoise and lapis lazuli. In its original state of May 1928 the central part of the lipstick case was set with a hollow Egyptian glazed faience amuletic bead in the form of a *wedjat* eye, the eye of the falcon god Horus, dating, as far as one can tell from the archive photograph (fig. 5), from the Third Intermediate Period, *c.* 950–700 BC. The faience ornament was taken out in August 1928 and reused on a colourful bracelet made as a special order for Mrs Cole Porter (fig. 6). Flanking the Egyptian faience bead were discs of lapis lazuli and turquoise beads; the bracelet itself was a flexible tube of diamonds. Mrs Cole Porter had previously purchased another Cartier Egyptian-style piece, the scarab belt buckle of 1926 (cat. 254).

Cartier and their rivals

The use of Egyptian faience is unique to Cartier, and in this their work differs radically from the Egyptian-style pieces made at the same time by other high-fashion jewellery houses such as Van Cleef & Arpels, in which tiny Egyptian figures are depicted in coloured gemstones on a diamond ground. Sections 5, 6 and 7 deal with the setting of stones carved in India or the incorporation of Chinese jade into objects that were overtly Indian or Chinese in taste, as well as into objects that were not historicist in conception.

Cartier's Indian-style pieces formed a very large part of their production, whether for stock or as special orders commissioned by both Indian and Western clients. In some instances pieces designed specifically for Indian clients inspired similar creations for Western clients (see cat. 106). Existing literature suggests that this was not true of Cartier's competitors, although some of these firms, among them the Crown Jewellers, Garrards, in London, and Boucheron and Chaumet in Paris, also had Indian clients, and sometimes they were the same as Cartier's. Between 1925 and 1928 the Maharajah of Patiala gave Cartier a huge number of stones from his treasury to be remounted in traditional Indian designs, but in platinum instead of gold, according to Western fashion (see pp. 31–3). In 1927 he gave Boucheron a similar commission for turban ornaments, necklaces, upper-arm bracelets, belts and so on.[1] Presumably the quantity of work was so great that no one firm could complete it. But this large commission appears to have had little effect on Boucheron's current stock production or on special orders for Western clients.

Chaumet's Indian clients, like Cartier's, were the wealthy Parsi families of Bombay and the Indian princes, in particular the Maharajahs of Indore, both before the First World War and after. The Chaumet archives contain designs of the 1920s and 1930s for jewel-studded turbans, tunics and a diamond and pearl jewel to wear with a sari; it had pearl strings across the bosom, rather like Cartier's shoulder sashes (see p. 68, fig. 52), but with one shoulder completely encased in diamonds and pearls.[2] However, apart from a design of c. 1925 for a shoulder jewel attached to a *bazuband* or Indian upper-arm bracelet, and a diamond pendant set with a carved Mughal emerald, published evidence suggests that the Indian influence did not play a great part in Chaumet's production.[3] Van Cleef & Arpels, too, had Indian clients, but their Indian-style pieces made for stock were exactly like their Egyptian-style pieces, with tiny gem-set figures on a diamond ground, and bore no relation to any Indian prototype.[4] Cartier were not alone, however, in producing multigem or 'tutti frutti' jewellery with carved ruby, sapphire and emerald leaves imported from India. Among their competitors in this field were the firm of Mauboussin.[5]

Similarly, a number of other high-fashion houses were influenced by the art of the Far East. During the 1920s rival Paris firms such as Boucheron made ring-and-tassel pendants with jade discs in the Chinese manner similar to those made by Cartier, as well as cylindrical vanity cases inspired by Japanese *inro*; like Cartier, too, they set carved jade plaques into cigarette cases.[6] Mauboussin also incorporated carved jade and lacquer panels into their vanity cases, as did Chaumet.[7] The Maison Fouquet, then under the direction of Georges Fouquet (1895–1937), mounted pieces of carved Chinese jade as brooch-pendants in the same way as Cartier. Fouquet, however, also created Chinese-style pieces in an entirely contemporary idiom of a kind never made by Cartier. An example is Georges Fouquet's famous *devant de robe* or long brooch of c. 1920–25 with a Chinese mask in jade-coloured enamel, with jade beads, diamonds and onyx, which is among the most sensational pieces of French jewellery of the 1920s.[8]

Finally, Cartier never adopted the sculptural, Constructivist brand of modernism that can be seen in the work of Fouquet, Dusausoy or Mauboussin in the 1920s and 1930s, all of whom worked in conventional materials: precious and semi-precious stones, rock crystal and platinum. Mauboussin, for example, made a series of 'machine-age' brooches in diamonds and rubies, created by their in-house designer, Marcel Mercier, c. 1931.[9] Georges Fouquet stands out for his enterprising employment of outside artists of considerable stature, such as Adolphe Cassandre and André Léveillé, the architect Eric Bagge, or the sculptor Jean Lambert-Rucki, to design jewels for his firm. An interesting demonstration of the different aesthetics of Cartier and the modernist jewellers is to be gained

TOP

FIG. 5. Archive photograph of lipstick tube (cat. 137) as originally made in 1928, with centre formed of an ancient Egyptian faience bead. The lipstick tube was contained in the hollowed-out bead. Cartier archive, Paris.

FIG. 6. Archive photograph of a bracelet set with the ancient Egyptian faience bead that originally formed the centre part of the lipstick tube (cat. 137). The diamond back part of the bracelet is of similar design and construction to cat. 212. Cartier archive, Paris.

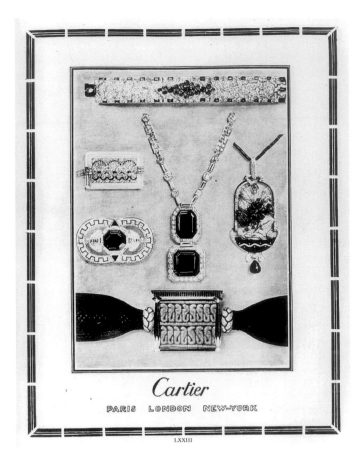

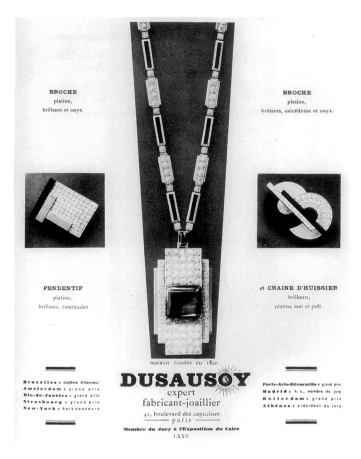

FIG. 7. Cartier advertisement from the catalogue of the French Exhibition in Cairo of 1929, showing a typical group of gem-set and Egyptian-style pieces from their current range.

FIG. 8. Dusausoy advertisement from the catalogue of the French Exhibition in Cairo of 1929, showing jewels in an abstract modernist style never adopted by Cartier.

by comparing the advertisements placed by Cartier and Dusausoy in the catalogue of the French Exhibition held in Cairo in 1929. Dusausoy's abstract, sculptural jewels, with their broad flat areas of colour, are quite unlike Cartier's exotic gem-set jewels incorporating either Egyptian faience or flower basket motifs (figs 7–8).

Clocks and watches

One area in which Cartier was pre-eminent throughout this period was the design and manufacture of clocks and watches. The technical virtuosity and the range of new models they introduced have been the subject of a previous monograph.[10] The examples included here are therefore by no means representative, but intended rather to relate to the themes of the catalogue.

So, for instance, some of Cartier's most spectacular clocks illustrate the firm's work in the Egyptian or Chinese styles, such as the clock in the form of an Egyptian temple gate (cat. 88) or that incorporating a Chinese carved jade screen (cat. 107). Cartier's celebrated mystery clocks with their transparent rock-crystal dials and invisible movements appear as examples of enamelled goldwork (cat. 69) or of Cartier colour combinations (cat. 124), while one of the series of impressive 'portico' mystery clocks is included as an example of the Chinese and Japanese styles, since it has elements of both in its design (cat. 123). Among the most original designs produced by Cartier were the cube desk clocks with doors that opened to reveal the dial. The folding dial was patented by Vergely; Cartier decorated these diminutive clocks with bold patterns enamelled on gold (cat. 70–71). Equally striking enamel patterns appear on Cartier's pocket-size travel clocks with hinged lids that formed a stand (cat. 72–3).

The watches included here have been chosen to show how Cartier incorporated them into fine jewellery to create a design that was both practical and the ultimate in fashion. Notable Cartier inventions, both dating from 1913, are a watch with carved rock-crystal mount (cat. 18) and a *tonneau* or barrel-shaped watch with a striking zigzag design (cat. 27). Both are attached to black grosgrain ribbon-bracelets with folding buckles in gold, introduced by Cartier in 1910. From the outside, all that was visible was a rectangular diamond-set clasp. The hinged buckle, which opened out and snapped shut, was hidden behind it (cat. 27.1). Equally characteristic of the Cartier style were the elegant pendant watches on long ribbons (cat. 174) and the slim-line gentlemen's pocket watches of the 1920s in onyx and diamonds (cat. 176). The 1920s also saw the tiny baguette movements made for Cartier by Jaeger, ingeniously concealed beneath hinged lids in diamond bracelets (cat. 210–12) or cleverly set as a bracelet centrepiece that could be removed and worn as a clip brooch (cat. 169).

There were many other inventions in wrist watches for everyday wear, as distinct from those that were also fine jewellery. Chief amongst these were the Santos-Dumont model, a flat, streamlined, square-shaped watch designed for the aviator Alberto Santos-Dumont and commercialised in 1911, and the Tank model of 1919, designed by Louis Cartier in the form of a rectangle with gold bars either side, recalling the tanks used in the First World War. In building up such a strong line in wrist watches, the essential accessory of the twentieth century, Louis Cartier wanted to create a modern image for the firm and this must have done much to draw in a new clientele.

Panther-skin ornament

It is perhaps significant that one of Cartier's new inventions in jewellery, the setting of onyx studs or chips into a background of pavé-set diamonds, which was eventually nicknamed 'panther-skin' ornament, was first used on a wrist watch in 1914. The spotted decoration surrounded the dial and was described simply as 'lunette onyx de forme irrégulière, le reste pavé roses' (border with irregularly shaped onyx, the rest pavé diamonds). There is no contemporary photograph, but a pencil sketch in the margin of the stock book shows it clearly (fig. 9). The earliest surviving piece with spotted decoration is also a watch, this time a pendant watch of 1915 (cat. 170). The first use of the term 'panther-skin' ornament or 'pavage peau de panthère' appears in 1917 for another wrist watch made for stock, with a border similar to that of the 1914 example. The idea of a flecked surface was eventually developed into a representation of a panther itself (see cat. 173), with the spots in black lacquer instead of onyx. Some of the most elaborate examples of panther-skin ornament, done on a curved surface, which required exceptional skill, were shown at the Paris Exhibition of 1925 (see section 9f, cat. 271 and 283).

New types of jewellery

Many new types of jewellery were shown at the 1925 Paris Exhibition (see section 9). Among them were the comb bandeau with orchids (cat. 271) and the long shoulder ornament (cat. 269).[11] But the exhibit that caught the attention of all the critics was the *broche de décolleté* or *fermeture de corsage* (dress clasp) designed to replace a conventional fastening for the front opening of a dress. At just over 15 inches, or 38 cm, this was almost certainly the longest *devant de corsage* ever made by Cartier (fig. 10). The design consisted of two stems joined at the base in a point, with stylised blossoms along the outer edge of each stem, and it was executed in diamonds, onyx and pearls set in platinum, with two melon-cut emeralds at the base. It appears as the centrepiece of an advertisement for Cartier's jewels at the Paris Exhibition, published in *Vogue*, 15 September 1925, with the caption: 'Cartier sponsors this new jewelled ornament to outline the front opening of the bodice. It is attached at the top with a pin clasp and may be fastened at intervals to the corsage with needle and thread.'[12]

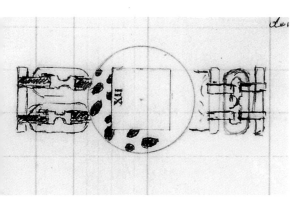

FIG. 9. Pencil sketch for a wrist watch made by Cartier Paris in 1914 incorporating the first example of Cartier's 'panther-skin' ornament. From the stock book for 1914. See cat. 170–73. Cartier archive, Paris.

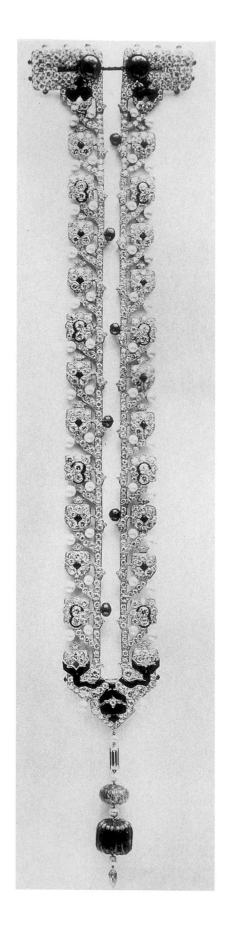

FIG. 10. Archive photograph of the 15-inch long *broche de décolleté* made for the Paris Exhibition of 1925. This corsage ornament was designed to replace conventional fastenings for the front opening of a dress. The ornament itself did not sell and was later broken up, but the idea was immediately borrowed by fashion designers (see fig. 11). Cartier archive, Paris.

FIG. 11. Fashion photograph from London *Vogue* for early November 1925, showing a dress designed by Nicole Groult copying Cartier's jewelled corsage brooch in embroidery. British Library.

Among the *haute couture* dresses in the Pavillon de l'Elégance was one by Worth with a deep *décolleté*, illustrating the plunging neckline which this brooch was designed to enhance.[13] By November 1925, the idea had caught on and dresses were being designed with ready-made Cartier-like corsage ornaments sewn onto the fabric in semi-precious stones. A dress by Nicole Groult advertised in *Vogue* was captioned: 'The new corsage line, sponsored by Cartier in one of the most magnificent pieces of jewellery shown at the Paris Exhibition, is carried out in this lovely black evening gown by embroideries of conventional flowers in crystal and coral.' Although the shape is identical, the 'conventional flowers' are a far cry from Cartier's subtle oriental-style stylised design (fig. 11).[14]

The Cartier décolleté brooch did not sell at the exhibition. It was known to have been broken up and it was thought that none of it survived. However, the belt buckle included here as cat. 180 bears a remarkable resemblance to the base of the 1925 Exhibition piece. A check in the archive revealed the following history. The décolleté brooch was first shortened to just over 12 inches, but still it did not sell. In October 1927 two of the pairs of stylised flowers were made into brooches. In November 1927 the rest was completely dismantled, except for the lower motif ending in a point. This was transferred to the stock of 'apprêts' (i.e. ready-made elements for reuse). In May 1928 it was indeed reused, as an onyx and diamond belt buckle, turned on its side and attached to a plaited black silk belt (cat. 180).

Diamond and precious-stone jewellery, in particular, is constantly altered or broken up because of its intrinsic value. Even if some of Cartier's most surprising creations were to survive, their intended function would not be obvious, and the fact that they were made at all would be hard to believe without the contemporary documentation. Take, for example, Cartier's 'diamants mystérieux', single diamonds mounted in a

FIG. 12. Cartier's 'Diamants mystérieux'. Photographs by Horst from Paris *Vogue*, September 1934. Each diamond was mounted individually with its own spring clip. Stones could be attached to as few as two or three hairs, and could even be worn in the eyebrows.

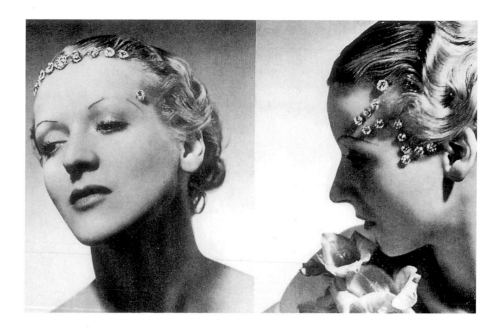

simple claw setting fitted with a sprung clip at the back (fig. 12). In September 1934 Paris *Vogue* published photographs by Horst demonstrating how they might be worn, with the following text:

> Jewellery can produce the most astonishing surprises . . . Mr Cartier should be proud of his latest creation, which he has perfected thanks to the extraordinary skill of his craftsmen. An ingenious fitting is fixed behind each stone – the tiniest but safest of platinum clips, rather like a hair-grip, with two prongs resting one against the other. The prongs are curved, making the grip even stronger. One is fixed, the other opens at the touch of a spring; you insert the hair, two or three hairs suffice, and release the spring to close the clip. Cartier suggests setting ten or twelve diamonds in this way and arranging them according to your taste – they can even be worn in the eyebrows. . . . In the hair, unexpected arrangements are possible. By placing the stones in a line the effect of a long brooch, comb, hair-slide or diadem can be created. Other dispositions recall no other jewel and completely turn upside down our idea of ornament. Here a flash of lightning is implanted, there the diamonds follow the hairline of a graceful brow, the largest in the centre with smaller ones either side and two to highlight the temples on each side. For a more simple arrangement three diamonds will do, asymmetrical or not, according to the shape of the face and its features.

Another scarcely believable invention, also of 1934, was the diamond curls worn vertically in the hair to form a crest down the centre of the head or a diadem across the front. They were advertised in American *Vogue* in November 1934, together with an all-purpose flexible bar brooch (fig. 13).

Cartier's all-purpose designs are among their greatest inventions, but because the materials – diamonds and platinum – are conventional, the originality of these pieces has often been overlooked. Convertibility in expensive diamond jewellery has a long history. Many a nineteenth-century tiara could be taken apart and worn as brooches or comb mounts, or removed from its frame, turned upside down and worn as a necklace. Cartier created convertible jewels from the beginning: examples dating from before the First World War are discussed in section 1. But it was during the inter-war years that Cartier's creative genius in this field reached a peak. A number of examples are included in section 8, such as the bandeau that converts to two bracelets (cat. 205), the sautoir that con-

FIG. 13. Advertisement from American *Vogue*, 1 November 1934, for Cartier novelties. The caption reads: 'Above, you see three of the uses of an amazing new flexible bar set with round and baguette diamonds – four inches long, and hinged so that it forms a clip, bracelet, an epaulet, or hair-ornament. The new hairpins at the right, like dazzling Tanagra curls, are paved with round and baguette diamonds. Wear them as you please – separately, down the part[ing] of your hair, or across as a tiara.'

verts to four bracelets (cat. 214), the rock-crystal bracelet with diamond centrepiece that can also be worn as a brooch (cat. 219), and the double clip brooches that could be worn singly or combined to make a brooch (cat. 221–3), or clipped to a black lacquer band to make a bracelet (cat. 292–4). Further examples, such as tiaras that convert to necklaces, are discussed in the introduction to section 8.

An astonishing number of large pieces of convertible diamond jewellery were produced in the 1920s and 1930s and recorded in the Cartier photograph albums. Cartier London dominated the production of large necklaces of diamonds or coloured stones; between 1933 and 1938 they produced approximately 280 necklaces, including 45 coloured bead sautoirs.[15] Little of this now survives. Among the most extraordinary inventions were the expanding diamond shoulder straps, always worn singly rather than

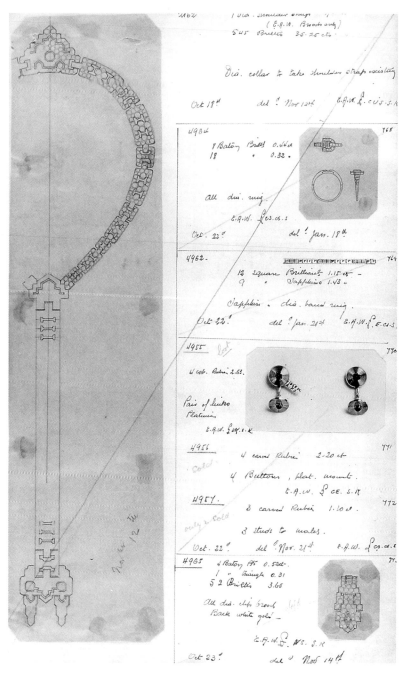

FIG. 14. Page from an English Art
Works job record book showing a
working pencil drawing for a
diamond shoulder strap and collar.
The expanding shoulder strap was
made in 1928; the diamonds have
been sketched in at the top and
bottom only. The collar was added
in 1929 so that the strap formed a
long pendant down the back,
to be worn with a backless dress
(see fig. 15). Cartier archive, London.

in pairs. In her memoirs Diana Vreeland remembered Millicent Hearst, wife of William Randolph Hearst, wearing emerald or diamond shoulder straps in the 1930s.[16] The English Art Works job record books record four examples made for Cartier London between October and December 1928. They all comprised a long flexible strip with larger elements at each end, which could be turned into a bracelet and a brooch formed from the two ends joined together. In 1929 one of them was given a diamond collar (fig. 14), to be worn as a necklace with the strap hanging down the back. It was made for stock, as were most of the others. A few years later, in 1934, a series of illustrations appeared in London *Harper's Bazaar* showing how such jewels might be worn. With titles such as 'Souper-Dansant', 'His Coming of Age', 'Her Eighteenth Birthday', Mummy Dresses for the Party', 'The Big Table', 'Bridge Four', 'Hen Luncheon' and 'Dinner Hour in the Grand Restaurant of the Queen Mary', they are wonderfully evocative of the social milieu of Cartier's clientele (fig. 15). All the Cartier favourites are shown, from cigarette holders and vanity cases to quintuple clip brooches, black lacquer bracelets, diamond curls in the hair, halo head ornaments, and jewels for the small of the back. This last fashion was remembered by Loelia, Duchess of Westminster: 'By the end of the twenties it had become essential to possess a pair of diamond, or pseudo-diamond, clips. They were clipped not only to hats but on to everything else, even the small of the back, where they served to keep underclothes out of sight.'[17]

Head ornaments are another category in which Cartier produced a number of new models. Cartier London seems to have made a speciality of head ornaments, possibly because the court or social occasions for which tiaras or other head ornaments were worn were more numerous and continued for a longer period than on the Continent or in America. At the very beginning of 1925, London *Vogue* printed a four-page advertisement for 'The New Jewellery' by Cartier. The idea of a comb bandeau for the back of the head had been introduced by 1923 (see cat. 202). But Cartier now proposed 'a band of tortoiseshell which fits across the back of the head and ends in large diamond loops at each side of the head, giving the effect of hairpins'. And indeed the effect was the same as a pair of *fourches* or two-pronged hairpins (see fig. 35), but the tortoiseshell band was designed for the new bobbed hair with short curls at the back and may have been

FIG. 15. 'Dinner Hour in the Grand Restaurant of the Queen Mary.' Illustration by A. K. Macdonald from *Harper's Bazaar*, 1935. The central figure wears a diamond collar and strap hanging down her back similar to that shown in fig. 14. A clip secures the base of her plunge-back dress. Her companion wears a black lacquer upper-arm bracelet. Cartier archive, London.

FIG. 16. Cartier advertisement for 'The New Jewellery' in London *Vogue*, 25 January 1925, showing a flat bandeau similar to cat. 204–5. The photograph is captioned: 'The small sleek head is the epitome of chic this season, and it would be hard to find a smaller or sleeker head than this one. Cartier has designed the magnificent diamond bandeau – which is flexible and supple as a ribbon – for the shingled head.'

attached to a sprung wire to keep it in place, rather than a comb. Even more radical than the bobbed head was the shingled head, cropped very close and short at the back. It was described as 'the epitome of chic this season'. Cartier designed for it 'a magnificent diamond bandeau – which is flexible and supple as a ribbon' (fig. 16). The extent to which this fashion caught on is again recorded by the Duchess of Westminster, who followed every craze as a young débutante in the early 1920s:

> Next a diamanté bandeau worn straight across the forehead became a must. These were made of pliable cardboard cut out in a design, such as Greek key-pattern, painted with glue, dusted with diamanté and backed with net to match one's hair. With cheap ones the diamanté came off and one found oneself with a flashing nose or eyebrows but on the whole it was a pretty fashion.[18]

The tortoiseshell headband mentioned above was one of a series of ornaments for short hair produced by Cartier London in the second half of the 1920s, all of them unprecedented in shape and decoration. Another tortoiseshell bandeau was designed to be seen from the back of the head (fig. 17). Three head ornaments were in the form of a continuous band that followed the brow and went round the back of the head; they were set with topazes and diamonds (see p. 261, fig. 81), with rubies, pearls and diamonds (cat. 256), or with emeralds and pearls. There was also a flexible band formed of three rows of coral batons with a central brooch ornament which encircled the head like a turban. These head ornaments, with their unusual materials such as tortoiseshell and coral, represented a radical break from convention and were no doubt aimed at society occasions. For court or official functions such as the state opening of Parliament a head ornament that was at least shaped like a traditional tiara was needed, and it had to be of diamonds or precious stones. But even then, Cartier succeeded in producing highly original designs, among them the halo head ornament (see cat. 80 and pp. 258–9, fig. 80). Equally original was the diamond Siamese-style head ornament of 1931, made by Cartier London and exhibited at the Exposition Coloniale in Paris that year. It is based on the front of the crown used in Thai dance. A publicity photograph taken by Cartier of the tiara on a wax model was illustrated in *Harper's Bazaar* for June 1931 with the caption 'A modern diamond tiara' (fig. 18).

FIG. 17. Archive photograph of a tortoiseshell bandeau shown on a wax model. Made by Cartier London in 1928 and designed to be seen from the back. Cartier archive, London.

FIG. 18. Publicity photograph of a Siamese style tiara made by Cartier London in 1931 and shown at the Exposition Coloniale in Paris in 1931. Cartier archive, London.

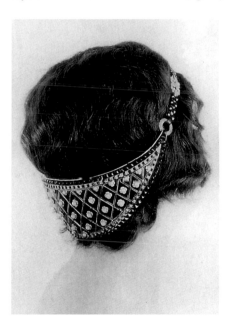

The 1937 Paris Exhibition and a change of style

In an article of 13 September 1937 on jewellery at the Paris Exhibition, the London *Times* singled out for special praise a diadem of diamonds and emeralds with arum lilies on a narrow circlet that weighed only 4 ounces. The *New York Times*, on the other hand (5 September 1937), complained about the lack of heavy and chunky jewellery on Cartier's display. All they thought worthy of mention was a lilac branch in diamonds with vibrating blossoms on a flexible mount. These two reports say much about respective tastes in London and New York. American *Vogue* echoed the sentiments of the *New York Times* but found a good deal more to talk about and illustrate on Cartier's stand:

> We've said it before, but we say it again (it's one of those great verities that bears repeating) – nothing strikes such a false note in this day and age as dinky, small-fry

FIG. 19. Cartier's giant diamond lilac clip shown at the Paris Exhibition of 1937. Photographed on a Schiaparelli dress by André Durst for American *Vogue*, 15 October 1937.

Huge solitaire sapphire – Cartier's new clip

Blackamoors in lieu of buttons – Cartier's gold-and-lacquer clips

FIG. 20. Illustration from American *Vogue*, 1 March 1937, of Cartier's new blackamoor clips, worn in lieu of buttons, as described by Diana Vreeland in her memoirs. The drawing also shows a large solitaire sapphire clip. British Library.

jewels. A wan string of molecule pearls, insignificant clips and bracelets – they count for precious little now. The real thing is . . . enormous, entertaining, ornamental, personal and witty.

Jewels no longer have a deadly seriousness, and even the most magnificent pieces are light-hearted. Look at those from Paris below: Cartier's giant clip of lilacs – dripping with diamonds, realistic enough to fool a bee – worn on Schiaparelli's dress [fig. 19].

The article continued:

Again, there's a great greed for gold – rich yellow gold and hoards of it. No little gram-weight nuggets content this age – your jewel pieces will be huge and affluent. You'll mix antique ones with modern. You'll wear one day all the gaudy riches of Hindu jewels; the next, modern gold studded with diamonds, emeralds or rubies. There's a fine free attitude about jewels today – just as about clothes – the only law is to be profligate, personal and entertaining. . . . Cartier of Paris beats gold into lifelike rosebuds – small rosebuds for earrings, and one huge one, with a diamond on the pistil, hanging from a gold safety-pin clip . . ..

But not all is gold. One of the most magnificent new necklaces in Paris is a woven chain of platinum – a chain more than a yard long – which wraps around your neck with the two loose ends hanging down on your chest. One end is a colossal rose of diamonds; on the other, a garland of diamond leaves. Keep your eye on these asymmetrical necklaces . . ..[19]

Another novelty at the Exhibition was featured by Paris *Vogue* in September 1937 (p. 35) with the title 'Somptueux mais pratique'. Six clips in the form of a flower could be worn as buttons down the front of a black dress during the day or, for the evening, be transformed into a pair of bracelets, mounted on platinum bands, three clips to each bracelet.

In light-hearted vein, Cartier had introduced earlier in the year gold and lacquer clips in the form of blackamoors, to be worn, like the flower clips, in lieu of buttons (fig. 20). Diana Vreeland, at that time fashion editor of *Harper's Bazaar*, recalled their popularity in her memoirs:

Have I ever showed you my little blackamoor heads from Cartier with their enamelled turbans? Baba Lucinge and I used to wear them in rows and *rows* . . . they were the *chic* of Paris in the late thirties. When I moved to New York, I made arrangements for Paris Cartier to sell them to the New York Cartier, and all I can tell you is that the *race* across the ocean – this was by boat, don't forget – was something so *fierce*. The Cartier ones were quite expensive, but then Saks brought out a copy of them that sold for something like, in those days, thirty dollars apiece, and it was impossible to tell them apart. So I bought the copies and wore them with the real ones, like decorations – I was *covered* in blackamoors![20]

By December 1937, *Femina* magazine recorded that the blackamoor heads had been replaced by Indian chieftains' heads and Indian squaws' heads with feather headdresses, all in lacquered gold and worn in a row along the shoulder line. The craze for them was such that on the same day at the Ritz in Paris they were worn by 'Princess J.-L. de Faucigny-Lucinge, Mme J. Ralli, the Duchesse d'Harcourt, Mme Fabre-Luce, the Comtesse de Castéja, etc . . ..'[21]

The trend towards large and chunky pieces is even more visible in Cartier's display at the New York World's Fair of 1939 (fig. 21). This change in style was marked by the dominance of big pieces, the use of gold (which was less expensive than platinum) and the introduction of figurative jewels such as the blackamoor clips or a lacquer hand holding a flower in coral and black enamel.[22] It is generally accepted that the guiding force behind it was Jeanne Toussaint (1887–1978), who had joined the firm in the early 1920s. Initially she directed the creation of a range of accessories in the Department 'S' (see section 3) and from 1933 she was put in charge of high jewellery. She was not a designer herself but seems to have had considerable input by suggesting new ideas. She was almost certainly responsible, for example, for the fashion for wearing imported Indian jewellery. In the late 1930s, quantities of gold and gem-set jewellery were purchased in India by Cartier London agents at her request (see section 5). After the Second World War, it was Toussaint who, in collaboration with the designer Peter Lemarchand (1906–70), developed the earlier panther motif into a three-dimensional representation of the animal studded with sapphires instead of onyx and seated on a huge sapphire for a brooch made for stock in 1949 and purchased by the Duke of Windsor as a present for the Duchess.[23]

FIG. 21. Archive photograph of one of Cartier's display cases at the New York World's Fair of 1939. Cartier archive, New York.

NOTES
1. Snowman (ed.) 1990, pp. 85 and 89; Neret 1988, pp. 104–7.
2. Scarisbrick 1995, pp. 174, 238–45.
3. Ibid. 1995, pl. 39, p. 253, and pl. 47, p. 263.
4. Snowman (ed.) 1990, p. 209.
5. See de Cerval 1992, pp. 90–94.
6. See Gabardi 1989, pp. 17, 23 and 73.
7. See de Cerval 1992, pp. 100–1, and Scarisbrick 1995, pl. 86, p. 283.
8. Paris 1983, p. 107.
9. See de Cerval 1992, p. 109.
10. Barracca *et al.* 1990.
11. At the 1925 Exhibition Boucheron showed a similar ornament in the form of a long band with no fastening, worn round the neck and crossed over on one shoulder, in the manner of a scarf. It was decorated with stylised flowers superimposed on stripes of diamonds and coloured stones. Whether it was inspired by Cartier's piece, or vice versa, is impossible to say (see Neret 1988, p. 87).

12. Cartier London also made versions of these long corsage brooches, though none approached 15 inches in length. One striking example was designed as a vase with a single stem of curved leaves; it came apart to form a brooch and bracelet. Another was very close to the 1925 design, with parallel flowering stems and a 'drawer-handle' brooch at the top.
13. *L'Art Vivant*, 1 August 1925, p. 27.
14. London *Vogue*, November 1925, p. 66.
15. These figures are quoted by Nadelhoffer 1984, p. 240.
16. Plimpton and Hemphill (eds) 1984, p. 91.
17. Westminster 1961, p. 97.
18. Ibid., p. 95.
19. American *Vogue*, 15 October 1937, pp. 75–7.
20. Plimpton and Hemphill (eds) 1984, p. 53.
21. *Jardin des Modes*, 1 February 1938.
22. See Gabardi 1989, p. 194, for a design of 1939 for one of these brooches.
23. See Paris 1989, col. pl. 1 and cat. 555.

3

CLIENTS

artier's huge success in the first half of the twentieth century was founded on its links with aristocratic clients from the 1890s onwards. Pre-eminent among these was Edward VII, who encouraged Cartier to establish premises in London and who awarded them their first royal warrant in 1904. From this starting point, Cartier rapidly assembled a client list of many of the wealthiest people in Europe. This was then extended to America and other parts of the world, in particular India. As further royal warrants were received, they were added to the firm's letterhead and to promotional material such as a leaflet issued by Cartier New York in 1917, advertising their services. The leaflet is titled 'How to increase the value of Your Jewels by Superior Workmanship and ever beautiful classical design'. At the top were six royal warrants, from the courts of England (1904), Spain (1904), Portugal (1905), Russia (1907), Siam (1908) and Greece (1909).[1] Cartier offered to remodel old-fashioned pieces, to create designs free of charge, to supply estimates with every sketch, to insure jewellery entrusted to their care, and to list and describe all stones before resetting them. All work was to be done on the premises in their own workshop.

Stock and special orders

Before discussing particular clients it is necessary to explain the distinction between items made for stock and items made as special orders. The vitrines in each shop would be filled with pieces made for stock, which were often highly adventurous, but Cartier was always willing to make pieces to commission, which ranged from the conventional to the outrageous. Special orders might be variations of something seen in stock made with stones supplied by Cartier. Alternatively, they might be entirely new creations made with stones supplied by the client, usually from earlier pieces that the client wanted to have reset in a current style. An example is the upper-arm bracelet commissioned by the Indian shipping magnate Sir Dhunjibhoy Bomanji in 1922 (cat. 99). He supplied a total of 859 diamonds, all of which were used except for a few tiny stones. Sir Dhunjibhoy Bomanji's convertible upper-arm bracelet, with its articulated openwork plaques, is very close in design and construction to the *devants de corsage* of the period *c.* 1912–14. Although the design is old-fashioned for 1922, it is nevertheless a very striking piece.

Because stock records were always kept separately from special order records, it has been possible to ascertain from the archive the origin of each piece, and this distinction is made in the catalogue entries that follow. In the case of pieces made for stock, the purchasers are also noted in the archive record. Thus a client's name can be associated with almost every item sold. In many instances the client's name is given in the entry, whether the piece was specially commissioned or whether it was purchased from stock. However, for reasons of confidentiality, Cartier has not wished some of the names to be published.

The execution of commissions between different branches

With an international clientele like Cartier's, a phenomenon that occurred regularly was the execution of commissions between different houses. This was especially common in the case of American clients, who travelled frequently between New York, London and Paris. The New York client files contain many examples of commissions begun in Paris or London and continued in New York, though they were not always completed. Generally the designs were made and approved in Paris or London and then sent to New York, where the piece would be executed, using the client's stones or stones from stock. Where a client's stones were to be used, the pieces might have been broken up in Paris or London and rearranged on wax to the approved design (see below). A number of cases are discussed under cat. 292, 294 and 297. Sometimes it was a question of where the client happened to be or the lack of time available to execute a piece during a European visit. But a financial reason also lay behind this practice: finished pieces set with gemstones were subject to duty on import to the United States. Unmounted gemstones, on the other hand, were not.[2] It was therefore much more economical for clients to take their own stones, unset, back to New York and have the jewel made there to designs prepared in Paris or London.

Often the designs sent to New York were accompanied by photographs showing the stones arranged on wax (see below, pp. 39–40). In July 1929, Marjorie Merriweather Post, then Mrs E. F. Hutton, ordered from Cartier London a ruby and diamond necklace, currently the height of fashion (see p. 164), the rubies taken from an old Indian ornament. London sent two photographs with different arrangements on wax, one rejected by the client because she did not like some of the stones suggested by Cartier, the other with stones that she had selected. Clearly the stones were being supplied by Cartier London, but as the final design had not been approved, the necklace was to be made in New York.[3]

Another aspect of this transatlantic trade was that pieces purchased in Paris were later altered to suit current taste in New York (see below, pp. 58–62).

The genesis of commissions

Many things could spark off a client's interest in commissioning a piece. It might be a short-lived fad for a particular gimmick, such as the cigarette case ordered by Mrs W. K. Vanderbilt in 1932 with a spring system that released each cigarette as required (cat. 91), or an unrepeated idea executed for one particular client only, such as the 'magic barometer vases' made for James de Rothschild as Christmas presents in 1926 (cat. 112). Another reason for a special order might be to complete a set, for example the pair of multigem clip brooches commissioned in 1935 by Mrs Cole Porter to match her two multigem bracelets of 1925 and 1929 (cat. 155–7). Alternatively, a client might have seen a special order for another client and wanted a similar piece. This was the case with the 'Hindu' necklace made for Daisy Fellowes in 1936 and based on one made in 1935 for the Maharajah of Patna (cat. 106). The pieces designed to incorporate Egyptian, Indian or Chinese objects owned by the client form a category of their own and are discussed in sections 4, 5 and 6.

FIG. 22. Daisy Fellowes wearing a pair of Cartier Indian-style fringe bracelets in diamonds and emeralds, of similar design to cat. 105. She wore them to Barbara Hutton's wedding in Paris in 1933. The photograph is captioned: 'Mrs Fellowes wears her heron feather collarette over pansy blue satin, Schiaparelli, and beautiful twin bracelets of diamonds, each dripping with a fringe of pear-shaped emeralds, Cartier.' From *Harper's Bazaar*, September 1933.

American clients

In 1908 Cartier's representative in Russia tried to persuade Alfred Cartier to open a shop in St Petersburg, but Alfred was then negotiating the opening of the New York shop and did not have enough staff for two new branches. He decided to limit the Russian business to two annual expeditions at Easter and Christmas, and to concentrate instead on New York.[4] This turned out to be a wise decision. The Americans were unquestionably the biggest spenders. English heiresses tended to wear inherited jewels, however old-fashioned. The novelist Elinor Glyn, writing in 1908, was impressed by the Americans who 'crossed the Atlantic twice a year to have their dresses fitted, and whose jewels were perfect, not a bit like the English sticking to their hideous early Victorian settings'.[5] In the years before the New York shop was opened in 1909, well-established clients of Cartier included such famous names as J. P. Morgan, Mrs Nancy Leeds, wife of the tin magnate W. B. Leeds (see cat. 45 and 232), and the great Vanderbilt dynasty. The Vanderbilts are notable for the number of large pieces of diamond jewellery commissioned by various members of the family in the period before the First World War. Mrs Cornelius Vanderbilt commissioned an elaborate diamond necklace with hexagonal pendants from Cartier Paris in 1908 (see below, p. 48, fig. 36). This was followed by many other orders, including a large shoulder sash in 1911, no doubt commissioned to keep up with Mrs W. K. Vanderbilt and Mrs F. W. Vanderbilt, both of whom had commissioned equally spectacular sashes the previous year (see p. 68, fig. 52). Mrs W. K. Vanderbilt (Virginia Graham Fair, died 1935) married W. K. Vanderbilt II in 1899 and is represented by three objects in this

FIG. 23. Portrait of Marjorie Merriweather Post, seated with her daughter, painted by Giulio de Blaas in 1929. She is wearing her emerald and diamond shoulder brooch (cat. 100). Hillwood Museum, Washington.

catalogue. She commissioned the spring-system cigarette case mentioned above (cat. 91) in 1932, and purchased the vanity case with onyx ring and coral plaque (cat. 190) in 1923 and the fruit bowl brooch (cat. 148) in 1927.

Among the regular American clients who appear in the catalogue entries are wealthy heiresses such as Daisy Fellowes (fig. 22), who inherited Singer sewing machine money through her mother, Isabelle Singer, and is represented by her famous 'Hindu' necklace (cat. 106) and a coral and emerald bracelet (cat. 142). Marjorie Merriweather Post, heiress to the Post cereal empire, is represented by another spectacular Indian-style piece

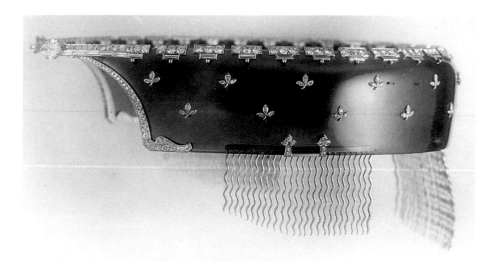

FIG. 24. Archive photograph of Barbara Hutton's wedding headdress of tortoiseshell studded with diamonds, made by Cartier Paris in 1933. The idea for the design came from the client and was inspired by headdresses she had seen on a recent visit to Bali. Cartier archive, Paris.

(fig. 23 and cat. 100), a ring (cat. 192) and designs for a diamond shoulder brooch (cat. 266). Barbara Hutton, granddaughter of F. W. Woolworth, is represented by a diamond-mounted tortoiseshell comb made by Cartier London – the largest one recorded in the archive (cat. 225). For her wedding in Paris in June 1933 to the Russian Prince Mdivani she wore a perfectly matched pearl necklace from Cartier, a present from her father, and a specially ordered exotic head ornament of tortoiseshell studded with diamonds (fig. 24). The wedding was described by the *Chicago Tribune*:

> One of the most effective touches was contrived by the bride herself. During her recent stay in the island of Bali, she was so struck by the hair ornaments, usually of wood, and forming a kind of crown, that she ordered one made of tortoiseshell of glowing amber colour. . . . On arriving in Paris, she suggested to the firm of Cartier that they should set small diamonds in the tortoiseshell to match the flowered designs in her wedding veil, and to finish the upper edge of the headdress with a row of fine brilliants. Louis Cartier eagerly adapted her tasteful and ingenious idea, and worked with her in carrying it out. This crown-like arrangement went perfectly with the ensemble, heightening the effect of her golden hair.

Other prominent clients represented here include the New York banker George Blumenthal and his wife (cat. 87, 90, 107 and 194) and the Chicago millionaire Harold Fowler McCormick and his wife, the Polish singer Ganna Walska (cat. 123, 144, 294 and 299).

A number of other American clients are not represented by objects in this catalogue but their taste and purchases from Cartier are sufficiently well documented to merit attention. Eva Stotesbury, of the Philadelphia banking family, has one of the most extensive client files in the Cartier New York archive. Among the pieces purchased before the First World War in New York was a bandeau with a 23.40 carat diamond projecting upwards at the centre. From Paris she had purchased a 'chaîne renaissance' formed of

wide diamond links with a large hexagonal pendant, and a necklace of nine large emeralds. Both Paris pieces were later completely altered in New York.[6] She also owned a
pocket watch of 1912 that showed the local times in Paris, London and New York. The
precision with which she planned and recorded each outfit gives some idea of the role
played by important jewels in the society to which she belonged. She was exceptional in
maintaining

> a full-time personal fashion designer and costume secretary whose talents included
> sketching her employer in her projected attire for an evening even down to the last clip
> and finger ring so that she might see how she was going to look without the trouble of
> dressing and could amend the whole arrangement without inconvenience. . . . Nor was
> Mrs Stotesbury willing to play second fiddle to Palm Beach hostesses who went to
> elaborate lengths to rotate their jewels and avoid appearing on successive occasions
> with the same combinations of necklaces, tiaras and bracelets. In a dressing room
> specially assigned for the purpose adjacent to her private apartments, her entire
> fabulous collection of ornaments was arranged, as in the window of a jewelry store, on
> the necks and wrists of mannequins with heavily annotated memoranda as to the date
> and occasions when they had last been worn.[7]

Possibly the biggest spender of all was Evalyn Walsh McLean (died 1947), daughter of
the gold prospector Thomas Walsh and wife of Edward McLean, heir to the *Washington
Post* millions. Mrs McLean was unusual among American clients in spending more
money on famous stones handled by Cartier than on elaborate commissions. In 1908 she
purchased from Cartier Paris a 94.80 carat diamond known as the 'Star of the East', traditionally said to have belonged to Sultan Abdul Hamid II, and two years later, again in
Paris, she first saw the celebrated 'Hope' diamond, so-called after its English owner,
Henry Philip Hope, in the early nineteenth century.[8] Although the settings in which these
stones were mounted are of little interest, Mrs McLean described the acquisition of these
pieces in her autobiography and paints a vivid picture of the polished salesmanship of
Pierre Cartier:

> Pierre Cartier came to call on us at the Hotel Bristol in Paris. He carried, tenderly, a
> package tightly closed with wax seals. His manner was exquisitely mysterious. I
> suppose a Parisian jewel merchant who seeks to trade among the ultra-rich has to be
> more or less a stage manager and an actor. Certainly he must be one great salesman.
> Of course, Mr. Cartier was dressed as carefully as any woman going to her first big
> ball. His silk hat, which he swept outward in a flourish, had such a sheen that almost
> made me believe it had been handed to him new as he crossed our threshold. His
> oyster-coloured spats, his knife-edged trousers, his morning coat, the pinkness of his
> finger-nails, all these and other things about him were made by him to seem to be for
> me – for Madame McLean – one French compliment.[9]

Yet despite Pierre Cartier's calculated performance, in which he concocted an exotic history for the stone, including its legendary curse, before even showing it to her, Mrs
McLean was not at first tempted. The negotiations continued in New York over several
months before a final selling price of $180,000 was agreed.

Another major American client was Elsie de Wolfe (1865–1950), a trend-setting American interior decorator who had made a fortune in New York before marrying Sir
Charles Mendl, British press attaché in Paris, in 1926. This extraordinary woman decorated the Villa Trianon which she rented at Versailles with leopard velvet and zebra skins
as early as 1919. The parties that she gave there in the 1920s and 1930s were grand
social occasions attended by figures from the world of art and fashion as well as other
Cartier clients, among them Barbara Hutton, Mrs Harrison Williams, Princess Karam of

Kapurthala, Lady Cavendish, Lord and Lady Milford Haven, Diana Vreeland, Elsa Schiaparelli, Mr and Mrs Cole Porter and Cecil Beaton. She was voted the best-dressed woman in the world by the Paris couturiers in 1935, when she was seventy. A photograph taken ten years earlier, in 1925, on her return to New York from Paris, shows her wearing one of Cartier's new 'temple of love' brooches pinned to her hat. This popular design was one of the first to use baguette-cut diamonds to represent architectural features.[10] It was for Elsie de Wolfe that Cartier Paris created one of the earliest models of vanity case. It took the form of a matching powder box and lipstick, the lipstick tube attached by

FIG. 25. Elsie de Wolfe putting on her lipstick and wearing her Cartier diamond curls (see fig. 13). Photograph from Paris *Vogue*, May 1935.

means of a chain, and was made in 1921, the year that Helena Rubinstein opened her Paris salons. An article in Paris *Vogue* for 15 January 1921 illustrated a sketch of Elsie de Wolfe's Cartier powder box and lipstick, the tube elegantly caught between the fingers as if it were a large ring, and gave the accompanying text:

Artists have given their imagination such free rein since it has become acceptable for women to wear powder that one would have thought all the forms of the powder box were exhausted. Nevertheless Cartier has created for Miss Elsie de Wolfe this charming beauty case containing a mirror and the inevitable lipstick tube. The octagonal mirror is covered in black enamel bordered with diamonds and engraved in the centre with a tiny wolf's head. The lipstick tube, also in black enamel with diamond border, is joined to the powder box with a fragile diamond and platinum chain.

This was the first of a series of fashions created by Cartier for Elsie de Wolfe. In 1935 she was photographed for *Vogue* wearing diamond spiral hair-clips made by Cartier to match her curls and putting on her lipstick from a vanity case (fig. 25). In the same year she ordered an aquamarine tiara and tinted her hair aquamarine to match it (see p. 263). Like Daisy Fellowes and Marjorie Merriweather Post, she succumbed to the prevailing fashion for exotic Indian-style jewellery, a fashion created by Cartier. In 1937–8 she went to India in the company of the English interior designer Syrie Maugham and brought back quantities of Indian jewellery. In Delhi she invited the jewellery merchants to her hotel, and bought:

a wide, flat collar of diamonds fringed with pearls and emeralds, a lacier collar of rubies, pearls, and emeralds, and another necklace that was a rigid tube of gold encrusted with pearls and diamonds. To fill out the hoard she later made a trip to the jewelry bazaar, where she toured the booths picking out an assortment of loose sapphires. Carefully arranging them on a sheet of paper heavily coated with wax, she carried the stones home to France and straight to Cartier for a more permanent setting.[11]

There must have been many other instances of clients bringing their own stones back from trips to India and having Cartier make them up into jewels, in the same way as the Indian clients did.

Indian clients

Another important group of clients was the Indian princes, who worked largely with Cartier London. An exception was the Maharajah of Patiala (fig. 26), who gave large commissions to Cartier Paris in the 1920s and 1930s. The Indian clients form a very particular, separate group in that most of their commissions were for the resetting of their own stones and so in many cases they were paying for the settings only. This made them very different from the Americans.

In requesting Cartier Paris to remodel his crown jewels between 1925 and 1928 the Maharajah of Patiala gave the firm its biggest single commission ever received from any one client. Discussed in more detail on p. 159, this included a colossal diamond necklace incorporating the 234.69 carat De Beers diamond (fig. 27), which passed to the Maharajah's heir on his death in 1938 (fig. 28). Rosita Forbes, writing in 1939, described a visit to the Patiala armoury where she was shown 'the famous Patiala emeralds, each as large as a dessert spoon, and a necklace which, when I tried it on, covered half my person with streams and lakes of diamonds. It was set by Cartier and contained pink, yellow, greenish and what I should call pale brown diamonds, all as large as my thumb-nails.'

FIG. 26. Photograph of the Maharajah of Patiala (Sir Bhupindra Singh, 1891–1938) taken in 1911 at the time of the Delhi Durbar. He is wearing the jewellery later reset by Cartier in the 1920s. Cartier Paris.

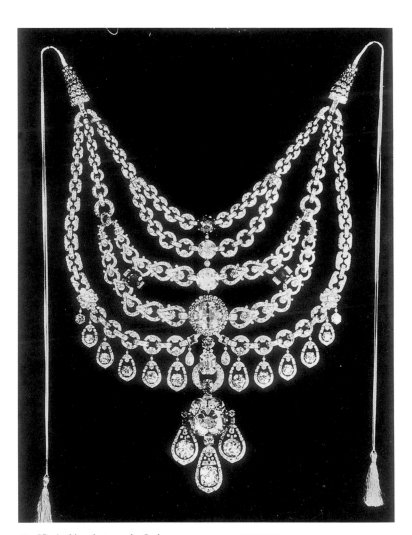

FIG. 27. Archive photograph of a large diamond necklace made by Cartier Paris for the Maharajah of Patiala (Sir Bhupindra Singh, 1891–1938) in 1925–8, using the Maharajah's diamonds. The necklace is of traditional Indian form with multiple strands, but set in platinum, instead of gold. Cartier archive, Paris.

OPPOSITE
FIG. 28. Photograph of the Maharajah of Patiala (Sir Yadavindra Singh, 1913–74), dated 1941. He wears the large diamond bib necklace (fig. 27) and diamond collar made by Cartier for his father. From the John Fasal collection.

Other major Indian clients were the Maharajahs of Kapurthala (see pp. 158–9) and Nawanagar, both of whom ordered their magnificent collections of diamonds and emeralds to be reset by Cartier London. The pieces made for the Maharajah of Nawanagar (died 1933), a celebrated cricketer, were designed purely to show the stones to advantage, with minimal settings. Presumably the Maharajah wanted it that way and was unwilling to pay for the extra stones of no particular interest that more elaborate settings would have required. For Jacques Cartier, the Maharajah's coloured diamonds enabled him to create 'the most extraordinary piece of the whole collection – a really superb realisation of a connoisseur's dream.'[12] Jacques Cartier was also especially proud of a collar of thirteen emeralds set with diamonds, containing twin rectangular emeralds at the centre, flanking a square one.

Papers in the Cartier London archive record trips made to India in the late 1930s and details of transactions, both successful and failed, with Indian clients and with Cartier's agents in India. They reveal, for example, that the twin rectangular emeralds in the collar made for the Maharajah of Nawanagar were not previously owned by him. In a letter of November 1932 to A. A. Javeri, Cartier's agent in India, E. W. Bellenger, manager of the London branch, writes:

> H. H. has favoured me with an important order – a short collar of emeralds and diamonds which I made for him from my two specimen emerald bracelets. They were for sale at £50,000 the pair, but I sold them to H.H. with another 10 carat emerald added in the centre and two more diamond links for £40,000. The emeralds as you will see are magnificent, and not dear at £500 a carat in average, the diamonds are the finest quality and come to £52 a carat in average, the largest baguettes have cost me £130 per carat.

This order must have been especially welcome, for in February 1932 the Maharajah of Nawanagar had postponed both the celebration of his silver jubilee and the marriage ceremony of his nephews. Cartier was already working on orders for these major celebrations and had purchased stones on the understanding that payment would be received in February or March, so this long delay was very serious. The wedding presents for the nephews were eventually sent via Javeri in December, together with diagrams showing how the different articles opened. Cartier's subtle and often invisible fastenings are not always immediately obvious, and such diagrams must have been essential when there was no Cartier salesman available to demonstrate their workings.

The London correspondence relating to the Indian trips of 1937 and 1939 reveals how transactions with clients were undertaken, from the submission and approval of designs to the supply and cutting of the stones. In 1937, Cartier's representative in India, C. W. North, was dealing with the Maharajahs of Kashmir, Jaipur, Gwalior, Udaipur and Nawanagar, and with a number of senior Indian officials and their wives. Often a client would request a design similar to one that Cartier had recently made for another client. One of the despatches received in London from Mr North in February 1937 reads 'Make designs and estimates for double clip brooch and pair earrings. Client has a quantity of emerald drops similar in size to ruby drops mounted 2 years ago as a double clip for Mrs K.S.P. Drops drilled sideways at point. Clips should be slightly larger than Mrs P's designs as more stones available. Post designs as soon as possible to C.W.N in Bombay.' Four alternative designs were duly posted later that month.

In January 1939 Jacques Cartier went to India with North, who had previously prepared a detailed list of all the Maharajahs and the possible marriages or events for which they might require jewellery, together with transactions already in progress. Things went well and in early February Jacques cabled London to send the designer Peter Lemarchand out to Bombay by air the following week. (Lemarchand had come to London from

Cartier Paris in 1935.) By the end of February North was able to record that Lemarchand had spent two days preparing designs for the Maharani of Jodhpur, who wanted pieces to match those made for her the previous year. At the same time, another transaction was under way with the Nawab of Bhawalpur. On 28 February, North wrote:

> We spent two days in Bhawalpur and had two interviews with H. H. At first we were shown by H. H. many bundles of pearls and also loose emeralds and diamonds which he has had cut in Bhawalpur from old stones and beads. He wanted to use up his pearls, with some emeralds and diamonds making a small set of jewels for a lady – actually to have ready for the time when his son, now fifteen years old, will marry. . . . Lemarchand prepared several suggestions and at our second interview H. H. approved designs for a necklace and two bracelets and a pair of earrings. There is also to be a brooch and perhaps two finger rings. We have to send finished designs and estimates for mounting only from London and H. H. will arrange to have all the small stones, including baton diamonds, cut in Bhawalpur. Delivery will be made personally to H. H. when he visits London in the summer of next year. . . . H. H. said that although it was a small order he hoped it was the beginning of happy business relations. He has a very large diamond crown which was made for his grandfather and he said that he thought some day of having it remodelled and that when this was done he would give us an opportunity of making suggestions. . . . He also intends to proceed slowly with the mounting of the best of his large stock of stones – mostly emeralds.

Transactions did not always come to fruition. From 1927 Cartier London engaged in an ambitious project to prepare a new crown for the Gackwar of Baroda. After eight years of complex negotiations, it was never made. Nevertheless, the correspondence provides a fascinating insight into how elaborate jewels were modelled and constructed from a distance.

Cartier's proposed design was to be in the traditional Indian form, with a sun motif in the centre.[13] The large diamonds were to be removed from the Gaekwar's existing jewels, while Cartier was to supply about 6,000 small diamonds, as well as the emeralds and rubies. The mounting was to be made in such a way that parts of it could be worn separately or together to fit the occasion: firstly, the whole crown, for durbars; secondly, without the dome, for big occasions; thirdly, only the front part, for important functions; fourthly, the central motif and tassel, for small occasions; fifthly, the sun motif only. Models of all the state diamonds used in connection with the crown were to be made in plaster by an Indian craftsman, who was to come to London to make the final model on which the work would be started. It was estimated that it would take a month to make the unpierced platinum blanks for the mounting. A mounter would then have to spend two months in Baroda to adjust the blanks, do the piercing for the large stones on site and bring back copper models of them. The setting would be completed in London. A setter would then be sent to Baroda for one month to add the large stones. Two wax models were to be made on site: one to take the large stones left in Baroda, the other to take the copper models made of the large stones. That way, any differences in the sizes between the actual stones and the models would be clear and the mount could be adjusted in London.

The negotiations began in March 1927. By October 1928 Cartier had submitted the model of the proposed crown, 'painted in exactly the way the stones would be set and the number of stones that will be used'. The copper model for the crown probably resembled those made by Chaumet for their tiaras. Chaumet's models, cut out in nickel silver (an alloy of copper, zinc and nickel) and painted in the same way, still survive in the Chaumet archive in Paris.[14]

Cartier advised the Gaekwar on which of his existing jewels were rare and ought not to be broken up to provide stones for the crown. The design was modified and Cartier supplied estimates for the various parts to be made in stages, together with photographs and design charts. One aspect that was a constant worry to Cartier, in this and many other transactions, was the changing market value of stones. If stones were specially purchased to carry out a commission, but were then rejected by the client and the market price subsequently fell, Cartier could suffer heavy losses.

Despite the failure of the new crown for the Gaekwar of Baroda, Cartier succeeded in making several important jewels for him. In December 1928, the Gaekwar ordered three pairs of diamond bracelets to be made from the best quality diamonds. Cartier had to purchase the stones specially; by May 1929 they had still only a small part of what was needed and the mountings could not be made until all the stones were available. Eventually they decided to make one bracelet as a sample, but warned that the prices of the remainder would have to be increased. Baroda wanted round brilliant cuts, but Cartier found that the cutters preferred 'to turn out square stones which are in great demand just now and for which they can get higher prices'. Finally Jacques Cartier wrote that he 'proposed to buy what the market has to offer instead of insisting on getting what the market has not got and is not interested in cutting from the rough'. In June 1929, Cartier sent copper models of six bracelets, comprising three pairs in three different sizes, for the Maharani and the Princess. They were damaged in transit and arrived oval instead of round, so a new set had to be sent. A photograph of the copper models and detailed description survives among the London papers, indicating the diamonds of different carats with which they were to be set. Despite sending the models, the bracelets for the Princess turned out to be too large and had to be remade with twenty-one instead of twenty-two diamonds.

It should be added that Indian clients frequently purchased jewellery made for stock that was not in the Indian style. Examples catalogued here include a cigarette case purchased by the Maharajah of Alwar (cat. 60), an Egyptian-style vanity case purchased by Princess Amrit of Kapurthala (cat. 79), an emerald, onyx and diamond brooch purchased by Sir Cowasji Jehangir (cat. 160), and an onyx and diamond brooch purchased by the Maharajah of Patiala (cat. 171).

Cartier's marketing

The archive records, together with information from contemporary magazines, throw considerable light on the methods used by Cartier to market their jewellery and accessories. Louis Cartier never wanted to put advertisements in magazines (this is not true of the London branch), but there were many other ways in which the various branches brought their creations to public attention.

One way was to lend jewellery for social occasions where it would be widely seen. For example, E. W. Bellenger of Cartier London recorded lending jewellery to clients for a charity ball in March 1939:

> There is a ball to-morrow which is called 'The Oxford & Cambridge' in aid of a Charity, the boat race being on Saturday. Miss Rowe came and told me that she was representing 'Oxford', then we had to lend her some jewellery of sapphires, and I made her a necklace with the bracelet we took back from Lady Castlerosse. I think it may be a chance of interesting her. . . . I also saw on the programme that Mrs Henry Dreyfus was to represent 'Cambridge', so I jumped on the 'phone and asked her if I could do anything to help her. She came in with Dr. Dreyfus, and they were both very pleased, and I am also doing something for her in aquamarines. I thought it would be a good way to make them spend a bit of money with us, as I have not seen much of them the last 18 months, and thought by obliging them it may lead to future business.[15]

Another method was to lend jewellery to actresses, either for stage performances or for

social occasions, in the hope that it would be photographed by the press. According to a newspaper cutting in the archive, Cartier New York lent 'over $60,000 worth of jewellery to the cinema actress Lola Galsworthy' for her appearance at the benefit for the Romanian war orphans at the Hotel Plaza in March 1922. In March 1924 Cartier London lent £400,000 of jewels to Alice Delysia, the French-born star of the revues presented by C. B. Cochrane at the London Pavilion between 1918 and 1931, for the 'Radiant Diamond dress' which she wore in 'Topics of 1923'. The jewels comprised a necklace, collar, stomacher, bandeau and many bracelets and rings.[16] In both instances the actresses were photographed and their jewels described as by Cartier.

A third method was to make jewellery available for fashion photography. As Cartier well knew, it would often be modelled by celebrities. In January 1923, the actress Ina Claire posed for London *Vogue* in three different outfits, each designed to show off Cartier novelties, such as a tassel necklace, hat brooch and seal-watch (see cat. 95.1). Cartier also knew that such photographs would not only be linked with the great couturiers but would often be taken by the leading photographers of the day, such as Baron de Meyer, P. Horst, Cecil Beaton, Man Ray (see p. 162, fig. 72) and Edward Steichen (fig. 29).[17]

A fourth method was to hold exhibitions, on Cartier's own premises and elsewhere. In April 1911, just two months before the coronation of George V, Cartier London held an exhibition of tiaras at their Bond Street shop. In 1913 there was an exhibition of Persian and Indian-style jewels at Cartier New York (see p. 157, fig. 68), and in 1928 Cartier Paris held an exhibition of the jewels made for the Maharajah of Patiala (see p. 160, fig. 70). Exhibitions elsewhere were aimed at new markets. Among the earliest was the series of exhibitions held in Moscow and St Petersburg from 1907 to 1914 (see p. 102, fig. 57). Other small-scale exhibitions of a very temporary nature were held at grand hotels in tourist resorts such as San Sebastian, Biarritz or Deauville. Branches were opened in St Moritz in 1929 and in Monte Carlo in 1935.

The admission fee of one guinea for the 1911

FIG. 29. A model wearing a Vionnet dress with Cartier jewellery and cigarette case. Photograph by Steichen from American *Vogue*, 1 October 1934, p. 52. For similar cigarette cases see cat. 85 and 121.

tiaras exhibition went to charity. Cartier London also lent their premises for charity functions organised by others, such as the Children's Jewel Fund launched by Consuelo Vanderbilt, Duchess of Marlborough, in 1917. Gifts of jewellery were assembled at Cartier's and then sold at Christie's.[18]

The different branches had to adjust to local markets. Cartier New York produced a series of trade catalogues throughout the 1920s and 1930s. Such catalogues do not seem to have been issued by Paris or London. The New York catalogues of the 1920s are titled 'Gift Suggestions' and include a wide range of objects, but no prices are given. A catalogue issued in 1932 at the height of the Depression, following the Wall Street crash of 1929, is titled 'Gifts one dollar upward'. One dollar purchased a pack of bridge cards. Eighteen dollars bought an enamelled gold Mickey Mouse charm on a child's bracelet of coral and gold beads, while the single page of 'jeweled articles' contained a bracelet for $5,100.

NOTES

1. A full list of Cartier's royal warrants is given in Hong Kong 1995, p. 12. They included Serbia (1913), Belgium (1919), Italy (1920), Monaco (1920), Romania (1928), Egypt (1929) and Albania (1939).

2. Finished pieces are still subject to duty today. Stones are sent separately from the mountings for reassembly in America. For an example of this practice, see cat. 30.

3. Letter of 9 July 1929 from Cartier London to Cartier New York, in Mrs E. F. Hutton's client file, Cartier archive, New York.

4. See Nadelhoffer 1984, p. 117.

5. Quoted in Scarisbrick 1989, p. 179.

6. For reference to the diamond bandeau and the emerald necklace, see Nadelhoffer 1984, pp. 74 and 238. For an illustration of the 'chaîne renaissance' of 1910, see Cologni and Nussbaum 1995, p. 97. According to her client file she had it altered several times to suit current taste, in 1928, 1930 and again in 1937.

7. Beebe 1967, pp. 362–3.

8. For full accounts of both these famous stones, see Balfour 1987, pp. 174 and 102–12.

9. McLean 1936, p. 195.

10. For the photograph of Elsie de Wolfe wearing the temple jewel, see Proddow and Fasel 1996, p. 72.

11. Smith 1982, p. 277.

12. Jacques Cartier, 'The Nawanagar jewels' in *The Biography of Ranjitsinji*, London n. d. (offprint in the Cartier archive). See also Nadelhoffer 1984, pp. 242–3.

13. According to Nadelhoffer (1984, p. 241), the design was by Frederick A. Mew, chief designer in the commissions department, and Ernest C. Frowde.

14. See Scarisbrick 1995, pls 47–8, p. 195: a design for a *kokoshnik* tiara and its nickel silver model; p. 340: an archive photograph of the models as displayed for the clientele; and p. 342.

15. Letter of E. W. Bellenger to Jacques Cartier, 30 March 1939, Cartier London archive. The annual Oxford and Cambridge boat race, in which the two university teams compete against each other, is still held every spring. The Oxford colour is dark blue, hence the sapphires, while Cambrige is light blue, hence the aquamarines.

16. *The Sketch*, 5 March 1924, p. 442.

17. Adolphe de Meyer (1868–1949) was a major contributor to *Vogue*, *Vanity Fair* and *Harper's Bazaar* during the First World War and the 1920s. He and his wife, Olga, were long-standing clients of Cartier and he may have been responsible for the regular features on Cartier jewellery in those magazines: see Nadelhoffer 1984, p. 64.

18. See Vanderbilt Balsan 1953, p. 178.

4

THE
PRODUCTION
PROCESS

This chapter looks at the function of the different kinds of design drawings, from the initial sketch to the working template, the use of wax models to arrange the stones, and the making of plaster casts from finished pieces as a three-dimensional record. It also looks at the different workshops that made the pieces in Paris, London and New York, and describes the marks that appear on them.

The design drawings and their function

A description of the different sorts of designs that survive in each of three Cartier archives and information about the designers is to be found on pp. 57–8 and in section 9.

The most preliminary types of drawing are the sketches made in museums or from books, for example cat. 233 and 235–6 by the designer Charles Jacqueau, or cat. 247, a page of studies copied almost line for line from Owen Jones's *Grammar of Ornament*. Generally these consisted of ornamental motifs, which might be translated into decorative patterns in diamonds or enamel, rather than sketches of actual jewels. The next stage was the initial sketch for a jewel. Several pen and ink sketches of this kind appear in Louis Cartier's Notebooks (see p. 53, fig. 40) and in the Jacqueau archive. If the idea was approved on the basis of this initial sketch, a finished coloured design would be produced.

The finished design would indicate the colours of the different stones and the overall appearance of the piece. In the case of a special order, the stones were generally accurately painted in. Either they were the client's stones (see cat. 265) or they were partly the client's and partly from stock, or entirely from stock if the client did not have his or her own stones. In the case of a stock piece the stones might or might not be accurately painted in, depending on whether the stones had already been selected. Sometimes the stones were not selected until the design was approved.

The design would then, where necessary, be passed to the stone department, where the stones would be selected. The stones would then be arranged on wax, following the design, to show how the piece would finally look. The wax arrangement enabled the stones to be carefully placed according to size, colour and quality. This too would need the approval of the relevant parties, whether the piece was for stock or for a special order.

The wax arrangement was then given to the workshop for execution. This procedure is precisely documented in the job record books in the London archive (see below, p. 58). In some instances the workshop appears to have received only the wax arrangement with the instruction 'Mount this arrange on wax as a necklace' ('arrangement' was often abbreviated to 'arrange'). Sometimes they were given both a wax arrangement and an accurate pencil drawing or template in which each stone was drawn. Sometimes they were only given a template drawing. These template drawings are pasted into the job record books with specific written instructions (figs 14 and 43). For example, an arrangement on wax and a template drawing for a diamond double clip brooch was supplied to Sutton & Straker in June 1937 with the instruction, 'These stones must be mounted ditto as the weights are exact.' A template drawing for a pair of clips, each with three large square-cut or 'emerald-cut' diamonds, was supplied with a list of the stones by carat indicating which was to be used for clip 'no. 1' and which for clip 'no. 2' and the instruction 'These emerald-cut brilliants must be kept in these positions.' These template pencil drawings are usually duplicates and a finished, coloured one has also been kept.

This process from design to manufacture is described in an article written in 1948 about Jules Glaenzer, then salesman and vice-president of Cartier New York, with reference to the way in which a special order might come about:

> About half the women who shop at Cartier's are looking for something the store hasn't in stock . . . the fussy woman might want, say, a certain kind of ruby-and-diamond braceclet. Well, Cartier's has a stock of about twenty-five ruby-and-diamond bracelets. The lady examines those in her price range and she finds none that equals her dream. She points to one of the pieces. She likes the style of it, but instead of nine small rubies, she would like three large rubies surrounded by tiny round diamonds and linked by circles of square-shaped diamonds. She leans over Glaenzer's desk and intently scribbles on a piece of paper to picture for him what is in her mind.
>
> Glaenzer then has a conference with Maurice Daudier, the head designer, who perches on a high chair at a draftsman's table on the fifth floor and supervises the work of the four designers, all of whom are French-born and Paris trained. . . . Daudier assigns an artist to make a sketch of the bracelet. He draws the outline in dark blue ink. Then the outline is filled in with colors, the proper color for each gemstone.
>
> If milady approves the watercolour sketch, it is sent to John Gorey, chief gemmologist. Glaenzer, in the margin of the sketch, has indicated the approximate size of each stone. The gemmologist then goes to a safe on the sixth floor. The safe is enormous – like the refrigerator in a butcher's shop. It extends from floor to ceiling. It is in a room caged in by a strong wire network. Admittance is only through an electrically-controlled door. The safe contains more than $150,000 worth of unset stones in small yellow envelopes – neatly catalogued by size and quality and color. The gemmologist then sifts rubies and diamonds, and finally selects those that match in size and color.
>
> Then the stones are pressed into wax, following the layout of the stones in the sketch. Now the effect is as the bracelet will look when it is done. Now the customer can see the overall effect of her brain-child.
>
> Maybe she thinks the rubies should be larger. Or the rubies changed to emeralds. Maybe she approves. She does not leave a deposit or sign a written order. She merely receives a letter stating: 'Following your instructions, we are executing the bracelet you ordered. The price will be $22,000 and you may expect delivery in five weeks.' This is legally binding. The sketch and the wax mold are then sent to the workrooms.[1]

Glaenzer was an extraordinary salesman, an astute businessman and a strong personality. In London, it was Jacques Cartier himself who supervised the designers. James Gardner, who worked as a young designer at Cartier London in the 1920s, recalled his experiences on arrival at Cartier in 1923:

> I was set up in a corner of his private office, which was rather like an antechamber to a Louis XVI boudoir, to work at a little ormolu table under a pink-ruched, silk-shaded lamp, within range of the maestro's enquiring eye. Though scared stiff, I soon found something I could hang on to. Jacques was what we then called a gentleman. He was excitable, had compassion, and he lived for design. . . . I must learn to use cribs. Everything grows from something that grew before and the room contained a library of things that had gone before; Chinese carpets, Celtic bronze work, Japanese sword hilts, arabesques – designed to delight emperors, samurai and caliphs . . . he would glance at my labours in the corner, then stride over and exclaim, 'What is that you are doing Gardinier? Dis-donc that is not a curve, see, a curve has purpose, it starts here – so – but it expresses, how you say – an intention . . . .' He would open the glazed bookcase, bring down a leather-bound volume of *Meubles Chinois*, and open it at an illustration of a black lacquer table. I must observe how the legs terminated. They were not amputated with a saw, but shaped with three tight little curves, which touched the floor lightly.[2]

The workshops

During the second half of the nineteenth century, stock was purchased from other manufacturers (see pp. 65–6). But once Cartier had set up their own design and manufacturing operation, around 1900, certain workshops began to work exclusively for them. By the end of the 1920s, all three Cartier houses in Paris, London and New York had established additional workshops that bore the name Cartier, those in New York and London being situated on the Cartier premises. Even after the Cartier workshops were set up, other workshops continued to carry out work for Cartier.

PARIS

The workshop responsible for each piece is recorded in the archives. The principal Parisian workshops for gem-set platinum jewellery in the period 1900–1918 were those of Charpentier, Harnichard, Lavabre, Picq, Andrey and Droguet. Edmond Lecas appears less frequently, his diamond jewellery of the 1880s was much praised by Henri Vever. Picq, Andrey and Droguet both continued to work for Cartier into the 1920s. According to Nadelhoffer, Henri Lavabre worked exclusively for Cartier from 1906 to 1921; the collaboration continued into the 1930s.[3] During the 1920s, Lavabre seems to have specialised in goldwork and enamelling, executing a very large proportion of the cigarette and vanity cases. Another major exclusive supplier after the First World War was the Renault workshop, which worked primarily on gem-set pieces rather than in goldwork or enamel. From 1929 Cartier's own workshop was established at 17 Rue Bachaumont; the workshop was probably that of one of its former exclusive suppliers, but it now bore the name Cartier. From the mid 1930s Cartier seems to have taken over as well the Linzeler workshop at 9 Rue d'Argenson, and these two workshops co-existed until the early 1940s, when they were integrated at Rue d'Argenson. They moved to Cartier's main premises at the Rue de la Paix from the 1950s until 1976, but the present workshop is no longer at this address. A number of specialist workshops used for work on hardstones are discussed on p. 103.

Specialist workshops were also required for the clocks and watches. The principal supplier of watches was the firm of Edmond Jaeger (1850–1922), with whom Cartier signed a contract in 1907, giving them exclusive rights to its output. All the watches catalogued here were made by Jaeger. For clocks, the main supplier was Maurice Couet (1885–1963), who supplied table clocks to Cartier from 1911. In 1919 he set up a Cartier clock workshop at 53 Rue Lafayette, employing thirty specialists, including enamellers, stone-setters,

FIG. 30. Photograph of Maurice Couet's workshop, c. 1927–8. The Egyptian-style temple gate clock (cat. 88) can be seen on the top shelf of the bookcase at the back. Cartier archive, Paris.

engravers and engine-turners. This explains why the workshop also made some of the finely enamelled vanity cases, for example, cat. 130. An archive photograph taken in 1927 of the Rue Lafayette workshop shows a crystal Chimaera clock being worked on and, on the shelf at the back, the Egyptian-style temple gate clock made by Couet in 1927 and sold in New York in 1929 (fig. 30). According to Nadelhoffer, Couet's workshop had its own designers and executed designs supplied by them as well as by the Cartier designers at the Rue de la Paix. From 1930 the workshop was housed in the Rue Réaumur, the premises occupied by the Renault workshop. At this time Couet was employing about twenty workmen, but in 1931 the recession forced him to lay some of them off.[4]

From 1919 the importing of Paris-made clocks and watches into America was handled by the European Watch and Clock Company, which was based in New York with an office in Paris. Pieces handled by this firm generally bear the initials E. W. C. Co. or the name of the company in full.

LONDON

Cartier's London workshop was called English Art Works and was established by 1922. Directed by Félix Bertrand, it was housed in Cartier's premises at 175–6 New Bond Street before moving to 105 New Bond Street. As the name suggests, the employees were all English. During the 1930s some sixty skilled craftsmen were employed (see fig. 31). The workshop is now one of the few surviving in Bond Street, though it is only about one-quarter of the size. The tradition of handing down expertise from generation to generation is maintained to this day, with fathers and sons working side by side.

Before the setting up of English Art Works, Cartier London used a number of differ-

FIG. 31. Photograph of English Art Works taken in 1930, showing over forty jewellers at the bench. The floor is covered with a grid to catch the scraps of precious metal. Cartier archive, London.

ent workshops, many of which continued to supply the firm after 1922. Chief among these were Wright & Davies in Rosebery Avenue, which specialised in cigarette cases, lighters and other goldwork, and Sutton & Straker in Bond Street, which supplied a range of goldwork as well as gem-set platinum jewellery. Much of their work of the 1930s is recorded in a series of job record books in the London archive. A number of other specialist firms worked for Cartier London in the 1920s and 1930s. Wilkinson and Eady both supplied rings, Cropp & Farr and Paton supplied studs and links, Messenger supplied buttons and charms, Edwards made amber and composition cigarette holders, Peake seems to have done much of the diamond setting, and Sampson Mordan & Co. supplied pens and propelling pencils. Many of these London suppliers are discussed in Culme 1987. The workshop ledgers provide ample evidence of the extensive trade in small and relatively inexpensive items such as gold rings and charms. Some of these bore delightful mottoes with punning combinations of letters and numbers in the tradition of eighteenth-century sentimental jewellery, for example a ring made in 1938 was inscribed inside 'M Moi 100 CC' (aime-moi sans cesser = love me for ever).

Many pieces were sent from London to be repaired in Paris, presumably by the workshops that made them, for example Lambert Frères, Georges Lenfant and Rubel Frères. The Lenfant workshop was a big supplier of gold and gem-set chains and bracelets to many firms, but its production included models exclusive to Cartier. One such example, supplied by Lenfant and bearing the Lenfant workshop mark, is in the Hull Grundy Gift to the British Museum – a bracelet of gold links and cabochon amethysts. It appears in a Cartier London archive photograph dated 1925.[5]

NEW YORK

Initially Cartier New York obtained its stock from Paris and London. The date when it established its first workshop is uncertain, but it must have been in existence by 1917, the date of a leaflet advertising the remodelling of old-fashioned jewels by their own workshops (see above, p. 26). By the 1920s they were known as American Art Works and were situated on the fifth floor of the New York premises (see fig. 32). The workshop employed up to seventy craftsmen under the supervision of Paul Duru (1871–1971). The chief stone-setter was Paul Maîtrejean (1883–1975). Unlike English Art Works, the jewellers were all French, many from Cartier's Paris suppliers. One such craftsman was a certain Bouquet, who had trained in the Charpentier workshop.[6] In 1925 a second workshop was set up, also on the Fifth Avenue premises, specialising in goldwork. It was called 'Marel Works', a combination of the names of Pierre Cartier's daughter, Marion, and his wife, Elma. In addition to these two Fifth Avenue workshops, Cartier Inc. also used outside workshops.

At the outbreak of the Second World War the number of employees in American Art

FIG. 32. Photograph of American Art Works, *c.* 1922, showing some thirty workmen. Cartier archive, New York.

Works was reduced to around twenty-five, and activity was temporarily interrupted in 1941. After the war American Art Works was replaced by Vors & Pujol, still on the fifth floor of the Cartier premises with many of the same craftsmen.

The marks

When a piece was completed, the Cartier reference number would be added together with the signature 'Cartier', usually finely engraved in cursive script or capitals. Each piece, whether made for stock or as a special order, bore an individual reference number. There were separate sequences of numbers for stock and special orders. Paris-made pieces also had by law to bear an assay mark, either for gold (eagle's head), silver (boar's head) or, from 1912, platinum (dog's head), applied by the Paris assay office to each separate piece. Those for gold and silver are restricted warranty marks, guaranteeing a minimum standard of 750 for gold (i.e. 18 carat) or 800 for silver. In practice the standards were often higher. Some of the larger pieces, such as boxes, bear the French third gold standard mark for 18 carat gold, which is a specific, not a minimum, standard.[7]

It was also obligatory for French work in precious metals to bear the *poinçon de fabricant* of the workshop that had made the piece. Although *poinçon de fabricant* is literally a

OPPOSITE

FIG. 33. Five pieces in their original tooled and gilded morocco leather cases, dating from 1911–13: cat. 6 (back), 18–19 (watch and hat-pin), 31 (right) and 51 (sleeping pig). The cases always bore an impressed and gilded CARTIER stamp on the outside, as well as an address label printed in gold on the silk lining to the lid or wings. The costs of the cases are given in both the stock records and the order books. Some of the more elaborate cases were very expensive to make.

FIG. 34. Six pieces in their original tooled and gilded morocco leather cases, dating from 1923–35. Front row: cat. 173 and 208. Back row: cat. 202, 163, 67 and 184.

maker's or manufacturer's mark, the term 'workshop mark' has been used here to avoid confusion with English practice. French pieces made for the big firms often bear the marks of other workshops, and Cartier is no exception. This is entirely different from the English tradition, where the jeweller who sells the piece sends it to be marked with his 'maker's mark'. Where legible, the French workshop marks are described in the relevant catalogue entries, and the archive record is often corroborated by the mark on the piece itself. Sometimes the mark is lacking, for example if the piece has been altered and the fittings, where the piece was often marked, have been changed.

The following list gives the Paris workshop marks that occur on the pieces included in this catalogue. French workshop marks take the form of a horizontal or vertical lozenge containing the manufacturer's initials with a central symbol, often a pun on the maker's name (where there is any uncertainty this is indicated).

Andrey	GA flanking a spray of mistletoe
Bellemans	JB flanking a bell
Boulon & Taragnat	BLT (illegible symbol)
Cartier	C between two crescents with the letter S above and A below[8]
Droguet	HD flanking a flower
Dubois	RD flanking three chevrons
Georges Harnichard	GH flanking a chariot
Holl	CH flanking a set-square
Edmond Jaeger	EJ flanking an hour-glass
Henri Lavabre	HL flanking a four-leaf clover
Edmond Lecas	E and L above and below K
Georges Lenfant	GL flanking a dice above a wing
Mathey	M & CIE above a bird
Henri Picq	HP flanking an ace of spades (Fr. *pique* = spade)
Pillard	PP (illegible symbol)
Ploujavy	PLJV (or PLJY) with a diagonal cross
Renault	R with a crescent and flame (?)
Varangoz	KBV flanking a vase (?)

The pieces made in New York generally have only the Cartier signature, usually in capital letters, and number. The law did not require the application of an assay mark or workshop mark. American law permitted the use of 14 carat gold, while in England 15 and 9 carat were also used.

English hallmarking laws are different again. Platinum jewellery made in Britain prior to 1975 did not have to bear a hallmark, so the London-made platinum pieces bear only the Cartier signature and number. Cigarette and vanity cases, however, as gold or silver work, were subject to assay. Examples made or sold in London usually bear a full set of hallmarks with date-letter and importer's or sponsor's mark JC for Jacques Cartier. This mark was entered at the London assay office in 1912. The term 'sponsor' is now generally accepted as more accurate than 'maker', since the retailer or manufacturer who submitted the piece for assay was rarely the same as the workshop that had made it. Some of the Paris-made boxes catalogued here bear London import marks in addition to the French assay and workshop marks because they were made in Paris for Cartier London, and their sale-date is recorded in the London archive (for example, cat. 197–8).

The plaster casts

The archive in Paris holds several hundred hitherto unpublished plaster casts made in the workshop from finished pieces to provide a three-dimensional record, as a supplement to the archive photograph. These casts date from the period *c.* 1900–1920 and most of them are in the various styles discussed in section 1. The plaster cast recorded the curvature of a diadem or necklace and the often considerable height of the stones, features

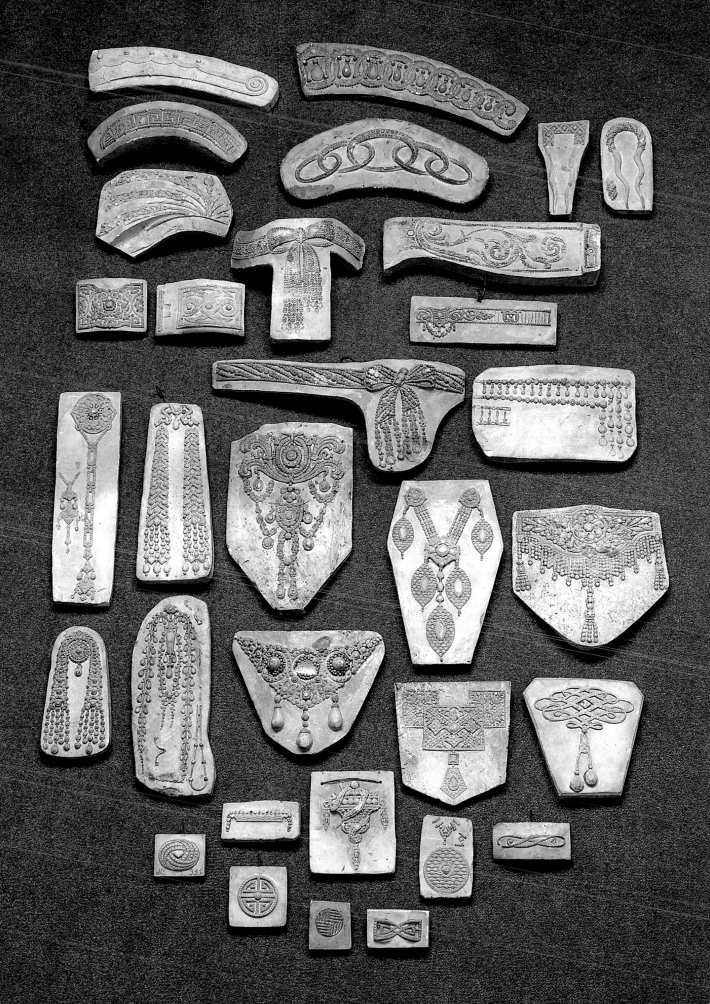

that would not be obvious from the archive photograph alone. The object was pressed into wax, leaving an impression in intaglio. From this the plaster cast in relief was made. Sometimes casts were taken of the blank mounting, before it was set with diamonds, but this tended to produce poor definition since the wax went through the holes.

The surviving casts are from pieces made for stock as well as pieces made as special orders, suggesting that there must once have been a complete series. Many of them have iron hooks at the back and must have been kept hung on the wall, possibly for display to clients in the same way as Chaumet's nickel silver models for tiaras (see p. 35). Most of the elaborate ones are annotated on the back with the date, the name of the client who commissioned or purchased the piece, the order or stock number, the workshop that made it and the price for mounting in the Cartier 'confitures' code, and the salesman's initials with sale number. The ten letters of the word confitures (preserves) represented the numbers 1 to 9 with zero at the end, i.e.: C = 1, O = 2, N = 3, F = 4, I = 5, T = 6, U = 7, R = 8, E = 9, S = 0. The letter K indicated a repeated number. For example, the cast from the devant de corsage made for Baronne de Gunzburg (illustrated with cat. 4) bears the client name, salesman's initials and sale number, the date of completion, the letter H for Harnichard stamped in blue and the workshop name 'Harnichard' written in, and the price code charged by the workshop for the mounting, CTSK, i.e. 1,600 francs.

FIG. 36. Plaster cast taken from the large diamond necklace with hexagonal pendants made for Grace Wilson, Mrs Cornelius Vanderbilt, in 1908 (greatly reduced).

The taking of plaster casts as records had been standard practice among many large firms since the nineteenth century, and is still done today by Cartier and others. However, it is extremely rare for casts of the nineteenth and early twentieth century to survive. One other comparable group was kept by the Frankfurt firm of Gertenbach & Kaiser and is displayed at the Frankfurt Historical Museum among the contents of the firm's workshop in the late nineteenth century. There is also the recently discovered group of plaster casts from the workshop of Alfred André in Paris.[9]

The Cartier casts provide an evocative record of great diadems or tiaras and necklaces that no longer survive. Examples include casts from the necklace with three hexagonal diamond pendants made for Mrs Cornelius Vanderbilt in 1908 (fig. 36) and from the diadem made for Mrs W. B. Leeds in 1913 (fig. 35, top centre).[10] The latter comprised a series of interlinked diamond and pearl circles, each with a pendant pearl hanging at the centre. The design of Mrs Leeds' diadem was based on the tiara of Grand Duchess Marie Pavlovna, made in Russia in the 1880s and temporarily deposited at Cartier Paris by the Grand Duchess for cleaning in 1911.[11] There are casts of many other famous pieces. A cast of part of a diamond sash made for Mrs W. K. Vanderbilt in 1910 is shown centre left in fig. 35. It comprises a circular brooch with a long pendant. Another complete diamond sash made for the same client is illustrated on p. 68. A cast of a devant de corsage made for the Countess of Hohenfelsen in 1908, with three huge button pearls and three pendant pear-shaped pearls, is shown towards the bottom of fig. 35, in the centre. She also wore it as a hat jewel with a white ostrich-feather aigrette.[12]

The cast of Mrs Leeds' diadem consists of just over half the tiara, including the central element and one side. This was standard practice for the casts of tiaras that encircled the head. Three other examples are shown top left in fig. 35, the first a steel diadem made for stock in 1914, similar to cat. 28; the second a Greek meander pattern sold to Pierre Cartier in 1909; the third a spray of wheat ears of 1909, sold to a Russian client from St Petersburg. In the case of a diadem for the front of the head only, a cast of the whole piece was taken, for example the frontlet of five interlinked circles immediately below Mrs Leeds' diadem in fig. 35.

Fig. 35 also shows two bow-knot necklaces of 1908 and 1910, both designed to be worn with the bow at the side. One of them is a cast taken of the blank mounting before it was set with diamonds. Next to these are two dog-collar necklaces of openwork diamond elements designed to be sewn to a black ribbon, and, to the right, a delicate necklace of pear-drop diamonds with a fringe of diamonds at the centre. All four necklaces were made as special orders by Lavabre, the right-hand one with central fringe for the Countess of Derby in 1909. Below this, on the right, is an extraordinary *devant de corsage* of 1907, with fringe and tassels, in the shape of a curtain pelmet. Other notable pieces include two corsage ornaments of 1911 in the form of double tassels (fig. 35, centre left), next to them a drooping vase brooch of 1911, and a 'devant de corsage japonais' of 1907 with overlapping squares and rectangles (bottom right). There are also examples of more modest pieces such as *plaques de cou* or the central ornaments of dog-collar necklaces of 1907 and 1909 (top left, below the diadems), *fourches* or two-pronged combs (top right), a group of small geometric brooches of *c.* 1907 (see cat. 22–5), and a vase draped with a garland and a brooch in the form of a flat fruit bowl, similar to those designed by Charles Jacqueau (see cat. 240–42).

In some instances the object from which the cast was taken survives. Where casts exist relating to objects catalogued here, they are mentioned in the relevant catalogue entry. Some are illustrated with the object itself (e.g. cat. 4 and 76–7). Fig. 37 shows three objects catalogued here with their related casts. The cast of the Japanese knot brooch is

FIG. 37. Cat. 22, 21 and 24 with their related plaster casts. The cast of the Japanese knot brooch (centre) is taken from a larger version of the brooch, not from the brooch illustrated here.

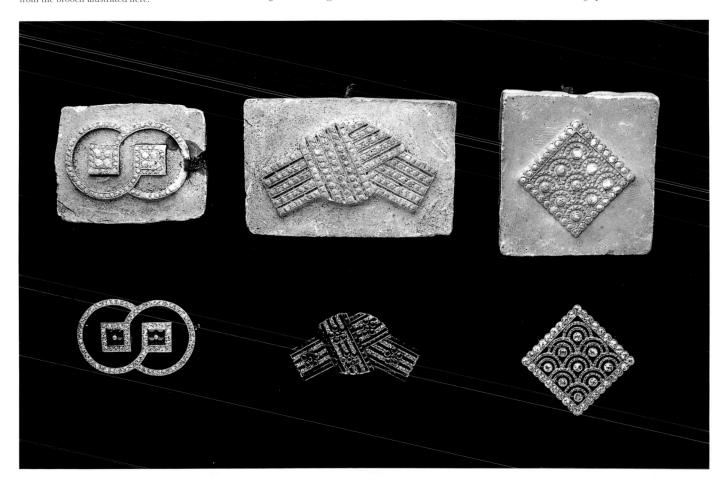

FIG. 38. The carved rock-crystal pendant (cat. 16) taken apart to show how the central element detaches for wear as a brooch.

FIG. 39. Plaster cast of the different elements of the carved rock-crystal pendant (cat. 16) made prior to assembly of the finished piece.

taken not from the brooch included here (cat. 20), but from a larger version. In the case of pieces that could be dismantled and worn in different ways, casts were sometimes taken of the component parts. This could provide a useful record if repairs were needed or if a similar example was executed at a later date. The rock-crystal pendant of 1912 (cat. 16) contains a central diamond oval which can be removed and worn as a brooch, with a separate brooch fitting with four spanner-head screws (fig. 38). The fitting has to be unscrewed from the back in order to detach the brooch and is then screwed back on afterwards. The cast shows the clasp lower left and the diamond oval element with central sapphire removed from the carved rock-crystal cartouche (fig. 39). The four screw-holes made in the crystal to attach the brooch are clearly visible in the cast.

NOTES

1. From Maurice Zolotow, 'Fine jewels are his business', *Saturday Evening Post*, 8 May 1948. Press clipping in Cartier archive, New York.
2. Gardner 1993, pp. 25–6.
3. Nadelhoffer 1984, p. 95 and ch. 6, n. 11.
4. Nadelhoffer 1984, p. 249 and ch. 16, n. 7, notes that Couet later moved into the Cartier workshop at the Rue d'Argenson, and eventually into the Rue de la Paix until 1956.
5. See Gere *et al.* 1984, cat. 1185.
6. Nadelhoffer 1984, ch. 2, n. 11.
7. Where the piece has been assayed by cupellation an accurate measurement is obtained. The restricted warranty marks are applied to items assayed by the touchstone, which is not as accurate and indicates a minimum standard only. See Tardy, *Les Poinçons de Garantie Internationaux pour l'Or, le Platine, le Palladium*, 10th edn, Paris 1981, pp. 31ff. and 160 ff., and Tardy, *Les Poinçons Internationaux pour l'Argent*, 10th edn, Paris 1981, pp. 199 ff.
8. The letters S and A in the Cartier workshop mark stood for 'Société Anonyme'. This was a shortened version of 'Société Anonyme à Responsabilité Limité' (SARL). The mark is illustrated in Nadelhoffer 1984 in his chronology under the year 1929 (unpaginated).
9. For the André plaster casts, see R. Distelberger *et al.*, *Western Decorative Arts*, Part I, National Gallery of Art, Washington, 1993, pp. 282–305. The casts are discussed with reference to jewels in the Renaissance style that André is thought to have made. One of the two examples illustrated is very similar in form to the Cartier casts.
10. The archive photograph of Mrs Vanderbilt's necklace is illustrated in Nadelhoffer 1984, pl. 25, p. 51, together with a photograph of her wearing it (pl. 14, p. 47). For the archive photograph of Mrs Leeds' diadem, see Nadelhoffer 1984, pl. 60, p. 71.
11. The tiara was acquired after the Grand Duchess's death by Queen Mary in 1921 and is now owned by Queen Elizabeth II. It was hung with pearls instead of diamonds and is illustrated, worn by the Grand Duchess, Queen Mary and Queen Elizabeth in Menkes 1985, pp. 78–9 and in Field 1992, pp. 24–5.
12. The archive photograph of Countess von Hohenfelsen's brooch is illustrated in Nadelhoffer 1984, pl. 34, p. 53, together with a photograph of her wearing it in 1912 as a hat brooch, pl. 53, p. 67. For the archive photograph of Mrs W. K. Vanderbilt's sash, see Nadelhoffer 1984, pl. 42, p. 57.

5

THE CARTIER ARCHIVE AND SURVIVING EVIDENCE

Each of the three Cartier houses in Paris, London and New York has kept its own records and the archive as a whole is exceptionally complete. All three houses maintained separate records of stock items and of special orders, as well as a remarkably comprehensive series of archive photographs of every piece made. The principal documents for the period 1900–1939 which have provided the basis for the catalogue that follows are described below.

Records of items made for stock

The Paris stock records often have a pen and ink sketch of the piece in the margin (see p. 17, fig. 9). They record the name of the workshop that executed the piece, the date of sale and the name of the purchaser. Where possible, this information has been given in the catalogue entries, so that the speed with which pieces were sold can be appreciated by comparing the date of entry in the stock book with the date of sale. If the piece did not sell and the stones were reused, this was also recorded. For examples of the reuse of stones see above, pp. 17–18, and cat. 136, 160 and 180, all of which incorporated stones or elements from pieces that did not sell. The complete history of cat. 269, the shoulder ornament made for the 1925 Paris Exhibition, can also be traced from the stock records.

Records of items made as special orders

The catalogue entries frequently refer to the Paris order books, which often contained pasted-in designs and photographs as well as records of modifications made according to changes in fashion (see figs 46–7 below). From the order books it has been possible to trace the continuous history of the 'collier hindou' made for Daisy Fellowes in 1936 (cat. 106), starting with the reuse of the stones from three different stock pieces handed back by the client and ending with the changes made to the necklace by her daughter in 1963.

New York special order records were kept in individual client files rather than ledgers for practical reasons: the customers made such frequent visits that the records had to be kept together. These client files are of particular value in that they contain all the alternative designs for each commission, including the rejected ones (see cat. 266, 298 and 299), as well as recording the changes made to pieces in later years.

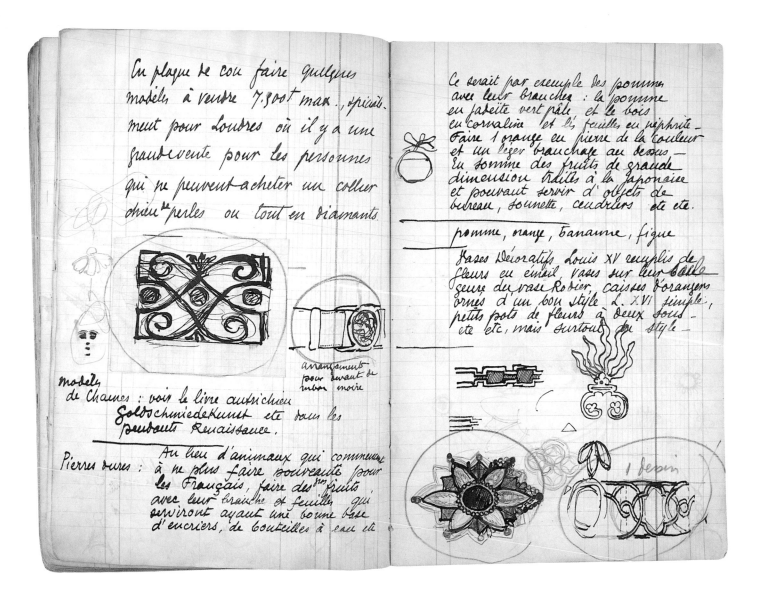

FIG. 40. Page opening from Louis Cartier's Notebooks (*Cahiers d'idées*), 1906–7, showing a sketch for a dog-collar plaque and notes for new models in carved hardstones. Cartier archive, Paris.

The photograph albums

The systematic photography of every piece – both stock and special orders – on delivery from the workshops began in the early 1900s. Actual-size prints were arranged in large albums. The 'Département S' (explained in section 3, p. 120) was always kept separate. In Paris alone a series of over 30,000 glass negatives survives from 1906 onwards. Some of the pieces catalogued here are described as 'dated by photographic negative number'; this refers to the photographs in these volumes.

Louis Cartier's Notebooks (*Cahiers d'idées*)

These four notebooks in the Paris archive cover the period *c.* 1905–25. They are not individually dated, but each book contains a number of dated notes. Much is by Louis Cartier himself, and the books have traditionally been described as his, since he directed all aspects of creation at that time, but many other hands also appear, for example in the commentaries on existing stock. In addition to sketches of ideas for jewels, the Notebooks give references to books used as sources of inspiration, analyses of current stock, notes of ideas for the new season's jewellery, notes of successful pieces to be repeated, and new inventions.

Fig. 40 shows a page opening in Louis Cartier's hand from the Notebook for 1906–7, with a sketch of a plaque for a dog-collar necklace annotated: 'Make some dog-collar plaques to be sold at 7500F max., specially for London, where they sell well to those who cannot afford a dog-collar necklace entirely of pearls or diamonds.' The page also includes Louis Cartier's note to himself to look at an Austrian book on goldsmiths' work with Renaissance pendants for models for chains, and his ideas for new models in hard-stone work:

Instead of animals, which are no longer new for the French, make large branches of fruit and leaves with solid bases that could be used as inkwells or scent bottles. For example, apple branches, the apples in pale green jadeite, the branch of cornelian and the leaves of nephrite . . . make large fruits in the Japanese manner that can be used as desk ornaments, bells, ash-trays etc. . . . . ornamental vases in the Louis XV style filled with enamel flowers, vases on plinths . . . boxes of oranges decorated in good and simple Louis XVI style, little flower pots for twopence, etc., etc. – but above all they must have style. . . . We should be busying ourselves with stock and not always looking for ideas of genius which are rare and which in consequence can produce a lot of unsaleable stock. We should be making sensible pieces: cuff-links in gold and gemstones that look as though they're worth the money but not as if they cost a king's ransom, cravat-pins with one or two stones that look expensive but simple.

For Autumn 1907, there were plans for bracelet-watches, blued steel chains, cord necklaces with ornamental slides, 'diamond chains like we sold to Mrs MacKay',[1] lavallières (see cat. 3), a big choice of items up to 250F for New Year's gifts, and a choice of items up to 1900F, 'the two choices always get forgotten'. It is indeed easy to overlook the huge range of modest gifts that must have been a very large part of Cartier's stock. There were always gifts for young girls, for confirmation or bridesmaids' presents – brooches, hair slides, medallions, pearl necklaces, and so on. By 1910–11 there were plans for sporting and yachting presents for young men, unspecified presents for 'messieurs âgés' as well as 'objets qui sont nécessaires aux dames tous les jours' (everyday necessities for ladies).

Not all the ideas in the Notebooks were taken up. A sketch for 'a long undulating bandeau with diagonal openings through which hair can be passed', contained in the Notebooks for 1908–9, does not appear to correspond to anything in the photograph albums. Other ideas appear in the Notebooks very much earlier than one might have expected. The list of New Year's Day novelties for 1910 included several varieties of double-headed cliquet pin: sketches in the margin show some in the form of arrows, others with twin heads. Examples rarely survive from this early date, however. Lipstick tubes are also mentioned at this date, though again none survives from before the First World War.

The last of the Notebooks covers the years 1915–25 and contains a detailed stock analysis made in September 1919. It is the only such analysis and presumably represents an assessment of the existing stock after the end of the war. Some of the pages are damaged and difficult to read, but the main points are summarised below. It describes what was actually in stock, what was to be broken up and what was currently in production. The main categories to be dismantled were dog-collar necklaces and plaques, by then long out of fashion. Among items that were lacking, the replacement of combs, bracelets and brooches was given a higher priority than that of necklaces or pendants. Smokers' accessories consisted entirely of bought-in pieces. Stocks of ladies' accessories were very low. Among items currently in production were cliquet pins, 'bracelets soudanais' (see cat. 187), necklaces for the upper and lower neck, and fancy earrings in onyx and diamonds (see cat. 177). One of the most interesting points to emerge is that in high jewellery it was thought that too many stones of different sizes and too much metal were tied up in large,

FIG. 41. Page opening from the Garland Style Design Scrapbook, I, p. 30, c. 1906, showing neo-classical style dog-collar necklaces. Cartier archive, Paris.

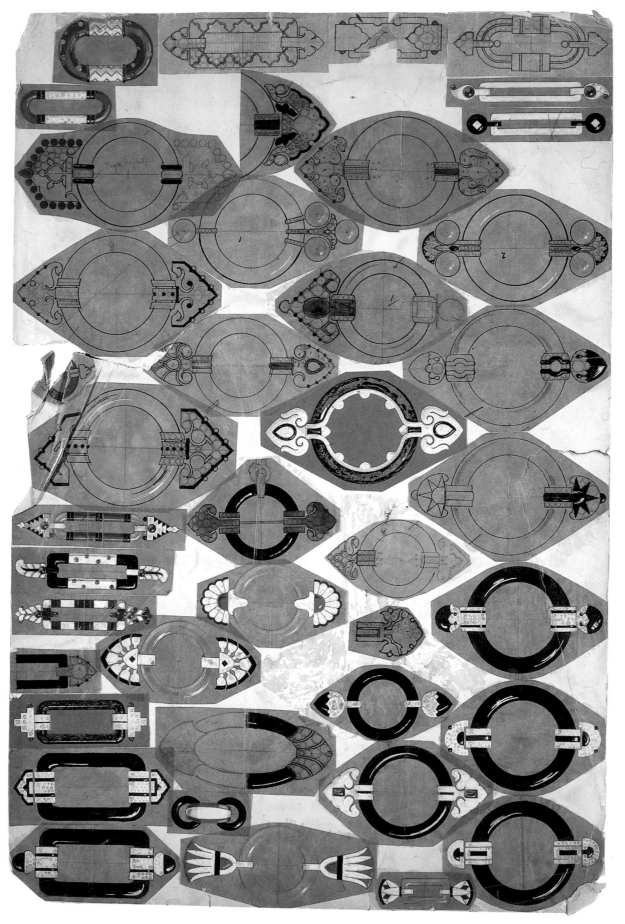

FIG. 42. Page of designs for brooches with onyx or rock-crystal rings or rectangles from the London Design Scrapbook, *c.* 1922–3 (see cat.162).

expensive stock pieces, and that such jewellery should consist of large stones which alone made up the value of the piece.

Finally there is a list of some forty new ideas for stock items for New Year's Day 1922, dated 8 September 1921 and showing how stock was constantly updated:

> . . . new designs for head ornaments, belt buckles with hardstones, belts, new designs for bracelets, pendants hung on long cords, seals, ash-trays, elaborate cigarette holders, enamel and diamond shoe-buttons, Japanese pins, cuff-links with demi-pearls, inexpensive hat-pins, fur bracelets, jewels for the back, dog-collars in jet (jet beads), resurrect the idea of objects in silver ribbon (have silver cords woven), look at Worth's silver fabrics, brooches to clip onto the coat or hat, inexpensive pendant watches [*montres régences*], use very pale and translucent horn, use amber, new objects to include pencils and pens, calendars, New Year's Day cards in gold with gold envelopes, find a suitable lightweight material to make netting for bracelets, necklaces or for the hair, cigar boxes with match compartments, match-boxes, spectacles, opera glasses, belts formed of a double cord of silver attached with diamond buttons and diamond terminals, Spanish combs, diadems with tiled pattern in ivory or other materials, chains formed of onyx tubes.

Many of these ideas were put into production, though perhaps not immediately. Jewels for the back, for example, appeared towards the end of the 1920s and continued into the 1930s (see pp. 20–21, figs 14–15). The plan to make New Year's Day cards in gold with gold envelopes was not carried out, but Louis Cartier kept the idea in his head and on leaving New York in 1927 sent his brother Pierre a gold 'thank you' card in a gold envelope, apparently the only one ever made (cat. 58).

The designs

The function of the various designs, ranging from sketches of source material to highly finished designs, is discussed above in the chapter on the production process. The designers are discussed in section 9 of the catalogue. The following is a summary of the different kinds of design illustrated in this catalogue.

Firstly, there are sketches of source material comprising studies of ornament made in museums or taken from books (p. 64, fig. 49, and cat. 247); some sketches of architectural ornament may have been made directly from the buildings themselves.

Secondly, there is a series of scrapbooks, some compiled at the time and more or less homogeneous, such as the Garland Style Design Scrapbooks, *c.* 1900–1912, in Paris. The drawings in these three volumes are not highly finished, being mainly in pen and ink with some watercolour and bodycolour, and do not correspond exactly to the jewels as executed. Fig. 41 shows a page with designs for dog-collar necklaces and *plaques de cou*, some of which are not unlike the casts shown in fig. 35. Other scrapbooks were compiled later and cover two or three decades. These generally contain finished designs. The three different Paris design scrapbooks illustrated here (see, for example, cat. 228–9, 249–50, 280 and 282), are described for reference purposes as Design Scrapbook I, II and III. This catalogue also includes a number of illustrations from a scrapbook with London pieces, referred to as the London Design Scrapbook (fig. 42, fig. 57 on p. 138 and cat. 252, 256). This scrapbook also contains the original design for the emerald and diamond shoulder brooch acquired by Marjorie

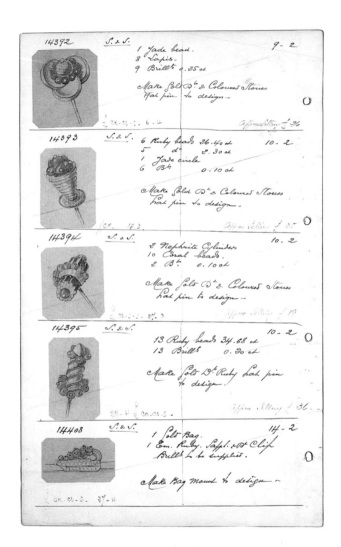

FIG. 43. Page from the job record book for Sutton & Straker, one of the workshops that supplied Cartier London, showing designs for gold hat-pins with jade, coral, rubies and diamonds, mid-1930s. Cartier archive, London.

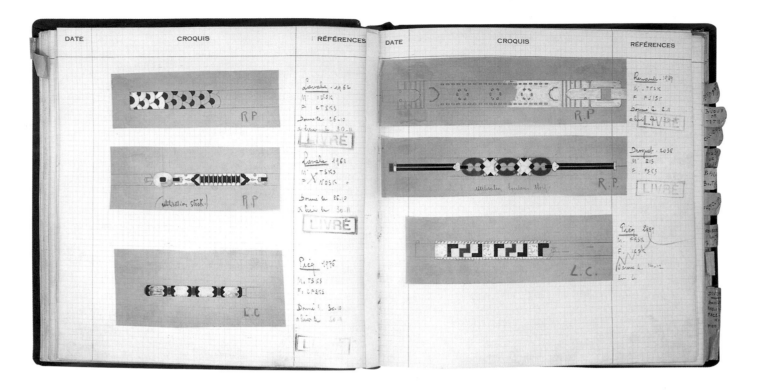

FIG. 44. Page opening from the Stock Design Record Book, 1922, showing designs for bracelets (cat. 259). The right-hand column records the workshop that made the piece and the manufacturing cost in code. Cartier archive, Paris.

OPPOSITE

FIG. 45. Diamond clip brooch in the form of a pyramid (cat. 220). One of a pair of clip brooches purchased by an American client from Cartier Paris in 1935.

Merriweather Post (cat. 100). Although the designs in these scrapbooks are not individually dated, many of those that were executed can be dated by matching them up with the archive photograph.

Thirdly, many designs are pasted into chronologically arranged volumes. Examples include the London workshop daybooks or job record books for English Art Works (see above, p. 21, fig. 14), and for other workshops that supplied Cartier London, such as Sutton & Straker (fig. 43).[2] Stock and special orders are mixed in these volumes. Paris has a similar sequence of dated designs in stock design record books (see fig. 44 and cat. 259) and in the order books mentioned above (cat. 258 and 300). The New York designs in this catalogue come from the New York client files (see above, p. 52).

Other miscellaneous records in all three archives include press cuttings and illustrations from contemporary fashion magazines, ephemera such as printed catalogues (see cat. 70–71 and p. 157, fig. 68) and invitations to exhibitions (see p. 102, fig. 57).

Tracing pieces between the different Cartier archives

The Cartier archive records can be used to document not only the changes and additions made to a single piece over a period of time, but also to show how the same client might patronise more than one Cartier house or how a piece ordered from one house might be completely altered in later years by one of the other Cartier houses. With the sequence of records described above, it is possible to trace the continuous history of a piece over several years and between the different houses. American clients, in particular, often had dealings with all three branches. Examples of commissions begun in Paris or London and continued in New York are to be found on p. 27 and in section 9 (see cat. 294, 296 and 298).

One surviving example that can be pursued from Paris to New York is the pyramid clip brooch in the Cartier collection (cat. 220; see fig. 45). It was initially one of a pair of clip brooches commissioned by an American client from Cartier Paris in 1935. The large double clip brooch made by Cartier Paris in 1935 could be worn as a single brooch or as

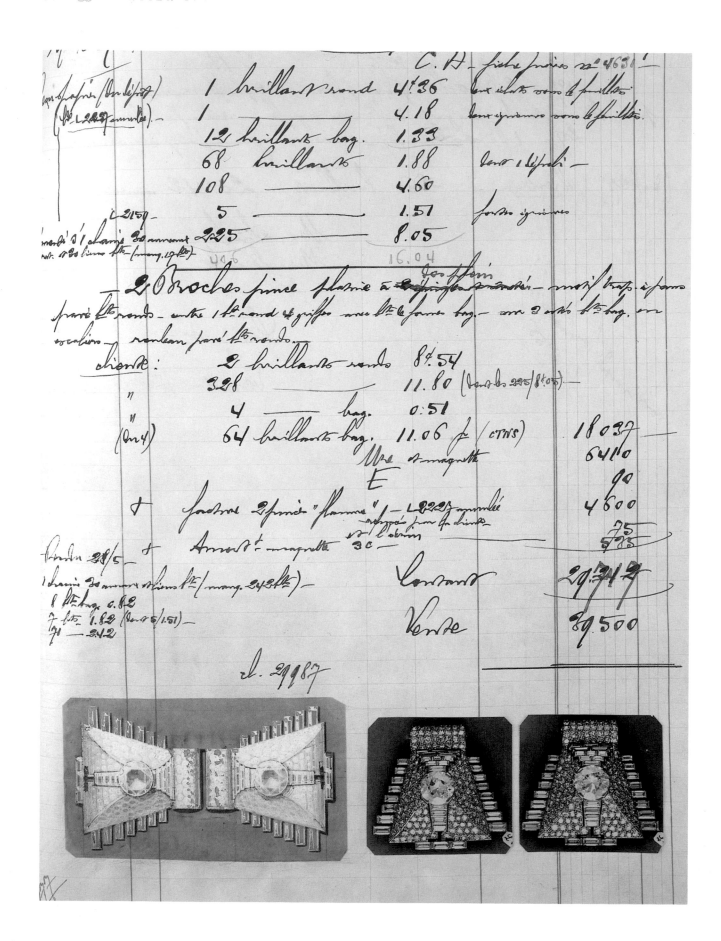

OPPOSITE

FIG. 46. Original design in bodycolour on buff tracing paper for cat. 220, one of a pair of clip brooches forming one brooch. From the order book for 1935. Cartier archive, Paris.

FIG. 47. Design for and photograph of the black lacquer bacelet designed to take one of the clips shown in fig. 46 (cat. 220). Order book, 1935. Cartier archive, Paris.

BELOW

FIG. 48. Two alternative designs from a Cartier New York client file for a gold necklace to take both pyramid clips (cat. 220). The designs were done for the same client who purchased the brooches in Paris in 1935 and date probably from the late 1930s or early 1940s. Cartier archive, New York.

two clip brooches. The original bodycolour design for the double clip brooch in white on buff tracing paper is in the Paris order book for 15 May 1935 (fig. 46). Later that year the client commissioned one of the newly fashionable black lacquer bracelets to take one of the clips. The original pencil, pen and ink design for the bracelet in black lacquer on white gold is in the same order book, for 23 December 1935. It shows two views, the top with clip and the side; the bracelet was to be in white gold, the wrist measurement of the client being duly recorded, as was customary with commissioned bracelets (fig. 47).

In New York, at a later unrecorded date, probably in the late 1930s or early 1940s, the client decided to update her clip brooches by turning them into ornaments for one of

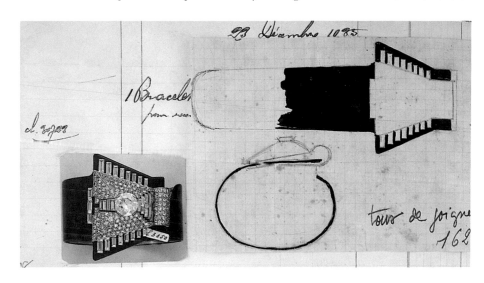

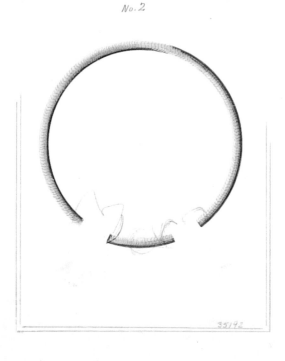

Cartier's most popular inventions of the 1930s, the flexible gold tubing for necklaces or bracelets known as 'tuyau à gaz', or gas-pipe, because of its coiled pattern. Cartier was producing it by 1936 and exhibited examples at the Paris Exhibition of 1937.[3] In the Cartier New York archive, designs for special orders are kept not in order books as in Paris, but in an alphabetical sequence of client files. Here, under the same client's name, are two original designs in pencil and bodycolour on white paper for a gold tube necklace to take both clips, either separately or together as a bow-shaped pendant in the front (fig. 48). The archive does not record whether either necklace design was ever executed, but that one of them was indeed made is suggested by an inner fitting inside the cylindrical hinge at the top of the clip to fit the chain. Necklaces of this kind were often designed to be worn alone or to take a series of detachable clips, sometimes as many as seven. A number of similar designs of the mid- to late 1930s for gold necklaces and clip pendants are to be found in the Cartier London archive.

Other sources of information

The volumes of press cuttings in the Cartier archive are an invaluable resource. They contain articles from the international press relating to the activities of all three houses and their staff, members of the Cartier family, important sales and deals, and so on. They also contain fashion photographs and articles from contemporary journals. The press cuttings seem to have been more systematically collected than the material from magazines. There is very much more information to be gleaned in all the relevant magazines such as *Vogue* (French, English and American editions), *Harper's Bazaar* (English and American editions), *Femina* (Paris), and the *Sketch* (London). Complete runs of these journals are not easily available, but the selective search that has been carried out for this catalogue has provided not only additional fashion photographs of models wearing Cartier jewellery, but also advertisements, pictures of Cartier clients wearing their jewels, and accounts of social occasions with descriptions of Cartier jewels that were worn.

Assembling information on Cartier clients is not an easy task. For British and American clients there are dictionaries of national biography and the volumes of *Who Was Who*. The best source for Continental European families is the *Almanach de Gotha*. This has revealed the many marriages of American heiresses into European aristocratic families. Much use has also been made of anecdotes from memoirs and biographies of Cartier clients or their circle.

Last but not least, Hans Nadelhoffer's monograph of 1984, *Cartier. Jewelers Extraordinary*, contains a wealth of information that is not available elsewhere. Much of it clearly comes from first-hand sources, although these are not always given.

NOTES

1. Mrs Clarence Mackay, a major American client in the early 1900s. The number of references in the Notebooks to pieces sold to Americans provides evidence of the importance of American clients in these years.
2. Further pages from these books are illustrated in Paris 1989, cat. 460–62.
3. See Gabardi 1989, p. 203 and p. 200, a fashion plate from the magazine *Femina*, with matching necklace and bracelets of gas-pipe tubing with bunches of grapes, all in gold.

NOTES ON THE CATALOGUE

The following format has been adopted in the catalogue entries. After each catalogue heading is given the name of the workshop (where known) that made the piece; which of the three Cartier branches it was made for – Paris, London or New York; whether it was made for stock or as a special order; and the year it was made. A description of the piece is followed by documentary information from the archive, for example the date the piece was entered in the stock book; the date it was actually sold; the name of the purchaser, if made for stock, or of the client who commissioned it (where Cartier has permitted this to be revealed); and the subsequent history of the piece, including any alterations, any later owners, and any auction sales in which it may recently have appeared. At Cartier's request, prices have been omitted.

Exhibitions referred to are mainly those organised by Cartier, and the catalogues are listed in the Bibliography under the section on publications devoted solely to Cartier (section A). Other exhibition catalogues and other literature are listed in section B of the Bibliography.

Finally, details are given of any related material in the archive, such as design drawings for the piece or plaster casts taken from it.

The measurements of the design drawings in section 9 refer to the size of the tracing paper or card on which the design is drawn, or to the whole page onto which the designs have been pasted, and not to the actual image.

All items are illustrated, many actual size or as near actual size as possible. Where illustrations are greatly enlarged or reduced, this is indicated.

1900–1918
THE EMERGENCE
OF THE
CARTIER STYLE

FIG. 49. Page from the
Sketchbooks showing
drawings of architectural
ornament and ironwork
c. 1905. Cartier archive Paris.

During Cartier's first half-century, from 1847 to 1900, the firm acted as retailers rather than as designers or manufacturers, and their stock was entirely bought in from several different suppliers. The stock comprised a wide range of jewels and *objets d'art* in all the revivalist styles then current, as well as traditional diamond jewellery. Cartier thus combined the two French traditions of *bijouterie* (fancy jewellery in gold, enamel and semi-precious stones) and *joaillerie* (high jewellery in diamonds and precious stones).

Around 1900 a dramatic change occurred that made the period from the turn of the century up to the end of the First World War one of enormous diversity and development. It is difficult to state exactly when this change took place because of the lack of documentation in these early years, but the move to the Rue de la Paix in 1899 seems to mark the transition from retailer to creator and the setting up of Cartier's own design studio. No designs survive from the nineteenth century, only thumbnail sketches of bought-in pieces in the margins of the stock books. From the early 1900s, however, a series of design scrapbooks survives, which make it possible to identify Cartier's own creations; but it is only from 1906, when the firm started to make a comprehensive photographic record of its entire output, that it is possible to make generalisations with any degree of accuracy. Even then, only the Paris house kept photographic records at this time. The range of stock was still extraordinarily diverse – including, for example, the Russian-style boxes and hardstone carvings discussed in section 2 – but nevertheless several different themes emerge clearly. The objects in this section have been grouped to illustrate some of these themes, most of which existed simultaneously and do not represent any chronological development.

The first point that needs to be made is the almost total absence of the Art Nouveau style in Cartier's stock in the years around 1900. An exception was a series of religious medallions bought in by Alfred Cartier, which were designed in the Art Nouveau style by the medallist Frédéric de Vernon and made by the workshop of Félix Duval. They were struck in gold or silver and then part-enamelled or pierced to take plique-à-jour enamel (an example of a gold medallion of the Virgin with a plique-à-jour enamel background is in the Hull Grundy Gift to the British Museum and is identical to those sold by Cartier).[1] Apart from these, a few specific pieces were supplied to Cartier, such as a gold and silver thistle-motif waist clasp of 1896 and a gold-mounted handbag of 1906. There was also a peacock pendant by Louis Aucoc, one of the greatest exponents of the Art Nouveau style, who favoured the new materials such as carved and tinted horn and plique-à-jour enamel.[2] The early photographic albums suggest that the Art Nouveau style was sometimes used for small diamond brooches, but not for large-scale pieces.

A glance through the pages of these albums shows how very different Cartier's production was from that of the other jewellers of the Rue de la Paix, as illustrated by Henri Vever in his authoritative history of French nineteenth-century jewellery.[3] The first theme that becomes clear is a highly individual interpretation of neo-classical and Empire-period ornament. Cartier's designs are derived not only from jewellery of the late eighteenth and early nineteenth century, but also from architectural ornament of that period (fig. 49). Louis Cartier encouraged his designers to make sketches of architectural details on the buildings of Paris, and the sketchbooks dating from this time include garlands of fruit from the Petit Trianon at Versailles. Nadelhoffer coined the term 'garland style' to describe the ubiquitous neo-classical swags and laurel wreaths in the Cartier design repertoire (cat. 4–7). The term 'neo-classical' has been adopted here to reflect the source of inspiration of a number of pieces in section 1a.

Louis Cartier owned copies of many of the standard ornament books printed in Paris in the late eighteenth century.[4] Bow-knots and tassels were derived from J. P. Pouget's *Traité des Pierres Précieuses* of 1762 (examples can be seen in the group of plaster casts taken from Cartier jewels shown in fig. 35 on p. 47). Pouget's designs for trophies of love included flower baskets, and these may have inspired the watch purchased by Nellie Melba in 1909 (cat. 14). Designs for stomachers by L. van der Cruycen (1770) were copied as *devants de corsage* in the form of an inverse triangle, one of which comprised a series of bows decreasing to a point at the base.[5] A pattern book issued by T. Bertren in 1771 contained frames which reappear on Cartier's invitation cards, as well as garlanded vases taken up by Charles Jacqueau (see cat. 240–41). Several designs for dog-collar plaques were derived from eighteenth-century designs for snuff-boxes, while a number of tiara designs incorporating acanthus scrolls, wreaths and drops were closely based on early nineteenth-century models (see cat. 7).

Cartier's so-called 'Russian diadem' (cat. 10) owes less to the Russian *kokoshnik* (a broad band that flared outwards from the head) than to the Empire-period diadem worn by Empress Josephine among others, formed of a vertical band that expanded towards the centre. These were known as 'Spartan' diadems in England, reflecting their classical origins.[6] The two combs (cat. 8 and 9) also derive from early nineteenth-century models. The wide, flat comb with ornamental band across the top (cat. 9) is a characteristic form of *c.* 1800–1810,[7] while the curved diamond meander (cat. 8) is inspired by frontlet ornaments of *c.* 1820–30, with hinged mounts so that the comb could be inserted horizontally into the piled-up hair, leaving the ornamental part visible, as if it were a small diadem.[8]

Another theme of the early 1900s is illustrated by cat. 1–2. The *devant de corsage* in the form of entwined lily and eglantine branches (cat. 2) is a fine example of detailed three-dimensional naturalism, and the open-back setting of diamonds on the curved surfaces of the leaves and petals is masterly. The use of open-back platinum puts it in the early twentieth century, but its design is entirely conventional and if it were in closed-back silver, with no other documentation, it could be taken for mid-nineteenth-century work. This is not the case with the fern-spray branches (cat. 1), where each element is fitted with a gallery, that is, a raised platinum frame at the back that lifts the piece off the body and allows light to pass through the stones. Cartier were not unique in constructing jewellery in this way, but they were certainly one of the first to introduce this method around 1900, and it

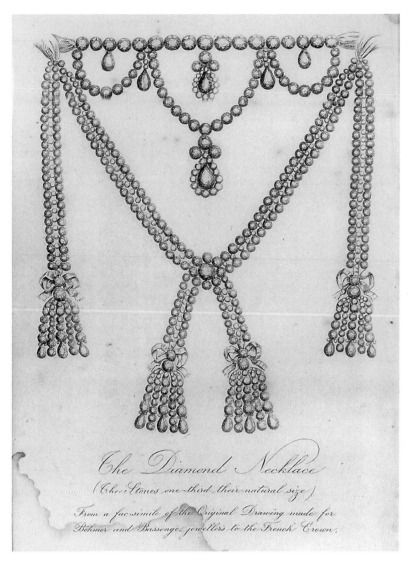

FIG. 50. Archive photograph of the diamond and platinum 'hair-net' necklace (*collier résille*) made by Cartier for Caroline Otéro in 1903, the design based on the celebrated diamond necklace that became the centre of a scandal devised to dishonour Marie Antoinette (see fig. 51).

FIG. 51. Nineteenth-century engraving of the diamond necklace commissioned by Louis XV for Madame du Barry in the 1770s. From H. Vizetelly, *The Story of the Diamond Necklace*, London 1881.

became a hallmark of their diamond jewellery of the period 1900–1918. Both pieces are beautifully articulated, so that they conform naturally to the curves of the body.

Such flexibility and lightness of construction would have been unthinkable without Cartier's pioneering use of platinum. Diamonds have traditionally been set in white metal, whether silver, white gold or platinum, in order to enhance their refractive properties. Gold might be used for a frame or stem of a plant spray, but not adjacent to the stones themselves. Silver, used throughout the eighteenth and nineteenth centuries for diamond jewellery, is a relatively soft metal. It bends easily and cannot support weight unless it is fairly thick. Platinum, on the other hand, is light and capable of being worked in very thin gauge while retaining its strength. It does not bend easily, so flexibility has to be obtained purely by constructing the jewel in several hinged elements. For this reason many of the bracelet or necklace clasps on Cartier jewellery, where extra flexibility was needed, are often of gold or white gold. According to Louis Cartier, the firm introduced platinum in 1896. In an interview for the *International Jeweler* in 1927 he had this to say:

> The thick settings of gold, silver and heavy woven strands that had been known since time immemorial were like the armour of jewelry. The use of platinum, which became its embroidery, an innovation introduced by us, produced the reformation; but it was

no easy task to transform the thin, light metal into a support of precious stones. It was not until we studied the mechanics of the springs and trusses that hold up the sleeping car, that we were able to adapt the metal to our purpose. Today, however, we have overcome the difficulty. We have even produced a hard platinum by adding nickel and iridium to the tips of the metal and platinum will remain the chosen metal for the worker until we find another, even lighter, with all its other good qualities.[9]

Louis Cartier's description of platinum as the embroidery of jewellery was aptly chosen. Nowhere was platinum used with more delicate, lace-like effect than in the series of *colliers résille* (literally 'hair-net' necklaces) made in the very first years of the century. Perhaps the most technically astonishing is that made for 'la belle Otéro' in 1903 with stones from the celebrated *boléro* (a sleeveless jacket that owed its name to her) made for her by Paul Hamelin in 1901. The tight, yet supple dog-collar, extended to a point at the front, was made entirely of solitaire diamonds held in a grid of thin platinum wires and punctuated by larger stones. Two long ribbons, formed of three rows of diamonds similarly set, cross over the breast and end in large bows and tassels (fig. 50). The idea of the knotted ribbons and tassels was directly inspired by the famous diamond necklace commissioned by Louis XV for Madame du Barry. It later became the subject of one of the great pre-Revolution scandals, in which Marie Antoinette was accused of trying to acquire it without the knowledge of Louis XVI (fig. 51).[10] Caroline Otéro (1868–1964) was one of many actresses who became customers of Cartier. Her collection of jewels, received from admirers such as Leopold II of Belgium, Albert of Monaco, the Shah of Persia and the Khedive of Egypt, was legendary. She wore pieces once owned by Empress Eugénie and the Empress of Austria, and continued to commission pieces from Cartier until 1919.[11]

A third theme of Cartier design at this period was the combination of diamonds with pearls, to achieve still greater lightness and delicacy. This was very much a taste of the period and not unique to Cartier, but Cartier created pieces of exquisite charm and elegance (cat. 10–13). The flat pearl and platinum chains often incorporated coloured pearls: cat. 11, the watch and chain, makes particularly subtle use of coloured grey and pinkish pearls to complement the matt grey surface of the platinum watch. This group illustrates the emerging fashion for the long chain or sautoir, another revival from the late eighteenth and early nineteenth century. Flat chains made of pearls or of woven or cut steel were characteristic of the period 1790–1810, and the octagonal diamond motifs punctuating the pearl chain of cat. 11

FIG. 52. Archive photograph of an *écharpe* or shoulder sash made in diamonds and pearls by Cartier Paris for stock in 1909 and sold to Mrs W. K. Vanderbilt in 1910. The same client owned another made entirely of diamonds, and at least two further examples were made for Mrs Cornelius Vanderbilt and Mrs Frederick William Vanderbilt. The top part was pinned to the shoulder and the lower part to the corsage. The strings could hang straight down, as in this photograph, or be draped right across the bodice.

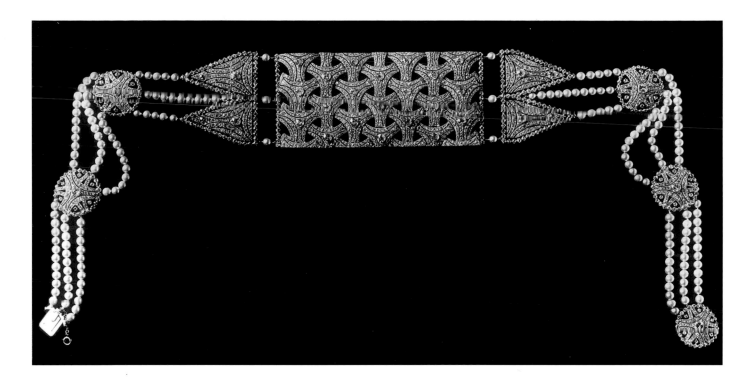

FIG. 53. Archive photograph of a 'Byzantine' head ornament of diamonds and pearls made by Cartier Paris to the order of Mrs W. K. Vanderbilt in 1909.

seem to be taken directly from neo-classical cut-steel chatelaine chains made both in England and in France.[12]

Sadly, the grandest and most unconventional pieces of Cartier's pearl, diamond and platinum jewellery do not survive. Chief amongst these must be the outsize *écharpe* or shoulder sash made for Mrs W. K. Vanderbilt in 1909–10 (fig. 52). Here, diamond elements were attached to festoons of pearls, pinned to the shoulder and then draped right across the breast like a sash. Necklaces were often pinned like a fringe across the bosom,[13] but the idea of a jewelled sash seems to have been a Cartier invention. In 1910 Mrs W. K. Vanderbilt commissioned another sash made entirely of diamonds, including five enormous pear-drops.[14] Several sketches for similar sashes appear in Louis Cartier's Notebooks for 1908–9, annotated 'écharpes genre Vanderbilt'. Mrs W. K. Vanderbilt also commissioned a spectacular 'Byzantine' head ornament of diamonds and pearls in 1909 (fig. 53). Worn low across the forehead, it anticipated the series of flat supple bandeaux produced from *c.* 1913.

Another theme that emerges from *c.* 1910–11 is the use of rock crystal carved and engraved in the Renaissance manner as the starting point for the creation of diadems, pendants, brooches, clocks, watches and hat-pins (cat. 16–19). The inspiration came from the carved and engraved rock-crystal vessels produced in Milan and Prague in the sixteenth and seventeenth centuries for the courts of Europe. Many such vessels entered the French royal collections and would have been familiar to the Cartier designers. The Cartier rock-crystal pieces were cut and engraved by the Berquin-Varangoz workshop.[15] Among the largest pieces were two diadems, one made for Baronne de Gunzburg in 1912, the other as a wedding tiara for the Russian Princess Irina, for her marriage to Prince Felix Yusupov in 1914.[16] Sometimes the rock crystal was cut into simple oval shapes for brooches and engraved with foliate scrollwork. Two examples are included among the designs of Charles Jacqueau (see cat. 234). But in the more elaborate pieces the crystal was cut into the shape of a Renaissance cartouche and mounted in diamond settings that might resemble Renaissance strapwork. Cat. 16 is superbly carved with grotesque heads and the crystal is matt, not polished. This gives a completely different effect from Renaissance carved crystal and from earlier French Renaissance-revival pieces incor-porating carved rock crystal made by jewellers such as Baugrand, who combined engraved crystal panels with enamelled gold in the 1860s and 1870s.[17]

Concurrent with all these revival styles was a completely unexpected approach that is impossible to categorise. It has been broadly labelled here as geometric and avant-garde design, and comprises two different strands. The first is a group of linear geometric designs produced *c.* 1906–10 (cat. 20–26). These are quite unlike the contemporary 'garland' or neo-classical style pieces in that they rely purely on simplicity of design. Some are inspired by Japanese motifs (cat. 20) or by Chinese ornament (cat. 24 and 25). Further examples of this linear style may be seen in the designs (cat. 228). The same designs were made into larger brooch-pendants by the addition of a chain and a smaller brooch at the top. Fig. 54 shows plaster casts taken from four long brooch-pendants of this kind.

Others, such as the bracelet imitating watered silk (cat. 26), are inspired by textile patterns in the same way as the lacework necklaces discussed above, but with bold abstract designs. The watered silk motif was used to best effect in a dog-collar necklace of 1907 (fig. 55). Each vertical element was articulated for flexibility, but from a distance the vertical divisions would have been invisible, leaving the impression that the wave pattern was floating on the black grosgrain ribbon support. According to Nadelhoffer, a similar bandeau made in 1912 was exhibited at the Canadian Exhibition of the same year. At $10,080 it was the most expensive item, and it was sold to Princess A. Bibesco.[18] Fig. 56 illustrates another dog-collar necklace, of 1909, which is one of the first examples of Cartier's overlapping scale pattern, which recurred time and again in bandeaux of the early 1920s.

Given that Cartier paid almost no attention to Art Nouveau, it is perhaps surprising that the firm was one of the first to introduce an avant-garde style. This lasted about ten years, from 1910 to 1920, and is not paralleled by anything being done by its competitors (cat. 29–36). It is also one of the few styles in which many pieces can be attributed with reasonable certainty to a particular designer, Charles Jacqueau. This is due to the survival of the Jacqueau archive, which is discussed in section 9 and which contains working designs for four of the brooch-pendants included here (cat. 29–32).

The novelty lies both in design and in colour. The brooch-pendants all consist of a two-pronged brooch with hanging elements which gave the effect of jewelled fabric, since the pins were hidden during wear; hence the term *broche draperie* sometimes applied to

FIG. 54. Four plaster casts taken from brooch-pendants of geometric design, *c.* 1909. The second from left (L. 15.5 cm) has a lozenge-shaped pendant with scale-pattern motif identical to that of cat. 24. The far right pendant is in the form of a Chinese bronze chime or gong (see p. 189, fig. 76). Reduced.

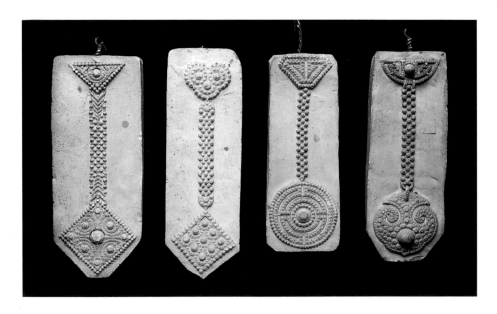

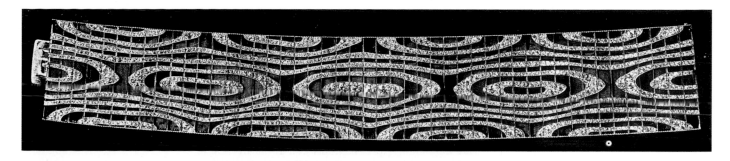

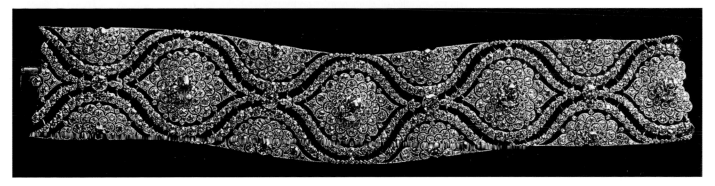

FIG. 55. Archive photograph of a dog-collar necklace of diamonds imitating watered silk, set on a backing of grosgrain ribbon, made by Cartier Paris for stock in 1907.

FIG. 56. Archive photograph of a dog-collar necklace of diamonds set in platinum made by Cartier Paris for stock in 1909. There is no ribbon backing: the central scale-pattern rosettes are held within the undulating wave motif by barely visible platinum stems.

these brooches. And the designs are truly startling. The bold simplicity of cat. 31 is remarkable, as is the long, thin, banner-shaped pendant of cat. 29, with its marquetry of jade and sapphires providing the blue and green colour combination popularised by Cartier in the 1920s. Cartier's colour combinations are discussed in section 7, but there are two other notable examples in this section, both also dating from 1913–14. Coral and black onyx appear together in cat. 32, while cat. 30 combines emeralds, diamonds and onyx, as well as Cartier's much-loved zigzag onyx border pattern, which is also found on the wrist watch of 1913 (cat. 27).

Needless to say, these daring pieces were almost all made for stock. The exceptions are the brooch with large sapphires (cat. 34) in which the client's own stones were reused, and one of the New York brooches (cat. 36), which was designed to take the client's cabochon sapphires.

NOTES
1. See Gere *et al.* 1984, cat. 1153.
2. For the clasp and bag see Cologni and Mocchetti 1992, pp. 36 and 52. The peacock pendant is mentioned in Nadelhoffer 1984, pp. 87–8.
3. Henri Vever, *La Bijouterie Française au XIXe siècle*, 3 vols, Paris 1904–8.
4. A number of these are listed by Nadelhoffer (1984, pp. 46–7) but the source of his information is not given and there appears to be no surviving record of Louis Cartier's library in the Cartier archive now.
5. An example of 1905 is illustrated in Nadelhoffer 1984, pl. 40.
6. See Bury 1991, vol. 1, col. pl. 9 and pl. 34.

7. See Bury 1991, pls 46 and 56.
8. For examples in the Hull Grundy Gift to the British Museum, see Gere *et al.* 1984, cat. 45–6 and 55–6.
9. Press cutting, *International Jeweler*, March 1927, Cartier archive, New York.
10. It inspired another pastiche made by Chaumet for Princess Yusupov in 1914: see Scarisbrick 1995, pl. 17, p. 173.
11. For a photograph of 'la belle Otéro', see Vever, op. cit., vol. III, 1908, p. 568. She is covered with jewels, though none is by Cartier.
12. For examples of cut-steel chains made by Boulton & Watt in Birmingham, *c.* 1780, see Bury, op. cit., pls 18–19.
13. See the photograph of Mrs Cornelius

Vanderbilt in Nadelhoffer 1984, pl. 14. She is also wearing her Cartier necklace with three large diamond pendants.
14. Nadelhoffer 1984, pl. 42.
15. Nadelhoffer 1984, p. 301, n. 2.
16. See Nadelhoffer 1984, p. 71, pls 62 and 64. The Yusupov tiara was among the jewels discovered in the former Yusupov palace in 1925, but has since disappeared without trace.
17. Baugrand exhibited at the Paris Universal Exhibition of 1867 an enamelled gold clock with carved crystal panels which was much praised at the time: see Mesnard 1867, pp. 140–42.
18. Nadelhoffer 1984, pl. 68.

1 Two fern-spray brooches

Made by Charpentier for Cartier Paris for stock as a diadem or two *broches de corsage*, 1903

Diamonds in open-back millegrain platinum setting. Two identical fern branches, the leaves pierced with a central vein. Each branch articulated for complete flexibility in all directions. The reverse with screw fittings along entire length to take a diadem frame or brooch fittings. There are four brooch fittings, a necklace clasp and the original spanner-head screwdriver.

Entered in Paris stock book on 20 November 1903. Sold 28 January 1904 to Sir Ernest Cassel. Sold Sotheby's London, 21 June 1990, lot 143, from the estate of the Countess of Brecknock (1900–89).

MARKS None.

L. 18.5 cm, W. 4 cm

Cartier collection, CL 114 A03

EXHIBITIONS Hong Kong 1995, cat. 7; Tokyo 1995, cat. 53; Lausanne 1996, cat. 167.

LITERATURE Nadelhoffer 1984, p. 77.

This ingenious ornament can be worn in four different ways and is one of the most successful designs for convertible diamond jewellery of this kind. The two branches can be worn either separately as brooches or together as *devant de corsage*, diadem or necklace (1.1, 1.3, 1.2). The original spanner-head or double-armed screwdriver survives for the brooch fittings, all of which have spanner-head screws (i.e. with two holes). The spanner-head screw is a precision fixing for engineering used, for example, in optical equipment, to obtain absolute positive location so that the screwdriver does not slip out and scratch the surface of the object. Its use in jewellery is exceptional and almost certainly an innovation of Cartier, characteristic of their attention to accuracy and fine craftsmanship.

The initial design was for the two branches joined at the wider part to be worn as a head ornament on a rigid frame. The original diadem frame no longer survives, but it is illustrated in a surviving archive photograph (1.3) and Cartier has made a modern reconstruction based on this illustration. Alternatively, the two branches could be worn as a flexible *devant de corsage*, which could follow the outline of the dress (1.1), attached at the centre with an oval fitting. The branches could also be worn singly as flexible brooches or *épaulettes*, pinned at the shoulder.

The brooch fittings comprise two pairs of V-shapes, both for the wider end: the longer

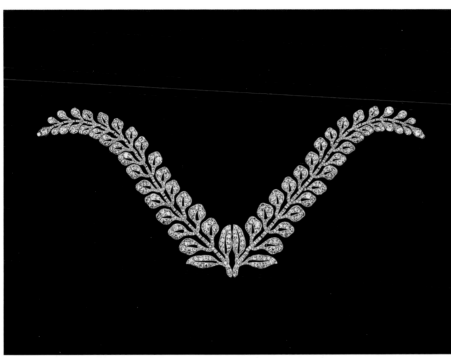

1.1 Cat. 1 as *devant de corsage*.

1.2 Cat. 1 as necklace, without fittings.

pair fixes the curve over three pairs of leaves instead of two. The supple construction of the sprays permits a variety of different curvatures. Characteristic of Cartier settings of the early 1900s is the use of a gallery or cagework support in platinum wire beneath each element. This raises the jewel to allow light to pass through the stones and provides a frame for the fittings (1.4).

Louis Cartier's Notebooks for 1906–7 refer to 'bretelles – bandes droites – pour les deux épaules, souple à droite à gauche, en avant en arrière, faisant chaînes avec motifs' (shoulder straps – stright bands – for both shoulders, flexible to the right and to the left, forwards and backwards, forming a chain with motifs). These two brooches demonstrate that flexibility of this kind was already developed by 1903. Whether Louis Cartier ever went ahead with the flexible shoulder straps is not recorded.

The financier Sir Ernest Cassel (1852–1921) had been widowed since 1881. His only daughter, Amalia, married Lt.-Col. Wilfred William Ashley in 1901 and died in 1911. According to the London archive records, Ernest Cassel gave the piece to his sister, 'Madame Cassel'. In March 1904, in London, he ordered the diadem fitting to be altered for her and at the same time requested fittings for a necklace. The surviving necklace fittings comprise various lengths of chain attached at the narrower ends of the branches. There is also a tiny diamond-set ring. The brooches appear to have passed to Lady Brecknock via Cassel's niece and Lady Brecknock's mother, Anna Isabella Jenkins (d. 1959). Her daughter, Marjorie Jenkins, married the Earl of Brecknock, heir to the 4th Marquis Camden, shortly after the end of the First World War. The Countess of Brecknock was a prominent socialite during the 1920s and 1930s and very close to her cousin, Edwina, Countess Mountbatten, who was Cassel's granddaughter. Both were heavily involved with the St John Ambulance Brigade. Lady Brecknock owned many other Cartier pieces, mostly inherited from her mother, including a turquoise and diamond 'garland style' brooch of 1904 (Sotheby's London, 21 June 1990, lot 125), now in the Cartier collection (see Lausanne 1996, cat. 133, also sold to Sir Ernest Cassel), and a ruby and diamond bandeau of 1925, convertible to a pair of bracelets (lot 123). When she posed in coronation robes for her photograph by Cecil Beaton in May 1937, she wore the ruby and

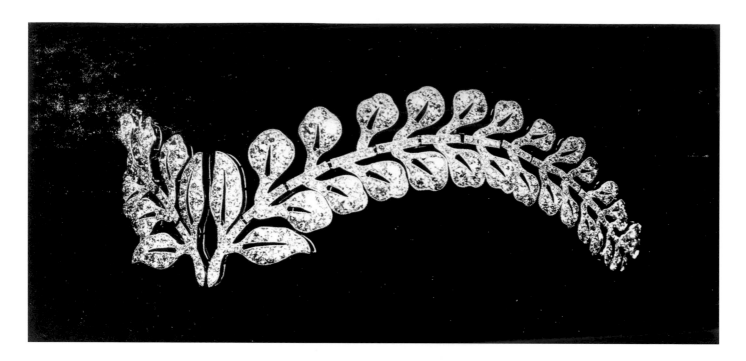

1.3 Archive photograph of cat. 1 mounted as a diadem.

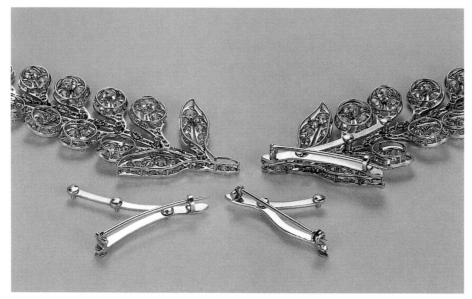

1.4 Detail of cat. 1 from the back, showing how the brooch fittings are slotted into the gallery, or raised platinum cagework. The spanner-head screws are also visible.

diamond bracelets together on one wrist and the fern-spray brooches pinned to the edge of her dress. The Beaton photograph is reproduced in the Sotheby sale catalogue.

This is one of two pairs of fern-spray brooches made by Cartier Paris. The second pair, also by the Charpentier workshop, was entered in the stock book on 8 November 1902 and sold on 19 December 1903 to Sam Lewis. By the mid-1930s it too was in England. Photographs of 1935 showing the two sprays, mounted on an entirely new diadem frame, are to be found in the Cartier London archive. The new frame was in the fashionable 'halo' form of the period. One photograph shows the halo ornament set vertically on its new frame. The other two show front and side views of it on a contemporary mannequin. The 1935 photographs were made for Mrs Koch de Gooreynd. Records indicate that she had acquired the two branches by July 1912, when she ordered '2 fittings for Diamond leaf ornament to be worn on hair with rings for hair pins and supplying 2 brilliants .064'. The 'leaf head ornament' appears again in the London records in June 1914: 'supply screws to armature of 2 diamond leaf ornaments and altering frame to take same'. The precise date when Mrs Koch de Gooreynd acquired the branches is not recorded in the London archive.

2 (greatly reduced)

2 Lily and eglantine *devant de corsage (ornement lys)*

Made by Guesdon for Cartier Paris to the order of Mrs Townsend, 1906

Diamonds in open-back millegrain platinum setting. Two articulated curving sprays: a branch of lilies wreathed with a branch of eglantine. At the intersection a large brilliant-cut diamond. The back with a series of screw holes, for a diadem frame or for brooch fittings. At the end of each spray a detachable brooch fitting. Completed in January 1906. Sold Sotheby's New York, 23 April 1991, lot 52, from the estate of Mrs Donald McElroy (Thora Strong Ronalds).

MARKS None.

L. of each branch 27.3 cm (w. spread wide approx. 40 cm)

Cartier collection, CL 134 A06

EXHIBITIONS St Petersburg 1992, cat. 22; Hong Kong 1995, cat. 2; Tokyo 1995, cat. 57.

LITERATURE Nadelhoffer 1984, p.55, fig. 37; Cologni and Nussbaum 1995, p. 99.

The 'Mrs Townsend' who ordered this piece in Paris must have been Mrs Richard H.

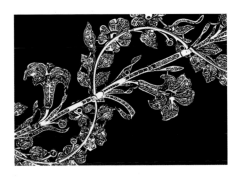

2.1 Detail of cat. 2 (front).

Townsend, great-aunt of Thora Strong Ronalds (see cat. 13).

The two sprays are shown here as they appear in the archive photograph album, spread wide across the top of the corsage. The construction of this piece is remarkable; the articulation works forwards and backwards as well as sideways, while the three-dimensionality of the flowers, with petals that curl back on themselves, involves the setting of diamonds on a curved surface (2.1–2).

A sketch for the lily sprays (without the wreath of eglantine) appears in Louis Cartier's Notebooks for *c.* 1906–7, almost certainly from an eighteenth-century source, the idea of crossed sprays deriving from a laurel wreath.

2.2 Detail of the back of cat. 2, showing the open-back bombé setting (i.e. on a curved surface).

3 Chaîne de Lavallière
Made for Cartier Paris, c. 1906

Diamonds in open-back millegrain platinum setting.
A long chain with interlace knot motif from which hang
two flexible pendants with openwork design of flower-
heads in the shape of lilies of the valley.

MARKS Rim of brooch engraved *Cartier Paris Déposé*;
CARTIER PARIS LONDRES on one of ring-bolts for chain.

L. 33.5 cm, L. of brooch with pendants 14.5 cm

Cartier collection, NE 02 C06

EXHIBITIONS Naples 1988, cat. 14; Paris 1989, cat. 104;
Rome 1990, cat. 18; St Petersburg 1992, cat. 25.

LITERATURE Proddow and Fasal 1996, p. 56.

The interlace knot with pendants attached is
removable for wear as a brooch, and is fitted
with a detachable brooch-pin. It unhooks from
a movable loop at the back of the adjacent link
of chain at the top of the knot; the loop is
turned sideways to enable the hook to slide out.

The pendants can also be removed, presumably for wear as earrings. Because the pendants
are detached at the end of their chains and not
at the knot, the brooch cannot be worn without
the pendants. A small length of chain has been
added at the top with two tiny diamond-set ring
bolts, one of which is set with diamonds on
both sides. This is a remarkable technical
achievement and typical of Cartier's attention
to detail (see cat. 14.1).

Although not recorded in either the stock
or order books, this piece can be dated from
the Cartier photograph albums. These long
chains with double pendants were a novelty in
1906–7 and are referred to in the Notebooks
for those years.

The flower-head motifs on the pendants are
an early form of Cartier's 'serti muguet' or
'lily of the valley setting'. Here, the settings
have the shape only, but the later version,
which had appeared by 1912, incorporated
four small diamonds round the lower edge of
a large circular diamond. The setting enclosed
all five stones in a lily of the valley shape, with
no setting between the large stones and the
smaller ones (see Cologni and Nussbaum
1995, pp. 100–101).

Bow-knot chains have traditionally been
called 'lavallières' after Louise de la Vallière,
one of Louis XIV's mistresses, who gave her
name to the lavallière ribbon-bow cravat.
Diamond necklaces of this kind then
became associated with the Second Empire
actress Eve Ferroglio, who took Lavallière as
her stage name.

3

4 Devant de corsage

Made by Harnichard for Cartier Paris to the order of Baronne de Gunzbourg, 1909

Diamonds in open-back millegrain platinum setting. A central rosette flanked by triangular wings containing foliate motifs held by thin platinum wires within a frame of collet-set diamonds which continues to form two pendant chains. Three further pendants with foliate motifs and a bow.

Completed in March 1909.

MARKS Rim engraved *CARTIER*, with workshop mark *GH* flanking a Roman chariot.

W. 9.6 cm, H. 12 cm

Cartier collection, CL 208 A09

EXHIBITIONS Lausanne 1996, cat. 159.

RELATED MATERIAL Original plaster cast in Paris archive.

The brooch fitting unscrews and there are the remains of a screw on the reverse of the central rosette.

4

4.1 Reverse of plaster cast of cat. 4, with workshop name, client name, date and price, for the setting only (*monture*, abbreviated *Mre*), in Cartier's code.

4.2 Plaster cast taken from cat. 4.

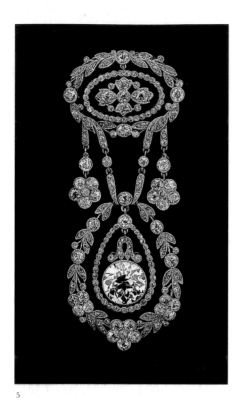

5

5 Brooch-pendant

Made for Cartier Paris, *c.* 1910

Diamonds in open-back millegrain platinum setting. Oval and tear-drop laurel wreaths, joined by a ribbon with two floral drops; each wreath contains an openwork movable pendant. The lower pendant set with a yellow old-cut diamond. Brooch detachable.

MARKS None.

W. 3.1 cm, L. 7.5 cm

Cartier collection, CL 198 C10

RELATED MATERIAL A closely similar fragmentary pencil sketch appears in the Garland Style Design Scrapbook, II, p. 9.

This brooch-pendant does not appear in the photograph albums and may possibly be an element from a larger piece, such as a necklace.

6

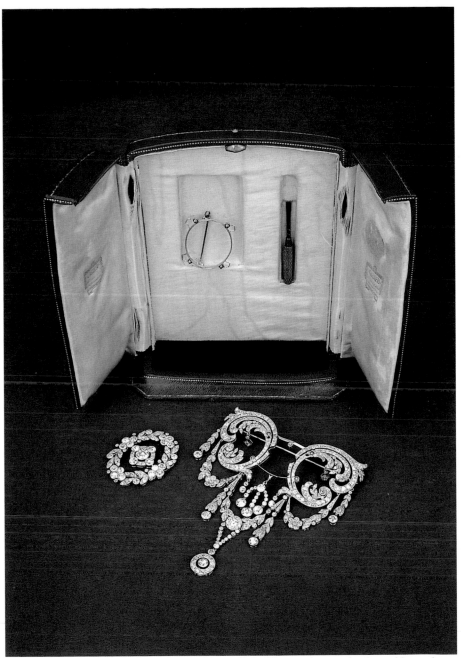

6.1 Case for cat. 6, with black velvet pad removed (see p. 45, fig. 33) to reveal spanner-head screwdriver and brooch fitting for the central oval (shown separately).

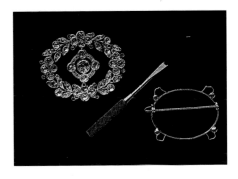

6 Devant de corsage

Based on a design of 1907 and made by Harnichard for Cartier Paris to the order of Mrs Meyer Sassoon, 1912

Diamonds in open-back platinum setting. Oval laurel wreath superimposed on scroll motifs with laurel-wreath swags and drops. The central oval wreath is detachable for wear as a brooch. Contained in the original case of red leather with gilt tooling in the form of a standing triptych with weighted base.

Completed in March 1912. Sold Sotheby's Geneva, 14 November 1990, lot 560.

MARKS *Devant de corsage*: upper rim engraved CARTIER PARIS; Paris eagle's head assay mark on gallery (used for platinum prior to 1912). Case: reverse stamped in gold CARTIER, base stamped MADE IN FRANCE; silk lining to each door printed in gold CARTIER, PARIS 13 RUE DE LA PAIX, LONDON 175 NEW BOND STREET, NEW YORK 712 5TH AVENUE.

W. 10 cm, L. 11.5 cm. Case: H. 17.2 cm

Cartier collection, CL 122 A12

EXHIBITIONS St Petersburg 1992, cat. 34; Hong Kong 1995, cat. 20; Tokyo 1995, cat. 69.

LITERATURE Cologni and Nussbaum 1995, p.81.

RELATED MATERIAL Original plaster cast in Paris archive.

Two closely similar but not identical designs are to be found in the Garland Style Design Scrapbook, I, p. 9, and III, p. 62. In both designs the oval wreath is interlaced with the C-shaped scrolls rather than superimposed on them. This would not have provided a detachable brooch.

A variant of this design appears to have been first executed as a *plaque de cou* in 1907, made as a special order, with diamonds and emeralds. It was then reinterpreted with minor variations at least six times. Three other versions were made, all as *devants de corsage* with interlaced wreath, in 1910, 1911 and March 1912, the same month as this example. A fifth, simplified, version was made in June 1912, with central emerald and pendant pearl. All five were special orders.

This piece incorporates diamonds from an earlier aigrette, a bracelet and two fans. A separate oval brooch fitting and spanner-head screwdriver survive (see also cat. 1). The piece is now fitted with a large brooch-pin across the top, but two screw fittings at each side suggest that it may also have been worn as a necklace.

FAR LEFT 6.2 Detail of reverse of cat. 6.

LEFT 6.3 Reverse of detached oval brooch with original screwdriver and fitting.

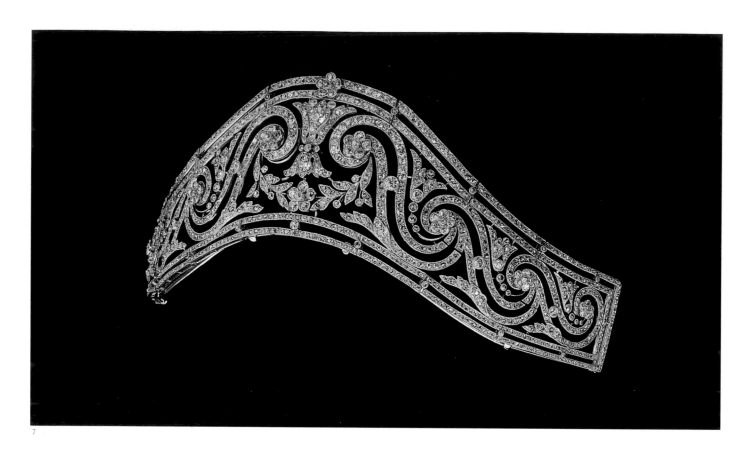

7

7 Diadem

Made by Lavabre for Cartier Paris as a special order, 1911

Diamonds in open-back millegrain platinum setting.
A running scroll with garlands and stylised buds, framed by a double row of diamonds.

Completed in February 1911.

MARKS Engraved *Cartier Paris Londres New York* on lower rim.

H. at centre 4.7 cm, at ends 2.6 cm

Cartier collection, JV 13 A11

EXHIBITIONS Munich 1989, cat. 257; Tokyo 1995, cat. 68; Lausanne 1996, cat. 52.

This piece is a small diadem for the front of the head and is designed to sit tilted slightly backward, on a piled-up slope of hair at the top of the head, the lower edge following the shape of the head. There are no obvious attachment loops and it was probably pinned on, being fairly small and light, but may have had a metal frame that sat below the diadem, as in cat. 10. Its subtle construction allows considerable flexibility. There are three hinges on each side; the scrolls are not hinged but made in sections, so that they move with the rim of the setting.

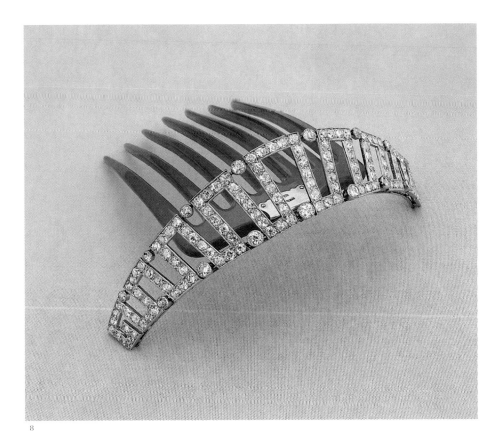

8

8 Comb

Made for Cartier Paris probably for stock, *c.* 1903

Diamonds in open-back millegrain platinum setting. A meander motif, expanding towards the centre, attached to a blonde tortoiseshell comb with a hinged gold fitting.

MARKS Gold mount: *BTE SGDG*; Paris eagle's head assay mark for gold; unidentified workshop mark *F D* flanking an illegible symbol. Platinum setting: French platinum import mark in use since 1927.

W. of jewelled mount 9 cm, L. of comb 7.3 cm

Cartier collection, JV 15 C03

EXHIBITIONS St Petersburg 1992, cat. 77; Tokyo 1995, cat. 81.

LITERATURE Cologni and Mocchetti 1992, p. 59.

This is a 'peigne de nuque' or comb for the nape of the neck; the diamond mount is hinged at right angles to the comb, which slides into the piled-up hair and is completely hidden. A description of a similarly constructed comb is recorded in the stock books in November 1903, made by the Saibène workshop. The description reads: 'vertical comb of blonde tortoiseshell, the upper part turned back at an angle and ornamented with rose-diamond plastics.'

9 Comb

Made by Césard for Cartier Paris for stock, 1905

Enamelled gold and diamonds set in open-back silver, mounted on blonde tortoiseshell. The mount in the form of a diamond wreath with ribbon of green enamel on an engine-turned ground, in a white enamel frame ending in Greek-style volutes.

Entered in stock book on 10 March 1905; sold 17 June 1905.

MARKS Cartier stock number only.

W. 10 cm, H. 8.3 cm

Cartier collection, AL 101 A05

Vertical combs of this kind were also made in sets of three in decreasing sizes; a number of such sets appear in the Paris archive photograph albums, in which the motifs are often reduced versions of those used for tiaras.

9

10

10 Russian diadem
(diadème russe)

**Made by Lavabre for Cartier Paris
for stock, 1908**

Diamonds and pearls in open-back platinum setting.
A curved crescent of alternating rows of diamonds and
pearls at top and bottom, within which hang fifteen
pear-shaped diamond drops. The drops hang freely and
move with the wearer. Fitted with a frame that sits below
the base of the diadem.

Entered in stock book on 21 May 1908; sold 27 May
1908. Sold Christie's London, 20 July 1988, lot 328.

MARKS None.

Max. W. 14.5 cm, H. 4.7 cm

Cartier collection, JV 06 A08

EXHIBITIONS Paris 1989, cat. 125; Rome 1990, cat. 25;
St Petersburg 1992, cat. 28; Tokyo 1995, cat. 63;
Lausanne 1996, cat. 149.

LITERATURE Cologni and Nussbaum 1995, p. 106.

RELATED MATERIAL Original plaster cast in Paris archive.

The frame that sits below the base of the
diadem was standard at this date. The hair
was passed over the frame and through the
gap to keep the diadem in place.

Although described as a 'diadème russe' in
the archive records, this diadem is more likely
to derive from neo-classical diadems of the
early nineteenth century in the shape of a vertical band that expanded towards the centre.
The description 'diadème russe' referred to
the Russian *kokoshnik* (literally, cockscomb), a
larger and more solid head ornament consisting of a broad band that flared outwards from
the head.

11 Sautoir

Made by Saibène for Cartier Paris for stock, 1907

Diamonds in open-back millegrain platinum setting; an openwork flat chain of platinum links and pearls with four hexagonal diamond-set motifs. In the centre an octagonal motif, from which hangs a polygonal pendant ending in miniature tassels.

Entered in stock book on 22 January 1907; sold 13 May 1907.

MARKS Engraved *CARTIER PARIS* on the clasp.

L. including chain approx. 40 cm; L. of central element from octagonal motif 10 cm

Cartier collection, NE 26 A07

RELATED MATERIAL Orignal pen and ink design for the polygonal pendant in the Garland Style Design Scrapbook, III, p. 10; another version as brooch-pendant in the Design Scrapbook, I, p. 35.

The chain is of the same design as that used for the pendant watch, cat. 12.

12 Pendant watch and chain

Made by Jaeger for Cartier Paris for stock, 1910

Platinum watch with diamonds in millegrain platinum setting, pearl chain. Square silvered engine-turned dial, mounted upside down so that it is correct for the wearer, with diamond-set winding button. On reverse of watch a monogram HEC in diamonds. Attached with a swivel setting to chain, a flat band of platinum links and pearls.

The watch entered in stock book on 8 September 1910; sold 23 September 1910.

MARKS Watch: *CARTIER PARIS* on dial. Chain: engraved *Cartier Paris*; Paris eagle's head assay mark (used for platinum before 1912) on triangular loop.

W. of watch 2.8 cm, L. of chain approx. 31 cm (double)

Cartier collection, WC 07 A10

EXHIBITIONS Milan 1988, p. 23; Paris 1989, cat. 140; Rome 1990, cat. 29; St Petersburg 1992, cat. 36.

LITERATURE Barracca *et al.* 1989, p. 21; Cologni and Nussbaum 1995, p. 104.

The monogram was added later by the purchaser.

11

12

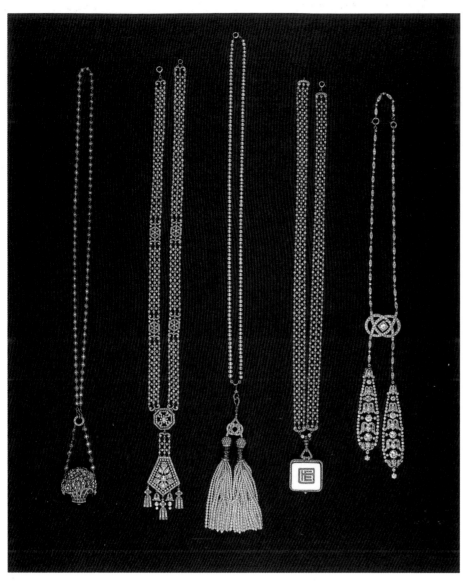

14.1 Cat. 11–14, showing full length of chains.

to President Roosevelt, and died in 1949. Records in the Cartier New York archive indicate that Thora Strong Ronalds already owned it by 1946.

The graduation of the seed pearls on the tassels is characteristic of Cartier's attention to detail. Another version of the tassel pendant, completed in June 1909, was included in the Cartier retrospective exhibitions in New York (1976, cat. 72) and Los Angeles (1982, pl. 5) with an elaborate necklace comprising 3,692 oriental pearls.

14 Flower basket watch and chain

Made by Jaeger and Naudet for Cartier Paris for stock, 1909

Diamonds, platinum and enamel. The watch in the form of a flower basket with rose-cut diamonds in openwork millegrain platinum setting, on a blue enamelled engine-turned ground, hung from a diamond-set ring. The watch lid opened by pressing the central diamond in the basket. Winding button at the base of the basket set with a rose-cut diamond. The dial mounted upside down so that it is correct for the wearer. Chain of round diamonds held at each side within openwork links.

Entered in stock book on 31 July 1909; sold 18 May 1910 to Nellie Melba. Bought back into stock on 16 July 1910 and sold to Prince Yusupov on 17 January 1912. Sold Christie's New York, 19 October 1988, lot 91.

MARKS Engraved *CARTIER* on the ring fasteners of the chain. Inside the lid *CARTIER PARIS* and on the dial *CARTIER*.

L. with chain approx. 38.5 cm, H. of watch 3.5 cm

Cartier collection, WC 14 A09

EXHIBITIONS Rome 1990, cat. 28; St Petersburg 1992, cat. 35; Lausanne 1996, cat. 39.

LITERATURE Nadelhoffer 1984, p. 254.

RELATED MATERIAL Pen and ink sketch in stock book for 1909 with dial uncovered, described as 'montre dans corbeille fleuri genre ancien . . . cadran visible, lunette roses, suspendu à une double chaînette, anneau roses' (watch in old-style flower basket . . . visible dial, bordered with rose-diamonds, hung from small double chain and diamond ring).

The flower basket is derived from mid-eighteenth-century jewellery designs. The setting of the watch dial upside down so that it can be easily read by the wearer is characteris-

13 Sautoir with pearl tassels

Pendant made by Lavabre, chain by Lenfant for Cartier Paris for stock, 1910

Diamonds and sapphires in millegrain platinum setting, pearl tassels and chain. A diamond knot motif from which hang two pearl tassels made of strings of graduated seed pearls held by calibré-cut sapphire and diamond rings. Four tiny sapphire rings and a diamond-set swivel fitting link pendant to pearl chain.

Chain entered in stock book on 14 October 1908. Pendant entered in stock book on 13 September 1910: chain and pendant sold together on 7 November 1910 to Mr Townsend. Sold Sotheby's New York, 23 April 1992, lot 13, from the estate of Mrs Donald McElroy (Thora Strong Ronalds).

MARKS Pendant: on hook at top Paris eagle's head assay mark (used for platinum before 1912) and workshop mark *HL* flanking a four-leaf clover. Swivel loop: *BREVETE*

SGDG. Chain: eagle's head assay mark and workshop mark *GL* flanking a dice and a wing.

Total L. approx. 44.3 cm, L. of pendant 12 cm

Cartier collection, NE 16 A10

EXHIBITIONS St Petersburg 1992, cat. 85; Tokyo 1995, cat. 86.

RELATED MATERIAL Preliminary sketch for a tassel pendant of this design, to be executed with rubies instead of sapphires, in Notebook for *c.* 1906–7.

The 'Mrs Townsend' who purchased this piece in Paris in 1910 must have been Mrs Richard H. Townsend (Mary Scott), great-aunt of Thora Strong Ronalds and a prominent member of Washington society (see also cat. 2). The piece may have passed directly to Thora Strong Ronalds, or via Mrs Townsend's daughter, Mathilde, who married Sumner Welles (1892–1961), Under-Secretary of State

tic of Cartier pendant watches: time-keeping was as important as the decorative effect. The open setting of the diamonds in the chain was known as 'loop' setting and made the diamonds look bigger. The working sketch and description indicate that the watch was made with visible dial and that the lid was added later.

The Australian prima donna Dame Nellie Melba (1861–1931), who kept this watch for only three months, made her début at Covent Garden in 1888; she sang regularly at the Paris Opéra until her retirement in 1926. The second owner of the watch, Prince Felix Yusupov (1887–1967), son of Princess Zenaïde, married Princess Irina, daughter of Grand Duchess Xenia and niece of Tsar Nicholas II, in Paris in 1914. He was one of the murderers of Rasputin in 1916.

14

13

15

16 Rock-crystal pendant
Made by Picq for Cartier Paris for stock, 1912

Rock crystal, diamonds, sapphires and pearls in open-back millegrain platinum setting. A carved matt rock-crystal cartouche with two grotesque heads at each side; a central oval motif in diamonds and pearls with large cabochon sapphire; three pendant pearls. Hung from a small sapphire-set diamond element on a black silk cord chain with diamond-set clasps (the present cord is a modern replacement). The central oval diamond motif can be removed for wear as a brooch, with detachable fitting (p. 50, fig. 38).

Entered in stock book on 29 February 1912; sold 14 May 1912.

MARKS Paris eagle's head assay mark (used for platinum before 1912) on gallery; workshop mark *HP* flanking an ace of spades on pendant loop.

W. 4.5 cm, L. of pendant 11.5 cm, L. of cord 20.7 cm. Total L. 32 cm

Cartier collection, NE 11 A12

EXHIBITIONS Rome 1990, cat. 69; St Petersburg 1992, cat. 87; Lausanne 1996, cat. 200.

RELATED MATERIAL Original plaster cast in Paris archive.

This pendant has its original case in the form of a standing triptych in tooled and gilded red leather (see cat. 6), with the standard Cartier stamp inside both wings.

It is one of a range of pieces incorporating Renaissance-style carved and engraved rock crystal introduced by Cartier around 1912 (see pp. 69–70 and cat. 17–19). For illustrations of this pendant with the oval brooch detached and the original plaster cast, see pp. 50–51, figs 38–9.

15 Lorgnette *(face-à-main)*
Made by Ballada for Cartier Paris for stock, 1909

Blonde tortoiseshell, diamonds in open-back platinum setting. The hinged folding eye-glasses released by pressing a diamond-set spring at top of handle. The tortoiseshell handle decorated with diamond-set wreaths of clover leaves alternating with a plain spiral. A suspension loop at the base.

Entered in stock book on 8 February 1909; sold 4 May 1910.

MARKS Paris boar's head assay mark for silver on hinge for lenses.

L. closed 13 cm, W. of lenses open 10 cm

Cartier collection, AL 79 A09

EXHIBITIONS Lausanne 1996, cat. 143.

LITERATURE Cologni and Mocchetti 1992, p. 52.

Lorgnettes were introduced in the late nineteenth century as a less conspicuous alternative to spectacles. The light hinged frames enabled them to be folded away when not in use.

15

17

17 Rock-crystal brooch-pendant

Made by Picq for Cartier Paris for stock, 1913

Rock crystal, sapphires and diamonds set in platinum. A shield-shaped pendant of rock crystal engraved with foliate scrollwork, with central faceted sapphire and diamond border, hung from pearl strings, with diamond and sapphire terminals.

Entered in stock book on 19 February 1913; sold 8 September 1913.

MARKS Pin engraved CARTIER; Paris eagle's head assay mark for gold on pin and pendant (this mark is sometimes found on platinum pieces at this date, although a separate mark for platinum had been introduced in 1912); workshop mark HP flanking an ace of spades.

H. 5.8 cm, W. 4.6 cm

Cartier collection, CL 213 A13

RELATED MATERIAL Original plaster cast in Paris archive.

18

18 Rock-crystal bracelet-watch

Made by Jaeger for Cartier Paris for stock, 1913

Rock crystal, diamonds and onyx in closed-back millegrain platinum setting; original watered silk bracelet with gold *boucle déployante* (folding buckle). Rock crystal engraved with foliate scrolls, curved to fit the wrist, with silvered dial in centre; diamond border and bars of calibré-cut onyx at join of bracelet; onyx clasp with diamond border.

Entered in stock book on 26 May 1913; sold 30 July 1913.

MARKS On dial CARTIER PARIS; on rim French dog's head assay mark for platinum; on clasp workshop mark EJ flanking an hour-glass and French third standard gold mark.

W. 2.9 cm

Cartier collection, WL 82 A13

EXHIBITIONS Tokyo 1995, cat. 111.

LITERATURE Nadelhoffer 1984, p. 274; Barracca *et al.* 1989, p. 64; Cologni and Nussbaum 1995, p. 105.

The dial originally had arabic numerals. The form of the rock-crystal surround echoes the barrel-shaped or *tonneau* form popular for gold wrist watches. The original case survives (see p. 45, fig. 33).

19

19 Rock-crystal hat-pin

Made by Droguet for Cartier Paris to the order of Sir Philip Sassoon, 1912

Diamonds and rock crystal in open-back millegrain platinum setting. Lozenge-shaped pin-head of engraved rock crystal with central diamond and diamond border. The pin has been shortened. Original specially shaped red leather case with gilded tooling (see p. 45, fig. 33).

Completed in December 1912.

MARKS Rim of pin-head engraved *CARTIER PARIS LONDRES NEW YORK*; French dog's head assay mark for platinum.

Pin: L. 12.8 cm, W. of pin-head 2.2 cm. Case: L. 21.8 cm

Cartier collection, AL 108 A12

This hat-pin is assumed on the basis of the description in the order books and the illustration in the archive photograph albums to be the one ordered by Sir Philip Sassoon in 1912, although the number on the object itself differs from that recorded in the archive in 1912.

Philip Sassoon's mother was the daughter of Baron Gustav de Rothschild. He inherited his father's fortune in 1912 and made several purchases from Cartier in that year. He died unmarried and his fortune went to his sister Sybil, who married the Marquis of Cholmondeley in August 1913. His Cartier purchases of 1912 could perhaps have been for his sister's engagement. However, he was intimate with many members of the royal family and often gave them expensive presents (see K. Rose, *Intimate Portraits of Kings, Queens and Courtiers*, London 1985, p. 258).

Hat-pin cases rarely survive. An example made in 1908, a gold hat-pin with pink enamel and diamond head in a very similar case, is illustrated by Nadelhoffer (1984, col. pl. 18). Usually the heads were transformed at a later date for wear as brooches (see cat. 25). The shape of the case is based on neoclassical hair-pin cases of the late eighteenth century.

20 Japanese knot brooch

Made by Lavabre for Cartier Paris for stock, 1907

Diamonds in closed-back platinum setting and rubies in open-back gold setting. Three rows of rose-cut diamonds between calibré-cut rubies; set with cabochon ruby flower-heads.

Entered in stock book on 25 February 1907; sold 8 March 1912.

MARKS Rim engraved *Cartier Paris*, with initials *MD* (stamped) for 'Métaux Divers' (mixed metals); Paris eagle's head assay mark for gold on gallery; workshop mark *HL* flanking a four-leaf clover.

L. 4.5 cm

Cartier collection, CL 23 A07

RELATED MATERIAL Original plaster cast of a larger version of this brooch without the flower-heads in Paris archive.

EXHIBITIONS Naples 1988, cat. 60; Paris 1989, cat. 153; Rome 1990, cat. 63; St Petersburg 1992, cat. 82; Tokyo 1995, cat. 83; Lausanne 1996, cat. 139.

LITERATURE Munn 1993, p. 97.

This brooch is in the form of a Japanese paper knot which, by Japanese tradition, cannot easily be untied and is therefore symbolic of love and marriage. A design for a similar Japanese knot in brown pen is in the Garland Style Design Scrapbook, I, in the Paris archive. At least two other variants of this model are recorded in the Paris photograph albums, each of different size and design (see p. 49, fig. 37).

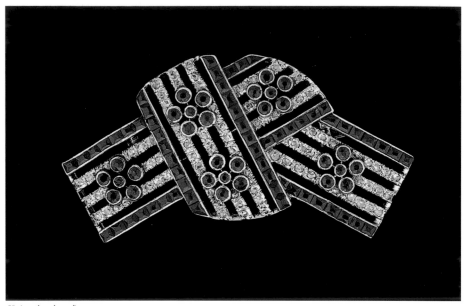

20 (greatly enlarged)

21 Bracelet

Made for Cartier Paris, *c.* 1907

Diamonds, rubies and pearls in open-back platinum and gold settings. A line of calibré-cut rubies and diamonds punctuated by lozenges set with a central pearl. The diamonds set in white metal, the rubies in gold.

MARKS Engraved *CARTIER PARIS* on edge of central lozenge.

L. 19.4 cm

Cartier collection, BT 03 C07

EXHIBITIONS Naples 1988, cat. 61; Paris 1989, cat. 152; Rome 1990, cat. 62; St Petersburg 1992, cat. 81; Tokyo 1995, cat. 84; Lausanne 1996, cat. 144.

A sketch for this design appears in Louis Cartier's Notebooks, 1906–7, while a bracelet of similar design with sapphires and gold setting was entered in the stock books in February 1907 and made by the Holl workshop.

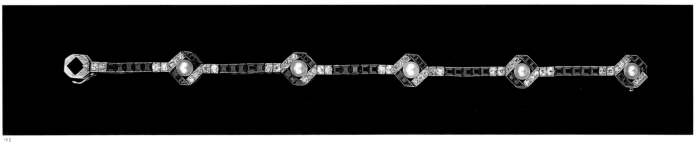

21

22 Brooch

Made by Andrey for Cartier Paris for stock, 1909

Diamonds and rubies in open-back millegrain platinum setting. Two circular motifs with square terminals each containing four calibré-cut rubies with a tiny central diamond.

Entered in stock book on 6 September 1909; sold 4 November 1912.

MARKS Rim engraved *CARTIER PARIS*; workshop mark *GA* flanking a branch of mistletoe (?) on the pin.

W. 4.2 cm

Cartier collection, CL 102 A09

RELATED MATERIAL Original plaster cast in Paris archive (p. 49, fig. 37).

EXHIBITIONS St Petersburg 1992, cat. 84; Tokyo 1995, cat. 85; Lausanne 1996, cat. 140.

22 (greatly enlarged)

23 Brooch

Made by Lavabre for Cartier Paris for stock, 1906

Diamonds set in platinum and sapphires set in gold, the settings open-back. Interlaced double circles with foliate motif in each, one in diamonds with central sapphire, the other in sapphires with central diamond.

Entered in stock book on 7 December 1906; no record of sale date.

MARKS *Cartier Paris* engraved on rim.

L. 6 cm

Private collection

LITERATURE Snowman (ed.) 1990, p. 194.

RELATED MATERIAL Original plaster cast in Paris archive.

Described in the Paris stock book as 'Broche 2 motifs gothiques, 1 en brillants centre 1 saphir, 1 en saphirs calibrés centre 1 brillant, monture platine et or' (brooch with two Gothic motifs, one in diamonds with sapphire in centre, one in calibré sapphires with diamond in centre, setting platinum and gold).

The Gothic inspiration of this brooch recalls the work of the Paris firm of Jules and Louis Wièse, who made a series of jewels in cast and chased gold with similar foliate motifs (see Munich 1989). Louis was still producing his father's designs of *c.* 1860 in the years around 1900, while Froment-Meurice included his Gothic revival designs of 1849–51 in the retrospective displays for the Paris Centennial Exhibition of 1900.

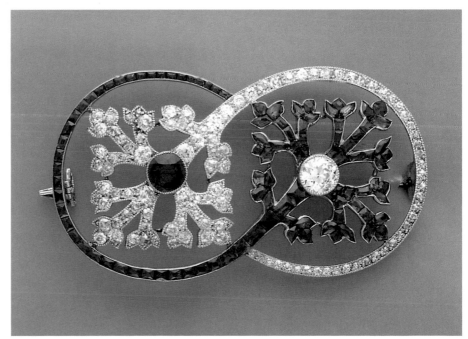

23 (greatly enlarged)

24 Lozenge-shaped brooch

Made by Lavabre for Cartier Paris for stock, 1907

Diamonds in open-back millegrain platinum setting. A frame with repeating openwork scale pattern, a round diamond within each scale, the scale pattern made separately and riveted into the frame.

Entered in stock book on 25 April 1907; sold 3 August 1907.

MARKS Reverse engraved *Cartier Paris Déposé*.

W. diagonally across lozenge 3.8 cm

Cartier collection, CL 99 A07

EXHIBITIONS St Petersburg 1992, cat. 79; Tokyo 1995, cat. 82; Lausanne 1996, cat. 156.

LITERATURE Cologni and Nussbaum 1995, p. 81.

RELATED MATERIAL Original plaster cast in Paris archive (see p. 49, fig. 37).

The scale pattern is derived from Chinese or Japanese sources.

24 (greatly enlarged)

25 Hat-pin head

Made by Andrey for Cartier Paris to the order of Baron Maurice de Rothschild, 1910

Diamonds and sapphires in open-back millegrain platinum setting. A pattern of vertical wavy ribbon motifs fills the circle, with a border of calibré-cut sapphires. The hat-pin no longer survives and the head is now fitted with a brooch-pin, but the hole for the hat-pin is visible in the centre at the back.

Completed in June 1910. Bought back for stock on 19 July 1910 and resold to Mrs C. Vanderbilt on 20 September 1911, as a hat-pin.

MARKS Rim engraved *CARTIER*; Paris eagle's head assay mark (used for platinum before 1912) and workshop mark GA flanking a branch of mistletoe (?) on gallery.

W. 4.1 cm

Cartier collection, CL 202 A10

The wavy ribbon pattern, probably inspired by Chinese or Japanese sources, was used for a series of pendants, all with a large central stone. The pattern could be set vertically or horizontally.

Mrs C. Vanderbilt was Grace Wilson (1870–1953). She married Cornelius Vanderbilt III (1873–1942) in 1896 (see San Francisco 1996, p. 353).

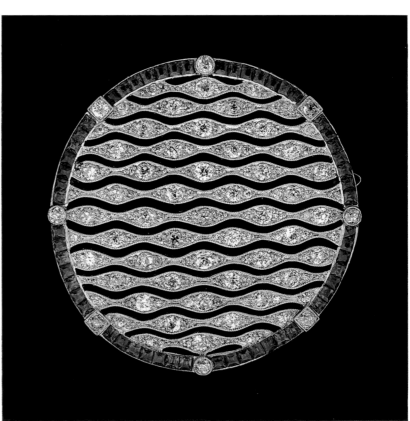

25 (greatly enlarged)

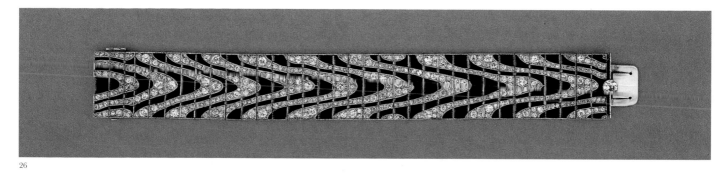

26

26 Bracelet

Made by Lecas for Cartier Paris for stock, 1907

Diamonds set in platinum, mounted on black ribbon, with gold tongue. A wave pattern of diamonds imitating watered silk, formed of a series of hinged elements for complete flexibility. The ribbon is modern.

Entered in stock book on 15 November 1907; sold 23 June 1908 to Mrs Vanderbilt.

MARKS On reverse of clasp *DEPOSE*, with workshop mark *E* and *L* above and below a letter *K* (i.e. 'к', for Lecas).

L. including tongue 10.1 cm

Private collection

EXHIBITIONS Paris 1989, cat. 119.

The original black fabric would have been a grosgrain ribbon. This is clearly visible in the Paris archive contemporary photographs, which include two other bracelets of this kind, both with patterns of concentric ovals and both made for stock in 1907 by the Lecas workshop. One was sold to the Princesse de

26.1 Cat. 26 shown closed.

Polignac, the other to the King of Siam. The concentric pattern also appears in a pencil sketch for a bow-knot necklace in the Garland Style Design Scrapbook, I, p. 4, and was used for a bandeau (illustrated in Nadelhoffer 1984, p. 73, fig. 68). According to Nadelhoffer, the bandeau was exhibited at the 1912 Canadian Exhibition as the most expensive item ($10,080) and sold to Princess Bibesco. For the Princesse de Polignac, see cat. 147.

27

27 Bracelet-watch

Made by Jaeger for Cartier Paris for stock, c. 1913.

Watch of gold-backed platinum set with diamonds and onyx in millegrain platinum setting, with original bracelet of black watered silk with *boucle déployante* (folding buckle) in gold with onyx and diamond rectangular clasp. Watch of so-called *tortue* (turtle) shape, bordered with zigzag pattern in calibré-cut onyx and diamonds.

A bracelet-watch of identical design was entered in the stock book on 10 November 1913.

MARKS On dial *CARTIER FRANCE*; Paris eagle's head assay mark for gold; workshop mark *EJ* flanking an hour-glass and *BTE SGDG* on folding buckle.

W. 2.2 cm

Cartier collection, WL 31 C13

EXHIBITIONS Los Angeles 1982, cat. 121; Naples 1988, cat. 130; Paris 1989, cat. 211; Rome 1990, cat. 101; Tokyo 1995, cat. 112.

27.1 Cat. 27 with folding buckle shown open. The grosgrain ribbon is original.

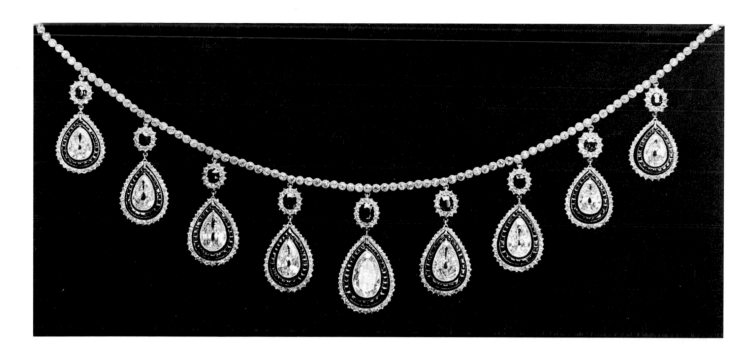

28 Steel diadem

Made by Picq for Cartier Paris to the order of 'Madame Marghiloman, sister of Queen Marie of Romania', in 1914

Steel inset with rubies and diamonds in platinum setting A curved oxidised or blackened steel band bordered at top and bottom with an inner line of calibré-cut rubies and an outer line of diamonds, reaching a peak at the front. Nine large pear-shaped diamonds bordered with calibré-cut rubies are set into the steel band, alternating with diamonds in collet settings. Upper row of diamonds and pear-shaped diamonds open-backed.

Completed in April 1914.

MARKS French dog's head assay mark for platinum on reverse, together with workshop mark *HP* flanking an ace of spades.

Max. W. 17.4 cm, H. at centre 4.1 cm, max. D. front to back 18.5 cm

Cartier collection, JV 20 A14

EXHIBITIONS Tokyo 1995, cat. 89.

LITERATURE Cologni and Nussbaum 1995, p. 107.

This is one of a group of diadems of *kokoshnik* form made of blackened steel and diamonds between 1913 and 1914. For the *kokoshnik* form, see cat. 10. The rubies and diamonds came from a necklace made for stock in February 1906 and sold to Lady Avery in October 1906. At some point before 1914 Cartier bought the necklace back from Lady Avery (the precise date is not recorded) and it was taken apart. It comprised nine pear-shaped diamonds edged with calibré-cut rubies and diamonds, strung on a simple line of diamonds (28.1). The diamond surrounds were not reused. Queen Marie of Romania acceded to the throne in 1914. This diadem may have been ordered for the coronation celebrations.

These steel diadems were originally kept in place with a cord at the back. On the reverse of this one are three hinged loops at the base for attachment. Four others were made for

28.1 Archive photograph showing the necklace of 1906 with pear-drop diamonds and rubies reused upside down in cat. 28.

stock in 1913 and 1914, one of which was sold to Melissa Doenkoff, while a fifth was ordered by Sir Philip Sassoon in 1914. It had a wreath of ivy in diamonds on the black steel ground, with a diamond border at the top and a central fitting possibly for an aigrette. They all appear to have been made by Picq. An alternative patination in green on copper is suggested by a design for a *kokoshnik* of this type that appears in the Workshop Estimate Book for 1913. Although the design is painted black, it is annotated 'étoiles brillants sur fond cuivre teint vert-de-gris' (diamond stars on a copper ground the colour of verdigris).

◀ 28

29

29 Brooch-pendant

Designed by Charles Jacqueau and made
by Picq for Cartier Paris for stock, 1913

Jade, turquoises, sapphires, diamonds and a pearl in
open-back platinum setting. Bar with two upturned ends
each set with a cabochon sapphire; pendant formed of
articulated jade plaques set with sapphires at the joins,
bordered with diamonds and turquoises, with a leaf-
shaped sapphire drop.

Entered in stock book on 23 August 1913; sold
30 August 1913 to Ira Nelson Morris. Bought back for
stock on 23 October 1913 and sold to Baron Henri de
Rothschild on 4 January 1919. Sold Sotheby's Geneva,
16 November 1994, lot 526.

MARKS Base of bar engraved *Cartier Paris*; French dog's
head assay mark for platinum and workshop mark *HP*
flanking an ace of spades.

L. 12.5 cm

Cartier collection, CL 193 A13

EXHIBITIONS Lausanne 1996, cat. 198.

LITERATURE Nadelhoffer 1984, col. pl. 31; Arwas 1992,
p. 122.

RELATED MATERIAL Original plaster cast and bodycolour
design in Paris archive; second unfinished design amongst
Jacqueau's working designs (private collection, no. 771).

The design in the Paris archive appears in the
Workshop Estimate Book for April 1913 with
an estimate from Lavabre for 935 francs.
There is no figure after Picq's name, but the
page is annotated 'Commande donné à Picq
par Mr Louis'.

Jacqueau's working designs also include a
design for a choker necklace with the same
motif of jade plaques and sapphire cabochons
(see cat. 238).

Cartier made several brooch-pendants in
which the brooch took the form of a bar with
upturned ends; they are often described in the
archive as 'broches étriers' or stirrup brooches
(see cat. 36).

The bold combination of green and blue is
usually associated with designs of the 1920s,
especially those of Georges Fouquet, for
example his bracelet of 1924–5 made of
hexagonal jade plaques set with lapis cabochons and edged with blue enamel, the hinges
concealed with diamonds (see Arwas 1992,
p. 126) or his rock-crystal and diamond pendant of 1923–4 with jade discs and lapis
cabochons (Paris 1983, p. 99). But Jacqueau's
brooch-pendant anticipates these by a decade,
and it is significant that Victor Arwas illustrated it in his book on Art Deco.

For Ira Nelson Morris, see cat. 86.

30 Brooch-pendant
(broche vase)

Designed by Charles Jacqueau and made
by Picq for Cartier Paris for stock, 1913.
Exhibited at Cartier New York in November
1913

Emeralds, pearls, onyx and diamonds in open-back
platinum setting. Vase formed of a polygonal emerald
of 11.90 carats with dogtooth pattern rim and scrolling

30

handles in diamonds and onyx, the fruit of cabochon emeralds; stirrup-shaped bar with pearl, diamond and onyx chain. Four pear-shaped emerald drops.

Entered in stock book on 29 May 1913, the emeralds removed from the setting in August 1913. Emeralds and setting sent separately to Cartier New York, where the jewel was remounted.

MARKS French dog's head assay mark for platinum and workshop mark *HP* flanking an ace of spades stamped several times.

L. 9.5 cm, W. 3.5 cm

Cartier collection, CL 183 A13

EXHIBITIONS Tokyo 1995, cat. 87; Lausanne 1996, cat. 182.

LITERATURE Nadelhoffer 1984, p. 186; Cologni and Nussbaum 1995, p. 102, with illustration of original design.

RELATED MATERIAL (1) Original design in pen and ink, watercolour and bodycolour on buff tracing paper in Workshop Estimate Book, 1913, in Paris archive. (2) Preliminary working sketch in pencil, pen and ink amongst Jacqueau's working designs (private collection, no. 771, identical to this example except for sapphires in centre of chain).

The Workshop Estimate Book has estimates from both Lavabre (600F) and Picq (455F).

The stones and setting were sent separately

31.1 Jacqueau's working sketch in pen and ink for cat. 31 (private collection). The annotation on Jacqueau's sketch, '1 saphir, cab. 35 ct', refers to the size of the stone before cutting. It is now 28.70 carats.

---

to New York in order to avoid the payment of duty on finished jewellery, as opposed to unmounted gemstones, which were regarded as raw materials and not generally subject to import duty in the USA at this time. The setting would have been sent in several pieces for reassembly; this would explain the stamping of French assay marks in several places. The piece was sent to New York for display in the exhibition held at Cartier New York on 11–15 November 1913. The catalogue, entitled *A Collection of Jewels created by Messrs Cartier from the Hindoo, Persian, Arab, Russian and Chinese*, included at the end a small section called 'From the Antique'. No. 50 is described as 'An Attic vase made of one triangular emerald of fine quality supporting a pyramid of fruit, set with pearls, diamonds and onyx. $ 3,850.'

A second, identical setting, also made in Paris, was used for a smaller emerald of 4.49 carats, the space left by the larger emerald being filled with calibré-cut onyx. This version was entered in the stock book on 12 March 1914 and sold on 31 March 1914 to Lord Wellesley, later 7th Duke of Wellington, who married Dorothy Ashton on 30 April 1914 and presented Apsley House to the nation in 1947.

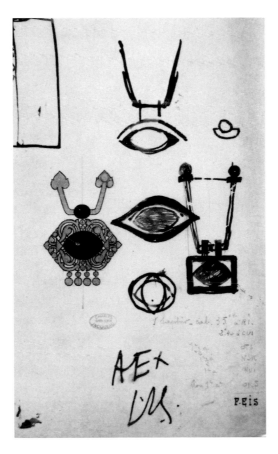

---

31 Brooch-pendant
(broche draperie)

Designed by Charles Jacqueau and made by Picq for Cartier Paris for stock, 1912

Sapphires and diamonds in open-back platinum setting. A large lozenge-shaped sapphire of 28.70 carats within a diamond rectangle bordered with calibré-cut sapphires; chain of square-cut diamonds in millegrain setting; brooch-pin (cliquet system) with further calibré-cut and two cabochon sapphires. Contained in original red leather case with gold tooling in form of standing triptych (see p. 45, fig. 33).

Entered in stock book on 19 September 1912; sold 12 November 1912.

MARKS Brooch: pin engraved *CARTIER*, with Paris eagle's head assay mark (used for platinum prior to 1912) and workshop mark *HP* flanking an ace of spades. Case: *CARTIER* stamped in gold on reverse, with standard printed Cartier mark inside both wings.

Brooch: L. 7.2 cm, W. 4 cm. Case: H. 10.5 cm, D. 1.6 cm

Cartier collection, CL 197 A12

RELATED MATERIAL Original pencil, pen and ink sketch (see 31.1) amongst Jacqueau's working designs (private collection, no. 561), annotated '1 saphir cab. 35 ct', with price codes and A EX (à exécuter).

The term 'broche draperie' is used in the firm's records to describe brooches usually with garlands draped from two separate elements. The elements are joined by the brooch-pin, which is invisible when worn. The type was introduced around 1910 and many other examples appear in Jacqueau's working designs.

31

32

32 Brooch-pendant
(broche draperie)

Designed by Charles Jacqueau in 1914 and made by Lavabre for Cartier Paris as a special order in 1922

Coral, onyx and diamonds set in platinum. A coral vase hung from a garland of leaves with coral and onyx berries.

Completed in November 1922.

MARKS Engraved *Cartier Paris*; French dog's head assay mark for platinum.

L. 13.8 cm

Private collection

EXHIBITIONS Los Angeles 1982, cat. 50; Paris 1989, cat. 185.

LITERATURE Nadelhoffer 1984, col. pl. 51.

RELATED MATERIAL (1) Original pen and ink and bodycolour designs for three slightly different versions in Workshop Estimate Book, 1914, pp. 82–3, in Paris archive, two in black and white (i.e. onyx and diamonds; for one of these, see Rome 1990, cat. 79), one with a pink or coral vase. (2) Unfinished designs for two further variants in watercolour and bodycolour among Jacqueau's working designs. One of these is included here as cat. 243.

33 Brooch

Made by Droguet for Cartier Paris for stock, 1913

Enamelled gold and sapphires; platinum brooch-pin. A central bar with two cabochon sapphires, with two chains formed of white enamelled links ending in green enamelled pendants, each with three cabochon sapphires.

Entered in stock book on 20 December 1913; sold 7 February 1914 to the Countess of Hohenfelsen. Sold Sotheby's Geneva, 14 November 1990, lot 192.

MARKS French dog's head assay mark for platinum and workshop mark *HD* flanking a flower on brooch-pin; Paris eagle's head assay mark for gold and workshop mark on pendants.

L. 5.3 cm, W. 1.8 cm

Cartier collection, CL 121 A13

RELATED MATERIAL Original plaster cast and original design in pencil, ink, watercolour and bodycolour on buff tracing paper in Workshop Estimate Book, 1913, p. 61, with initials LC for Louis Cartier. The pendants and upper bars in pale blue instead of green. Both cast and design in Paris archive.

Estimates for three versions of this piece, one enamelled (no. 2), another with diamonds (no. 1) and one with calibré stones (no. 3), were supplied by two workshops, Lavabre and Droguet, as follows:

Lavabre:

tout le blanc émail	no. 2	190F
haut et bas brillants et roses	no. 1	275F
avec calibrage	no. 3	275F

Droguet:

tout émail	no. 2	150F
avec brillants et roses	no. 1	180F
avec calibrage	no. 3	250F

The cheaper estimate from the Droguet workshop bears a cross indicating the approval of Louis Cartier.

The Countess of Hohenfelsen was born Olga Valerianovna Karnovitch. She became Olga von Pistohlkors and then married secondly Grand Duke Paul of Russia (1860–1919) in 1902. The marriage was morganatic. She was a major client of Cartier in the period 1900–14; her celebrated *devant de corsage*, commissioned in 1908, contained three enormous pear-shaped pearls and three large pearl buttons (Nadelhoffer 1984, p. 53, fig. 34). She also commissioned a tiara with seven pear-shaped diamonds in 1911 (Nadelhoffer 1984, p. 66, fig. 53, and p. 71, fig. 61).

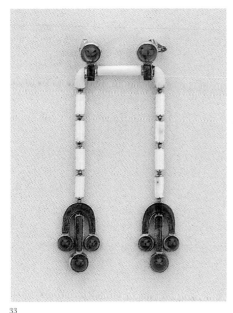

33

34 Brooch-pendant
(broche draperie)

Made by Droguet for Cartier Paris to the order of Countess Palffy-Daun of Hungary, 1913

Sapphires and diamonds in open-back millegrain platinum setting. A double draped chain and hexagonal pendant set with five faceted sapphires. The large sapphire in the pendant has a calibré-cut sapphire border.

Completed in March 1913.

MARKS Rim engraved CARTIER PARIS; French dog's head assay mark for platinum and PT 950 on pin; workshop mark HD flanking a flower on the setting of one of sapphires.

L. 11.6 cm, W. 6 cm

Cartier collection, CL 105 A13

EXHIBITIONS Hong Kong 1995, cat. 22.

The brooch uses client stones from an earlier necklace and pendant. Possibly the stones were reset on the occasion of the marriage of Marie-Amélie, Countess Esterházy (1895–1928) to Joseph-Guillaume Palffy-Daun (born 1892) in 1913. Alternatively, the brooch may have been made for Eléonore, Countess Nugent (born 1867), who married Joseph-Guillaume's father, Guillaume Léopold Palffy-Daun (1867–1916), in 1889.

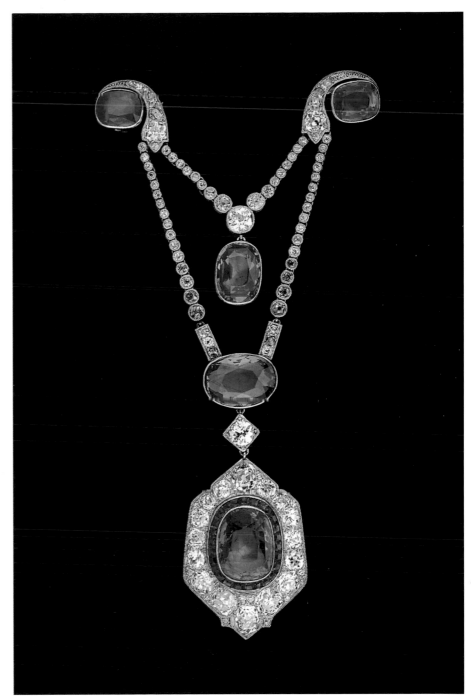

34

35 Brooch-pendant

**Made for Cartier New York for stock,
c. 1920**

Diamonds, sapphires and onyx in open-back platinum
setting. A bar with articulated pendant decorated with a
tree in a pot, the trunk and pot in specially shaped
pieces of onyx, the fruit of sapphire cabochons.

MARKS Engraved *CARTIER N.Y.* on pendant loop.

L. 10.1 cm, W. 3.6 cm

Cartier collection, CL 160 C20

EXHIBITIONS New York 1976, cat. 94.

LITERATURE Nadelhoffer 1984, col. pl. 10.

36 Brooch-pendant
(broche étrier)

**Made for Cartier New York as a special
order, 1920**

Onyx, diamonds and sapphires in open-back millegrain
platinum setting. A stirrup-shaped brooch with two
cabochon sapphires and rigid pendant with
geometrically cut onyx plaque set with three cabochon
sapphires.

Although designed as a special order, this piece was not
purchased by the client, but entered into New York stock
on 15 September 1920 and eventually sold on 26 May
1925.

MARKS On rim of brooch *CARTIER.*

L. 7.2 cm, W. 2.8 cm

Cartier collection, CL 07 A20

EXHIBITIONS New York 1976, cat. 93; Los Angeles 1982,
cat. 30; Paris 1989, cat. 181; Rome 1990, cat. 83;
St Petersburg 1992, cat. 82.

LITERATURE Nadelhoffer 1984, col. pl. 10.

RELATED MATERIAL Original design in pencil, watercolour
and bodycolour on brown tracing paper in client file in
New York archive, annotated 'OK Lynch' for the
salesman W. Lynch, and 'II', indicating that there must
have been an alternative design that no longer survives.

Lynch was a major salesman at this date.
Many of the New York client designs are
annotated with his initials and 'OK', indicating that the client had given permission to
proceed with the execution of the piece.

35

36

THE
RUSSIAN
STYLE

In the winter of 1902–3, the recently married Duchess of Marlborough (Consuelo Vanderbilt) visited Russia. The palatial interiors of the houses of the St Petersburg nobility were not to her liking: they 'lacked the perfect taste one finds in France. One could not imagine oneself in a French house any more than one could mistake a Fabergé jewel for one set by Cartier.'[1] The Duchess was probably thinking of the diamond and platinum jewellery in which Cartier excelled, in both design and technique. With *objets d'art* the comparison is less clear-cut.

Little has as yet been written on the similarities and differences between Cartier and Fabergé hardstone carvings or enamelled gold *objets d'art*, and on the difficulty of distinguishing the work of the two firms. Existing discussions have been in publications on Fabergé, where Cartier is viewed as a rival, at best, or mere imitator, at worst. The materials used and the types of object made are often identical. And, indeed, many objects produced by Cartier are closely inspired by Fabergé models, though rarely are they direct copies. The problem with trying to make the distinction is that while hundreds of Fabergé objects are fully documented in collections worldwide, and there is a vast body of literature on them, relatively few documented works by Cartier in the Russian style survive and even fewer are published.

Nevertheless, a close inspection of what does survive, together with contemporary photographs in the Cartier archive, reveals the development of a highly original style, particularly in the hardstone flowers from *c.* 1906. Many models remained in production well into the 1920s, while new models were created after 1918, and many of them are totally different from anything produced by Fabergé. Fabergé's London shop closed in 1917. The same clientele, which had previously bought indiscriminately from Fabergé and from Cartier, transferred its custom to Cartier.

In his 1984 monograph on Cartier, Hans Nadelhoffer devoted two whole chapters to the influence of Fabergé and to Cartier's activity in St Petersburg, based for the most part on correspondence and records in the Cartier archive which the present author has not consulted. The information given below on Cartier's Russian suppliers and the firm's exhibitions in Russia is derived largely from Nadelhoffer's text.

The first contact seems to have been Pierre Cartier's visit to St Petersburg and Moscow

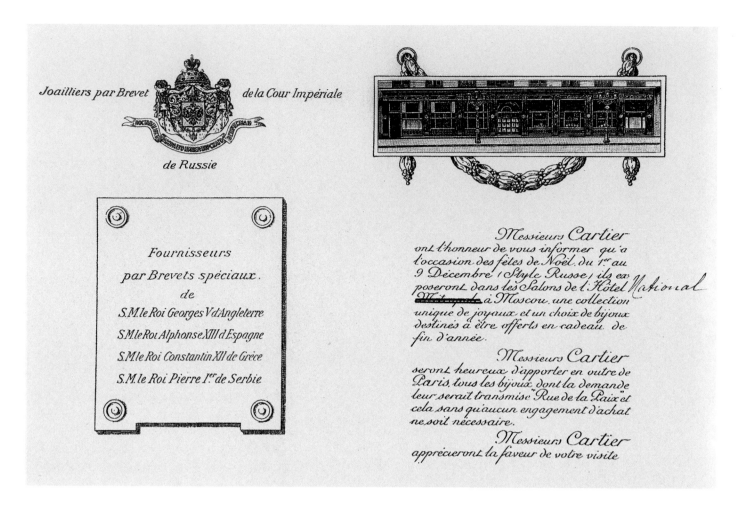

Joailliers par Brevet   de la Cour Impériale

de Russie

Fournisseurs
par Brevets spéciaux.
de
S.M. le Roi Georges V d'Angleterre
S.M. le Roi Alphonse XIII d'Espagne
S.M. le Roi Constantin XII de Grèce
S.M. le Roi Pierre Iᵉʳ de Serbie

Messieurs Cartier
ont l'honneur de vous informer qu'à
l'occasion des fêtes de Noël du 1ᵉʳ au
9 Décembre (Style Russe) ils ex-
poseront dans les Salons de l'Hôtel National
à Moscou, une collection
unique de joyaux et un choix de bijoux
destinés à être offerts en cadeau de
fin d'année.

Messieurs Cartier
seront heureux d'apporter en outre de
Paris, tous les bijoux dont la demande
leur serait transmise "Rue de la Paix" et
cela sans qu'aucun engagement d'achat
ne soit nécessaire.

Messieurs Cartier
apprécieront la faveur de votre visite

FIG. 57. Invitation issued by Cartier Paris to a Christmas exhibition at the Hotel National in Moscow, *c.* 1911.

in 1904–5. Initially, Cartier sold objects imported from Russia. The Moscow lapidary Svietchnikov supplied Cartier with animals made either to his own or to Cartier's designs. So did Karl Woerffel of St Petersburg, who was also Fabergé's supplier for hardstone goods. At the same time, Cartier Paris was corresponding with another Moscow manufacturer, Yahr, who did the goldwork and enamel for Svietchnikov, requesting samples of his enamel colours. Yahr then supplied Cartier directly with a range of enamel objects (see cat. 37). Other Russian suppliers included Ovchinnikov (for hardstones, although the firm was known for its enamelling), Denissov-Uralski and Fabergé himself. Geza von Habsburg has also noted an English supplier of Fabergé items called Stopford, whose name appears in the Cartier ledgers.[2] Nadelhoffer notes that when Grand Duchess Marie Pavlovna, wife of Grand Duke Vladimir, fled Russia, she entrusted her jewels to the same man, Albert Stopford.[3]

Following their first exhibition of jewels in St Petersburg in 1907, Cartier rented premises, with the help of their representative in Russia, Désiré Sarda, for two exhibitions a year, for the Easter and Christmas seasons, starting at Christmas 1908 and ending in spring 1914. They chose to exhibit in St Petersburg so as not to compete with their fellow jewellers of the Rue de la Paix, Boucheron, who had opened a branch in Moscow in 1899. For the 1908 exhibition over 500 letters of introduction and invitations were sent out. One such surviving invitation, for an exhibition in the Hotel National in Moscow, dates probably from 1911, when Louis Cartier and Charles Jacqueau received prospective customers there (fig. 57). These exhibitions showed the latest Paris fashion in delicate platinum jewellery as well as objects in the Russian taste.

A number of Russian clients had already become patrons of Cartier's shops in Paris and London prior to the exhibitions in Russia. Early clients of Cartier Paris included Grand Duke Alexis (from 1899), Grand Duchess Marie Pavlovna (from 1900), Grand Duke Paul (from 1901), Grand Duchess Xenia (from 1906) and Empress Marie Feodorovna (from 1907). But from 1908 they added to their clientele Grand Duke Michail Michailovich, the prime minister Stolypin (assassinated in 1911), Count Alexis Orlov and many more. Cartier not only gained access to Fabergé's Russian clients. By the early 1900s the firm's ledgers reveal the same European and American clients as appear in Fabergé's books. Recent studies by Geza von Habsburg of Fabergé's American clients and of surviving ledgers from Fabergé's London shop for the period 1907–10 repay detailed study by those interested in Cartier's clientele of that period. The names in the ledgers of both firms are almost identical.[4] They were all buying the animals and other small objects to give to each other as presents.

Cartier began making their own Russian-style objects around 1906. The main specialist workshop for gold and enamel was that of Henri Lavabre, who worked exclusively for Cartier from 1906 to 1921.[5] Despite requesting Yahr's palette of enamel colours, Cartier never produced the variety of enamel colours seen in the work of Fabergé. They employed the same technique of building up the enamel in layers over an engine-turned base to obtain the required intensity of colour and produced some very refined pieces of enamelwork, for example the opalescent enamel box, cat. 41; they also introduced new colour combinations such as mauve and green (cat. 40).

Cartier also produced a range of cigarette cases in coloured gold marquetry, another Fabergé speciality adopted by a number of Paris firms. An example with a Russian inscription is to be found in section 3 (cat. 56).

The main lapidary workshop was that of Berquin-Varangoz (see cat. 44–5, 47–9), taken over in 1918 by Aristide Fourrier (1875–1941). Fourrier remained the firm's principal lapidary throughout the 1920s and 1930s, for all inlay and hardstone work (cat. 50 and 53). The workshop's consummate hardstone inlay work is represented in many other sections of this catalogue (for example, cat. 136–7).

Ivory carvings were bought in from the Paris branch of the Japanese dealer Yamanaka, possibly for resale or perhaps as models for small scale animal carvings. Fabergé certainly used *netsuke* as models, resulting in minutely observed animal carvings in which every feather or hair is represented. In general, Cartier animals are not as minutely observed; nor do they exploit the inclusions in the stone to suggest the natural markings of animals in the same subtle way as Fabergé. The stones are often very homogeneous in colour.

Cartier's own designs for animals, as distinct from those bought in from Russian suppliers, are sometimes very close in style to Fabergé models, such as the rose-quartz sleeping pig (cat. 51) made by the Taillerie de Royat. But while rose quartz was popular with Cartier, it was not favoured by Fabergé, who liked to use Russian stones wherever possible. The Cartier birds on perches (cat. 48–50), made mostly by the Berquin-Varangoz workshop or later by Fourrier, were probably their most popular and long-lived line in animal carvings, produced between 1906 and c. 1925. Some of the later designs executed by Fourrier display an unexpected individuality, for example the kingfisher perched on a dead branch above a rock, made in several versions c. 1925. One of them is in the Cartier collection.[6]

Nadelhoffer rightly recognised the originality of the Cartier flower pieces. Unlike Fabergé's, they are all housed within glass cases with decorative gold corners, on raised ivory or wood bases carved in the Chinese manner. The arrangements tend to be in the form of bunches or branching elements, or very tall single stems climbing up a stake, rather than the simple stems favoured by Fabergé. And the pots only rarely copied Fabergé's clear rock crystal imitating glass flower vases with the water line visible (fig. 58).

FIG. 58. Group of Fabergé carved hardstone flowers
with vases of rock crystal imitating glass, *c.* 1900.
Wartski, London.

Cartier pots were usually carved in opaque hardstones, often in the form of square
troughs or handled buckets containing hardstones specially chosen to simulate earth.
Many of the arrangements have an asymmetry that was unquestionably intended to look
Japanese, and indeed the titles often confirmed the intention: 'un pommier japonais' (cat.
47), or 'un magnolia du Japon', for example. The materials used were generally more
varied than those used by Fabergé and the flowers themselves differed, concentrating on
rare and exotic blooms rather than Fabergé's delicate wild flowers. A further Japanese
touch, reflecting the Japanese taste for patinated metals, was the use of oxidised or blackened stems (fig. 59, 'lys martagon'). Sadly, very few identified Cartier flowers survive.
Published examples include a hyacinth, lilies, carnations, lily of the valley, morning glory

FIG. 59. Archive photograph of a glass-covered exotic lily stem with enamel flowers, oxidised metal stem and aventurine leaves, climbing an ivory stake. Made by Fourrier for Cartier Paris, 1926.

and cacti in the Lindemann collection, all *c.* 1925,[7] and a double flower-pot in the Musée des Arts Décoratifs, Paris,[8] bequeathed, like cat. 47, by Mlle Yznaga. Three others in the Cartier collection include an astonishingly fragile hydrangea, the petals made of enamel alone.[9] It survives with its original fabric-covered box, adding to the Japanese effect.

NOTES
1. Vanderbilt Balsan 1953, p. 167.
2. St Petersburg/London 1993, p. 166.
3. Nadelhoffer 1984, p. 123.
4. San Francisco 1996, pp. 27–43 and 339–54.
5. Nadelhoffer 1984, p. 296, n. 11.
6. Tokyo 1995, cat. 52.
7. See New Orleans 1988, pls XXXI–XXXVI.
8. Possémé 1993, p. 59.
9. For a similar one, see Nadelhoffer 1984, col. pl. 1.

37

enlisted in the war against Japan, but that help never arrived. Thus it is not clear how many of these 160 objects were actually supplied (Nadelhoffer 1984, pp. 90–91). However, the letter of February 1904 from Cartier to Yahr provides evidence for at least fifty of them. This letter, signed on behalf of Pierre Cartier by J. Lebault, specifies which of the accompanying stones were to be used for which object. The objects include table bells, paper-knives, pin-boxes, cigarette cases and ash-trays, magnifying glasses, scent bottles and parasol handles. The letter also refers to the enclosure of new designs for objects and to 'all the objects that Mr Pierre Cartier has purchased from the Woerffel shop in St Petersburg'. Pierre Cartier purchased several items from Karl Woerffel, Fabergé's supplier, in 1904.

38 Card case

Made by Chailloux for Cartier Paris for stock, 1906

Gold with sapphire cabochon push-piece. Engraved with a sunburst on both sides. The push-piece releases a sprung flap which folds back to reveal the cards, held in place by a pierced gold bracket. The interior engraved with a monogram CP (?).

A similar, but not identical, piece entered in stock book on 7 May 1906; four further examples entered on 30 May 1906. This example sold Habsburg Feldman, Geneva, *The Art of Cartier*, 28 June 1988, lot 45/105.

MARKS Engraved on bracket inside *CARTIER Paris London DÉPOSÉ*; French third standard gold mark and workshop mark *BC* (or *RC*) flanking an illegible symbol.

L. 9.3 cm, W. 6.1 cm

Cartier collection, AG 36 C06

37 Photograph frame in the form of a miniature camera

Made by Yahr in Moscow for Cartier Paris, 1904

Gold, enamel, ruby and wood. Chased and coloured gold camera on tripod, the lens plate enamelled white on an engine-turned ground, the frame white with green gold garlands, the lens set with a cabochon ruby and four small rubies at each corner; the back plate glazed to take a photograph with frame of green translucent and white beaded enamel. The tripod with coloured gold and silver garlands, the bellows of carved wood. The original Cartier case survives.

Not recorded in stock or order books but assumed to be the 'appareil photo B', mentioned in a letter from

Cartier Paris to Yahr of 24 February 1904 enclosing stones for specific pieces ordered by Cartier Paris. Sold Sotheby's Geneva, 12 November 1987, lot 424.

MARKS Underside of camera engraved *CARTIER*.

H. 10.1 cm

Cartier collection, IV 39 A04

LITERATURE Cologni and Mocchetti 1992, p. 51.

The Yahr workshop in Moscow specialised in gold and enamel objects, supplying firms such as Ovchinnikov. Nadelhoffer notes that in 1904 Yahr was expected to supply some 160 objects to Cartier and that he wrote to Cartier requesting help from the Paris workshops to replace some of his best craftsmen, who had

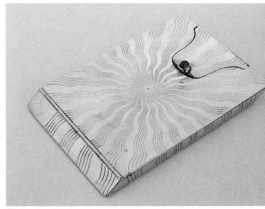

38 (greatly reduced)

39

39 Easter egg

Made by Picq, Césard and Guesdon for Cartier Paris for stock, 1906

Enamelled gold, fluorite, diamonds and pearls set in platinum. Enamelled and chased gold plinth, carved pale green fluorite cushion with diamond edging and tassels, on which sits the egg, surmounted by a diamond-and pearl-set crown. The egg enamelled purple on an engine-turned ground, with central band enamelled white and set with cypher of Nicholas II; diamond-set palms above and below. The egg opens to reveal a hinged miniature frame with diamond border containing a photograph of Tsarevich Alexis. Mounted on a modern onyx plinth.

Entered in stock book on 5 December 1906; sold 18 May 1912 to the City of Paris. Later acquired by Laird Shields Goldsborough, who bequeathed it to the Metropolitan Museum in 1951.

MARKS Gold plinth signed on underside *Cartier Paris*; Paris eagle's head assay mark for gold on on rim of base of egg and inner flange of lid.

H. 11.6 cm, plinth 6.2 × 6.2 cm

The Metropolitan Museum of Art, New York, Department of European Sculpture and Decorative Art, 51.91.1, Bequest of Laird Shields Goldsborough, 1951

EXHIBITIONS Munich 1986, cat. 621; Paris 1989, cat. 44; Tokyo 1995, cat. 22.

LITERATURE Snowman 1952, p. 97, fig. 336; Habsburg 1979, fig. 117; Nadelhoffer 1984, col. pl. 2, pp. 92 and 122.

According to Nadelhoffer (p. 122), this Easter egg of 1906 was taken to Russia by Louis Cartier in 1910 as a showpiece. In 1912, on the occasion of an official visit of the Paris City Council to Moscow, the egg was presented to Nicholas II. The City Council wanted to honour the Tsar with a gift that symbolised not France but the host country. Nadelhoffer also states that the presentation took place at Tsarskoe Selo, but gives no source for this information.

This egg may also have been considered an appropriate gift for the Tsar because its design was inspired directly by Fabergé pieces shown at the Paris Exhibition of 1900: firstly, the imperial Easter eggs, and secondly, the miniature replicas of the imperial regalia. Fabergé's miniature regalia (now in the State Hermitage, St Petersburg) comprised two diamond crowns and orb, each set on buff velvet cushions mounted on chased silver plinths (see St Petersburg/London 1993, cat. 113). Here Cartier has substituted an imperial Easter egg in the Fabergé taste for the regalia.

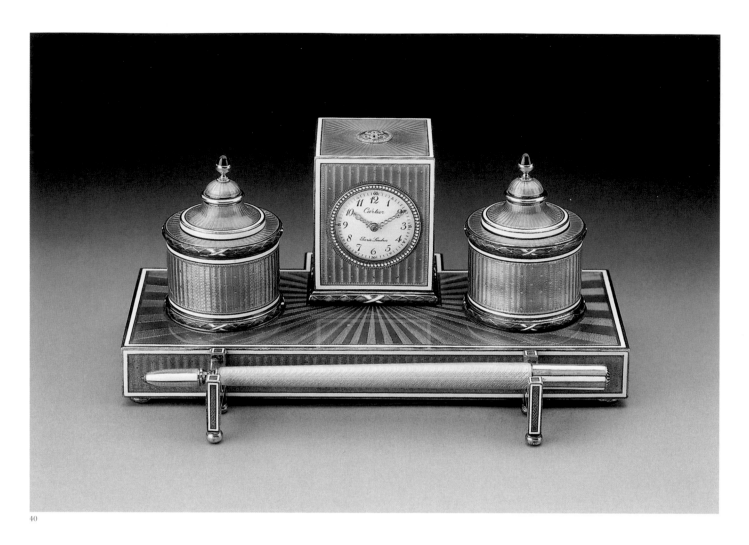

40

40 Desk set

Made by Prévost and Bako for Cartier Paris for stock, 1908

Enamelled gold and silver, with sapphire cabochons for the inkwell lids. A rectangular tray with clock and two inkwells; in front a pen-holder and pen. All in lilac and blue enamel on an engine-turned ground, with borders in white and translucent green enamel. Decorative monogram in diamonds on top of clock. The original case, in the form of a roll-top bureau, survives.

Entered in stock book on 28 April 1908; sold 3 May 1913.

MARKS *Cartier Paris Londres* on dial.

L. 18.5 cm, W. 7 cm, H. 8.3 cm

Private collection

EXHIBITIONS Los Angeles 1982, cat. 108.

LITERATURE Nadelhoffer 1984, col. pl. 5; Snowman (ed.) 1990, p. 195; Cologni and Mocchetti 1992, p. 58.

The monogram on top of the clock may have been added later.

41

42

41 Powder box

Made by Lavabre for Cartier Paris for stock, 1911

Enamelled gold with diamond thumbpiece. Pale pink ombré enamel on an engine-turned ground, the lid edged in white enamel; applied chased gold Imperial Russian arms.

Entered in stock book on 27 April 1911; sold 5 July 1911.

MARKS Partly visible workshop mark on rim of lid

DIAM. 4 cm

Cartier collection, IV 101 A11

EXHIBITIONS Tokyo 1995, cat. 30; Lausanne 1996, cat. 131.

In most of these Russian-style enamels, several layers of enamel were fired successively to achieve the desired strength of colour without losing the translucency, so that the gold or silver base with its complex engine-turned patterns remained visible. The ombré, or shaded, enamel on this powder box was achieved by varying the thickness of successive layers of enamel as they were applied. This gave an iridescent or opalescent surface effect.

The Russian arms appear to have been added later, since the stock book describes a 'reserved shield' in the centre.

42 Trump marker

Made by Varangoz (hardstone base) and Mathey (enamelled gold) for Cartier Paris for stock, 1907

Silver-gilt and enamel, with pink quartz base and moonstone at top of push-button. Stem and disc in blue enamel on an engine-turned ground; on both sides a window with revolving inner disc activated by the push-button to show the four aces enamelled in red and black on white.

Entered in stock book on 9 October 1907; sold 24 December 1913.

MARKS On base of stem and rim of disc, Paris boar's head assay mark for silver and workshop mark *M & Cie* with a bird for Mathey et Compagnie.

H. 13 cm, base 5 x 5 cm

Cartier collection, IV 117 A07

EXHIBITIONS Tokyo 1995, cat. 26; Lausanne 1996, cat. 37.

43

43 Cigarette case

Made by Lavabre for Cartier Paris for stock, 1907

Enamelled gold. Flat and curved in shape to fit in a back pocket. Royal blue enamel on an engine-turned ground with three sections continuing round both sides, each bordered with a wavy line of white enamel, divided by two bands of green and white enamel circles. Rosette in centre of top; two lids, both with diamond thumbpieces, the smaller lid presumably for matches since there is a strike-a-light on the nearest edge, but the interior now has no compartments.

Entered in stock book on 26 August 1907; sold 26 October 1909.

MARKS Inside rim of lid engraved *Cartier Paris*; Paris eagle's head assay mark for gold and illegible workshop mark.

L. 9.7 cm, W. 5.6 cm

Cartier collection, CC 41 A07

EXHIBITIONS London 1988, cat. 97; Naples 1988, cat. 87; Paris 1989, cat. 50; Rome 1990, cat. 36, pl. XXII; Lausanne 1996, cat. 17.

The enamel decoration of this piece is taken directly from that found on gold boxes and *étuis* (flat cases for notebooks or implements) made in Paris or Geneva in the late eighteenth century: see, for example, S. Grandjean *et al.*, *The James A. de Rothschild Collection at Waddesdon Manor. Gold Boxes and Miniatures of the Eighteenth Century*, London 1975, nos 63–5. The collection of boxes owned by Edmond de Rothschild (1845–1934) in Paris, which came to Waddesdon through his son James, was one of several collections of such boxes in Paris that would have been familiar to Cartier designers. The characteristic decoration of translucent enamel over an engine-turned ground, with the borders of chased gold and opaque relief enamel, was also copied by Fabergé. The use of a curved shape to fit a back pocket goes back to the early nineteenth century. For a Cartier enamelled gold box owned by Edmond de Rothschild, see cat. 130.

44 (greatly reduced)

44 Perfume-burner (*lampe à parfum*)

Made by Varangoz for Cartier Paris for stock, 1907

Aventurine, silver-gilt, enamel and sapphires. The base of carved green aventurine, the lid of aventurine and enamelled silver-gilt, with blue enamel on an engine-turned ground, the rim enamelled white with four palmettes and cabochon sapphires round the side, the knop with four white circles containing further sapphires.

Entered in stock book on 28 September 1907.

MARKS Base engraved *Cartier Paris Londres*; Paris boar's head assay mark for silver and workshop mark K (H?) BV flanking a vase.

H. 13.1 cm

Cartier collection, IV 59 A07

EXHIBITIONS St Petersburg 1992, cat. 43.

This urn-shaped vessel is described as a 'lampe à parfum' in the stock book. It is the only object so described in the Paris ledgers. There are, however, two mentions of a 'vase brûle-parfum', in 1906 (Mathey workshop)

and in 1907 (Varangoz and Mathey workshops). The latter, in grey agate and green enamel with applied gold garlands, appears to be similar to the present example. Presumably the vessel contained a wick soaked in perfumed oil; the lid would be removed and the wick pulled out as required.

45 Jade cigarette case

Made by Lavabre (gold mounts) and Varangoz (carved jade) for Cartier Paris for stock, 1914

Jade, with gold and enamel mounts, thumbpiece set with graduated calibré-cut onyx. The box carved out of one piece of jade, including the lid. A compartment for matches at the top end with a strike-a-light inside the lid; black silk tinder-cord with tassel at the end attached to a gold chain at the top, with a gold ball to pull it up through the hollow spine of the box. The gold ropework borders outlined in black enamel.

Entered in stock book on 31 March 1914 with diamond thumbpiece; sold 16 April 1914 to the 'Comte de Quinsonas'. Bought back for stock on 15 May 1914, thumbpiece changed to onyx, sold for second time on 2 October 1916 to Mrs W. B. Leeds.

MARKS On gold tube for tinder-cord, Paris eagle's head assay mark for gold and fragmentary workshop mark.

L. 11 cm, W. 6.7 cm

Cartier collection, CC 61 A14

EXHIBITIONS Hong Kong 1995, cat. 17.

This box, carved out of one piece of jade, is a masterpiece of lapidary work. The tinder-cord functioned as a wick. After lighting a match on the strike-a-light, the cord would be lit in order to provide a longer-lasting flame for use out-of-doors or to pass round in company. Once the tinder-cord was pulled back down into the hollow spine, the flame was extinguished. The cords were generally made with an inner cord of cotton soaked in saltpetre to make it burn, which was then wrapped in silk. They were frequently replaced, and few such boxes survive with the original cord. The cord on this box is probably a replacement. The original cord had a ring to pull it up by, instead of a ball.

The fashion for cigarette boxes with tinder-cords started around 1900. Although such boxes are particularly associated with Fabergé, they were popular elsewhere in Europe. The tinder-cords had an additional function: the boxes could be pulled out of the pocket by the cord, which gave them a foppish elegance.

Nancy Mary (May) Stewart (1873–1923),

widow of the American tin magnate William Bateman Leeds (1861–1908), was one of Cartier's most regular clients, residing at Grosvenor Square in London and entertaining lavishly, with fellow-American Lady Paget as her social sponsor. She also patronised Fabergé's London shop, where her purchases between 1907 and 1917 included eight cigarette cases in enamelled gold and hardstone (San Francisco 1996, pp. 347–9). She owned showy pieces with large stones, as well as an exquisite diamond and platinum 'embroidery' bandeau of 1912 (Nadelhoffer 1984, p. 73, fig. 67). W. B. Leeds was her second husband. In 1920 she married Prince Christopher of Greece and became Princess Anastasia. Philip de Laslo's portrait of 1921 shows her wearing her Cartier tiara and necklace (1921) of diamonds and emeralds (Nadelhoffer 1984, p. 69, fig. 58).

45

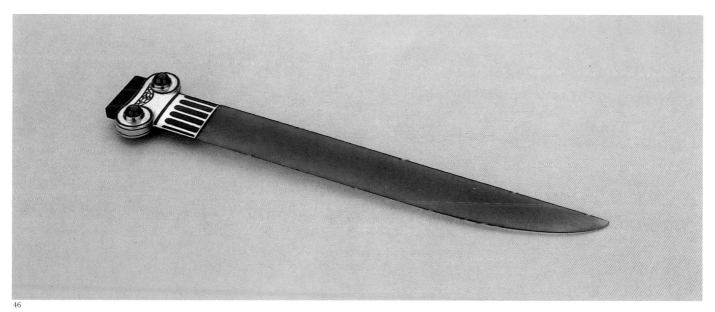

46

46 Paper-knife

Made by Allard & Meyer for Cartier Paris for stock, 1913

Jade and enamelled gold. The blade in carved jade, with gold mount in the form of an Ionic capital, decorated with black enamel, the volutes set with four cabochon sapphires, two on each side.

Entered in stock book on 19 December 1913; sold 23 December 1913 to H. H. The Aga Khan III. Bought back into stock on 21 January 1916 and sold for the second time on 22 December 1916.

MARKS Paris eagle's head assay mark for gold on mount.

L. 13.3 cm

Cartier collection, IV 24 A13

EXHIBITIONS Los Angeles 1982, cat. 72; London 1988, cat. 109; Naples 1988, cat. 53; Paris 1989, cat. 191; Rome 1990, cat. 89; Hong Kong 1995, cat. 28.

Jacqueau's working designs include a paper-knife with a mount in the form of an Ionic capital, but the blade is much wider than on this example.

47

47 'Japanese apple blossom' *(pommier japonais)*

Made by Berquin and Lavabre for Cartier Paris for stock, 1907

A blossoming branch in a rectangular pot, the branch in stained ivory, the flowers of pink enamel with gold stamens and diamond or moonstone centres, the pot of pink quartz in an ivory stand with rubellite earth, within a glass case on a wood base.

Three similar examples, all described as 'pommier japonais', entered in stock book in November 1907: (1) sold 14 December 1907; (2) sold 10 June 1908 to C. Vanderbilt; (3) unsold. From the archive descriptions, no. 2 is the closest to the example catalogued here. There is a contemporary archive photograph for one of the three only, which also corresponds most closely to no. 2, but has a number of differences.

MARKS An applied gold square plaque enamelled CARTIER on the wooden base inside the glass case.

H. 15 cm

Musée des Arts Décoratifs, Paris, inv. no. 36247.70, given by Mlle Yznaga in 1949

LITERATURE Possémé 1993, p. 59.

Although described in the archive records as an apple branch, the branch itself is inspired by Japanese pine branches. This model was taken up again in the 1920s; four examples made by the Fourrier workshop are recorded in the Paris stock books and illustrated in the photograph albums, but they are all significantly different from the present example.

The Yznaga sisters from Cuba lived in Paris and London. One of them was also a regular client of Fabergé London and bequeathed two Fabergé animals to the Musée des Arts Décoratifs, along with two Cartier flower pots, of which this is one. Other objects owned by her were sold at Christie's Geneva between 1979 and 1984 (see St Petersburg/London 1993–4, p. 127).

48 Owl on a perch

Made by Varangoz for Cartier Paris for stock, 1906

Agate, ivory, gold, silver-gilt, enamel, emeralds, sapphires and diamonds. The owl of carved grey agate with emerald eyes and chased gold feet; ivory perch with gold caps ringed in green enamel and set with two sapphire cabochons; agate plinth in silver-gilt base with laurel-leaf borders set with diamonds.

Entered in stock book on 1 February 1906; sold 30 March 1906 to Lady Rothschild.

MARKS None.

H. 7.8 cm

Cartier collection, AS 10 A06

EXHIBITIONS St Petersburg 1992, cat. 65.

49 Pair of love birds (inséparables)

Made probably by Varangoz for Cartier Paris for stock; model created 1907, this example c. 1910

Quartz, ivory, gold, diamonds Two birds, one in white, the other in yellowish grey quartz, with chased gold feet and diamond eyes; ivory perch with pink quartz terminals; stand of carved pink quartz.

Similar, but not identical, piece made by Varangoz in fluorine and grey agate entered in stock book on 4 March 1907; sold 27 May 1907. Another thirty variants of this model with different components recorded in the Paris stock books between 1907 and 1930. Sold Christie's Geneva, *Russian Works of Art*, 14 May 1986, lot 399.

MARKS None

H. 18.4 cm

Cartier collection, AS 03 C10

EXHIBITIONS Paris 1989, cat. 96; Rome 1990, cat. 56 (pl. XXVII).

LITERATURE Cologni and Mocchetti 1992, p. 64.

Varangoz made a number of different models with birds on perches: two cockatoos (1905); a pair of parrots (1906); *inséparables* (1907); two parakeets in a ring (1910). Of these, only the *inséparables* model appears in the photograph albums.

48–50 (greatly reduced)

50 Two budgerigars on a perch

Designed probably in 1918 and made by Fourrier for Cartier Paris for stock, 1927

Fluorite, ivory, agate, gold, spinels. The birds carved from one piece of fluorite with chased gold feet and spinels for the eyes, ivory perch and agate plinth.

Entered in stock book on 30 September 1927; sold 20 February 1928.

MARKS Stock number on base only.

H. 8.6 cm

Cartier collection, AS 04 A27

EXHIBITIONS London 1988, cat. 74, pl. XIII; Milan 1988, p.77.

LITERATURE Cologni and Mocchetti 1992, p. 64.

51 Sleeping pig

Made by the Taillerie de Royat for Cartier
Paris for stock, 1911

Pink quartz. Contained in the original green leather
case with tooled gilding.

Entered in stock book on 20 November 1911;
sold 31 December 1912.

MARKS Pig: none. Case: stamped *CARTIER* in gold on
reverse, with standard Cartier stamp printed in gold
inside each door.

Pig: L. 6.7 cm. Case: L. 9.8 cm

Cartier collection, AS 01 A11

EXHIBITIONS Munich 1986, cat. 632; London 1988,
cat. 73, pl. XII; Milan 1988, p. 67; Naples 1988, cat. 44;
Rome 1990, cat. 57; St Petersburg 1992, cat. 71;
Lausanne 1996, cat. 58.

51

52 Seated bulldog

Made probably by Bozzachi and Lenfant for
Cartier Paris for stock, *c.* 1912

Carved smoky quartz, with olivine eyes, collar of gold
set with sapphires, pendant pearl.

A seated bulldog made by Bozzachi (carved stone) and
Lenfant (setting of collar and eyes) recorded in stock
book in 1912.

MARKS None.

H. 6.5 cm

Cartier collection, AS 11 C04

LITERATURE Cologni and Mocchetti 1992, p. 64.

This is a highly accomplished piece of carving
and is markedly different in quality from the
birds on perches.

52   52

53 Two penguins

Made probably by Fourrier for Cartier Paris for stock, c. 1923–4

Agate, rubies. Carved from one piece of agate, with ruby eyes.

Similar but not identical pieces entered in stock book on 15 December 1923 (Renault workshop for the gem-setting, origin of hardstone not given) and on 17 November 1924 (Fourrier workshop), the latter sold on 26 December 1924 to Baron Lambert.

MARKS None.

H. 7.9 cm

Cartier collection, AS 15 C23

53

54 Pekinese dog

Made for Cartier New York (workshop unknown), c. 1925

Carved jade dog on a gold plinth with white enamel motifs, set with cabochon sapphires, contained in glass case with wooden stand; the gold corners of the case with white enamel motifs and sapphires as on plinth.

Sold Christie's Geneva, 16 May 1985, lot 43.

MARKS Stand engraved *CARTIER NY*.

H. 11.4 cm, L. 13.1 cm, W. 8.5 cm

Cartier collection, AS 02 C25

EXHIBITIONS Naples 1988, cat. 106; Paris 1989, cat. 97; Rome 1990, cat. 58; Lausanne 1996, cat. 57.

54 (greatly reduced)

FASHIONABLE ACCESSORIES

IN GOLD AND ENAMEL

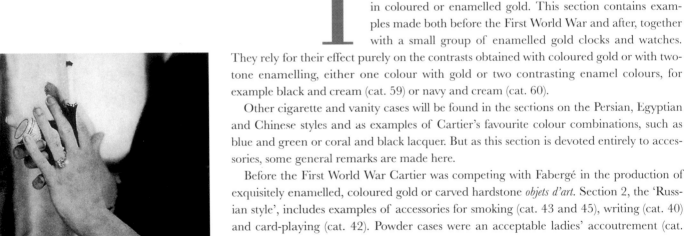

FIG. 60. How to carry a Cartier vanity case and cigarette holder. Photograph from London *Vogue*, August 1925.

The flat surfaces of cigarette and vanity cases provided the Cartier designers with a vehicle for abstract patterns, whether in coloured or enamelled gold. This section contains examples made both before the First World War and after, together with a small group of enamelled gold clocks and watches. They rely for their effect purely on the contrasts obtained with coloured gold or with two-tone enamelling, either one colour with gold or two contrasting enamel colours, for example black and cream (cat. 59) or navy and cream (cat. 60).

Other cigarette and vanity cases will be found in the sections on the Persian, Egyptian and Chinese styles and as examples of Cartier's favourite colour combinations, such as blue and green or coral and black lacquer. But as this section is devoted entirely to accessories, some general remarks are made here.

Before the First World War Cartier was competing with Fabergé in the production of exquisitely enamelled, coloured gold or carved hardstone *objets d'art*. Section 2, the 'Russian style', includes examples of accessories for smoking (cat. 43 and 45), writing (cat. 40) and card-playing (cat. 42). Powder cases were an acceptable ladies' accoutrement (cat. 41), but probably for the dressing table rather than for use in public. The wearing of lipstick was still taboo. But the emancipation of women during the First World War made it acceptable not only to wear cosmetics, but to apply make-up in public, at all times of day. Similarly, women were also now permitted to smoke in public and so required cigarette cases, previously an almost exclusively male preserve.

By 1921, when Helena Rubinstein opened her Paris salons, cosmetics were big business. One of the first and simplest models was an octagonal powder box and matching lipstick, the lipstick tube attached by means of a chain, created for Elsie de Wolfe (1865–1950) in 1921 (see p. 31). Examples of the octagonal or circular powder box of the 1920s are included in sections 6 and 7. Fig. 61 shows two of them open. Both have mirrored lids and contained loose powder; inside are the original powder puffs with hinged gold loop handles. The octagonal one has an extra lid to keep the powder from spilling. An illustration in London *Vogue* for August 1925 shows how they could be carried, looped over the fingers (fig. 62).

By 1920, Cartier had developed one of their most sophisticated models, the combined

FIG. 61. Two powder boxes and lipstick tubes shown open. Left: cat. 116; right: cat. 131.

FIG. 62. How to carry a Cartier powder box and lipstick tube. Photograph from London *Vogue*, August 1925.

cigarette and vanity case (cat. 63–5). This was usually oval in shape, to give the required depth inside, and might be designed to incorporate its own cigarette holder, with compartments at the ends (see also cat. 268, a design for a vanity case of this kind), or to contain the usual powder and rouge compartments in the base and cigarettes in the lid. An illustration in London *Vogue* for August 1925 demonstrated how the oval shape enabled it to be cradled comfortably in the hands, while the decoration of thin stripes gave added elegance (fig. 60). A multi-compartment vanity case of this kind would be carried instead of an evening bag.

Cigarette holders were made of black jet, amber and a wide variety of hardstones. Examples included in other sections are made of jade (cat. 125), coral and lapis lazuli (cat. 140) and coral and black jade (cat. 196). The hardstone examples appear to have been made in Paris, but the workshops are not recorded in the Paris ledgers and none of the examples included here bears a workshop mark. Cartier London ledgers confirm that hardstone cigarette holders were imported from Paris, but there were also a number of London suppliers, such as J. Edwards & Company, who were supplying examples in amber and black composition. Although contemporary illustrations almost always show women carrying cigarette holders, they were not an exclusively female accessory. The composer Igor Stravinsky was bitterly upset at the loss of his Cartier cigarette holder in Chicago in 1925, during a reception following a concert: 'I realised that my cigarette holder, a delightful jewel given me by the Princesse de Polignac about 10 years ago, had been stolen. I cried with fury.'[1]

Lipstick tubes could be purchased on their own (see cat. 136 and 199), often designed with matching but separate vanity case. Mostly, however, they were snugly fitted into the

FIG. 63. Three vanity cases shown open.
Left: cat. 92; centre: cat. 121; right: cat. 126.

OPPOSITE
FIG. 64. Advertisement for Cartier vanity cases from
Harper's Bazaar, London, August 1932, p. 55.

interior of a vanity case, either with their own spring fitting so that as the lid was lifted the tube sprang up, or clipped inside the lid of a tiny compartment. The owner would have had to have these minute lipstick tubes replaced by Cartier when they ran out. Fig. 63 shows three characteristic arrangements of the various compartments. The central vanity case still retains its original gauze sifters to prevent spillage from the powder and rouge boxes. The lids are lifted with the fingernail. In the other examples the lids have sunken hinged handles, sometimes sprung so that they lift up automatically when the box is opened. Often there was a long, thin space for a tiny gold-mounted tortoiseshell comb, but these rarely survive. Exceptions are cat. 89 and 200. By around 1930 compact powder was in use, hence the term 'powder compact' (see cat. 198 for an example). All examples with loose powder are described here as powder boxes.

In August 1932, *Harper's Bazaar* was advertising 'Still more varieties of vanity'. A whole page illustration, 'All from Cartier', was captioned: 'Ancient Chinese lacquer plaques are embodied in the powder box, top left; lipstick and tiny scent bottle spring out at the sides. Severely elegant is the flat triple box, in white gold with motifs in periwinkle blue enamel. The black case, lacquer on silver, has a clasp which may be hinged back to form a handle. A flick of the finger opens the gold lipstick' (fig. 64). An example of the clasp that hinges back to form a handle may be seen in cat. 200.

There was an understood etiquette that certain materials were appropriate for differ-ent times of day. According to *Adam, La revue de l'homme* for February 1928, patterned enamel cigarette cases were considered suitable for daytime use and traditional coloured or engine-turned gold for the evening. Similarly, women would carry vanities of enamel or semi-precious stones such as jade or coral during the day, while diamonds and black

onyx would be reserved for the evening. American *Vogue* for 1 October 1934 advertised a Vionnet dress of black taffeta worn by a model with carefully poised cigarette in one hand, no fewer than three diamond bracelets on the same wrist, a diamond brooch, and in the other hand a smart black vanity or cigarette case with diamond border and central circle (p. 37, fig. 29). The jewellery and accessories were all from Cartier. For similar vanity cases, see cat. 79 and 121. Cartier examples are described either as vanity cases or as nécessaires or powder boxes in the archive records. The term *minaudière* (from *minauder*, to simper), sometimes applied to the multi-compartment vanity case, was coined by the firm of Van Cleef & Arpels in the early 1930s.[2]

The prices varied enormously depending on the materials and the work involved. The vanity cases, with their complex and time-consuming interior construction, were very much more expensive than a cigarette case with similar exterior. The production costs of a cigarette case with all-over enamelling, such as cat. 59, were about half those of a vanity case with all-over enamelling, such as cat. 92, where twice the quantity of gold was used and the cost of labour was more than twice as much. Both examples were made in 1927. A cigarette case with complicated hardstone work as opposed to enamel might be as expensive as an enamel vanity case such as cat. 137.

Most of the items discussed so far have been in gold. From 1923, a separate department was set up, known as Department 'S', for silver, to produce a cheaper range of goods such as smokers' and desk accessories, evening bags and vanity cases. An advertisement in London *Vogue* in November 1926 for Cartier's 'New Department', on the first floor at Bond Street, illustrates a cigarette case and a vanity case with lipstick tube on a chain in 'Chinese lacquer' on silver.

Sales in the 'S' department increased dramatically following the Depression of 1929–30. Nadelhoffer has noted that between 1928 and 1930 the turnover of gold and silver cigarette lighters rose by some 50 per cent, while the sales of expensive enamelled, gem-set and hardstone cigarette cases fell by the same amount (1984, p. 205). The New York 'S' department had an especially enthusiastic clientele and this is reflected in the wide range of catalogues of 'inexpensive gifts' issued by Cartier New York in the 1930s.

NOTES
1. From a letter written by Stravinsky in November 1925, quoted in Lausanne 1996, pp. 106–7.
2. See Snowman (ed.) 1990, p. 208, and Raulet 1986, pp. 277–81.

55 Cigarette case

Designed probably by Charles Jacqueau and made by Wollès for Cartier Paris for stock, 1913

Silver with applied coloured gold. Flat silver case with rounded edges and reeded decoration; both sides made in five separate pieces and applied with bands of alternating red and yellow gold forming rectangles. Interior with silver-gilt bar to hold cigarettes, decorated with laurel wreath and berries.

Entered in stock book on 24 October 1913; sold 12 July 1916.

MARKS Inside rim engraved *CARTIER PARIS LONDRES NEW YORK*; Paris eagle's head and boar's head assay marks for gold and silver, together with mixed metals mark in use since 1906; workshop mark *BW* flanking a hunting horn.

L. 13 cm, W. 8.5 cm

Cartier collection, CC 59 A13

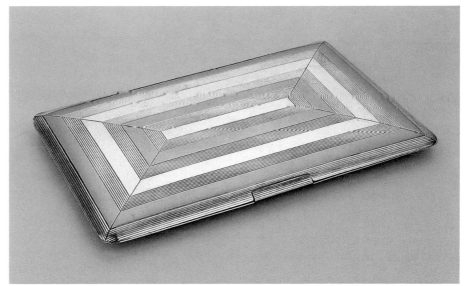

55 (greatly reduced)

Jacqueau's working designs include two for similar boxes with coloured-gold applied rectangles on a reeded ground.

The workshop of Benjamin Wollès is recorded from 1892, when the mark that appears on this cigarette case was registered. This case is one of four similar cigarette cases made for stock on the same day; they each had different applied gold decoration. Wollès specialised in silver and gold accessories, for example a series of silver-gilt waist-buckles designed by the sculptor Gustav Obiols around 1900, two of which are in the Hull Grundy Gift to the British Museum (see Gere *et al.* 1984, cat. 1133–4).

56 Cigarette case

Designed probably by Charles Jacqueau and made by Boulon & Taragnat for Cartier Paris for stock, 1927

Coloured gold and sapphires. Flat case with rounded edges, a patchwork in red and green gold with a geometric pattern of interlaced octagons. Push-piece set with three cabochon sapphires. Lid engraved inside with a Russian presentation inscription in Cyrillic script and the date 20 November 1927. Interior with hinged clip to hold cigarettes.

Entered in stock book on 25 May 1927; sold 12 November 1927 to a Russian client.

MARKS Inside rim engraved *Cartier Paris Londres New York*; Paris eagle's head assay mark for gold and workshop mark *BL* and *T* flanking an illegible symbol.

L. 12.3 cm, W. 8.5 cm

Cartier collection, CC 31 A27

EXHIBITIONS Naples 1988, cat. 64.

This is a fine example of coloured gold mar-

56 (greatly reduced)

quetry. A sheet of red gold was inlaid with green gold, and the two colours soldered together to create a new sheet, from which the box was made. The pattern is always visible on the inside. The technique was used for gold boxes in Paris in the eighteenth century and was revived in the 1920s by other Paris firms, such as Lacloche. A cigarette case with geometric marquetry in coloured gold and palladium made by Lacloche in 1927 is in the Hull Grundy Gift to the British Museum (Gere *et al.* 1984, cat. 1175).

Both Cartier and Lacloche were probably inspired by Fabergé, who were producing coloured gold marquetry boxes in the early 1900s (see St Petersburg/London 1993, cat. 291).

Jacqueau's working designs include a number for similar boxes with coloured gold patchwork, the different colours of gold indicated in near primary tones – pink for red gold, blue for white gold and green for green gold – as in designs by mid-eighteenth-century Paris box-makers (see K. Snowman, *Eighteenth Century Gold Boxes of Europe*, Woodbridge 1990, p. 71).

57 Cigarette case and matching lighter

Designed probably by Charles Jacqueau and made by Lavabre (?), the cigarette case for Cartier Paris for stock in 1912, the lighter made in Paris *c.* 1913–15

Enamelled gold, onyx and diamonds set in platinum. Both of flat form with rounded edges, enamelled all over with a pattern of white and black dashes. Case with diamond and onyx push-piece; lighter with diamond push-piece. Interior of case with pierced gold hinged bar to hold cigarettes in place. The lighter with strike-a-light on base and engraved inscription inside: 'L. A. Aug. 25th 1915'.

A photograph of an identical cigarette case in the Paris archive photograph albums is datable from the negative number to July 1912. The identical decoration appears on a cigarette case of 1913, made by Lavabre, hence the attribution to this workshop. The lighter has not been traced in the Paris archive and may have been made for Cartier London or New York.

MARKS Inner rim of both items engraved *Cartier Paris Londres New York*; Paris eagle's head assay mark for gold and third standard gold mark on both.

Cigarette case: L. 9 cm, W. 8 cm. Lighter: L. 4.9 cm, W. 4.4 cm

Cartier collection, CC 76 A12 and LR 18 A13

Jacqueau's working designs include a number of similar boxes of this shape with geometric enamel all-over patterns. The flat, rounded shape was described as 'forme coussin' (cushion shape) in the archive records and first appeared in 1903.

58 Visiting card with envelope

Made for Cartier New York to the order of Louis Cartier, 1927

Gold, engraved and enamelled. Miniature stamped addressed envelope, the address and postmark engraved and enamelled in black, the 2 cent stamp enamelled in red and white. The address reads: 'Monsieur et Madame P. Cartier, 15 East 96th Street, New York City', with postmark 'NEW YORK N.Y. MAR 26 1927'. On reverse of envelope a red enamel seal with CC monogram forming a hinged clasp. The envelope flap hinged at top, with further small hinged section at the front so that it folds back allowing easy removal of card. The gold visiting card with 'MR & MME L. J. CARTIER' in the centre, and an inscription above and below: 'Merci, de tout coeur, pour votre charmant accueil, et notre délicieux séjour parmi vous Toute notre affection Louis Jacqui.'

MARKS None.

L. 8.3 cm, W. 5 cm

Cartier collection, AG 73 A27

57 (greatly reduced)

58 (greatly reduced)

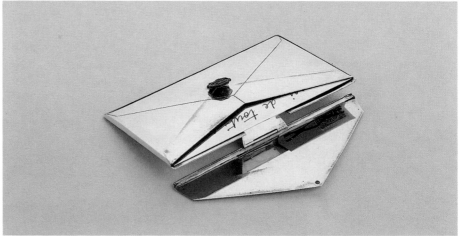

58

This envelope and visiting card was made for Mr and Mrs Pierre Cartier at the request of Louis Cartier and his second wife, Jacqueline Almassy, on leaving New York, to thank his brother for 'your charming welcome, and our delightful stay with you'. Presumably Louis Cartier wrote the message on his visiting card with his and his wife's printed name and gave the card in an addressed envelope to Cartier New York before leaving, so that both card and envelope with his handwriting could be copied in gold. An interview with Louis Cartier, published in the *International Jeweller* for March 1927, records that this was his first visit to the United States (Press Clippings Book, New York archive).

Miniature envelopes with messages inside were popular as love tokens throughout the nineteenth century. Indeed, Cartier themselves produced them as watch-chain or bracelet charms in the 1920s. At the end of 1921 Louis Cartier was planning to make New Year's Day cards in gold with gold envelopes (see p. 57), but they were never made, and this 'thank you' card seems to have been the first and almost unique example made by Cartier, though envelope-shaped accessories were made by others, such as Paul Flato of New York. Records of one other envelope with message have come to light so far, created by Cartier New York as a special order in 1938. It contained no separate visiting card but opened on hinges to reveal inside an engraved 'thank you' message for weekend hospitality.

A similar idea was carried out in a series of gold cigarette boxes in the form of stamped addressed envelopes made in the late 1920s and early 1930s. For an example made in 1932 and addressed to Randolph Churchill, see Paris 1989, cat. 476.

59

59 Cigarette case

Made by Renault for Cartier Paris as a special order, 1927

Enamelled gold with baguette diamond push-piece. An all-over optical illusion pattern of black and cream cylinders on a gold ground, the ends enamelled black, one with gold monogram. Integral hinge.

Completed in September 1927.

MARKS Inside rim engraved *Cartier Paris Londres New York*; Paris eagle's head assay mark for gold, illegible workshop mark.

L. 8.1 cm, W. 5.8 cm

Cartier collection, CC 30 A27

EXHIBITIONS Naples 1988, cat. 74; Limoges 1992, cat. 118.

RELATED MATERIAL Original design for a similar box, but with agate ends, in pencil, ink, watercolour and bodycolour on buff tracing paper in Stock Design Record Book for 1927, p. 75b, in Paris archive.

This special order of September 1927 is a close copy of a box created for stock in March 1927. The stock version had pale agate plaques at each end and was also made by Renault. Three further examples were made for stock, all with agate ends. This one was presumably given enamel ends so that the owner's monogram could be incorporated.

60

60 Cigarette case

Made by Renault for Cartier Paris for stock, 1928

Enamelled gold with agate ends, push-piece set with calibré sapphires. An all-over geometric pattern in dark blue and cream enamel. Integral hinge.

Entered in stock book on 30 July 1928; sold 13 November 1929 to the Maharajah of Alwar.

MARKS Inside rim engraved *Cartier Paris Londres New York MADE IN FRANCE*; Paris eagle's head assay mark for gold and illegible workshop mark.

L. 8.8 cm, W. 5.8 cm

Cartier collection, CC 73 A28

EXHIBITIONS Lausanne 1996, cat. 258.

This geometric pattern of squares is taken from a Japanese source, possibly a textile. For a Cartier cigarette case with a closely similar pattern, executed in black and red enamel imitating red lacquer, see Christie's New York, 21 October 1992, lot 611.

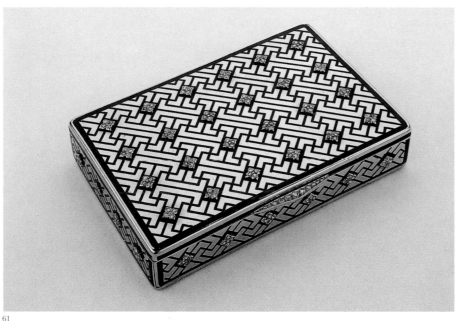

61

61 Vanity case

Made by Lavabre for Cartier Paris for stock, 1927

Enamelled gold set with diamonds mounted in platinum. On each side a Chinese-style geometric pattern in black enamel, the front set with flower-heads of rose-cut diamonds; diamond push-piece. Interior with mirrored lid, two compartments for rouge and powder and a space for a comb.

Entered in stock book on 31 May 1927; sold 22 July 1927 to Baron Eugène de Rothschild.

MARKS Engraved *Cartier Paris Londres New York*; Paris eagle's head assay mark for gold and workshop mark *HL* flanking a four-leaf clover.

L. 8.5 cm, W. 5.5 cm

Cartier collection, VC 10 A27

EXHIBITIONS Paris 1989, cat. 348; Hong Kong 1995, cat. 200; Tokyo 1995, cat. 200.

RELATED MATERIAL Original design in pencil, ink, and bodycolour on buff tracing paper in Stock Design Record Book for 1926, p. 68a, in Paris archive.

At least four other boxes of similar design were made for stock in 1927–8. The comb, now missing, was of blonde tortoiseshell with gold back. The geometric pattern may have been taken from Japanese *inro*, where the same pattern of Chinese origin is often found, usually in gold on a black lacquer ground.

62

62 Cigarette case and lighter

Made by Renault for Cartier Paris for stock, 1928

Case: enamelled gold, emeralds, moonstones, diamonds. Chinese-style engraved pattern all over, with deep blue enamel palmette motifs on each side, set with diamond-encrusted carved emeralds on the front. The ends in blue enamel with four matt-polished moonstones, two of which act as push-pieces; integral hinge and 'Kodak' system opening. Lighter: oval section, decorated as above, single blue enamel cartouche set with emerald on front.

An identical cigarette case made by the Renault workshop entered in stock book on 31 July 1928 and transferred for sale to New York on 3 October 1928.

MARKS Case: Engraved inside rim *Cartier Paris Londres New York MADE IN FRANCE*; Paris eagle's head assay mark

for gold and Cartier workshop mark, *C* between two crescents with the letters *S* and *A* above and below. Lighter: on base *CARTIER 10K US PAT 1671311 Bettini 70019.*

Case: L. 8.9 cm, W. 5.7 cm. Lighter: H. 3.6 cm, W. 3.7 cm

Cartier collection, CC 34 A28

EXHIBITIONS Naples 1988, cat. 117.

LITERATURE Cologni and Mocchetti 1992, p. 119.

The US patent is presumably for the automatic mechanism of the lighter, in which the narrow arm on top is pulled out to release the wick cover and turn the wheel at the same time. The term 'Kodak system' refers to the 'shutter' mechanism by which the lid springs open when the ends are pushed in. The appearance of the Cartier workshop mark suggests that repairs were carried out after 1929, when the mark was registered.

63

63

63 Cylindrical cigarette and vanity case

Made by Lavabre for Cartier Paris for stock, 1920

Enamelled gold, diamonds set in platinum, lacquer; tortoiseshell cigarette holder. The oval-section body enamelled all over with thin black stripes (*émail pékin mille raies*), the ends in black enamel bordered with diamonds and a band of floral ornament in white on a black ground. The lid applied with a diamond-set monogram DAW and diamond push-piece; gold chains with black lacquer links and diamond-set suspension ring. Interior for cigarettes with clip-in diamond-mounted cigarette holder; both ends open to provide compartments for powder with mirrored lid (right) and matches with strike-a-light (left).

Entered in stock book on 29 October 1920, the chains originally set with an onyx bead flanked by two pearls; sold 7 December 1920. Monogram added 14 December 1920.

MARKS Inner rim of base engraved *Cartier Paris Londres New York*; Paris eagle's head assay mark for gold on rim, French dog's head assay mark for platinum on suspension ring. Workshop mark HL flanking a four-leaf clover inside one end lid. The cigarette holder engraved *Cartier Paris* on end.

L. 11.9 cm, W. 4.5 cm, L. with chain extended approx. 21.5 cm

Cartier collection, VC 17 A20

EXHIBITIONS London 1988, cat. 173; Paris 1989, cat. 193; Rome 1990, cat. 90; St Petersburg 1992, cat. 96; Tokyo 1995, cat. 99.

LITERATURE Cologni and Mocchetti 1992, p. 79.

The idea of a multi-compartment box opening at both ends as well as in the centre goes back to the early nineteenth century. Similar examples were made in Geneva around 1830, usually of square or octagonal section (see Christie's Geneva, 17 May 1994, lot 24, and 14 May 1996, lot 274).

The oval form, taken from the Japanese *inro*, was especially popular for Cartier's combined cigarette and vanity cases, precisely because lid and base both provided sizeable compartments. The small end compartment for powder must have been intended for *papiers poudrés* or small patches of paper impregnated with powder. They would have fitted snugly into the space, whereas loose powder would have spilled out unless the case was held vertically, and was only practical for vanity cases that were placed flat on a table while in use.

64

64 Cylindrical cigarette and vanity case

Made by Lavabre for Cartier Paris for stock, 1922

Enamelled gold, onyx and diamonds set in platinum. The oval-section body enamelled all over with black circles and dots, diamond borders, onyx and diamond push-piece; the ends in black enamel with a diamond circle on the top end. The chain of two onyx rods between black enamel links, a double attachment loop of diamonds joined by an onyx bar, on an onyx suspension ring. Interior designed to hold cigarettes in lid with pierced gold bar to keep them in place, the base with two lidded compartments, the left one for matches with strike-a-light inside the lid, the right for powder with mirror on top of lid.

Entered in stock book on 17 October 1922, originally with a black silk tassel hanging from the onyx ring; sold 15 December 1922.

MARKS Inner rim of base engraved *Cartier Paris Londres New York*; on lid of powder compartment, Paris eagle's head assay mark for gold and workshop mark *HL* flanking a four leaf clover.

Case: L. 8.7 cm, W. 4.1 cm

Cartier collection, VC 19 A22

EXHIBITIONS London 1988, cat. 174; Naples 1988, cat. 128; Paris 1989, cat. 195; Rome 1990, cat. 92; St Petersburg 1992, cat. 98; Tokyo 1995, cat. 100.

Like the previous two items, this vanity case is inspired by Japanese *inro*, both in shape and in the decoration of circles and dots, often found on *inro* in gold wire or gold dust inlaid into black lacquer. The black silk tassel, however, that originally hung from the onyx ring would never have been found on a Japanese *inro*. The idea came from Chinese pendants. The diamond circle on the top was intended to take a monogram if the purchaser so desired.

65 Cylindrical cigarette and vanity case

Made by Cartier New York, *c.* 1924

Enamelled gold, diamonds set in platinum. White enamel stripes all over (*émail pékin*) and at each end a band of black enamel with zigzag motif reserved in gold. In the centre a diamond initial C within a diamond border on black enamel ground. Hung from a chain with white enamel links. Black enamel push-piece. Interior with space for cigarettes in the lid and two compartments in the base, the left with a strike-a-light, the right with mirror, and between them a lipstick tube with lid, the lid engraved 'Amour Ben d'or '24'.

MARKS Inside rim of lid engraved *Cartier*, rim of base with *CARTIER N.Y.*

L. 8.6 cm, W. 4 cm

Cartier collection, VC 39 C24

EXHIBITIONS Hong Kong 1995, cat. 24.

65

This combined cigarette and vanity case is traditionally said to have been given by the Duke of Westminster to his mistress Coco Chanel (1883–1971) in 1924. The initial C may or may not refer to Chanel. That it was a gift from the Duke of Westminster is indisputable because of the inscription. Hugh Grosvenor, 2nd Duke of Westminster (1879–1953), was nicknamed Bend Or after his grandfather's famous racehorse which won the Derby in 1880. The name was derived from the arms, azure a bend gold (or), borne by the Grosvenors. It may have been deliberately misspelt in the inscription to conceal the donor's identity or may simply be an error on the part of the engraver.

65

The Duke's third wife, Loelia, whom he married in 1930, recalled meeting Chanel on a trip to Paris, just after her engagement to the Duke had been announced. He took her off

to visit an old friend of his, Mademoiselle Chanel . . . She had more or less invented costume jewellery, specializing in most attractive ropes of imitation pearls, clasped at intervals with bunches of rubies and emeralds. When I saw her she was hung with every sort of necklace and bracelet, which rattled as she moved. Her sitting-room was luxurious and lavish, and she sat in a large armchair, a pair of tall Coromandel screens, now to be seen in her Paris showroom, making an effective backcloth. I perched, rather at a disadvantage, on a stool at her feet feeling that I was being looked over to see whether I was a suitable bride for her old admirer – and I very much doubted whether I, or my

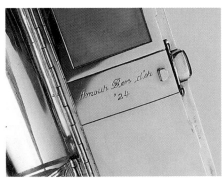

65.1 Inscription on cat. 65.

tweed suit, passed the test. (Westminster 1961, p. 159)

Chanel's private life was as spectacular as her design career. Grand Duke Dimitri was another of her lovers; her close friends included Misia Sert (see p. 164), and she designed costumes for Gloria Swanson (see cat. 217–18).

Originally, the suspension chain would have been longer, with a ring at the end.

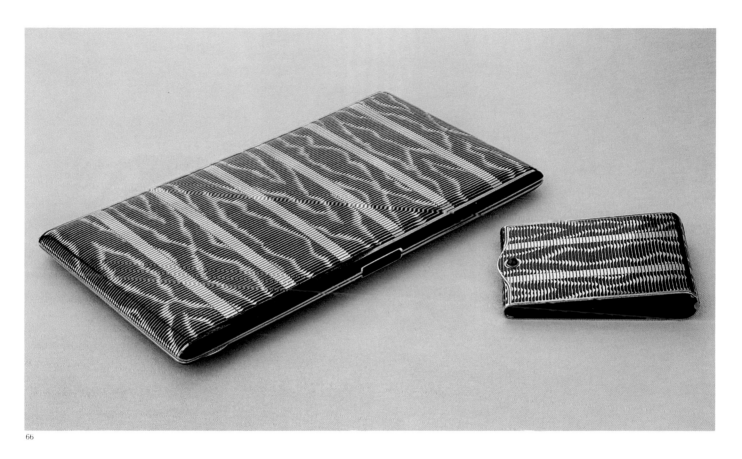

66

66 Cigarette case and match case

Made by the Cartier workshop for Cartier Paris as a special order, 1932

Enamelled gold, sapphire. All-over pattern in black champlevé enamel imitating watered silk. The long sides of both items enamelled black, the cigarette case with black enamel push-piece and thumb-catch at right side, the match case with a cabochon sapphire stud-catch. Interior with pierced bar to hold cigarettes in place. Lid engraved inside with later presentation inscription dated 1961. The match case with similar later inscription.

Completed in September 1932. Not purchased by client and transferred to stock on 8 June 1933; sold 18 October 1936. Sold Christie's Geneva, 16 November 1989, lot 164.

MARKS Cigarette case: inner rim engraved *Cartier Paris MADE IN FRANCE*; Paris eagle's head assay mark for gold and workshop mark *c* between two crescents with the letters *s* and *A* above and below. Match case: engraved inside lid *Cartier MADE IN FRANCE*; gold assay mark and workshop mark as above.

Cigarette case: L. 15 cm, W. 8.5 cm. Match case: L. 6 cm, W. 4.3 cm

Cartier collection, CC 55 A32

EXHIBITIONS Lausanne 1996, cat. 259.

A design of *c*. 1912 for a Russian-style cigarette box with tinder-cord, decorated with a watered silk pattern in black, suggesting enamel, appears in the Garland Style Design Scrapbook, III, though no enamel pieces with similar patterns survive from this early date.

67 Cigarette lighter

Made by the Cartier workshop for Cartier Paris for stock, 1935

Gold. A rectangular tube with vertical ridges and raised thumbpiece.

Entered in stock book on 30 November 1935; sold 11 January 1936. Sold Christie's Geneva, 16 May 1995, lot 3.

MARKS Base engraved *Cartier Paris*, BTE SGDG; Paris eagle's head assay mark for gold.

H. 7 cm, W. 2 cm

Cartier collection, LR 50 A35

A similar lighter appears in the Paris order book for 24 December 1935, described as '1 briquet tube rect. automatique or décor gros godrons' (1 automatic lighter with rectangular tube, wide gadroon decoration). Cartier took out a number of patents for the improvement of lighters, including one in 1932 for a 'slim-line lighter with hinged lid' (briquet à encombrement réduit avec couvercle à charnière) which may have been similar to this one. The action of pushing back the hinged lid automatically opened the wick and turned the wheel.

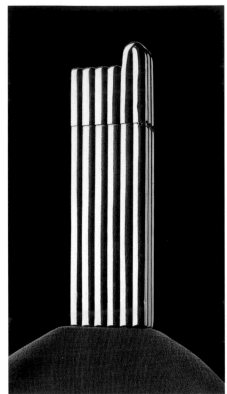

67

68 Cigarette case

Made for Cartier London, 1938

Coloured gold, formed of a ridged sheet of alternate yellow, green and white gold strips, with invisible hinge and baguette-cut sapphire push-piece.

MARKS Engraved *Cartier London* on inside rim; London hallmarks and date-letter for 1938, maker's mark JC for Jacques Cartier.

L. 11.2 cm, W. 8 cm

Cartier collection, CC 14 A38

EXHIBITIONS Paris 1989, cat. 480.

As for cat. 56, the coloured gold marquetry sheet would have been prefabricated and the box cut from it.

68

69 Mystery clock

Made by Couet for Cartier Paris for stock, 1922

Enamelled gold, rock crystal, onyx, diamonds set in platinum. Rock-crystal dial bordered with blue enamel, diamond-set hands and numerals, on onyx stem with Persian-syle lappet motif in black enamel round the top; base of stem in black enamel with blue enamel line at bottom, the plinth of onyx. Reverse of dial bordered with black enamel lappet motif.

Entered in stock book on 30 June 1922; transferred to the European Watch and Clock Co. for sale on 6 June 1923; sold by Cartier New York.

MARKS Base engraved *CARTIER N.Y.* and *European Watch and Clock Co. Inc. France*; Paris eagle's head assay mark for gold on dial and plinth.

H. 19.7 cm. Base: 8.9 × 4.6 cm

Cartier collection, CM 02 A22

LITERATURE For a similar clock, with gold numerals, see Nadelhoffer 1984, col. pl. 60; Barracca *et al.* 1989, p. 100, and Naples 1988, cat. 109.

Couet supplied table clocks to Cartier from 1911, inventing a number of illusory mechanisms prior to developing the true mystery clock in 1912–13. The movement operated on a lateral double-axle system housed in a vertical frame. According to Nadelhoffer, production of this first mystery clock model began in 1913, but an example of 1912 has recently been noted by Eric Nussbaum. In 1919 Couet set up a Cartier workshop, making cigarette and vanity cases as well as clocks (see cat. 130).

This example was the second mystery clock model, created by Couet in 1920. The second model used a single central axle which ran through a tall shaft, as in this example, or through a hollow ball at the base. Although the dial appears to be one piece of rock crystal, it is in fact two pieces with two glass discs sandwiched between, one for the hours and one for the minutes. Either each disc had a toothed edge cut into the glass itself, or they were fitted with a brass ring with teeth round the edge which was concealed by the frame. The teeth engaged with two separate mechanisms going up the central shaft from the drive housed in the base, so that each disc revolved at the correct rate.

Like the carved hardstone animals and flowers, the smaller mystery clocks were tremendously popular as presents. The disastrous fate that befell one such clock was

69

described by Loelia, Duchess of Westminster, in 1935, in her recollections of quarrels with the Duke of Westminster, whom she had married in 1930:

Raging scenes went on and on through long hours of the night. Objects flew through the air . . . A friend had given me a Cartier clock made of crystal with diamond hands as a wedding present; an exquisite little thing which seemed to work by magic. One night, during a nightmarish argument, it

was hurled against the wall and shattered into a thousand pieces. I let the debris lie among the plaster which had been dislodged from the wall, feeling too weak and aghast to trouble about 'keeping it from the servants'. Half an hour later Benny burst in again, waste-paper basket in hand, to scrape up the fragments saying he was going to take jolly good care that I didn't save so much as a diamond hand. (Westminster 1961, p. 232)

70 Cube desk clock with folding dial

Made in Paris (workshop unidentified) for Cartier New York or London, c. 1928

Enamelled gold, diamonds set in platinum. Enamelled in black with geometric borders. On front, two black enamel motifs flanking a diamond-set motif, the top and base of onyx. The diamond motif is in fact a clasp for a pair of doors that spring open to reveal a square dial, enamelled in blue and white and continued on the inside of each door; a second pair of doors at the back gives access to the movement.

This example is not recorded in the Paris archive, but an identical clock is illustrated in the Paris photograph albums, datable by the negative number to 1928.

MARKS On dial CARTIER BREVETÉ; inside back doors CADRAN BREVETÉ MADE IN FRANCE, with Paris eagle's head assay mark for gold and workshop mark VR & Cie, flanking the Roman numeral XII.

H. 6 cm. Base: 3.4 × 2.8 cm

Cartier collection, CD 36 A28

EXHIBITIONS Venice 1986, cat. 187; London 1988, cat. 260; Naples 1988, cat. 126; Paris 1989, cat. 412; Rome 1990, cat. 190; St Petersburg 1992, cat. 192.

LITERATURE Barracca et al. 1989, p. 177.

These small desk clocks were described in the London archive records as 'gold and enamel triptique clocks'. An example was sold by Cartier London to Mrs E. F. Hutton (Marjorie Merriweather Post) on 30 August 1928.

A Cartier New York catalogue of 1929 advertised a similar clock with a dial on the front of the doors as well as inside them. When closed, the doors were cut out to reveal the hands, so that the time could be read whether the doors were shut or open (70.1). The idea of having a small set of numbers on the outside of the case together with a larger set inside, to make it easier to read the time, was patented by J. Vergely of Paris on 28 August 1925.

71 Cube desk clock with folding dial

Made in Paris (workshop unknown) for Cartier London, 1928

Enamelled gold, sapphires. Same form as cat. 70 with double doors on each side, front doors opening to reveal dial; enamelled both back and front with a Chinese-style geometric motif in blue within two black semicircles, with sapphire clasps at front; the sides enamelled with interrupted lines in blue, echoing those on the front, so that when the doors are open a completely different

70, 71

70, 71

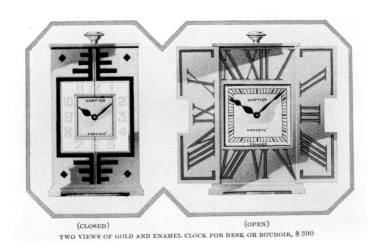

(CLOSED)　　　　　(OPEN)
TWO VIEWS OF GOLD AND ENAMEL CLOCK FOR DESK OR BOUDOIR, $390

70.1 Page from a Cartier New York catalogue, *Book of Gifts* of 1929, showing a desk clock with folding dial.

motif is created. Top and plinth of onyx. Dial with black numerals.

Entered in London stock book on 6 February 1928; sold 14 July 1931.

MARKS On dial CARTIER BREVET; inside back doors CADRAN BREVETÉ MADE IN FRANCE; Paris eagle's head assay mark for gold and workshop mark CM (?).

H. 5.8 cm. Base 3.5 × 2.8 cm

Cartier collection, CD 84 A28

EXHIBITIONS London 1988, cat. 261; Naples 1988, cat. 127; Paris 1989, cat. 413; Rome 1990, cat. 191; St Petersburg 1992, cat. 193; Tokyo 1995, cat. 232.

LITERATURE Barracca et al. 1989, p. 177.

The London stock sheet describes this clock as follows: 'Pendule, cubique, or poli, décor lignes Chinois et Grecques émail noir et bleu. Fermoir à saphir, socle et dessus onyx, cadran déployant' (clock, polished gold, Chinese and Greek decoration in lines of black and blue enamel. Clasp with sapphire, base and top onyx, folding dial). The semicircular geometric motif is inspired by motifs found on Chinese furniture.

For another triptych clock of this type, see Nadelhoffer 1984, col. pl. 70.

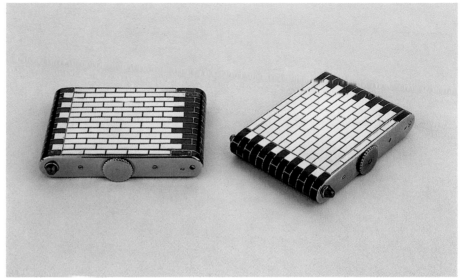

73, 72

73, 72

72 'Kodak' travel clock

Made by Jaeger for Cartier Paris for stock, 1929

Enamelled gold, sapphires. Enamelled all over in black with brick pattern, in black lines on gold on front and back, reversed at the sides as gold lines on black; two sapphire cabochon push-pieces release the lid, which revolves to form a stand when in use. Dial with arabic numerals. Engraved inside the lid: 'To Vernon Herbert from Mary & Douglas'.

Entered in stock book on 19 October 1929; sold 31 October 1929 to Douglas Fairbanks.

MARKS On dial CARTIER FRANCE; inside lid, Paris eagle's head assay mark for gold.

L. 4.3 cm, W. 3.1 cm

Cartier collection, CT 08 A29

EXHIBITIONS Los Angeles 1982, cat. 117; London 1988, cat. 269; Hong Kong 1995, cat. 41.

LITERATURE Barracca et al. 1989, p. 149.

Douglas Fairbanks Jr (1883–1939) and Mary Pickford (1893–1979) were both Hollywood film stars of the 1920s and 1930s. They married in 1920 and divorced in 1936.

The name 'Kodak' refers to the 'shutter' mechanism by which the lid springs open when the push-pieces are activated. Cartier

took out a patent in England in July 1926 for a clock with its lid adapted to support the device in a display position.

73 'Kodak' travel clock

Made by Jaeger for Cartier Paris for stock, 1929

Enamelled gold, sapphires. Enamelled all over in deep blue with brick pattern, in blue lines on gold on front and back, reversed at the sides as gold lines on blue; two sapphire cabochon push-pieces release the lid, which revolves to form a stand when in use. Dial with Roman numerals.

Entered in stock book on 14 December 1929; sold 22 September 1930.

MARKS On dial CARTIER FRANCE; inside lid Paris eagle's head assay mark for gold and workshop mark EJ flanking an hour-glass.

L. 4.4 cm, W. 3.1 cm

Cartier collection, CT 04 A29

EXHIBITIONS London 1988, cat. 268; St Petersburg 1992, cat. 212; Lausanne 1996, cat. 97.

LITERATURE Barracca et al. 1989, p. 149.

74 'Eclipse' watch

Made by Jaeger and Haas for Cartier Paris for stock, 1929

Enamelled gold. Blue zigzag pattern round the face and in centre of back, horizontal lines above and below. Two blue enamel push-pieces at top and bottom to release the sliding shutters, which cover the dial above the glass and automatically slide shut unless the push-pieces are held in.

This watch does not appear to be recorded in the Paris archive, but an identical watch was entered in the stock book on 18 July 1929 and sold on 2 September 1929 to the Pasha of Marrakesh.

MARKS On dial *CARTIER FRANCE*; Paris eagle's head assay mark for gold on side.

L. 4.1 cm, W. 2.8 cm

Cartier collection, CT 01 A29

EXHIBITIONS Paris 1989, cat. 434; Rome 1990, cat. 207; Hong Kong 1995, cat. 40; Tokyo 1995, cat. 251.

LITERATURE Barracca *et al.* 1989, p. 148.

Cartier introduced their eclipse watches, designed to go in a pocket or handbag, in 1929. For a group of contemporary archive photographs of further eclipse watches, see Barracca *et al.* 1989, p. 150.

75 'Eclipse' watch

Made by Jaeger and Frontin for Cartier Paris for stock, 1929

Enamelled gold, sapphires. Enamelled in black with dogtooth pattern at top and bottom, with sapphire cabochon push-pieces at each end. Sliding shutters as cat. 74, but below the glass, remain shut unless push-pieces are held in.

Entered in stock book on 7 February 1929; bought back into stock on 16 September 1929 and sold again on 5 November 1929.

MARKS On dial *CARTIER*; Paris eagle's head assay mark for gold on side.

L. 4.1 cm, W. 2.8 cm

Cartier collection, CT 05 A29

EXHIBITIONS Paris 1989, cat. 435; Rome 1990, cat. 208; Tokyo 1995, cat. 252.

LITERATURE Barracca *et al.* 1989, p. 148.

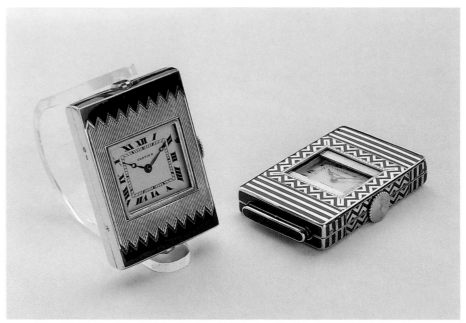

75, 74

75, 74

THE
EGYPTIAN
STYLE

This section contains two distinct groups. One comprises gem-set objects whose design is based on Egyptian motifs such as the lotus or the pylon. This category began to be produced around 1910, a decade before the discovery of the tomb of Tutankhamun in 1922, and continued into the 1930s (cat. 76–80). The other group consists of highly original objects incorporating actual Egyptian antiquities such as blue-glazed faience scarabs or other amulets (cat. 81–7). This second category does not appear to have been produced before 1922; there then came a flood of pieces in the mid- to late 1920s. Designs for objects from both groups are included in section 9 (cat. 247–54).

The first group reflects both the continued taste for Egyptian-style jewellery in France following the opening of the Suez Canal in 1869 and the revival of interest in the Egyptian discoveries of the late eighteenth and early nineteenth century, stimulated by the Franco-Egyptian Exhibition of 1911 at the Louvre. The examples that follow represent some of the pre-Tutankhamun Egyptian-style pieces made by Cartier, dating from 1913 (cat. 76–7), as well as one of the last, a typical Cartier London halo head ornament with lotus flowers of 1934 (cat. 80).

Gem-set Egyptian-style pieces were also produced by other Parisian jewellers, but generally the shapes used were conventional and the designs often figurative, which made them very different from those of Cartier. For example, Van Cleef & Arpels set tiny Egyptian figures in coloured stones into a diamond ground.[1] They are not in any way historically accurate. What distinguishes Cartier jewels is their close reliance on the major source books for Egyptian art, many of which Louis Cartier must have owned. The most important and lavish of these was the *Description de l'Egypte*, which published in a series of volumes the results of Napoleon's expeditions of 1798. The design for the Egyptian temple gate clock (cat. 88), Cartier's outstanding Egyptian-style piece, was almost certainly inspired by an engraving of the gate of the temple of Khons at Karnak from the *Description de l'Egypte*. Another major source book was Owen Jones's *Grammar of Ornament* of 1856. This inspired two pages of sketches in the Cartier Paris archive: one of them is included here as cat. 247.[2] Even after the discovery of Tutankhamun's tomb, the *Grammar of Ornament* remained a book to which the Cartier designers returned time and again. For

THE "TUTANKHAMEN" INFLUENCE IN MODERN JEWELLERY.

REPRODUCED BY COURTESY OF CARTIER, LTD., 175, NEW BOND STREET, W.I.

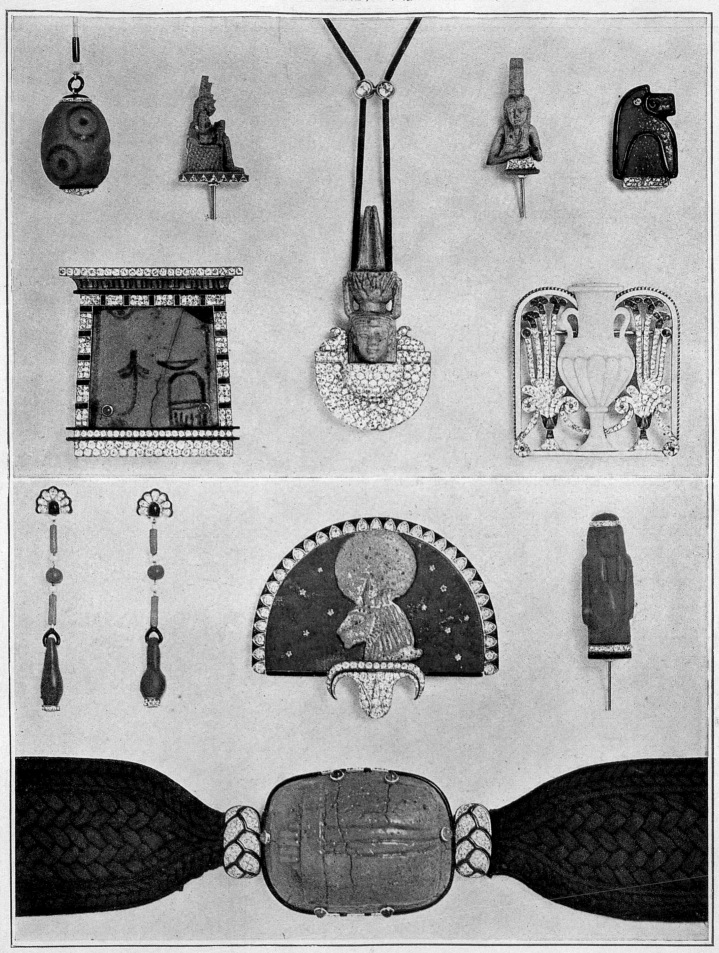

EGYPTIAN TRINKETS FROM 1500 TO 3000 YEARS OLD ADAPTED AS MODERN JEWELLERY: BROOCHES, PENDANTS, EARRINGS, AND HAT=PINS SET WITH REAL ANTIQUES, AND A TUTANKHAMEN REPLICA.

FIG. 65. Advertisement for Cartier Egyptian-style jewellery made by Cartier London, from the *Illustrated London News*, 26 January 1924.

example, the sarcophagus vanity case of 1925 (cat. 87) is decorated with a frieze of alternate lotus blossoms and grape bunches interspersed with stylised daisies, which combines two similar friezes in the *Grammar of Ornament*, one with lotus flowers and grapes, the other with papyrus flowers and daisies,[3]

Charles Jacqueau made several sketches of Egyptian objects from a number of other sources. These survive among his working designs, together with sketches for Egyptian-style jewels. One of his sketches is annotated 'pl. 145, Art égyptien de Capart'. This was the first volume of J. Capart's *Art Égyptien*, published in 1911; plate 145 showed a painting from the tomb of Prince Djihutihotep, depicting his daughters, one of whom wears a crown of lotus blossoms which must have inspired a Cartier bandeau of lotus blossoms in onyx and diamonds of 1923.[4] The designs for the lotus bandeau and many other Cartier Egyptian-style pieces were included in the exhibition 'Egyptomania' at the Louvre in 1994.[5]

The objects incorporating Egyptian antiquities have an entirely different fascination. Not only is there the challenge of creating a contemporary jewel round an ancient piece, but also the ancient pieces themselves can sometimes be of significant interest, like the carved Indian emeralds used by Cartier for their Indian-style jewellery (see section 5). And, like the emerald pieces, many of the Egyptian style-pieces were made for stock. This is true of all those catalogued here except for the brooch with a lotus flower deity (cat. 84), made as a special order by Cartier New York using a faience fragment belonging to the client. According to Nadelhoffer, Louis Cartier collected Egyptian antiquities from various dealers in Paris. One of them, Kalebdjian, sold him a whole series of pieces in 1914.[6] This collection must have served as a rich source of raw material for Cartier designs. Glazed faience fragments were perhaps obviously attractive items to set as jewellery. Much less obvious was the Egyptian carved calcite amulet, split into two halves to form the front and back of a vanity case (cat. 86); this is an exceptional piece and the idea was never repeated.

An advertisement in the *Illustrated London News* for 26 January 1924 gives an indication of the range of pieces with ancient fragments produced by Cartier London just a year and a half after the opening of Tutankhamun's tomb in November 1922 (fig. 65). The page is headed 'The "Tutankhamen" influence in modern jewellery' and captioned below 'Egyptian trinkets from 1500 to 3000 years old adapted as modern jewellery: brooches, pendants, earrings, and hat-pins set with real antiques, and a Tutankhamen replica'. The pieces are individually described. At the top were four small glazed faience objects: a bead, a figure of Isis and child and a head of Isis, both set as hat-pins, and the monkey-headed god Hapi. At the top centre was a faience head of Nefertem with a lotus on his head, misdescribed as Isis (see cat. 84). Other faience pieces were described as a 'miniature temple in glazed faience', a 'sacred ram' set as a semicircular brooch, a gem-set scarab forming the clasp for a twisted silk belt (see cat. 81–2), and earrings of lotus seeds and glazed faience tubes. On the right was 'a figure of Ta-urt [Taweret], in sardonyx'. The only object that was not an actual Egyptian antiquity was 'a miniature replica of the most beautiful alabaster vase found in Tutankhamen's tomb'.

Some of these descriptions need further explanation. The 'miniature temple' is in the form of a pylon, the rectangular truncated pyramidal building that flanked a temple gateway. Within the gem-set frame is a fragmentary faience plaque, mounted upside down. The hieroglyphs translate as 'wife of the king', but the name is missing. This same brooch was illustrated in American *Vogue* for 8 December 1928, worn by Lady Abdy on a dress with trimmed corsage, together with an emerald and diamond bracelet by Chaumet and a matching ring by Cartier.

The 'sacred ram' in fig. 65 is in fact a faience head of a lion with a sun-disc, set against a semicircle with a diamond ram's head below. It is one of two brooches made by Cartier

FIG. 66. Archive photograph of a brooch in the form of an Egyptian fan set with a glazed faience plaque bearing an inscription relating to Mentuemhat, mayor of Thebes. Made by Cartier London in 1923.

FIG. 67. Original design by Cartier London for a winged scarab belt buckle with multigem wings, 1925. From the London Design Scrapbook.

London in the form of the top of an Egyptian fan, or flabellum. The second piece, made for stock in November 1923 and sold in January 1925, contained an Egyptian semicircular inscribed faience plaque with border of papyrus in diamonds and a similar diamond-set ram's head below (fig. 66). Here the inscription bears the name of Mentuemhat, mayor of Thebes c. 600 BC.[7]

Among the more daring of the London designs was the setting of a faience scarab in 1925 as a convertible brooch or belt buckle like cat. 82, but in this instance the wings were of diamonds, onyx, emeralds, rubies, topaz and citrine. The setting of the stones was no doubt intended to recall Egyptian inlay work, though the colour scheme is Cartier's. The brooch survives, but without its silk belt.[8] Fig. 67 shows the original design.

Cartier's display at the French Exhibition in Cairo in 1929, organised by Jacques Cartier of London, included further pieces set with ancient faience (see p. 16, fig. 7), but Egyptian-style designs provided only a small part of the display. Most of the jewels shown were either typical diamond and gem-set pieces or earlier pieces that had not sold at previous exhibitions.

Cartier's ostentatious Egyptian-style designs were made during barely a decade, but the colour combinations derived from Egyptian antiquities permeated many other areas of their production. The combination of lapis and turquoise, inspired both by the Egyptian use of the stones themselves and by faience with combined pale and deep blue glazes, was perhaps the most striking and original (see cat. 137–8).

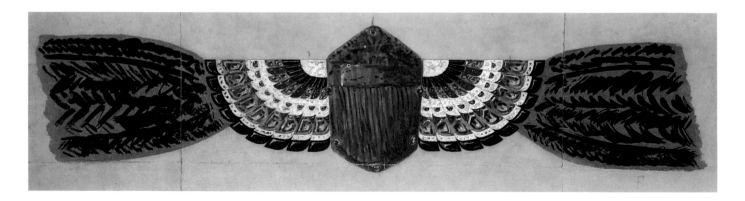

NOTES
1. See Gabardi 1986, p. 117, and Raulet 1986, pp. 167–9.
2. For the other, see Paris 1989, cat. 144.
3. Owen Jones, op. cit., pls VII and VIII.
4. Paris 1994, cat. 357, illustrating the design for the bandeau, the archive photograph of the finished object and the painting from Capart 1911, pl. 145. For a better colour illustration of the painting see Andrews 1996,

pl. 52. The princess also wears a necklace copied almost exactly in one of Jacqueau's sketches, see Paris 1989, cat. 168.
5. They are all illustrated in the excellent exhibition catalogue *Egyptomania*, Paris 1994, cat. 350–66, 368–71 and 373.
6. Nadelhoffer 1984, p. 152. Nadelhoffer gives no sources for any of his information about the dealers and the pieces they sold to Louis Cartier.

7. The inscription was published in 1961 with the information that the plaque on which it appeared was exhibited at the Victoria & Albert Museum (then the South Kensington Museum) in 1893, as in the Wallis collection, see J. Leclant, *Montouemhat*, Cairo 1961, p. 153, doc. 34. What happened to the plaque between 1893 and its acquisition by Cartier is unknown.
8. See Snowman (ed.) 1990, p. 200.

76 Pylon pendant

Made by Picq for Cartier Paris for stock, 1913

Diamonds and onyx in open-back platinum setting; black silk cord (replacement). A pylon-shaped frame with cavetto cornice containing a vase with central papyrus bud, formed of a pear-shaped diamond, and drooping papyri and Egyptian lilies. At base, pendent lotus motifs. Hinged loops at top.

Entered in stock book on 6 March 1913; sold 7 July 1913.

MARKS Engraved on rim *Cartier Paris*; French dog's head assay mark for platinum and workshop mark *HP* flanking an ace of spades on gallery.

H. of pendant (without loops) 7 cm

Cartier collection, NE 01 A13

EXHIBITIONS London 1988, cat. 212; Naples 1988, cat. 120; Paris 1989, cat. 170; Rome 1990, cat. 78; St Petersburg 1992, cat. 90; Paris 1994, cat. 353; Tokyo 1995, cat. 88; Lausanne 1996, cat. 179.

LITERATURE Nadelhoffer 1984, col. pl. 25.

RELATED MATERIAL Pencil sketch on buff tracing paper in the Sketchbooks, p. 258, in Paris archive.

A variant of this pendant made in Paris in 1920 was attached to a long pearl sautoir (Nadelhoffer 1984, p. 64, fig. 52). Another variant made for Cartier New York had a large stone forming the vase. The group of original plaster casts includes a further variant: the pylon is squatter in shape and contains a vase with four scrolling stems ending in blossoms (see 77.1, overleaf).

The pylon shape is inspired by Pharaonic pylon pectorals, both actual examples and examples depicted on mummies. The idea of the drooping papyrus stems may come from the bunches of drooping lotus on carved ivory toilet spoons of the New Kingdom, but the motif of the flower vase with drooping fronds is entirely twentieth-century.

76

77.1 Plaster casts taken from variants of cat. 76 and 77. The cast on the left is similar to cat. 76 but has a different motif in the centre; the cast on the right is taken from the 1913 version of cat. 77, which had a single pearl at the base.

77 Pylon and sphinx pendant

Designed in 1913 and made by Lavabre for Cartier Paris as a special order, 1921

Diamonds, onyx, rubies, emeralds, pearl and moonstone in open-back platinum setting. A pylon-shaped frame with cavetto cornice in onyx, containing stylised lotus flowers in rubies and emeralds on a pavé-set diamond ground, surmounted by a sphinx in carved moonstone and pavé-set diamonds, with ruby and emerald crest. Onyx loops and large pearl attach pendant to black cord with a row of collet-set diamonds and onyx cylinders. Six collet-set diamonds at base.

Completed in March 1921. Sold Phillips Geneva, 17 May 1994, lot 290.

MARKS On lower edge *Cartier Paris Londres New York*; on top edge French dog's head assay mark for platinum.

W. of pendant 4 cm, L. (without loops) 6.1 cm

Cartier collection, NE 21 A21

EXHIBITIONS Hong Kong 1995, p. 33; Tokyo 1995, cat. 94; Lausanne 1996, cat. 180.

LITERATURE Cologni and Nussbaum 1995, p. 132.

RELATED MATERIAL Original plaster cast for 1913 version in Paris archive (see 77.1).

Although this pendant was made in 1921, the design dates from 1913. In November of that year, a pendant of identical design was ordered from Cartier Paris by Lady Paget: the contemporary photograph suggests that the sphinx's face was of onyx instead of moonstone; there is a single pearl at the base instead of a line of diamonds, the chain also has pearls instead of diamonds, and instead of the large pearl a dark stone attaches the pendant to the chain. The plaster cast shown in 77.1 relates to the 1913 version with a single pearl at the base. The stone that attached the pendant to the chain is clearly visible on the cast and is a scarab, possibly an ancient one made of faience.

78

78 Egyptian *'flabellum'* cliquet pin

Made by Renault for Cartier Paris for stock, 1920

Onyx, coral, sapphires and diamonds in open-back platinum setting. Onyx plaque bordered with diamonds and encrusted with coral cabochons; central ziggurat motif of diamonds set with calibré-cut sapphires.

Entered in stock book on 22 March 1920; sold 7 June 1920 to Mrs Orme Wilson.

MARKS Rim and pin-catch engraved *Cartier*; Paris dog's head assay mark for platinum and workshop mark R with a crescent and flame (?) on gallery.

L. 10 cm

Cartier collection, CL 49 A20

EXHIBITIONS Los Angeles 1982, cat. 31; London 1988, cat. 168; Naples 1988, cat. 31; Paris 1989, cat. 180; Rome 1990, cat. 82.

The shape of the pin-head is derived from the Egyptian *flabellum*, a long-stemmed fan formed of ostrich feathers attached to a semi-circular base (see cat. 247).

This piece was purchased by an American client, Alice Wilson (née Borland), married in 1910. Orme Wilson (1885–1916) was in the American foreign service.

79 Vanity case with the goddess Maat

The vanity case made by Lavabre for Cartier Paris for stock in 1928–9; the figure of Maat made originally as a diamond brooch by Lavabre for stock in 1928 and added to the vanity case in 1930

Enamelled gold, round and baguette diamonds set in platinum. Enamelled black all over, with diamond borders. In the centre an applied seated figure of the goddess Maat holding an *ankh* emblem set with a pear-shaped diamond in her hand, her shoulder indicated by a shaped semicircular diamond, and triangular diamonds for the headdress. Diamond push-piece. Interior with mirrored lid and compartments for powder and rouge, the slot in front probably for a small comb.

Brooch of goddess Maat entered in Paris stock book on 23 October 1928. Vanity case without goddess Maat sold in 1929–30 and bought back into stock on 23 October 1930. Vanity case with goddess Maat sold 2 July 1931 to Princess Amrit of Kapurthala.

MARKS Lid engraved inside *Cartier Paris Londres New York MADE IN FRANCE*; Paris eagle's head assay mark for gold. Interior compartments with full set of London import marks, date-letter for 1929 and importer's mark J.C for Jacques Cartier.

L. 8.3 cm, W. 4.9 cm

Cartier collection, VC 28 A28/29

EXHIBITIONS New York 1976, cat. 70; London 1988, cat. 214; Naples 1988, cat. 121; Paris 1989, cat. 359; Paris 1994, cat. 363; Tokyo 1995, cat. 207; Lausanne 1996, cat. 181.

LITERATURE Nadelhoffer 1984, col. pl. 43; Cologni and Nussbaum 1995, p. 150.

RELATED MATERIAL Original design for brooch of goddess Maat in pencil and bodycolour on grey-green tracing paper in Stock Design Record Book, 1928, p. 28a, given to Lavabre on 1 August 1928 for delivery on 30 August 1928, in Paris archive, with initials R. R. for René Révillon.

The early history of this piece and the appearance of the London hallmarks need some explaining. It is one of a series of black vanity cases decorated with a simple diamond border and a central motif, which might be either in diamonds or coloured gems. It is clear from the photograph albums that many of the central motifs could be used interchangeably as brooches or box ornaments. In this instance the vanity case was originally made without a

79

79.1 Original design in pencil, watercolour and bodycolour on buff tracing paper for a coloured-stone brooch of the goddess Maat, Cartier Paris, 1927. This version is a more accurate representation of the goddess than the diamond motif on cat. 79. Cartier archive, Paris.

central motif, with a matching lipstick on a chain. At some point between June 1929 and April 1930 it must have gone to London in order to have acquired the London hallmarks for that year (London date-letters are changed in May). There is no record of its first sale date, but it was bought back from a client for stock by Cartier Paris in October 1930. In December 1930 the brooch of the goddess Maat, made in 1928 but still unsold, was added to it. It was still another six months before the vanity case was sold for the second time, to Princess Amrit of Kapurthala in July 1931.

The motif of the goddess Maat with the *ankh* or sign of life in her hand is based on Pharaonic models found on papyri or coffins; there are numerous examples in the Louvre. However, the representation here is significantly modified, or perhaps simply misunderstood. The face is correctly shown in profile, but the shoulders should be in full frontal position. Maat's ostrich-feather emblem does not appear on the headdress, and the distinction between the raised and the folded knee is blurred. A much more accurate version was made by Cartier as a gem-set brooch in 1927 (see Paris 1994, cat. 362), executed in diamonds, emeralds, coral, onyx and lapis lazuli (79.1).

80 'Halo' head ornament

Made by English Art Works for Cartier London for stock, 1934

Diamonds in open-back platinum setting. A vertical frieze of graduated lotus flowers and buds ending in upturned scrolling buds at the base, with a projecting band of geometric zigzag ornament in baguette and brilliant-cut diamonds which can be detached and worn as a bandeau.

Job given to Wallace of English Art Works on 12 October 1934, completed item entered in stock book on 26 November 1934. Sold to H. H. The Aga Khan III on 29 November 1934. Purchased for the Cartier collection at Christie's Geneva, *Magnificent Jewels from the collection of his late Royal Highness Sir Sultan Mohamed Shah Aga Khan III*, 12 May 1988, lot 705.

MARKS None.

W. at base 17 cm, H. 16 cm, max. W. of lotus frieze 3.4 cm, max. W. of removable bandeau 0.9 cm

Cartier collection, JV 19 A34

EXHIBITIONS Hong Kong 1995, cat. 50; Tokyo 1995, cat. 259; Lausanne 1996, cat. 270.

LITERATURE Cologni and Nussbaum 1995, p. 180.

RELATED MATERIAL Two pencil working drawings in English Art Works job record book for 12 October 1934 in London archive, showing front and side view.

'Halo' head ornaments, worn vertically at the front of the head like an alice band or halo, were especially popular with the London clientele. The archive records suggest that most of the diadems of this type were made for Cartier London between 1934 and 1936. They were often transformable into necklaces, with detachable centres that could be worn as brooches. This example, with projecting removable bandeau, is unusual. It was secured with elastic, which is clearly visible in the contemporary archive photograph and was

attached to two loops at each end of the halo.

H. H. Aga Khan III married Mlle Andrée Carron in 1929 and was a regular client of Cartier (see also cat. 46).

The halo was sold only three days after it entered stock. An annotation 'urgent' in the job record book suggests that although the piece was intended for stock, it may have been completed with this particular client in mind.

A similar Cartier halo ornament, with a frieze of scrolls, was purchased by Queen Elizabeth the Queen Mother, then Duchess of York, in 1936; it was set with 1,311 round and baton-cut diamonds. For a photograph of her wearing it, taken shortly before King Edward VIII's abdication, see Field 1992, p. 20.

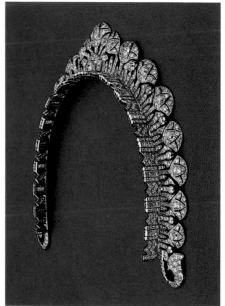

80.1 Side view of cat. 80 showing the forward-projecting band which can be detached and worn as a bandeau.

80.2 'The wife of Bahram's owner': photograph by Fayer of Vienna of H. H. the Begum Aga Khan wearing her lotus halo head ornament. *The Sketch*, 3 July 1935, p. 23. Bahram was the racehorse that had won the Derby that year. British Library.

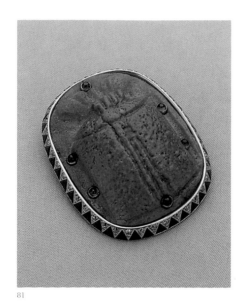

81

81 Scarab brooch

Made by English Art Works for Cartier London for stock, 1924

Egyptian blue-glazed faience scarab with emerald, sapphire, ruby and amethyst cabochons; zig-zag border of onyx and diamonds set in platinum. Gold backing engraved 'To Dorothy Xmas 1926 Luxor Henry'.

Entered in stock book on 12 February 1924.
Sold on 26 November 1924. Sold Christie's Geneva, 15 November 1990, lot 344.

MARKS Rim engraved *Cartier Ltd London*.

H. 4.8 cm, W. 4 cm

Cartier collection, CL 125 A24

EXHIBITIONS Lausanne 1996, cat. 218.

LITERATURE Cologni and Nussbaum 1995, p. 126.

The Egyptian faience scarab dates from the second half of the first millennium BC and is a typical funerary scarab of the kind attached to the wrapping over the chest of a mummy (see Andrews 1994 for full discussion and illustration of comparable examples). Generally, such scarabs were made entirely of faience. The Cartier archive photograph albums record a number of other pieces

incorporating ancient Egyptian scarabs; one brooch similar to this one could also be worn on a chain as a necklace.

The two names in the inscription, added two years after the piece was sold, cannot be identified from the archive records; the purchaser's name does not appear to correspond with either name.

82 Winged scarab brooch

Made by English Art Works for Cartier London for stock in 1924, to be worn as either brooch or buckle

The scarab cut in smoky quartz with emerald eyes, the wings in Egyptian blue-glazed faience and pavé-set diamonds, with black enamel outlines and cabochon emeralds. At top and bottom of scarab a frieze of geometric ornament in black enamel and diamonds. The diamonds set in platinum, other settings in gold. Fittings at back for wear as brooch or belt buckle.

Entered in stock book on 12 February 1924;
sold 16 May 1924 as brooch.

MARKS None.

L. 13.3 cm

Cartier collection, CL 32 A24

EXHIBITIONS Minneapolis 1971, cat. 1221 (not then identified as Cartier); Venice 1986, cat. 109; London 1988, cat. 213, pl. XXXI; Paris 1989, cat. 249; Rome 1990, cat. 118; St Petersburg 1992, cat. 137; Paris 1994, cat. 265; Tokyo 1995, cat. 139; Lausanne 1996, cat. 219.

LITERATURE Nadelhoffer 1984, col. pl. 14, p. 153; Barracca *et al.* 1989, p. 83; Cologni and Nussbaum 1995, pp. 126–7.

RELATED MATERIAL Original pencil, ink, watercolour and bodycolour design in London Design Scrapbook.

The Egyptian faience wing pieces are from a typical funerary scarab of the second half of the first millennium BC. Winged scarabs made entirely of faience were attached to the wrapping over the chest of a mummy. Cat. 82.2 shows a complete faience scarab in the British Museum. In this example the base is made in

one piece with holes at the edge for stitching onto the mummy, and the body of the scarab slots into the base (EA 58992; Andrews 1994, fig. 58).

A similar winged scarab brooch made for Cartier Paris in 1926 was sold to Mrs Cole Porter (see cat. 254). Both scarab and wings were in Egyptian faience. In one instance an Egyptian faience scarab was combined with multicoloured gem-set wings imitating Egyptian *cloisonné* jewels and probably inspired by the jewels painted on mummy cases. The brooch was made by Cartier London in 1925 and the wings were set with citrines, topazes, rubies, emeralds, onyx and diamonds (see Snowman (ed.) 1990, p. 200). The original design survives in the London Design Scrapbook (see fig. 67 on p. 138; also illustrated in Paris 1994, cat. 354).

All these winged scarab brooches could be converted to buckles and mounted on plaited black silk or enamelled gold chain belts. This brooch appears in the archive photograph albums both as a brooch and as a buckle, attached to a gold chain belt with black enamel links (82.3). The chain was entered in the stock book on 22 February 1924, but was not purchased with the brooch in May 1924 and was still unsold in April 1925.

Most of these scarab jewels were made for stock in the mid-1920s under the influence of Howard Carter's recent discoveries, but there were occasional later commissions for scarab jewellery, not always successful. One such example is a necklace ordered from Cartier Paris in 1932 and set with a glazed steatite scarab formerly owned by the French Egyptologist Gaston Maspero (1846–1916). The client supplied the diamonds and 856 pearls for the chain, as well as the scarab. The heavy diamond setting, combined with what was then a very old-fashioned pearl chain, has none of the elegance of the 1920s stock pieces (see Nadelhoffer 1984, col. pl. 14).

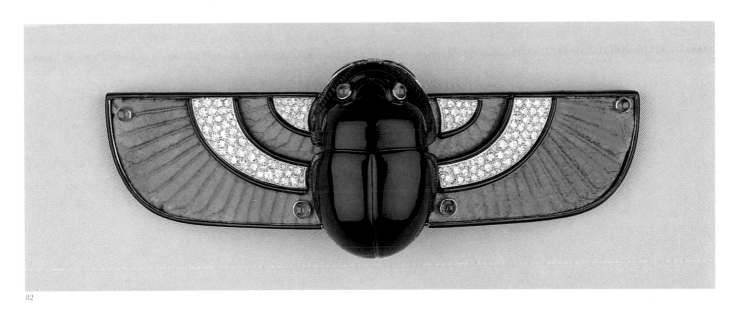

82

82.1 Detail of cat. 82, showing geometric ornament on mount of scarab.

82.2 Ancient Egyptian glazed faience winged scarab, w. 14.9 cm. British Museum, EA 58992.

82.3 Archive photograph showing cat. 82 as a belt-clasp on an enamelled gold belt, 1924. Cartier London.

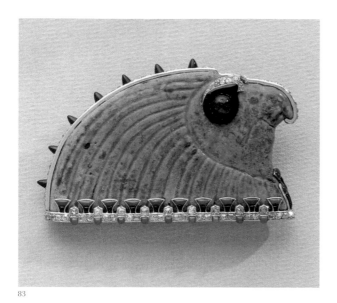

83

83 Horus head faience brooch

Made by Lavabre for Cartier Paris for stock, 1925

Egyptian blue-glazed faience with diamonds, coral and onyx set in platinum and gold. Onyx and emerald eye, onyx studs along top of head, and a row of stylised lotus flowers along the base.

Entered in stock book on 30 June 1925; sold 20 October 1925.

MARKS *Cartier Paris*, with French dog's head assay mark for platinum and Paris eagle's head assay mark for gold.

L. 7 cm

Private collection

LITERATURE Snowman (ed.) 1990, p. 201.

RELATED MATERIAL Original design in pencil, ink, watercolour and bodycolour on buff tracing paper in Stock Design Record Book, 1925, p. 13a, in Paris archive (see Nadelhoffer 1984, col. pl. 16, and Paris 1994, cat. 358).

The Egyptian faience head of Horus, the falcon-headed deity, dates from the second half of the first millennium BC. It was originally a terminal of a so-called 'falcon collar of gold', one of the prescribed pieces of jewellery to be taken into the other world. The falcon heads are generally longer, suggesting that part of this one was lost.

The falcon collar of gold comprised a multi-strand necklace with falcon-headed terminals and was frequently incorporated into the decoration of the coffin. Funerary examples were generally made of faience rather than gold, unless for royal burials. For an

83.1 Gold falcon-head terminals on a collar from the burial of the wives of Thutmose III, Thebes, 18th Dynasty; in lesser burials the falcon heads would be of glazed faience. A faience falcon-head terminal from a similar collar is used in cat. 83. Metropolitan Museum of Art, New York, 26.8.70/58.153.

example with faience heads in the Cairo Museum, see Paris 1994, cat. 358. For an example with gold falcon heads in the Metropolitan Museum of Art, see 83.1. See also Andrews 1996, pp. 120–21.

84 Lotus flower deity brooch

Made in Paris (workshop unknown) for
Cartier New York to the order of Mrs
William Scoville Moore, 1927

Egyptian blue-glazed faience head with enamel,
diamonds, emeralds, rubies and onyx set in platinum;
gold back and brooch fitting. The faience head emerges
from a lotus flower flanked by two buds, in enamel set
with diamonds, emeralds, rubies and a row of onyx at
the base of the head. Headdress of pavé-set diamonds
studded with onyx; at centre, a lotus with emerald at
base. Behind the head, a palmette in black enamel
studded with cabochon emeralds.

Dated to 1927 by archive photograph negative number.

MARKS Reverse engraved *Cartier Paris MADE IN FRANCE*;
Paris eagle's head assay mark for gold and French dog's
head assay mark for platinum.

H. 5 cm, W. 3.5 cm

Cartier collection, CL 161 A27

EXHIBITIONS Paris 1994, cat. 366; Lausanne 1996,
cat. 220.

LITERATURE Cologni and Nussbaum 1995, p. 133 (with
illustration of design).

RELATED MATERIAL Original design in pencil, watercolour
and bodycolour on brown tracing paper in New York
archive, showing front and side view.

The faience head is part of a figure of the
goddess Isis, dating probably from the late
period, 26th Dynasty, *c.* 600 BC or later. Cat. 84.1
illustrates a seated figure of Isis in the British
Museum (EA 63797) of the Late Dynastic or
Early Ptolemaic period, *c.* 400–300 BC. In this
example the goddess has a temple on her
head, but she is usually depicted with a temple
or a sun-disc. The fragmentary faience head
used in the Cartier brooch appears to be
incomplete beneath the setting at the top and
probably also once had such an emblem. The
headdress and palmette are inventions.

Although the Cartier faience head depicts
Isis, it has been set on a lotus flower and thus
transformed into Nefertem, the god on a lotus,
who symbolises the rising sun. The inspiration
for this design may have come from a fragmentary bronze statuette in the Louvre
depicting Nefertem on a lotus (see Paris 1994,
cat. 366, fig. 2). But it is also possible that the
idea was taken from glazed faience figures of

Nefertem, which show the god with a lotus on
his head. Such figures are relatively common.
Indeed, Cartier London incorporated the
upper half of such a figure in a pendant. It
appears in a full-page illustration of Cartier
Egyptian-style jewels in the *Illustrated London
News*, 26 January 1924, misdescribed as a
head of Isis (fig. 65 on p. 136). This confusion
on Cartier's part may explain why the New
York piece combines a head of Isis with a
lotus flower.

The Cartier faience head was purchased
from the Parisian antique dealer Kélékian,
who, together with another dealer, Kalebdjian,
supplied Louis Cartier with Egyptian antiquities, which were displayed in his apartment in
the Rue Saint-Guillaume.

84

84

84.1 Egyptian seated figure of Isis in
glazed faience, Late Dynastic or Early
Ptolemaic period, *c.* 400–300 BC.
H. 12 cm. British Museum, EA 63797.
A head of a similar figure is
incorporated into cat. 84.

85 Figure in shrine vanity case

Made by Lavabre for Cartier Paris for stock, 1924

Gold, mother-of-pearl, coral, lapis lazuli, onyx and diamonds, with Egyptian blue-glazed faience figure playing a double pipe set against a lapis lazuli background and surmounted by a coral, onyx and diamond lotus. The four sides set with mother-of-pearl plaques engraved with hieroglyphs, framed by coral papyrus columns and cornice, on an onyx base, with lapis lazuli panel on top. The back identical, with plain panel of lapis lazuli. Hung from an onyx finger-ring and leather thongs with lotus attachments. Interior slides out from base, with mirror in lid, two compartments and a lipstick.

Entered in stock book on 13 May 1924; sold 30 September 1924 to the perfumier Coty.

MARKS Engraved *CARTIER PARIS*; workshop mark *HL* flanking a four-leaf clover.

L. of box 9.5 cm, with ring and thongs 19 cm

Private collection

EXHIBITIONS New York 1976, cat. 43; Los Angeles 1982, cat. 7.

LITERATURE Nadelhoffer 1984, col. pl. 15 and p. 153.

RELATED MATERIAL Original design in pencil, ink, watercolour and bodycolour in the Stock Design Record Book, 1923, p. 94, in Paris archive (see Paris 1994, cat. 370).

The Egyptian faience figure, possibly Bes, dates from the Ptolemaic period, probably the last 300 years BC. Intended as an amulet, it has been treated here as a deity and placed in the centre of a shrine. The idea is taken from miniature bronze shrines with incised hieroglyphs and a central deity. For examples in the British Museum, see Andrews 1994, pl. 9a. The hieroglyphs depicted on the vanity case are readable, though inaccurate, and depict the name and titles of Thutmose III.

85

86 Vanity case

Made by Lavabre for Cartier Paris for stock, 1927

Enamelled gold, coral, lapis lazuli, emeralds and diamonds set in platinum, with an incised Egyptian calcite plaque on each side. On the front, Horus the Child, as Saviour, carrying a scorpion and a lion, with a vertical column of hieroglyphs down each side; on the back, a magical spell. The plaques surrounded by pieces of emerald; above and below, a band of lapis lazuli set with carved emerald flowers and edged with black and turquoise-blue enamel dogtooth ornament, within coral frames. The top and bottom edge with bands of diamonds and black enamel, the sides with lapis lazuli plaques, cabochon emeralds and black enamel push-piece. Interior with mirrored compartment.

Entered in stock book on 28 June 1927; sold 19 July 1929 to Ira Nelson Morris. Sold Christie's New York, 18–19 October 1993, lot 491.

MARKS Engraved *CARTIER PARIS*; Paris eagle's head assay mark for gold and workshop mark *HL* flanking a four-leaf clover.

H. 9.8 cm

Private collection

RELATED MATERIAL Original design in pencil and watercolour on buff tracing paper in Stock Design Record Book, 1927, p. 57b, in Paris archive (see Nadelhoffer 1984, col. pl. 16).

The two carved plaques originally formed back and front of an Egyptian *cippus* or amulet of the late period, *c.* 500 BC, with raised relief in front of a plaque, the reverse inscribed with a magical incantation invoking the protection of Horus. Such spells were usually designed to protect against poisonous bites. The *cippus* has simply been split vertically down the middle to provide the two plaques. The Cartier designer would have seen similar examples in the Louvre. Two examples in the British Museum are shown in 86.2, from the front (left) and from the back (right). In these examples the head of Bes is clearly visible above the figure of Horus. The two plaques used on the Cartier vanity case are fragmentary and only part of the head of Bes survives.

The colours of the gemstones and enamel were perhaps intended to evoke those used in ancient Egypt. Lapis lazuli and turquoise, for example, both sigified joy, while turquoise, as the colour of fresh vegetation, also signified regeneration. Emerald, however, was never used in ancient Egypt and coral only rarely.

Ira Nelson Morris (1875–1942), diplomat and author, was born in Chicago and married Constance Lily Rothschild in 1898 (see also cat. 29).

FAR RIGHT
86.1 Back of cat. 86, showing reverse of ancient Egyptian amulet (*cippus*) with inscribed magical incantation. Cartier archive, Paris.

86

86.2 Two ancient Egyptian amulets (*cippus* type) of the kind used in cat. 86, showing the head of Bes above the figure of Horus. British Museum, left, EA 36260 (H. 9.5 cm); right, EA 60960, showing inscription on back.

87 Sarcophagus vanity case

Made by Lavabre for Cartier Paris for stock, 1925

Enamelled gold, bone, emeralds, onyx and diamonds set in platinum. Curved bone lid carved with female figure and tulip, framed by emerald, onyx and pavé-set diamond columns with carved emerald palm-leaf capitals. The sides with champlevé enamel frieze of lotus flowers, daisies and gold bunches of grapes. At each end, a sphinx with carved emerald face and paws, onyx beard, sapphire headdress with diamond cobra and diamond body encrusted with onyx. On the base a gold plaque with gold wire cloisonné decoration of a female Egyptian alms bearer with ibis, carrying a basket and lotus flowers. The interior with mirrored lid and cigarette compartment.

Entered in stock book on 20 May 1925. Sold 11 June 1925 to Mrs George Blumenthal.

MARKS Engraved *Cartier Paris Londres New York*; workshop mark *HL* flanking a four-leaf clover.

L. 14.5 cm

Private collection

EXHIBITIONS Los Angeles 1982, cat. 22.

LITERATURE Nadelhoffer 1984, col. pl. 13 and p. 153; Snowman (ed.) 1990, p. 200; Cologni and Mocchetti 1992, pp. 74–5.

RELATED MATERIAL Original design in pencil, watercolour and bodycolour in Stock Design Record Book, 1923, p. 95, in Paris archive (see 87.1 and cat. 253).

The curved bone lid is now thought to be modern (Paris 1994, cat. 371), but at the time Louis Cartier thought that he had bought a piece of Egyptian ivory from a Paris antique dealer (see Snowman (ed.) 1990, p. 200). It was no doubt intended to recall the curved wooden lids raised on four posts of Egyptian coffins of the 26th Dynasty onwards (see C. Andrews, *Egyptian Mummies*, London 1984, fig. 56). The raising of Egyptian coffin lids on four posts may have inspired the design of a stand for this vanity case, ordered by Mrs Blu-

87

menthal in October 1926, some sixteen months after she had purchased it; the whole object was raised on four posts set with sapphires above a mirrored base so that the underside could be seen (87.4).

The sphinx at each end wears a royal headdress with lappets of alternate blue and yellow stripes, executed in sapphires set in gold. The frieze of lotus flowers, daisies and bunches of grapes along the sides may have been copied from the *Grammar of Ornament*, pls VII and VIII, published by Owen Jones in 1856. Similar friezes illustrated in this source book are described as taken from mummy cases in the British Museum and the Louvre.

The scene on the base combines a number of different sources of inspiration. Figures bearing baskets on their heads and lotus flowers over their arms, usually male, are commonly found on Old Kingdom scenes of offering bringers. But the offerings they carry are all edible. The ibis included here is not edible and does not occur in Egyptian representations of food bearers (although it looks more like a crane, the colouring is definitely

that of an ibis). The female figure is based on Late period Ptolemaic female offerers, while the ibis may be intended to evoke Thomas Moore's poem *Alciphron*, which inspired Edwin Long's painting of Alethe, priestess of Isis, depicted with a basket on her head and an ibis at her side (1888; see Paris 1994, cat. 336). Moore's poem of 1827 was published in French the same year; a second edition published in 1865 was translated by Théophile Gautier and illustrated by Gustave Doré. The design for this vanity case (87.1) shows that the underside was originally intended to be enamelled, presumably in cloisonné enamel, but the enamelling was never done and the gold cloisons remain unfilled (87.2).

Only one other similar vanity case appears to have been made. It was sold by Cartier Paris in January 1923. The lid contained a carved ivory plaque within an enamelled gold frame depicting two ivory-wreathed columns either side and birds at the top.

For Mrs George Blumenthal, see cat. 90.

87.1 Design for cat. 87, showing, from left to right, the lid, the side, the base and, below, one end with sphinx (see cat. 253).

87.2 Base of cat. 87.

87.3 Detail of one end of cat. 87, showing sphinx.

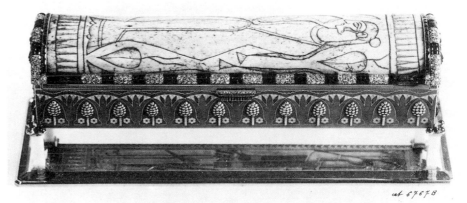

87.4 Archive photograph of the raised mirrored stand made for cat. 87 in order to show the underside.

88 Egyptian temple gate clock

Made by Couet for Cartier Paris for stock, 1927

Mother-of-pearl, lapis lazuli, coral, enamelled gold. In the form of an Egyptian temple gate, covered on all four sides with mother-of-pearl plaques engraved on the front with various scenes and mock hieroglyphs, and round the base with papyrus umbels and buds with stylised Egyptian lilies in the middle. The gateway itself occupied by the clock, framed in coral papyrus stems, the dial of mother-of-pearl plaques, the hands in the form of a lotus flower and bud, radial Roman numerals in gold. At the base an enamelled gold scene of offering bearers. The lintel with white enamel stripes and a winged goddess in enamelled gold. Top and base of lapis lazuli, with carved coral bamboo handles set in lapis lazuli lugs.

Entered in stock book on 30 October 1927; transferred to the European Watch and Clock Co. in September 1929 and sold by Cartier New York on 30 September 1929. Sold Christie's New York, 24 April 1991, lot 303.

MARKS The case with Paris assay mark for gold and workshop mark *MC*. Movement engraved *European Watch and Clock Co. No. 95504.*

H. 23.8 cm, W. 15.8 cm, D. 12.7 cm

Private collection

LITERATURE Nadelhoffer 1984, p. 155 and fig. 135, p. 249.

This is unquestionably Cartier's most spectacular piece of 'Egyptomania'. The design is based on a temple gate of the Ptolemaic or Graeco-Roman period. (The temple gate was the gateway through the enclosure wall and not part of the temple itself.)

This clock has previously been described erroneously as based on the temple of Khons at Karnak (Nadelhoffer 1984, p. 155 and Christie's sale catalogue), which dates from the New Kingdom. However, the temple gate of Khons, as distinct from the temple itself, is indeed Ptolemaic (*c.* 246–222 BC) and its shape is closely comparable with that of the Cartier clock (see J.-C. Golvin and J.-C. Goya, *Les Bâtisseurs de Karnak*, Paris 1987, p. 61, and K. Michalowski, *Karnak*, London 1970, pp. 63 and 81). A detailed engraving of the Khons temple gate was published in the *Description de L'Egypte*, A, III, pl. 51, and this may have provided the source of inspiration for Cartier (88.1).

The incised scenes on this clock are clearly from a different source, as yet unidentified. Some of the scenes have been split into two: for example, in the first side panels below the long panel across the top of the clock, standing kings are shown offering, but to no one, while, in the next panel down, the god Amun is shown seated but with no one offering to him. It may be that the scenes combine a number of different sources. None of the hieroglyphs is readable, while the papyrus frieze at the base, representing the marshes in which all creation began, should not include the Egyptian lily.

The goddess stretching her wings at the top is either Maat (usually shown with the *ankh* or sign of life in her hand) or Nut, the sky goddess, but in Egypt neither would ever be found

88.1 Engraving of the Khons temple gate from the *Description de l'Egypte*, Paris 1808 ff.

in such a place: all such gates have a protective winged sun disc. The winged goddess form has been taken from a funerary context such as a mummy case or coffin.

For a contemporary photograph of this clock in Couet's workshop, see p. 42, fig. 30.

The Cartier archive in Paris includes a design for another smaller temple gate clock, but it was never executed (see Paris 1994, cat. 368).

THE PERSIAN AND INDIAN STYLES

Cartier were producing jewels and *objets d'art* in both the Persian and the Indian styles by 1913, and these two styles were to dominate many of their designs until the end of the 1930s. The terms used in Cartier's own records are always 'décoration perse' or 'arabe'. The styles are never described as Islamic, although Persia (present-day Iran), Mughal India and much of the Arab world all come under Islam. Similarly, Cartier did not appear to make a distinction between Mughal and Hindu India. The terms 'style indien' or 'hindou' seem to have been used interchangeably to lend an aura of exoticism.

The main source of inspiration for Cartier's Persian-style jewels was the collection of Persian miniatures owned by Louis Cartier. Equally influential were the Ballets Russes of Diaghilev, and in particular the ballet *Sheherazade* with music by Rimsky-Korsakov, first performed in Paris in 1910. Its colourful costumes and set designs by Léon Bakst evoked a sultan's harem. Nadelhoffer records Jacqueau's obsession with the Ballets Russes, which he followed with bated breath and sketchbook in hand. The couturier Paul Poiret created costumes with billowing Turkish trousers and turban ornaments topped with feather aigrettes. Many of Cartier's bandeaux with aigrettes must have been designed with such costumes in mind, to be worn on appropriate occasions such as the series of *bals persans*, or Persian balls, held in Paris around 1912–13 by a number of society hostesses.[1] For a Cartier aigrette in the Chinese style, see p. 189, fig. 76. Others were attached to a thin headband.

The role played by the Indian style in Cartier's work was greater and more wide-ranging than the Persian, and can be seen to have four different aspects. Firstly, there were the commissions received from Indian clients and the influence of those commissions on the design of other Cartier pieces; secondly, Cartier's use of stones imported from India, in particular carved Mughal emeralds; thirdly, Cartier's imports of Indian jewellery, antique and modern, which was resold unaltered; and lastly, Cartier's creation of a fashion for Indian-style jewellery among non-Indian clients.

Many of these aspects are illustrated by the objects catalogued in this section. However, because the styles were so embedded in the Cartier design repertoire, objects with Persian or Indian elements in their design will also be found in other sections of this catalogue. For example, there are two diamond pieces based on Persian motifs in section 8, a bandeau (cat. 205) and a bracelet (cat. 208), while section 7 contains the dragon-head bracelet based on Indian Jaipur enamel examples (cat. 144), together with several pieces incorporating carved Indian emeralds (cat. 149, 150, 163, 165–7 and 168), and section 9 includes designs for pieces with carved emeralds which no longer survive (cat. 270, 275 and 287). In using engraved Indian emeralds and other carved gemstones for their contemporary designs, not just for jewels in the Indian taste, Cartier made one of their most original contributions to twentieth-century jewellery design.

The starting point for any discussion of Cartier jewels in the Persian and Indian styles must be the exhibition held at Cartier New York's Fifth Avenue premises in 1913. This exhibition lasted only five days, 11–15 November 1913, and was accompanied by a colour-printed catalogue entitled *Catalogue of a Collection of Jewels… Created by Messieurs Cartier… from the Hindoo, Persian, Arab, Russian and Chinese*. The front cover design was taken directly from a Persian bookbinding, while the title-page was decorated with motifs from Persian and Indian miniatures (fig. 68).

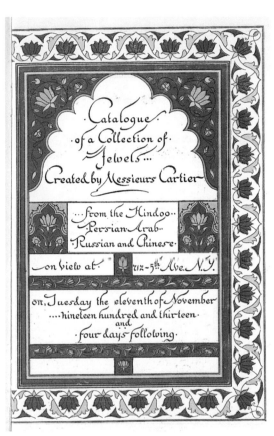

FIG. 68. Title page from the catalogue of an exhibition held at Cartier New York in 1913.

The exhibition comprised fifty pieces in all, of which twenty were described as 'From Indian Art'. They included carved white jade brooches and Mughal jades inlaid with precious stones and set as pendants. One of the necklaces was made of large pearls, ruby beads and emeralds, with 'a large engraved emerald of unusual shape'. The most expensive piece was 'A collection of eighteen large brilliants of the best quality, mounted as a bracelet such as worn by the Maharanee of Gwalior'. It cost $30,500.

These twenty Indian style pieces were followed by ten described as 'From Persian Art'. Again, jewels incorporating antique elements, such as a pair of pearl bracelets with 'an old Persian enamel clasp', were shown side by side with original Cartier designs. These included a pearl and diamond hair band with seven-branch aigrette, and a series of brooches or pendants in the shape of coloured-stone vases with foliage and fruits.

It would no doubt be possible to match up many of the descriptions in the 1913 catalogue with the contemporary archive photographs to provide a complete picture of the exhibition. But the descriptions alone demonstrate the different areas of Islamic and Indian art to which Cartier looked for inspiration. It is also apparent that at this early date Cartier was already selling genuine oriental pieces in Cartier settings and resetting stones imported from India, two aspects that are discussed more fully below.

That Cartier should hold such an exhibition in 1913 is significant. It followed the 'Exposition des Arts Musulmans' held at the Musée des Arts Décoratifs in Paris in 1912. Two earlier exhibitions with the same title had been held at the Musée des Arts Décoratifs, in 1903 and 1907. But the 1912 exhibition had 227 paintings, manuscripts and bookbindings. Such a quantity had never been seen together before, and the accompanying two-volume illustrated catalogue, written by two distinguished collectors, Georges Marteau and the jeweller Henri Vever, did much to heighten awareness of Islamic art as well as intensify competition amongst collectors.[2]

It is perhaps no coincidence that two of the leading Paris jewellers of the day were collectors of Persian miniatures. Henri Vever was one, the other was Louis Cartier. The jewel-like quality of the paintings must have had the same appeal to both of them. The date when Louis Cartier began his collection of Persian miniatures is not recorded, but he was certainly collecting by 1912–13. At least two of his paintings were included in the 1912 exhibition, and many are now in the Fogg Art Museum in Harvard, having been acquired by John Goelet, who gave them to the Fogg in 1958. They include two pages from the sixteenth-century Quintet of Nizami, one of the most sumptuous Safavid court manuscripts ever to have been created.[3]

How was this collection of Persian miniatures used as inspiration for the design of jewellery? Firstly, the designs on the bookbindings, usually in tooled and gilded leather, were copied in different materials on cigarette or vanity cases, for example cat. 89. Many appear among Jacqueau's working designs. The scroll patterns inhabited by animals and the foliate arabesques that appear in Islamic miniatures inspired the patterns executed by Cartier in enamelled gold (see cat. 91–2). Perhaps less obvious is the way in which border patterns or motifs from architectural elements were copied in diamonds as flat strap bracelets or bandeaux, as on cat. 208, a broad strap bracelet with alternating lotus flowers, a pattern common throughout the Islamic world.

Cartier's initial contacts with Indian princes visiting London or Paris were made in the early 1900s. The firm's first commission for an Indian-style piece came not from an Indian client, but from Queen Alexandra in 1901. Cartier was asked to reset Indian jewellery in the Royal Collection for the Queen to wear with three Indian gowns sent her by Mary Curzon, wife of the Viceroy of India. Cartier Paris (the London branch was not opened until 1902) created a necklace of pearls, emeralds, rubies and two square emeralds described as 'talismans', suggesting that they were carved.

In 1909 all aspects of the Indian business, including contacts with Indian clients as well as the purchase of stones, were handed over to Jacques Cartier and the London house. Jacques Cartier's first visit to India was made in 1911, the year of the Delhi Durbar for the coronation of George V. On this first visit, he dealt with the Maharajahs of Kapurthala and Nawanagar, the Nizam of Hyderabad, the Aga Khan, the Nawab of Rampur and the Gaekwar of Baroda. Nadelhoffer notes that the Indian rulers were exclusively interested in fashionable Parisian jewellery and accessories such as pocket watches for men, and had no hesitation in handing over their family treasures to be remounted.

But there is another significant factor at play. The Indian tradition has no concept

FIG. 69. Turban ornament of emeralds, pearls and diamonds made for the Maharajah of Kapurthala in 1926, incorporating the Maharajah's emeralds. Contemporary advertisement in the *Spur*. Cartier London.

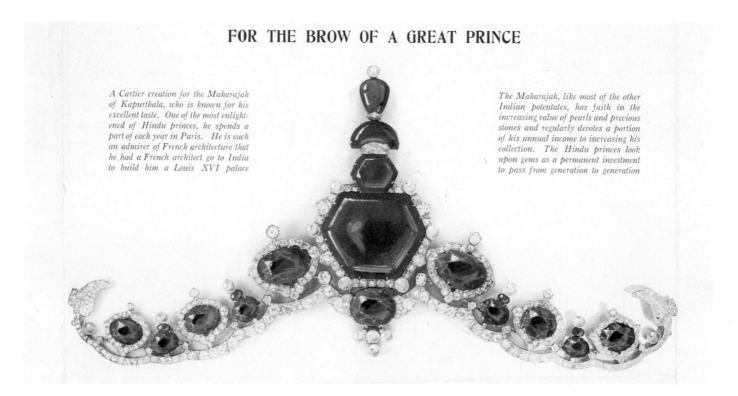

FOR THE BROW OF A GREAT PRINCE

A Cartier creation for the Maharajah of Kapurthala, who is known for his excellent taste. One of the most enlightened of Hindu princes, he spends a part of each year in Paris. He is such an admirer of French architecture that he had a French architect go to India to build him a Louis XVI palace

The Maharajah, like most of the other Indian potentates, has faith in the increasing value of pearls and precious stones and regularly devotes a portion of his annual income to increasing his collection. The Hindu princes look upon gems as a permanent investment to pass from generation to generation

of ancestral jewellery handed down from generation to generation, as in Europe. In India second-hand jewellery cannot be offered as gifts to a new bride; it has to be newly set, even if using ancestral gems, for it is the gems that are valued and collected. Perhaps the most startling aspect of Cartier's Indian commissions was that the Maharajahs wanted their gems set in platinum, as opposed to gold. Gold had previously been sacred to the Hindu tradition, but the westernisation of India had made platinum acceptable.[4]

Space does not permit mention of all these numerous commissions, but among the most spectacular was the emerald, diamond and pearl turban ornament made by Cartier London for the Maharajah of Kapurthala in 1926, shown in an advertisement in the *Spur*, entitled 'For the brow of a great Prince' (fig. 69).[5] The ornament incorporated fifteen large and unusual emeralds, with a central hexagonal emerald of 177.40 carats, surmounted by a smaller hexagon, a half-moon cut emerald and a pear-shape at the top. The accompanying text emphasises the importance attached in India to the stones themselves:

> The Maharajah, like most of the other Indian potentates, has faith in the increasing value of pearls and precious stones and regularly devotes a portion of his income to increasing his collection. The Hindu princes look upon gems as a permanent investment to pass from generation to generation.

The emeralds have been described as 'among the legendary jewels of India', and the Maharajah of Kapurthala wore his turban ornament at the Silver Jubilee of George V in 1935 and at the Coronation of George VI in 1937.[6]

The biggest single commission from an Indian client was the remodelling of the crown jewels of the Maharajah of Patiala (Sir Bhupindra Singh, 1891–1938), by Cartier Paris. Begun in 1925, the work continued until 1928, when an exhibition of the finished pieces was held at the Rue de la Paix (see fig. 70). There were two enormous diamond necklaces, one of uncut stones and one with the De Beers diamond of 234.69 carats (see p. 32, fig. 27), diamond collars, pearl and ruby bead necklaces, bracelets for the upper and lower arm, belts, buttons, rings, earrings, etc., some using the traditional forms of Indian jewellery, others in an entirely modern idiom. As a record of their work, Cartier compiled a sumptuous photograph album with tooled leather cover. The frontispiece was a photograph of the Maharajah in 1911, wearing some of his existing jewellery before transformation by Cartier. This and a photograph of his heir, Sir Yadavindra Singh, Maharajah of Patiala (1913–74), wearing the diamond necklace with the De Beers diamond are illustrated on pp. 32–3 (figs 26 and 28). The elder Maharajah of Patiala gave Cartier another sizeable commission, again using his own stones, in 1935 (cat. 102).

Although the upper-arm bracelet was a traditional item of Indian jewellery, Cartier received surprisingly few commissions for them. One of the few to survive is the example made for the shipping magnate Sir Dhunjibhoy Bomanji in 1922 (cat. 99).

The second aspect of Cartier's contacts with India was the importing of stones for resetting. The huge quantities of stones imported from India gave Cartier jewellery a character distinct from that of their contemporaries. Perhaps best known is Cartier's multigem or 'tutti frutti' jewellery. Rubies, sapphires and emeralds were carved into leaves probably in India at Cartier's request and set as fruiting leafy branches or flower bowls from *c.* 1924 to the late 1930s. This section includes the 'collier hindou' commissioned by Daisy Fellowes in 1936 (cat. 106). Other examples will be found in section 7b, in the context of Cartier colour combinations, since the designs are not in the Indian style.

The suppliers of these carved coloured gemstones are not easily identifiable from the archive records. With imported pearls, however, the situation is different. A Cartier

Crown Jewels designed and Mounted for H.H. The Maharaja Dhiraj of Patiala by Cartier

Cartier
PARIS
NEW-YORK
LONDON.

FIG. 70. Advertisement for an exhibition at Cartier Paris in 1928 of jewels made for the Maharajah of Patiala. Cartier Paris.

FIG. 71. Page from a Cartier New York catalogue of *c.* 1925, advertising pearls imported from India, with a pearl fisher diving from 'Mr Cartier's boat'. The catalogue offered pearl stringing on the premises or at home by appointment. Cartier employed several freelance pearl stringers. The wife of the designer Charles Jacqueau was a pearl stringer for Cartier Paris.

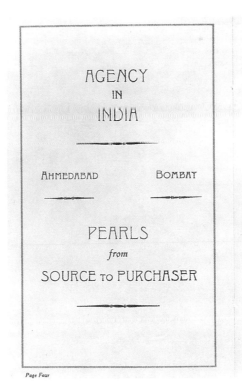

Diver descending
from Mr. Cartier's boat

Page Four   *Page Five*

New York catalogue of *c.* 1925 advertised an 'agency in India' at Ahmedabad and Bombay that supplied 'pearls from source to purchaser', 'in bunches as imported'. This was probably the Bombay Trading Company, an autonomous Cartier subsidiary, which developed trade between India, Europe and America.[7] Nadelhoffer mentions the Parsi pearl specialist Sethna in Calcutta and Bombay, while Cartier London records contain correspondence of the 1930s with another major supplier of pearls, Alibhai Abbabhai Javeri of Jamnagar and Rajkot.

Of all the Indian stones incorporated by Cartier in their jewellery, perhaps most striking was the astonishing number of large carved emeralds. Most of them are typical carved Mughal emeralds decorated with floral sprays. A particular rarity is the large emerald carved with a Hindu figurative scene (cat. 101). The emeralds themselves are Colombian and had been imported into India since the late seventeenth century. Those carved on both sides and along the edges were intended to be hung from a necklace and usually have a drilled suspension hole (see cat. 150 and 169). It is often difficult to date them with any accuracy, but in general they date from the seventeenth to the nineteenth or early twentieth century. An exception is the large carved emerald in the shoulder brooch made by Cartier London in 1923 and later acquired by Marjorie Merriweather Post (cat. 100), which bears an inscription referring to Shah Abbas of Persia. This is probably Shah Abbas II (ruled 1633–67) and so, if the inscription is genuine, the emerald can be dated to those years. Very few of the emeralds used by Cartier for stock pieces appear to have been inscribed, though this was not always mentioned in the records and, as the inscriptions are usually on the back or the edge, they are not visible in the archive photographs.

Carved Mughal emeralds also featured prominently in the jewels shown by Cartier at the Paris Exhibition of 1925; indeed, many of the star pieces in the exhibition were designed round emeralds of outstanding quality, the most spectacular of which was the so-called 'collier Bérénice' (cat. 269), containing three enormous rectangular carved emeralds. This object did not sell and was eventually dismantled, but the central and most important emerald has recently come to light and is discussed and illustrated under cat. 269. The 1925 Exhibition contained at least six other pieces with significant carved emeralds. Designs for some of them may be found in section 9 (cat. 270, 275 and 287). Apart from the use of the emeralds, the designs are not otherwise inspired by Indian jewellery. It must be emphasised that these pieces were almost all made for stock and represented a considerable risk, in that so much capital was tied up in them.

Special orders occasionally provided other exceptional pieces, such as the two emeralds inscribed with texts from the Qu'ran and mounted by Cartier Paris for the Aga Khan III in 1930. One, of 142.20 carats, was set as a brooch. The other, of 76 carats, formed the centrepiece of a bracelet. But neither of these inscriptions enable the emeralds to be precisely dated. They were both sold at Christie's Geneva, 12 May 1988, lots 703–4, and are among the few provenanced emeralds set by Cartier. No study has yet been made of the sources from which Cartier's carved Indian emeralds were acquired. The London correspondence of the 1930s suggests that some certainly were acquired in India. But they appear to have been purchased mostly from dealers and so the Indian families from which they came cannot be traced.

Cartier also used Indian emerald beads with simple decorative carving. The most popular were the irregular oblate melon-cut beads.[8] The 1925 Exhibition contained a necklace made up entirely of such beads, together with rubies and diamonds. The diadem worn by the 'Bérénice' mannequin incorporated vertical rows of melon-cut emeralds (cat. 269.1), and the big *décolleté* brooch (p. 18, fig. 10) had two melon-cut emeralds at the base. Other examples are to be found on the bracelet with coral dragons' heads, catalogued with other coral and emerald jewellery in section 7b (cat. 144). The emeralds in section 7c include pear-drops with chevron pattern carving (see cat. 163), a popular Indian form, and an unusual circular emerald carved with a lotus blossom, set as the back of a pendant watch (cat. 166).

Besides imported stones, Cartier also incorporated genuine Indian enamels into jewellery, cigarette cases and vanity cases (see cat. 93–4). Small enamel plaques from Jaipur, decorated with birds in flowering branches in characteristic colours of red, green and white, made ideal motifs for cigarette and vanity cases. Cat. 94 is a particularly early example of 1911. It is set with a Jaipur enamel plaque taken from an Indian box purchased from the Hungarian art expert Imre Schwaiger. Schwaiger divided his time between Delhi and London and negotiated the purchase of Indian jewels and *objets*

FIG. 72. Photograph by Man Ray of a mannequin with Indian jewellery sold by Cartier. From *Harper's Bazaar*, September 1935, p. 68.

d'art for Cartier. He also sold important Mughal jewels and other Indian objects to the Victoria & Albert Museum in the 1920s.

Another aspect of Cartier's regular trade with India was their purchase from Indian dealers, and indeed from the Maharajahs themselves, of a wide range of antique Indian

jewellery for resale. Both the London and Paris branches sold Indian jewellery unaltered, as well as remounting it in fashionable forms. While the Indian potentates had been resetting all their precious stones in platinum, Western clients were now avidly buying Indian jewels set in gold. Whether this was merely part of an independent reappearance of gold as a fashionable material, or whether the taste for Indian jewellery actually stimulated the reuse of gold is hard to say. In 1934–5, *Vogue* and *Harper's* ran a series of features entitled 'Bijoux hindus de Cartier' or 'The Jewels of India come West'. In September 1935 the London edition of *Harper's Bazaar* published a Man Ray photograph showing a mannequin with Cartier jewels: a diadem formed of an Indian necklace composed of gold and gem-set plaques, no doubt enamelled on the back, with a jewelled gold pendant and strings of beads cascading out of a jewel casket (fig. 72). The March 1935 issue of Paris *Vogue* showed a model in a Schiaparelli dress with necklace and bracelet of Indian pieces put together by Cartier. One of the chief suppliers seems to have been the Indian Arts Palace in Delhi, from which a huge quantity of enamelled gold and gem-set jewellery was purchased in the late 1930s for Jeanne Toussaint in Paris, including enamel bangles of the kind that inspired the dragon-head bracelet (cat. 144) purchased by Ganna Walska, who also owned a large collection of Indian jewellery. This included five Jaipur enamel bangles, possibly also purchased from Cartier. They were sold at Sotheby Parke Bernet on 1 April 1971, lots 33–5.

There were also special orders, from both Indian and Western clients, in which the client's own Indian pieces were mounted by Cartier. In 1934 Princess Karam of Kapurthala, wife of the fourth son of the Maharajah of Kapurthala, ordered a necklace from Cartier Paris comprising her own gold and gem-set pendant and six motifs, mounted on a gold chain. A photograph of her wearing it was published in American *Vogue* for 26 December 1934 (fig. 73).

The creation by Cartier of the fashion for Indian-style jewellery among non-Indian clients reached a peak from the late 1920s to the late 1930s. By 1928, a report in American *Vogue* suggested that Cartier's Indian-style jewellery was part of an:

increasing vogue for barbaric Indian jewellery with stones of irregular shapes, strung like valueless beads. Mrs Ali MacIntosh, who was Miss Lela Emery, has four new bracelets from Cartier that are perfect examples. They look like strings of beads, but, of course, they are made of precious stones. One bracelet has a melon-cut emerald in the centre, flanked by little diamond rouleaux and gold beads encrusted with rubies. It is fastened by a clasp powdered with diamonds. Another is made of irregularly shaped ruby beads, and two others are of sapphires with rubies and emeralds strung between. Mrs Reredon Havemeyer has an emerald necklace made of several strings of emerald beads, twisted like a rope, and caught with a gorgeous barbaric clasp of emerald and sapphire mosaic. Mrs Reginald Fellowes wears a twisted rope of large and small pearls, tied with a silver metal ribbon. Each end passes through three rubies and ends in a silver metal tassel. Cartier is favouring this new fashion for barbaric Indian jewellery, and, in the manner in which he presents it – always arranged with beautiful clasps and a surprising combination of stones – nothing could be more distinguished.

The jewellery was 'barbaric' because it used precious stones that were not cut or faceted. The strange effect that this created to a Western eye is revealed by the reaction of the Marchioness of Dufferin and Ava, wife of the Viceroy of India, in the 1880s to a 'fine collection of native jewels' that she saw in a Calcutta jeweller's shop: 'To our ideas they are positively ugly, and one can only wonder at the way in which the precious stones are treated – enormous rubies, emeralds and pearls bored through and strung like beads; diamonds cut perfectly flat and looking like glass.'[9]

Some of the necklaces with strings of beads were of dramatic proportions. A necklace of ruby beads with diamond clasps made by English Art Works for Cartier London for stock in March 1929 measured a total of 20 inches (51 cm), including the tassels that hung down the back. There is a pencil working sketch in the English Art Works job record book and a full-scale coloured design (fig. 74). It is described as follows: 'Ruby and diamond sautoir to take 5 rows of ruby beads strung on silk, diamond and ruby motifs to be supple, all rubies at back strung on chain, rubies in tassels strung on silk.' The stones were listed as 616 ruby beads, 2 cabochon rubies (set in the diamond clasps), 17 baton diamonds, 10 square diamonds, 112 brilliant-cut diamonds and two pearl and diamond tassels. This necklace was exceptionally large for a stock piece; it sold two years later in March 1931. In May 1934 Cartier Paris made for Misia Sert a necklace with no fewer than thirteen strands of ruby beads hung from ruby palmettes with a silk cord down the back. They were her own beads. Misia Sert (1872–1950) was married from 1893 to 1904 to Thadée Natanson, editor of *La Revue Blanche*. After a brief second marriage to the English businessman Alfred Edwards, from 1905 to 1909, she married thirdly the Spanish artist José-Maria Sert, from 1920 to 1927. Painted by Renoir and Lautrec in her youth, she became a central figure in Parisian artistic life and a close friend of Diaghilev, Stravinsky and Chanel. Cat. 105 is not such a grand-scale piece as these two, but is one of the very few surviving multiple strand necklaces with ruby beads. It was made for Mrs Ronald Tree, later Nancy Lancaster, an American who settled in England and became a sought-after interior decorator, eventually purchasing the famous decorating firm of Colefax & Fowler. Another American interior decorator, Elsie de Wolfe, acquired her own stones in India and took them to Cartier Paris for setting (see p. 31).

There is no doubt that Cartier's Indian-style jewellery had found its pre-eminent market among fashionable and artistic society. To judge from

FIG. 74. Design for an Indian-style necklace with multiple strings of ruby beads, the tassels designed to hang down the back, 1929. Cartier London.

FIG. 75. Miniature powder box and matching lipstick with stylised trees in carved rubies on a black enamel ground. Made by Cartier Paris as a special order in 1931 and 1933. Private collection (cat. 104)

repeated references in fashion journals alongside information from the Cartier archive, one of the firm's biggest clients for Indian-style jewellery was Daisy Fellowes. This section ends with a detailed account of her 'collier hindou' (cat. 106), which is given special emphasis not only as an Indian-style bib necklace copying one recently made for an Indian client, the Maharajah of Patna, but also as an example of the client returning items previously purchased at Cartier to be reset according to current fashion.

NOTES

1. See Nadelhoffer 1984, p. 82, and Pringué 1950, pp. 125 and 72, a photograph of the Comtesse de Montesquiou-Fezensac dressed for a Persian ball of 1913 with a bandeau and huge feather aigrette.

2. G. Marteau and H. Vever, *Miniatures persanes exposées au Musée des Arts Décoratifs Juin-Octobre 1912*, 2 vols, Paris 1913. For an account of the development of interest in and collecting of Islamic miniatures, with particular reference to the collections of Henri Vever, see G. Lowry and S. Nemazee, *A Jeweler's Eye. Islamic Arts of the Book from the Vever Collection*, Arthur M. Sackler Gallery, Smithsonian Institution, Washington, D.C., 1988.

3. See M. Shreve Simpson, *Arab and Persian Painting in the Fogg Art Museum*, Fogg Art Museum, Harvard University, Cambridge, Massachusetts, 1980, nos 17 and 18. The two paintings included in the 1912 Paris Exhibition are nos 15 and 19. Some of Louis Cartier's Persian miniatures were included in an exhibition of Persian miniature painting at Burlington House, London, in 1931.

4. For a fuller account of this aspect of Cartier's work for Indian princes, see Susan Stronge, 'Indian jewellery and the West: stylistic exchanges 1750–1930' in *South Asian Studies* 6, 1990, 143–55.

5. Illustrated in colour in Nadelhoffer 1984, pl. 29.

6. See Forbes 1939, p. 63.

7. Nadelhoffer 1984, p. 178. Nadelhoffer's account of Jacques Cartier's early Indian trips appears to be based on papers in the Cartier archive which the present author has not seen.

8. For an Indian necklace of melon-cut emeralds dated to the seventeenth century in the Kuwait National Museum, see Pal *et al.* 1989, pl. 141.

9. The Marchioness of Dufferin and Ava, *Our Viceregal Life in India*, London 1893, quoted by Gere and Culme 1993, p. 58.

89 Turquoise and pearl vanity case

Made by Renault (goldwork and applied mother-of-pearl) and Fourrier (turquoise inlay) for Cartier Paris for stock, 1924

Enamelled gold, mother-of-pearl, turquoises, pearls, emeralds and diamonds set in platinum. Front and back with Persian-style motif in mother-of-pearl inlay edged with black enamel and diamonds, surrounded by turquoise inlay, the corners with diamond motifs and cabochon emeralds; pearl and white enamel borders. The front with central cartouche of diamonds and black enamel containing a large carved emerald leaf on a ground of turquoise, and two smaller emerald flowers with diamond and enamel borders. The sides with further mother-of-pearl inlay and black enamel set with pearls, diamonds and emeralds. Interior with mirrored lid, two compartments, lipstick holder, and slot at front with the original gold-mounted tortoiseshell comb.

Entered in stock book on 19 December 1924, originally with gold chain and onyx ring, and a Persian miniature in the centre of the cover. The large emerald leaf replaced the miniature on 24 June 1926; date of sale not recorded.

MARKS Rim of base engraved *Cartier Paris Londres New York* and *JC*; *750* stamped on rim and comb with Paris eagle's head assay mark for gold on compartment lids and comb; workshop mark *C* between two crescents with the letters *s* and *A* above and below on rim, lipstick, and comb; workshop mark *R* with a crescent and flame (?) on compartment lids and comb.

L. 10.8 cm, w. 5.8 cm

Cartier collection, VC 34 A24

EXHIBITIONS New York 1976, cat. 15; Venice 1986, cat. 132; London 1988, cat. 218, pl. XXXII; Naples 1988, cat. 114; Paris 1989, cat. 320; Rome 1990, cat. 143; St Petersburg 1992, cat. 160; Tokyo 1995, cat. 181.

LITERATURE Nadelhoffer 1984, col. pl. 34.

RELATED MATERIAL Original design in pencil, ink, watercolour and bodycolour on buff tracing paper in Stock Design Record Book, 1923, p. 104, with initials L.C for Louis Cartier. The design shows the onyx ring and diamond attachment loop for the gold chain.

Designs for several cigarette cases and vanities with similar Persian-style cartouches are to be found amongst Jacqueau's working designs. They are all derived from Persian bookbindings of the fifteenth to seventeenth centuries, or from Turkish or Indian bookbindings copying Persian examples. Louis Cartier was an avid collector of Persian manuscripts, and the design for this vanity case may have been inspired by a binding in his own collection. Cat. 89.1 shows a seventeenth-century bookbinding from the collection of a fellow jeweller, Henri Vever, in leather filigree over a

89

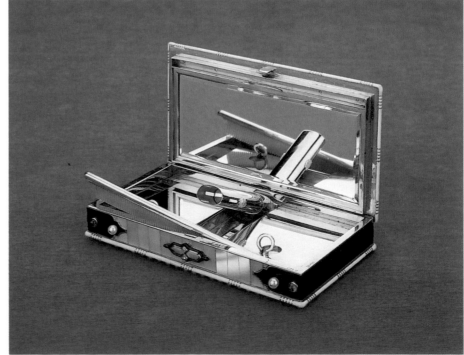

89

multicoloured paper ground (see G. D. Lowry and M. C. Bleach, *An Annotated Illustrated Checklist of the Vever Collection, Arthur M. Sackler Gallery*, Washington 1988, no. 475). For other examples with similar designs of a central cartouche within a frame in tooled and gilded leather, see D. Haldane, *Islamic Bookbindings in the Victoria and Albert Museum*, London 1983, pls 78 and 86.

The miniature comb inside is one of the few surviving examples. The interior underwent several repairs in the 1930s, which may explain the appearance of the Cartier workshop mark, registered in 1929.

90

89.1 Turkish leather bookbinding of Persian type, from the collection of the jeweller Henri Vever. Bookbindings of this kind inspired the design of cat. 89. Arthur M. Sackler Gallery, Smithsonian Institution, Washington, D.C.

90 Cigarette case

Made by Renault for Cartier Paris to the order of Mrs George Blumenthal, 1925

Enamelled gold and diamonds set in platinum. The sides pierced with a pattern of triangles within Persian-style cartouches, the ends with arabesques and the sides with a flowering tree in cream enamel. Black enamel borders and diamond initial B on front. The right-hand end forms a lid that opens backwards, the hinge along the long side.

Purchased by Mrs Blumenthal without the diamond initial on 14 May; diamond initial completed on 29 May.

MARKS Inside rim engraved *Cartier Paris Londres New York*; Paris eagle's head assay mark for gold and workshop mark *R* with a crescent and flame (?).

L. 12.3 cm, W. 6.1 cm

Cartier collection, CC 22 A25

EXHIBITIONS Tokyo 1995, cat. 188.

In October 1925 Mrs Blumenthal ordered an *en suite* match case, also made by Renault. A box and match case of identical design, but with unpierced decoration, was made as another special order in 1931.

George Blumenthal (1858–1941), banker and collector, emigrated from Germany to America in 1882. He became a director of the Wall Street investment bank Lazard's and, in 1905, a Trustee of the Metropolitan Museum of Art. This cigarette case was made for his first wife, Florence (1873–1930), whom he married in 1898. They were patrons of several French decorative artists in the 1920s, and owned major pieces by Cartier (see cat. 87, 107 and 194). George Blumenthal became President of the Metropolitan Museum of Art in 1934, and married secondly Mary Ann Payne in 1935.

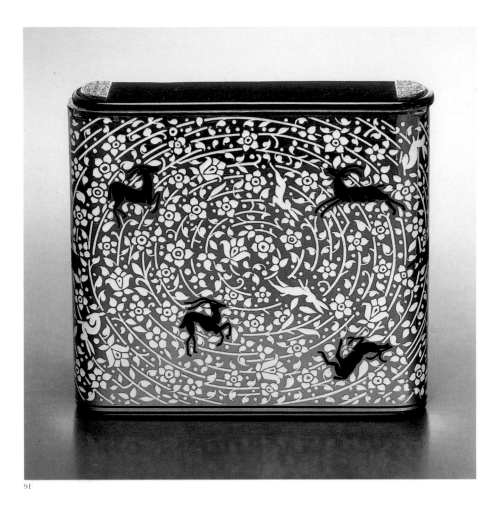

91

92

91 Cigarette case

Made by the Cartier workshop for Cartier Paris to the order of Mrs Graham Fair Vanderbilt (Mrs W. K. Vanderbilt), 1932

Enamelled gold with diamonds set in platinum on the lid. A white enamel floral scroll with rabbits in white and leaping deer in black enamel. The lid slides open, while the base is fitted with a spring system so that each cigarette pops out as the lid slides back. Both lid and base enamelled black, the lid with two semicircular diamond motifs at the ends.

Completed in October 1932.

MARKS Inside lid CARTIER PARIS; Paris eagle's head assay mark for gold.

L. 9 cm

Private collection

EXHIBITIONS New York 1976, cat. 60.

LITERATURE Cologni and Mocchetti 1992, p. 101.

RELATED MATERIAL Original pencil, ink and bodycolour design in order book for 1932 in Paris archive.

The two-colour decoration is inspired by patterns common to many branches of Islamic art, for example, on Safavid inlaid metalwork of the sixteenth and seventeenth centuries, usually inlaid in black composition into copper or brass (see A. S. Melikian-Chirvani, *Catalogue of Islamic Metalwork in the Victoria and Albert Museum*, London 1982, nos 155 and 166). Similar interlaced scroll patterns also occur in sixteenth-century Persian manuscripts. Examples were shown in the exhibition 'L'Art Musulman' held at the Union Centrale des Arts Décoratifs, Paris, in 1903 (see *Les Arts*, April 1903, p. 29). Inlaid ivory work is another possible source of inspiration, but Persian manuscripts are the most likely, in view of Louis Cartier's own superb collection.

The spring system is described in the archive record as a 'système élévateur de cigarettes pour Abdullah épaisses' (cigarette push-up system for thick Abdullahs). A similar model had been made for stock in May 1932, also by the Cartier workshop but without the spring system, and was sold to the Gaekwar of Baroda in 1935. The shape, however, is much

earlier. Two cigarette cases of the same shape
are in the Cartier collection, one of 1924,
with arabesques in black enamel, the other of
1929, with arabesques in cream enamel (Paris
1989, cat. 368).

Virginia Graham Fair (d. 1935), daughter of
James Graham Fair, one of the original dis-
coverers of the Comstock Lode, married
William K. Vanderbilt II (1878–1944) of New
York in 1899. They separated in 1909 and
were divorced in 1927 (San Francisco 1996,
p. 353).

92 Vanity case

**Made by Renault (goldwork and enamel)
and the Cartier workshop (setting of gems)
for Cartier Paris for stock, 1930**

Enamelled gold, diamonds and emeralds set in
platinum. All-over pattern of translucent green enamel
arabesques and cream enamel foliate scrolls; the sides
enamelled black, with diamond corner motifs, push-
piece with diamond baguette between two emeralds;
integral hinge. Interior with mirrored lid, powder
compartment with sunken handle and lipstick holder
(see p. 118, fig. 63).

Entered in stock book on 13 February 1930;
sold 25 February 1930.

MARKS Inner rim engraved *Cartier Paris Londres New York
MADE IN FRANCE*; Paris eagle's head assay mark for gold
and workshop mark *R* with a crescent and flame (?) on
lid, base and lipstick tube.

L. 8.5 cm, W. 5.5 cm

Cartier collection, VC 50 A30

EXHIBITIONS Lausanne 1996, cat. 228.

The pattern of flowers and arabesques is
inspired either by Safavid inlaid metalwork or
by Veneto-Saracenic ornament of the
sixteenth century.

93

93 Powder box

**Made for Cartier New York (workshop
unknown), c. 1925**

Enamelled gold, diamonds set in platinum. Enamelled
all over with thin white stripes (*émail pékin*), central
rectangular plaque enamelled with Persian-style floral
design, surrounded by four diamond motifs; diamond
push-piece.

A piece of similar design made for Cartier New York
appears in the New York archive photograph albums.

MARKS Inner rim engraved *Cartier*.

L. 8.4 cm, W. 6.4 cm

Cartier collection, AL 08 C25

EXHIBITIONS Paris 1989, cat. 396; Rome 1990, cat. 149;
St Petersburg 1992, cat. 162; Tokyo 1995, cat. 189.

The colour palette and foliate motifs of the
central enamel plaque are very close indeed to
Indian enamels of the nineteenth century,
probably from Murshidabad in East India
rather than Jaipur, and it is almost certainly a
genuine Indian enamel plaque mounted by
Cartier. The diamond cartouche that surrounds the plaque is, however, more Islamic in
inspiration.

94

objets d'art and jewellery for Cartier. Deep-blue enamel, as distinct from the traditional red, white and green, tends to occur in later Indian enamels of the second half of the nineteenth century onwards. The enamel plaque thus has every likelihood of being a genuine Indian enamel reused from a late nineteenth-century Indian box. For enamel plaques with comparable motifs of birds on flowering branches, on the reverse of an early nineteenth-century necklace, see Brussels 1982, cat. 71.

To complement the Indian enamel plaque, the running scroll round the edge is taken from Jaipur enamels of the nineteenth century. For a similar running scroll on a nineteenth-century pendant from Jaipur, see Stronge *et al.* 1988, no. 80. The cartouche round the enamel plaque on the front and the pseudo-Arabic inscription on the back are, however, more Islamic in inspiration.

95 Pendant watch

Made by Lavabre (enamelled dial) and Jaeger for Cartier Paris for stock, 1925

Enamelled gold, onyx, coral and diamonds set in platinum. Onyx bar, the ends set with diamonds and coral; black silk cord with diamond loops and slide, the watch hung on loop set with diamonds on each side and calibré onyx round the edge; the gold watch case enamelled in black, the dial with green and white enamel border; inner seal enamelled with Jaipur-style floral motif of a flower vase in green and white on a red ground on the reverse, the face enamelled with two parrots.

Entered in stock book on 30 September 1925, originally on silk cord necklace; mounted as lapel watch on 14 October 1926; sold 5 November 1926. The enamel plaque with parrots on the inner seal is a later addition.

MARKS On dial; *CARTIER*; French dog's head assay mark for platinum and workshop mark *EJ* flanking an hourglass on reverse of watch and on brooch-pin.

L. 9.7 cm, W. 2.7 cm

Cartier collection, WB 01 A25

EXHIBITIONS New York 1976, cat. 68; Los Angeles 1982, cat. 100; Paris, 1989 cat. 422; Rome 1990, cat. 196.

LITERATURE Nadelhoffer 1984, col. pl. 79; Barracca *et al.* 1989, p. 96; Cologni and Nussbaum 1995, p. 136.

Both this and the following watch are in the form of seals. Louis Cartier appears to have first thought of making seal-watches in about 1918, and recorded his ideas in his Notebooks. But most examples seem to have been made in the 1920s. They were advertised as new in

94 Cigarette case

Made by Lavabre for Cartier Paris for stock, 1911

Enamelled gold, diamonds set in platinum. In the centre an Indian-style enamel plaque with birds on flowering branches in red, green, yellow and white on a deep blue ground with diamond border, superimposed on a lozenge with arabesques reserved in gold on a blue enamel ground, with white enamel border. Round the edge and on all four sides an Indian running scroll reserved in gold on a white ground with blue border; palmettes at top and bottom. The reverse with the same blue and white enamel border and the same lozenge design, but engraved and not enamelled, the central square engraved with a pseudo-Arabic inscription.

Sapphire push-piece. Match compartment at top with strike-a-light inside lid.

Entered in stock book on 27 December 1911; sold 10 June 1912.

MARKS Inside rim of lid engraved *Cartier Paris Londres New York*; French Mercury head export mark on rim of match compartment; partly visible workshop mark *III.* flanking a four-leaf clover inside base.

L. 11.1 cm, W. 6.4 cm

Private collection

According to the archive records, the enamel plaque came from an 'Indian box' entered for stock on 21 August 1911. The box was supplied by Imre Schwaiger, the Hungarian expert who negotiated the purchase of Indian

95

London *Vogue* in January 1923, p. 46: 'Cartier spawns the newest watch, in form a tiny seal-ring, with the watch face for the seal and the ring of black and white enamel.' They were worn on a long black cord (see 95.1).

95.1 The actress Ina Claire wearing a Cartier seal-watch on a black silk cord and fastening a cliquet pin in her hat. London *Vogue*, January 1923. British Library.

96 Pendant watch

Made by Renault (brooch and chain) and Jaeger for Cartier Paris for stock, 1926

Enamelled gold, onyx, rock crystal, rubies; diamonds set in platinum. A semicircular black enamel bar with diamond terminals set with cabochon rubies forms the brooch; the chain of onyx cylinders and diamond-set links with a ruby cross. Watch attached to chain with rock-crystal ring. Watch enamelled black with Jaipur-style floral enamel on reverse in red, white and green on a white ground, scroll motif round sides reserved in gold, the dial white.

Entered in stock book on 20 January 1926, as a watch with crystal ring; brooch and chain added 25 November 1926; ruby cross motif added later, date unknown; sold 25 May 1941.

MARKS On dial: CARTIER; Paris eagle's head assay mark for gold and French dog's head assay mark for platinum on pin and chain; workshop mark EJ flanking an hour-glass on watch.

L. 11.6 cm, DIAM. of watch 2.2 cm

Cartier collection, WB 04 A26

EXHIBITIONS Paris 1989, cat. 427; Rome 1990, cat. 201; St Petersburg 1992, cat. 205.

LITERATURE Barracca *et al.* 1989, p. 151.

Although the shape and overall design is entirely of the 1920s, the floral enamel on the back of the watch and the running scroll round the side are inspired by Jaipur enamels of the nineteenth century.

This appears to have been a popular model. Other examples recorded in the Paris photograph albums were made as pendants with black silk cords in 1925; one example has an enamelled slide matching the enamel on the back of the watch.

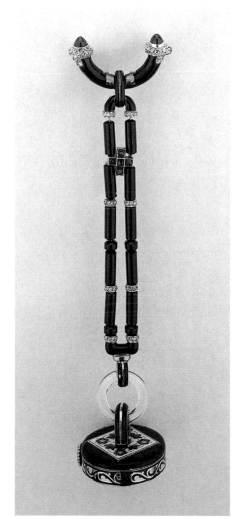

96

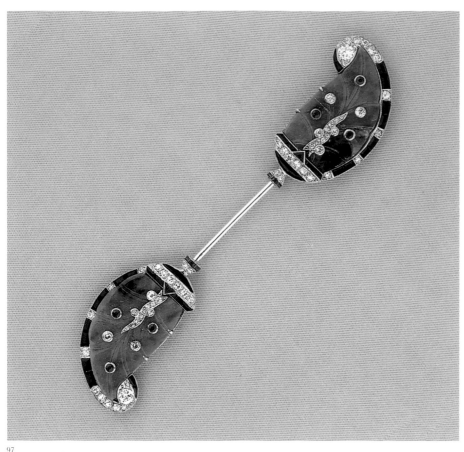

97

97 Double-headed cliquet pin (*broche cliquet*)

Made by Lavabre for Cartier Paris for stock, 1923

Jade, rubies, onyx and diamonds in open-back platinum setting. Two carved jade oriental palm leaves encrusted with diamonds and rubies, mounted in diamonds and calibré-cut onyx. A triangular-cut ruby at base of each leaf.

Entered in stock book on 21 August 1923; sold 29 August 1923.

MARKS Rim engraved *Cartier Paris*; French dog's head assay mark for platinum and workshop mark *HL* flanking a four-leaf clover.

L. 9 cm

Cartier collection, CL 106 A23

EXHIBITIONS St Petersburg 1992, cat. 127.

RELATED MATERIAL Original pencil, ink, watercolour and bodycolour design on buff tracing paper in Stock Design Record Book for 1923 in Paris archive. Initialled RR for René Révillon and stamped VENDU.

For another cliquet pin made by the Renault workshop in 1925, with a single jade palm and smaller leaf at the other end, see Nadelhoffer 1984, col. pl. 31, and Snowman (ed.) 1990, p. 197. The palm leaf, or *boteh*, in the form of a cone shape bent over at the point, is found in many branches of Mughal art, from Persian carpets to Kashmir shawls.

98 Head ornament

Made by English Art Works for Cartier London to the order of the Hon. R. H. Brand, 1935

Turquoises and diamonds in open-back platinum setting. Two tiers of turquoises in the form of oriental palm leaves and buds on a diamond base, with scrolling ends and three larger double-leaf motifs at centre and on each side. On reverse, two loops for a ribbon or elastic.

Job given to Wallace on 20 December 1935. Completed in January 1936. Sold Christie's Geneva 16 November 1989, lot 487, which states that 'According to a family tradition, this tiara was probably made on commission for the Hon. R. H. Brand.'

MARKS Reverse engraved *Cartier*.

H. at centre 4.8 cm, max. W. 16.7 cm

Cartier collection, JV 12 A36

EXHIBITIONS St Petersburg 1992, cat. 221; Tokyo 1995, cat. 266; Lausanne 1996, cat. 231, pp. 89 and 147.

LITERATURE Cologni and Nussbaum 1995, p. 181.

RELATED MATERIAL Working sketch in pencil and blue crayon in English Art Works job record book for 20 December 1935 in London archive.

For other examples of the palm leaf motif, see cat. 97 in carved jade, and cat. 258, a design for an elaborate necklace for the Maharajah of Patiala, with diamond palm leaves.

This is one of two head ornaments made by Cartier London and incorporating carved turquoise palm leaves. It was made in London for the Hon. R. H. Brand, and is described in the archive as a 'turquoise and dia head ornament, 100 turquoise fancy shapes, 538 brilliants'. Robert Henry Brand (1878–1963), banker and public servant, a director of Lazard's and Lloyd's, married Phyllis Brooks, née Langhorne, of Virginia in 1917. She was one of five sisters famed for their beauty, one of whom, Irene, married the illustrator Charles Dana Gibson who created the 'Gibson girl' image that became a standard of feminine attractiveness. Phyllis Brand died in 1937, a year after this head ornament was purchased, and it may have passed to one of her two daughters. Phyllis Brand's niece was Nancy Lancaster, who also married an Englishman as her second husband; she became a regular Cartier client (see cat. 105).

The other head ornament with carved turquoise leaves is earlier and was made for stock in 1930 using an existing diamond bandeau and adding a row of turquoise leaves. The diamond bandeau, described as a 'head ornament, 3 large round diamonds in the centre, in Boucheron case', was purchased by Cartier London in June 1929 from a regular client. The job of adding the turquoises was given to English Art Works on 6 November 1930, and a working sketch for the upper row of turquoises is in the English Art Works job record book for that date. The finished piece was entered in the stock book on 21 November, and sold on 31 December 1930.

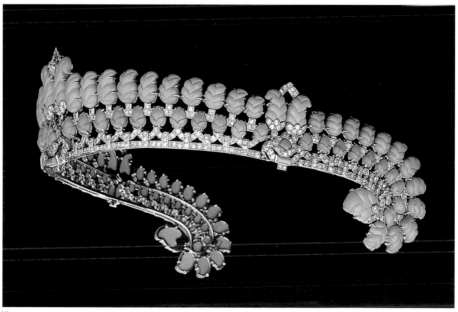

99 Part of an upper-arm bracelet

Made by Renault in Paris for Cartier London to the order of Sir Dhunjibhoy Bomanji of Bombay, 1922

Diamonds in open-back platinum setting. A central flexible plaque with three detachable pendant leaf-shaped elements on large pavé-set rings. Each element with openwork geometric trellis pattern attached with very thin platinum wires. The central plaque has six vertical hinges.

Completed in October 1922. Originally with three extra diamond rings forming the back of the bracelet.

MARKS French dog's head assay mark for platinum and workshop mark R with a crescent and flame (?) on the pendant loops.

W. of central plaque and flanking rings 12.5 cm

Cartier collection, BT 08 A22

EXHIBITIONS London 1988, cat. 233; Naples 1988, cat. 17; Paris 1989, cat. 184; Rome 1990, cat. 85; St Petersburg 1992, cat. 95; Tokyo 1995, cat. 96.

LITERATURE Cologni and Nussbaum 1995, p. 140.

RELATED MATERIAL Original pen and ink drawing of complete object, together with two pencil, ink and watercolour designs for the front part and back part (see 99.4–5 for the pen and ink drawing and one of the two watercolour designs). Loose designs, Paris archive.

These elements, the central plaque and three leaf shapes, are the surviving parts of an elaborate upper-arm bracelet that could be worn in four different ways, as bracelet, brooch, *devant de corsage* or pendant (see 99.4).

The use of openwork plaques goes back to designs of the 1910s and at first glance the design of this piece seems conventional, as was often the case with special orders. But this example is the earliest recorded upper-arm bracelet made by Cartier. The use of openwork plaques for an upper-arm bracelet demanded much greater flexibility than for a diadem or corsage ornament, and the innovation here lies not only in the form itself but also in the exceptional flexibility of each element. This was achieved by constructing each element in several thin vertical strips, each attached by very thin platinum wires.

According to a revealing stock analysis of September 1919 in Louis Cartier's Notebooks, bracelets for the upper arm had already been conceived by this date, but no examples appear in the photograph albums before this one of 1922. The idea does not seem to have been widely adopted, as very few were made, apart from the matching wrist and upper-arm bracelets with coral and emeralds designed for the 1925 Paris Exhibition (see cat. 287) and another diamond upper-arm bracelet made for the Maharajah of Patiala in 1935.

The upper-arm bracelet is a traditional form of jewellery in Mughal India, worn by men and women alike. It usually comprised a larger central element – a large stone or group of stones – attached to plaited cords round the back of the arm.

Although made in Paris, this piece was ordered and sold in London. The client was the Parsi millionaire and philanthropist Dhunjibhoy Bomanji of Bombay, who died in April 1937, aged 75. He ran the firm of shipping contractors established by his father, and owned vast estates in India as well as an estate in England, 'The Willows' at Windsor. He financed the dispatch of Indian contingents to South Africa during the First World War, helped to fund visits of British royalty to India and supported charitable causes both in India and in England. He was awarded a knighthood by the government of India in 1922, the year in which this commission was given to Cartier (information from obituary in the *Evening News of India*, Cartier archive, London).

Bomanji provided an astonishing number of diamonds to be made up. The finished design used almost all of them, a total of 859. The few small diamonds that remained were carefully returned to the client. The large old-cut raised diamonds in each element are extremely yellow in colour and have been cleverly arranged to form a pattern within the trellis work.

Originally three diamond rings (now missing) enabled the bracelet to be fastened round the upper arm. A full-size pen and ink drawing in the Cartier archive describes it thus: 'Bracelet du haut du bras formant broche, devant de corsage, ou pendant à executer aussi souple que possible' (upper-arm bracelet forming brooch, *devant de corsage* or pendant, to be executed as supple as possible). The drawing shows the bracelet's actual size with three small sketches indicating the three transformations (fig. 99.4). When worn as an upper-arm bracelet, the lower pendant leaf shape and its ring were removed while the two other leaf shapes were turned horizontal and joined round the back of the arm by the three diamond rings (99.1). At the tip of each leaf on the reverse can be seen the screw fitting for the three rings (99.3). The three small sketches

99.1 Cat. 99 with the centre leaf removed and the two flanking leaves turned sideways for wear as a bracelet.

are annotated 'broche' (the central plaque only), 'pendant' (the central plaque turned vertically and one leaf shape at the bottom, 99.2) and 'devant de corsage' (with the three back rings removed and the third leaf shape added, as it is now).

The full-size pen and ink drawing has various instructions indicating the sophisticated construction of this piece: on the left-hand ring 'anneau entièrement pavé pour permettre à la partie A de balancer' (rings pavé-set all round to allow element A [the leaf shape] to swing) and on the two joining links 'Ressorts pour l'extensibilité' (springs for extension). Thus the piece at the back that is now missing could be expanded to fit the arm. The full-size sketch is stamped SERVICE DE LONDRES; it is not clear whether this means that the drawing was done in London for execution in Paris or whether the drawing was done in Paris (according to Betty Jais, the quality of the paper suggests a London origin for this sketch). The piece may have been made in Paris because the Paris workshops were more experienced in executing elaborate flexible work of this kind.

The archive also contains two watercolour designs for the front of the bracelet (central plaque and two leaf shapes) and the back of the bracelet (the two leaf shapes joined by three rings). These would have been executed in addition to the pen and ink drawing in order to show the openwork construction, which would not have been obvious without colour (99.5).

99.2 Cat. 99 with two leaves removed for wear as a pendant. One of the two leaves is shown detached at the top.

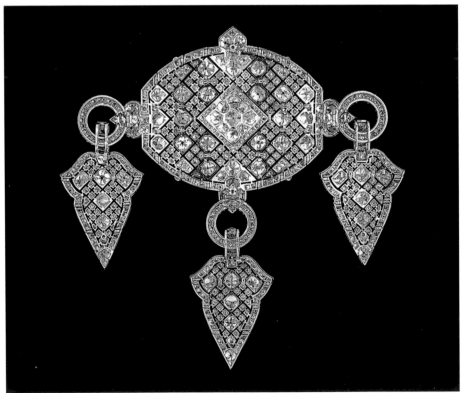

99.3 Reverse of cat. 99, showing construction and screw fittings.

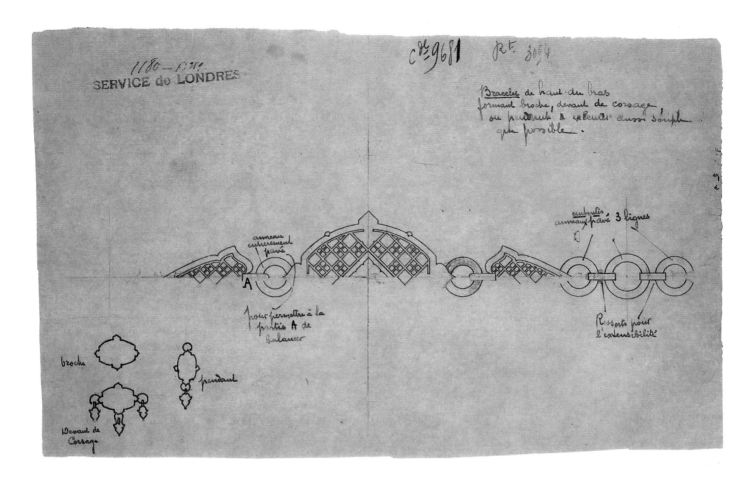

ABOVE 99.4 Pen and ink drawing for cat. 99, showing the back part, now missing, with sketches of its three transformations as brooch, pendant and *devant de corsage*. Cartier archive, Paris. See cat. 255a.

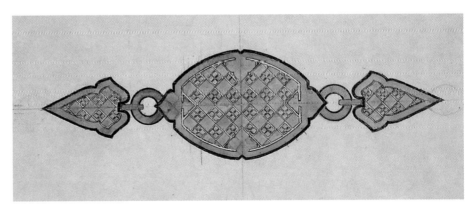

RIGHT 99.5 Two watercolour designs for the front and back parts of cat. 99. Cartier archive, Paris. See cat. 255b.

100 Shoulder clip brooch

Made by Cartier London for stock in 1923.
Altered by Cartier New York to the order of
Mrs E. F. Hutton (Marjorie Merriweather
Post), 1928

Emeralds, diamonds and black enamel in open-back
platinum setting. A large buckle and clasp motif,
studded with emeralds on a pavé-set diamond ground,
with lines of calibré emeralds at the join. At its base, a
polygonal carved Mughal emerald, from which hang
five articulated emerald drops, four of them melon-cut,
all with pavé diamond calyces edged in black enamel
and calibré emerald stems. In the centre a vase motif,
the upper part with handles in diamonds, the base
formed of an oval carved emerald. Double-prong clip
brooch fitting.

Made for Cartier London in October 1923 and sold
to Godfrey Williams on 30 April 1924. Acquired by
Mrs E. F. Hutton in 1928.

MARKS: CARTIER on reverse of mount of central emerald.

L. 19.5 cm. Large carved emerald 3.2 × 3 cm

Hillwood Museum, Washington

LITERATURE Nadelhoffer 1984, p. 183.

RELATED MATERIAL (1) Original pen and ink and
watercolour design for 1923 brooch in London Design
Scrapbook. (2) Pencil, pen and ink design in New York
archive for 1928 extension to brooch. Both on buff
tracing paper.

Marjorie Merriweather Post (1887–1973), sole
heiress to the Post cereal empire and philanthropist and art collector, acquired this brooch
together with an emerald and diamond
sautoir made by Cartier London in 1928
(Nadelhoffer 1984, p. 183, fig. 99). The sautoir
(owned by the Smithsonian Institution, Washington, and currently on loan to Hillwood),
was altered in 1941 and in its present shortened form has lost much of its original character. But the brooch remains in its 1928 form
and is among the most spectacular surviving
pieces of Cartier Indian-style emerald and
diamond jewellery.

The carved emeralds are all reused Indian
stones, carved in India probably in the nineteenth century. The idea of using a large stone
for the body of a vase goes back to 1913 (see
cat. 30). The large emerald carved with a
Mughal flower spray is exceptional in that it
bears an inscription which translates as 'the
servant of Shah Abbas'. This could be either
Shah Abbas I (reigned 1557–1629) or Shah
Abbas II (reigned 1633–67), but is perhaps
more likely to be the later ruler, as large emer-

100.1 Archive photograph of cat. 100 as originally made by Cartier London in 1923.

alds of this type were much admired by his contemporary Shah Jahan of India. Thus, if the inscription is genuine, the emerald can be dated to the mid-seventeenth century (100.2).

The brooch In its original form had a diamond circle studded with nine emeralds at the top instead of the buckle and clasp motif (see 100.1); it was sold with a 'three line brilliant loop (detachable) to use as a pendant'. The first purchaser, Godfrey Williams, had addresses in central London and at the South Western Hotel in Southampton, and so may have been a visiting American. The records do not indicate when or where Mrs Hutton acquired it, but it seems to have been in its original form, to judge by a photograph of it in her client file in the New York archive. The New York archive also contains photographs taken in 1928, when an extra element was added below the vase to extend the emerald drop at the base, and the top part was changed to the buckle and clasp motif.

Mrs Hutton wore her emerald and diamond brooch when she sat to Giulio de Blaas for her portrait in 1929 (p. 28, fig. 23). The massive and heavy brooch dominates the painting, and one wonders whether its attachment to such a flimsy dress was effected by a sturdy hidden undergarment.

The sautoir was made for Cartier London stock in April 1928, with a lyre-shaped pendant incorporating a large polygonal carved emerald of 47.20 carats. It was described in the records as 'Flexible line, barrel shaped *pavé* set diamond motifs with round emerald beads on the inside and baroque emerald beads on the outside.' It was illustrated in a fashion photograph for London *Vogue* on 3 October that year, but it does not appear to have sold. The pendant was removed and reused in November 1928 as the centrepiece of a bandeau formed of rectangular diamond links. In 1930 a crest of emerald beads was added to the bandeau (see Nadelhoffer 1984, p. 183, fig. 98).

Marjorie Merriweather Post was married first to Edward Bennet Close, from 1905 to 1918. She married E. F. Hutton in 1920; they divorced in September 1935. In December 1935 she married the attorney Joseph E. Davies, whom she divorced in 1955. Davies was US Ambassador to the Soviet Union in 1937–8, and it was then that his wife began the collection of Fabergé and Russian *objets d'art* for which she is best known (see San Francisco 1996, pp. 171–90). But she also owned a distinguished group of jewellery and objects by Cartier. Of these the most outstanding were the present brooch and its accompanying necklace, but she also owned a pair of diamond *devants de corsage* which she wore on her shoulders on the occasion of her presentation at court to George V and Queen Mary in June 1929 (see Rubin 1995, photograph between pages 208 and 209). One of these was later altered to make a diamond and pearl necklace. In 1937 she acquired a sapphire and diamond necklace, boldly designed with square-cut stones and very different from the 1920s pieces. Perhaps her most individual Cartier objects were a series of frames commissioned from Cartier New York in the late 1920s, each specially designed to hold a portrait miniature, painted on ivory from a photograph, the colours of each frame complementing the portrait it contained.

100.2 The inscription on the edge of the large carved emerald. It reads 'the servant of Shah Abbas'.

101 Emerald and pearl tassel necklace

Made for Cartier New York (workshop unknown) as a special order, 1925.

Emeralds, pearls, diamonds in platinum setting. A long single-strand pearl chain, the clasp in the form of a carved emerald leaf, with a short length of collet-set diamonds and emerald beads at the base. The detachable pendant formed of a polygonal carved emerald of 86.71 carats and a pearl tassel with emerald beads, small pear-drop emeralds and a large carved pear-drop emerald of 27.50 carats at the base. The large central emerald, with hatched sides and faceting on the reverse, is carved with a Hindu scene of Shiva and Parvati. The pendant loop is set with a baguette diamond.

Completed in October 1925.

MARKS Pendant loop engraved CARTIER.

L. of pendant (with loop) 16.5 cm. Total L. (with chain double) 56.5 cm. Carved emerald 3.6 × 3.9 cm

Cartier collection, NE 17 A25

EXHIBITIONS New York 1976, cat. 4; Los Angeles 1982, cat. 80; Tokyo 1995, cat. 142

LITERATURE Nadelhoffer 1984, col. pl. 30.

RELATED MATERIAL Original design in pencil, watercolour and bodycolour on cream tracing paper in client file in New York archive. The design shows only one emerald bead on each side at the base of the chain, instead of two.

Most Indian emeralds were carved with standard floral engraving in the Mughal rather than the Hindu tradition, and these were the stones most easily available for Cartier to use in their stock pieces (for example, cat. 165 and 169).

The central Hindu emerald, however, is a rare example of figurative carving quite unlike the stones normally found in Cartier jewellery. It belonged to the client and is a reused Indian stone of the eighteenth or nineteenth century, drilled at the top with a bow-drill for suspension. The shape was presumably suggested by the natural shape of the crystal. Shiva is depicted with the river Ganges flowing through his hair, referring to the story of how he caught the river as it came down from heaven. The two deities are shown on a tiger-skin, the seat of ascetics, with its paws either side and tail below. Around Shiva's neck is a rosary of sacred beads. One of the few comparable examples of Indian emeralds with figurative carving is illustrated in Brussels 1982, p. 140 (no location given).

The design of this necklace is very Indian in inspiration, but tassels on an Indian necklace usually function as ties and are smaller.

101

Larger tassels such as this were generally worn in India as head ornaments. The carved pear-drop emerald at the base of the tassel is a typical Indian stone of the late nineteenth or early twentieth century.

102 Pair of earrings

Made by Dubois for Cartier Paris to the order of the Maharajah of Patiala, 1935

Diamonds, rubies and pearls in open-back platinum setting. In the form of chandeliers; four discs edged with calibré-cut rubies from which hangs a row of pearls. At the top a dome of pavé-set diamonds, linked by three calibré-cut rubies to a single diamond stud.

Completed in June 1935.

MARKS Engraved *Cartier Paris*.

L. 5.5 cm

Cartier collection, EG 10 A35

These earrings are based on Indian models of the nineteenth century, executed in enamelled gold with pearls, or entirely in gold filigree with pendant sheet-gold strips, see Stronge *et al.* 1988, nos 52 and 56. They were made with the Maharajah's stones: 200 calibré rubies, 38 brilliants and 68 pearls. Cartier added four pearls only.

For a belt buckle in onyx and diamonds owned by the Maharajah of Patiala, see Hong Kong 1995, cat. 53. For an onyx and diamond brooch sold to the Maharajah of Patiala, see cat. 171.

103 Bracelet

Made by English Art Works for Cartier London as a special order, 1939

Diamonds in open-back platinum setting, gold and pearls. A double row of diamond rosettes, flanking a row of large pearls in alternate circular and four-petal diamond settings, with a frieze of pearls riveted with gold along the top. The whole set on a gold trellis, with triple pearl pendants on gold stems hanging from the lower row of gold rings. Contained in the original gold-tooled red leather case with standard Cartier stamp on gold on the silk lining to the lid.

Completed in August 1939.

MARKS Clasp engraved *Cartier*.

Bracelet: L. 19 cm. Case: L. 21.5 cm

Cartier collection, BT 51 A39

This bracelet combines the traditional Indian taste for gold jewellery with diamonds and platinum. It is much closer to Indian models

103

102

than many other Cartier pieces in the Indian taste, and is inspired by the Indian *guluband* or marriage necklace, formed usually of a row of square-shaped diamond and gold motifs with a row of pearls above and pearl drops or clusters below. Sometimes the drops were of emeralds and pearls. For eighteenth-century examples, see Brussels 1982, cat. 1 2 and 58. The reverse of the square motifs was usually decorated with red, white and green enamel.

This bracelet was made almost entirely of stones belonging to the client: 306 diamonds and 93 pearls.

A similar pair of Indian-style fringe bracelets made by Cartier was owned by Daisy Fellowes. She wore them for the wedding of Barbara Hutton and Prince Mdivani in Paris in June 1933, and was photographed wearing them for *Harper's Bazaar* in September 1933 (p. 28, fig. 22).

104 Powder box and matching lipstick

Made in Paris for Cartier New York as a special order, the powder box by the Cartier workshop in 1931 and the lipstick by Levoyer and the Cartier workshop, 1933

Gold with black enamel, rubies, diamonds set in platinum. Applied stylised trees of carved rubies set in gold, with border of round and baguette diamonds and cabochon rubies.

Completed in November 1931 (powder box) and May 1933 (lipstick).

MARKS Powder compact: *Cartier Paris*, MADE IN FRANCE, with Paris eagle's head assay mark for gold. Lipstick: *Cartier Paris*, with assay mark for gold and workshop mark C between two crescents with the letters S and A above and below.

L. of each 4.7 cm

Private collection

EXHIBITIONS Los Angeles 1982, cat. 44.

LITERATURE Nadelhoffer 1984, col. pl. 43.

The powder case bears an inscription dated 24 November 1931. In 1933 the same client commissioned Cartier Paris to execute the matching lipstick.

Illustrated on p. 165, fig. 75.

105 Necklace

Made probably by English Art Works for Cartier London to the order of Mrs Ronald Tree (later Mrs C. G. Lancaster), 1930.

Rubies, pearls and diamonds in open-back platinum setting. The front formed of five alternating rows of ruby beads and pearls terminating in six carved rubies at the ends of the three ruby strings. At each side, two large hinged diamond clasps set with carved ruby leaves, continuing with three rows of ruby beads to a pair of smaller diamond clasps. The back formed of two rows of ruby beads with two small diamond elements and a larger diamond element at the centre of the back set with carved ruby leaves and a central ruby cabochon. Both sets of side clasps come apart to form a bracelet made of the two larger and the two smaller clasps with their three rows of ruby beads. The length with two rows only round the back attaches to the front to make a smaller necklace. Alternatively, the back part can be worn as a choker by adding both lengths with three rows of ruby beads together, with one of the large side clasps as the central element.

Completed in March 1930; sold 31 March 1930 to Mrs Ronald Tree.

MARKS *Cartier London* engraved four times on reverse of clasps.

w. of large diamond clasps 2.4 cm

Cartier collection, NE 27 A30

The client's seventy-six pearls were incorporated in the two rows at the front. Cartier supplied all the remaining stones, which included '154 brilliants, 2 square brilliants, 19 ruby beads, 3 cabochon rubies, 23 ruby leaves'. The remaining ruby beads are not mentioned.

English Art Works made a number of similar necklaces, all with 'back part forming bracelet', in 1929 and 1930. They all consisted of rubies and diamonds only, except one, which also had pearls. They have no direct models in Indian jewellery. The balance of red is too great: an Indian necklace would comprise strands of pearls interrupted by coloured stones, and not alternate strings as here. Nevertheless, the multiple strands of beads were clearly intended to give an ethnic effect, or 'barbaric' look, as it was termed at the time. A closely similar necklace of 1929, with cabochon rubies in collet settings rather than strung as beads, was illustrated in a Cartier advertisement in *Harper's Bazaar*, London, June 1930, p. 107. There were earrings, a bracelet and a ring to match. The most Indian in taste of all Cartier's ruby necklaces was a large sautoir formed of multiple strands of ruby beads, with large diamond clasps at the side and ending in cords with tas-

105.1 Cat. 105 reassembled as a shorter necklace and a bracelet.

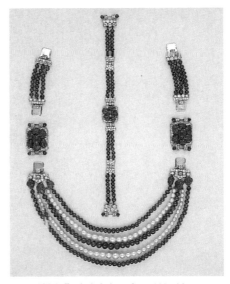

105.2 Exploded view of cat. 105 with constituent parts shown separately.

sels down the back (p. 164, fig. 74). It was made by Cartier London in 1929.

Mrs Ronald Tree, née Perkins (1897–1994), was born into a prominent family from Virginia. Her uncle, the Hon. R. H. Brand, purchased the turquoise tiara, cat. 98. Her second marriage, to Ronald Tree, an American by birth, in 1920 brought her to England, where she developed a flair for decorating and interior design. She was a great society hostess and decorated her own houses. In 1945, after marrying C.G. Lancaster (a Con-

servative MP), she purchased Colefax & Fowler, the decorating firm founded by Sybil Colefax (see R. Becker, *Nancy Lancaster*, New York 1996). The present Colefax & Fowler showrooms at 39 Brook Street contain her drawing-room of the 1930s. Colefax & Fowler decorated the home of the Duchess of Westminster, a celebrated Cartier client, and American *Vogue* for 15 August 1937 (p. 10) gave two illustrations of the Duchess in her home, wearing a remarkably similar multi-strand bead necklace with diamond clasps.

106 'Hindu' necklace (collier hindou)

Made by Lavabre for Cartier Paris to the order of Daisy Fellowes in 1936, with alterations of 1963 by the Cartier workshop to the order of her daughter, the Comtesse de Castéja

Emeralds, sapphires, rubies and diamonds in open-back cagework platinum setting. A heavy collar with inner row of alternate emerald and sapphire diamond-studded beads, to which is attached a narrow band of pavé-set diamonds with an upstanding 'ruff' of melon-cut emerald buds in diamond calyces, the emeralds with collet-set diamonds at the tips. From the diamond band hangs a fringe of articulated diamond-set stems with carved sapphire and ruby leaves and diamond-studded ruby, sapphire and emerald beads, ending in thirteen elliptical faceted sapphires. At the centre, two square carved emeralds; the clasp formed of two carved sapphires of 50.80 and 42.45 carats in the form of buds. The hinged stems set with baguette diamonds; two marquise-cut diamonds on clasp.

Completed in May 1936, using stones from three earlier pieces. Originally with Indian-style cord fastening round the back instead of a complete collar of gems (106.4), and with different arrangement of the larger stones. Necklace modified to its present form 29 June 1963. Sold Sotheby's Geneva, 15 May 1991, lot 390.

MARKS Reverse engraved *Cartier Paris*; Paris eagle's head assay mark for gold on white gold tongue and workshop mark *c* between two crescents with the letters *s* and *A* above and below on tongue and central pendant.

L. at centre 5.5 cm, max. DIAM. 19 cm

Cartier collection, JV 18 A36

EXHIBITIONS St Petersburg 1992, cat. 220; Hong Kong 1995, cat. 36; Tokyo 1995, cat. 267; Lausanne 1996, cat. 269.

LITERATURE Nadelhoffer 1984, col. pl. 45; Markevitch 1987, pp. 104–5; Cologni and Nussbaum 1995, pl. 159.

RELATED MATERIAL Original design in pencil, watercolour and bodycolour on grey paper in order book for 1936, Paris archive (see 106.3).

This necklace incorporated stones from three earlier pieces all purchased from Cartier by Daisy Fellowes: (a) a necklace of 1928, (b) a bracelet of 1929, and (c) an unidentified bracelet. The first two items each have their own documentation, given below.

(a) Necklace of 1928

A string of emerald and sapphire beads with thirteen elliptical faceted sapphires with platinum mounts

Entered in stock book on 20 June 1928; sold to Daisy Fellowes on 27 June 1928.

RELATED MATERIAL: Original design in pencil, watercolour and bodycolour on buff tracing paper in Stock Design Record Book, 1928, p. 45a (see 106.5).

All stones reused. The elliptical faceted sapphires retained with their petal-shaped mounts and baguette stems, but separated from the emerald and sapphire beads which formed the inner row of the 1936 necklace.

106.1 Detail of cat. 106, showing angle of 'ruff'.

106.2 Detail of back of cat. 106, showing hinged articulated elements.

(b) Bracelet of 1929

Formed of a wreath of carved emerald buds in diamond calyces, each bud set with a small ruby or turquoise bead at the tip, each stem ending at the centre in carved ruby leaves, with two large carved sapphires

Entered in stock book on 27 June 1929; sold to Daisy Fellowes on 31 October 1929.

RELATED MATERIAL: Original design in pencil, watercolour and bodycolour on buff tracing paper in Stock Design Record Book, 1928, p. 38b, with initials R.R. for René Révillon (see 106.6).

All stones reused except for the tiny turquoise beads. The two large sapphires, now forming the clasp of the 1936 necklace, were originally set in the centre of the necklace as part of a detachable clip brooch together with the two marquise-cut diamonds now in the clasp (106.4). The emerald buds were retained with their platinum calyces to form the 'ruff'. The rubies were set into the articulated stems.

The order book entry for the 1936 necklace lists all the stones, both the client's and those supplied from stock.

The stones are as follows:

Stones supplied by client

13 pendeloque briolette saphir, étrier		
1 brillant baguette, 1 bt carré et Bts ronds, monture platine		
2 saphirs feuille		93.25
24 " "		55.58
16 saphirs boule [bead]		37.07
22 rubis feuille		30.07
19 rubis boule		8.60
2 émeraudes carrées		12.06
6 "		3.26
67 "	boule	134.22
2 brillants navette		0.83
3 "	trapèze	0.34
7 "	baguette	0.97
6 "	carrés	0.90
594 "	ronds	10.62

Stones supplied by Cartier

101 "		2.34
96 "		1.01
18 "		0.27
23 "		0.15
1 rubis feuille		1.27
7 rubis boule		1.79

106.3
Original design in pencil,
watercolour and bodycolour
for cat. 106. Order book, 1936,
Cartier archive, Paris.

Although the above list describes the elliptical faceted sapphires as 'briolette', this term is normally applied to a pear-shape. The two square carved emeralds and the navette or marquise-shaped diamonds were not in the two identified pieces of 1928, and must therefore have come from the unidentified bracelet.

Daisy Fellowes (1890–1962), born Marguerite Descazes, was the daughter of the 3rd Duc Descazes and Duke of Glücksbjerg (1864–1912) and Isabelle Blanche Singer (1869–96), heiress of Singer sewing machine millions. She was married firstly to Prince Jean-Anatole de Broglie (1886–1918), from 1910 till his death in action in 1918. In 1919 she married an Englishman, the Hon. Reginald Ailwyn Fellowes JP (1884–1953), brother of the 3rd Baron de Ramsay and grandson of the 2nd Baron de Ramsay. The necklace passed to her eldest daughter, Emeline de Broglie (born 1911), who had become the Comtesse de Castéja by 1934. Daisy Fellowes, who was famous for her malicious remarks,

was on more than one occasion named one of the twenty 'Best Dressed Women of the World' by the Parisian couturiers during the 1930s. Reportedly she wore her 'collier hindou' only once, at a grand masked ball in Venice in 1951, hosted by the Mexican millionaire Carlos de Beistegui to celebrate his restoration of the Palazzo Labia. For photo-graphs of her wearing it on that occasion, see Hong Kong 1995, p. 65, and Tretiack 1996 (unpaginated).

The alterations made by her daughter in 1963 have completely destroyed the original appearance of the necklace by turning it into a solid collar and removing the cord strings which gave it its Indian character and provided flexibility in wear: it could be tied tight around the neck or worn looser and lower. But as a documented example of the remounting of earlier pieces over five decades it is unparalleled, and because such detailed records survive, it would be possible to return the necklace exactly to its original form of 1936.

In its original form, this necklace was without

doubt based on one commissioned from Cartier in June 1935 by the Maharajah of Patna, a son-in-law of the Maharajah of Patiala. Incorporating several of the Maharajah's old-cut diamonds, carved rubies and emeralds, it took the form of a bib with waving articulated diamond stems set with ruby leaves and increasing in size towards the base. At the bottom was an antique diamond drop, and it was fastened around the back with strings of beads. Daisy Fellowes's necklace was closely similar in conception, with a narrow collar from which hung a bib of graduated diamond stems set with carved gemstone leaves. She would certainly have been shown the design for, and photographs of, the Maharajah of Patna's necklace, and would have been well aware that her 'collier hindou' was a direct copy of it. But the necklaces differ significantly in the colours of the gemstones. The Maharajah of Patna's necklace combined the traditional red, white and green of Indian jewellery, while Daisy Fellowes's necklace placed great emphasis on huge carved sapphires and sapphire briolettes. The sapphire is an unlucky stone in the Indian tradition and would never have been worn by an Indian client, even one who wanted his stones reset in the Western style.

The Paris order books reveal many other Indian-style pieces made to order for Daisy Fellowes during the 1930s. These include a pearl choker necklace with pearl tassel of 1932, the emerald fringe bracelets of 1933 (see p. 28, fig. 22), and her 'Maharajah brooch' of 1936, an agate figure against a turquoise screen (illustrated in Nadelhoffer 1984, col. pl. 74). In 1928 American *Vogue* noted that she wore twisted pearl ropes (see p. 164), and in February 1934 *Harper's Bazaar* published a photograph of her wearing 'Old Indian jewellery imported by Cartier'. Whether she owned the Indian pieces or was simply posing in them is unclear.

Daisy Fellowes also owned more conventional diamond pieces, such as a necklace convertible to a tiara formed of three daisies on a metal frame covered with deep brown velvet, ordered from Cartier Paris in June 1938 (a sketch of her wearing the daisies as brooches, two in her hat and one on her lapel, appeared in London *Vogue*, 30 November, 1938, p. 116), and bizarre creations such as a bracelet made of actual panther fur with gemstone centre, ordered in 1935, also from Cartier Paris.

106.4 Archive photograph of cat. 106 as originally executed in 1936, showing the Indian-style cord fastening round the back.

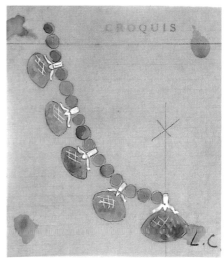

106.5 Original design in pencil, watercolour and bodycolour for a necklace with thirteen faceted sapphires purchased by Daisy Fellowes from Cartier Paris in 1928. All the stones were reused in her 'collier hindou' of 1936. Cartier archive, Paris.

106.6 Original design in pencil, watercolour and bodycolour for a multigem bracelet purchased by Daisy Fellowes from Cartier Paris in 1928. All the stones were reused in her 'collier hindou' except the tiny turquoise beads. Cartier archive, Paris.

THE CHINESE AND JAPANESE STYLES

Like the Egyptian-style pieces, the items included in this section divide themselves into two distinct groups: those that incorporate actual Chinese or Japanese elements, such as carved jade (cat. 107–10) or lacquer panels (cat. 111–13), and those that use Chinese or Japanese motifs in their design but were made entirely by Cartier. The second group comprises pieces made in an astonishing variety of colourful materials, such as the Chinese garden vanity case (cat. 115), as well as more restrained diamond jewellery and accessories (cat. 118–21). They all date from the 1920s.

The carved Chinese jade items in this section include a jade screen adapted as a desk clock (cat. 107), a Chinese belt hook adapted as a brooch (cat. 108) and a Chinese seal adapted as a pendant watch (cat. 109). Jade is a broad term for two distinct minerals, nephrite and jadeite. To identify them accurately requires scientific examination, and all the pieces catalogued here are therefore simply described as jade. Many other examples of carved Chinese jade will be found elsewhere in this catalogue. For example, many carved jade plaques and buttons of the eighteenth and nineteenth centuries were set into boxes and vanity cases, often combined with blue enamel or lapis lazuli to make one of Cartier's most characteristic colour combinations, blue and green. These pieces will be found in section 7a.

Similarly, many other pieces whose design is based on Chinese and Japanese motifs will be found in other sections. Chinese and Japanese patterns had so permeated the Cartier design repertoire that they are to be found as all-over decoration in enamel or engraved gold on boxes and vanity cases, such as cat. 62, which has an engraved Chinese geometric pattern, and cat. 130, which has an enamelled Japanese cloud pattern. In one instance, trellis patterns on Chinese furniture have been cleverly adapted in enamel to decorate the doors of a cube desk clock with folding dial, so that the pattern varies as the doors are opened (cat. 71).

Cartier's striking ring and tassel pendants (or brooches) are also derived ultimately from Chinese pendants. Several examples are included in section 9 (cat. 261–2 and 265), while a pendant with onyx ring, coral tube and pearl tassel is to be found in section 7e (cat. 188). Other Chinese motifs adopted by Cartier included the handled flower basket, many versions of which were executed as multigem brooches (see cat. 153).

FIG. 76. Chinese-style aigrette in diamonds with calibré-cut ruby border and feather plume, described in the archive record as a 'gong chinois' after Chinese bronze chimes or gongs of this shape. Cartier archive, Paris.

Chinese and Japanese motifs were already familiar in the Cartier repertoire before the First World War. The Japanese knot brooch (cat. 20) and the diamond lozenge brooch with overlapping scale pattern (cat. 24), both of 1907, are two examples. It could be argued that Far Eastern linear patterns provided the inspiration for Cartier's geometric-style diamond pieces of the first decade of the century.

But many other motifs were adopted from the Far East before 1914. One of these was the Chinese bronze chime or gong in the form of a *ruyi* symbol signifying 'as you wish', which appeared as gem-set aigrettes (fig. 76) or brooch-pendants (p. 70, fig. 54).[1] The New York Exhibition of 1913, already mentioned with regard to the Persian and Indian styles, also included a section called 'From Chinese Art'. There were pendants of carved jade and three pieces decorated with 'blue and green Chinese enamel'. What Cartier had in mind here is unclear, since both Canton enamel and Chinese cloisonné enamel use other colours in addition to blue and green. Whatever the source of inspiration, blue and green enamel was thought to be Chinese, and it appears time and again on Chinese-style pieces, for example the vanity case with Chinese vase (cat. 117), the lacquer lipstick and powder box (cat. 111), and the cigarette case with Chinese-style gem-set motif in section 7a (cat. 129). In each case the blue and green enamel is used as border decoration.

The diamond jewels incorporating Chinese motifs continued into the 1920s. Especially popular were dragon motifs derived from archaic Chinese bronzes (see cat. 118–19). These had been collected in Paris since the nineteenth century, and Cartier designers would have known the Guimet and Cernuschi collections. The London Design Scrapbook has some particularly intricate designs for diamond bracelets with interlaced dragons which must derive from similar sources.

Cartier's use of Chinese jade created a new category of semi-precious jewellery and accessories, for example simple jade bead necklaces, pendants of carved jade often combined with rubies,[2] and belts made of jade discs.[3] The taste for jade seems to have been part of the 1920s aesthetic. Other jewellery houses created contemporary designs with jade, while jade green became a favoured colour for evening wear. At a London ball in March 1926 Mrs Harold Pearson wore 'deep coral with embroideries of jade beads', while at Lady Headfort's ball in June of that year the hostess wore 'a white dress embroidered in jade green' and her guests included Princess Arthur of Connaught 'in a crystal-beaded jade frock'.[4] American *Vogue* advertised imported Chinese jade jewellery with the caption 'East meets West when the ultra-smart woman of today, with her slick hair, coral lips and finely lined eyebrows, wears jewels of the Orient.'[5]

During the 1920s Cartier also produced their celebrated series of mystery clocks designed round large-scale Chinese jade sculptures. These included figures of a mandarin duck, an elephant and the Chinese goddess Kuan Yin.[6] Perhaps most original of all is the conversion of a Chinese jade screen such as would have stood on a scholar's desk, mounted on a stand, into a clock. The mechanism that turned the hands was hidden within the carved jade. It remains a desk ornament, but with an entirely different function (cat. 107).

Cartier's reuse of lacquer inlaid with tinted mother-of-pearl (*lacque burgauté*) was equally original. The tinted mother-of-pearl could provide vivid contrasts of green and purple. Sometimes these were boldly combined with coral.[7] One rare case of lacquer combined with amethyst to enhance the purple tones of the mother-of-pearl inlay is to be found in a design for an octagonal powder box in the London Design Scrapbook. It had an amethyst ring and cabochon amethysts all round the edge. No example of lacquer combined with amethyst survives, so it is difficult to judge how successful this would have been. In the examples selected here, the *lacque burgauté* is combined either with red lacquer or carnelian, both of which were less strident than coral (cat. 112–13), or with blue and green enamel, perhaps the ideal colours to complement the tones of the tinted inlays (cat. 111). To judge by the large number of small objects decorated with lacquer produced by Cartier, they must have been extremely popular. In one instance a client ordered thirty-four lacquer vases as Christmas presents (cat. 112).

The lacquer panels were taken from bowls, trays or tables made in China or, more probably, in the Ryukyu islands or in Japan, which became the centre of the industry in the nineteenth century. There were a number of dealers in Paris who acted as suppliers for Cartier. These included C. T. Loo, Michon, the Compagnie de la Chine et des Indes and the Japanese dealer Yamanaka of Kyoto, who had outlets in New York and other American cities as well as in Europe and Japan. Sometimes Cartier used Western inlays made of tinted mother-of-pearl and a variety of hardstones inlaid into a pale mother-of-pearl ground. The effect was very different from that of the black *lacque burgauté*. These Western inlays are generally attributed to Vladimir Makowsky (1884–1966), a Russian based in Paris.[8]

The influence of Japan on Cartier design is less immediately obvious than that of China. One class of object, the cigarette and vanity case, was, however, decisively influenced by the Japanese *inro*, a small case for personal effects comprising a series of compartments that slotted together and were held in place by a cord. The cord was tightened with a sliding bead or *ojime* and attached to the belt with a carved *netsuke*. Cartier adapted the shape of the *inro*, whether rectangular or cylindrical, to suit the vanity case. The Japanese silk cord was replaced by a chain and the *netsuke* was replaced by a ring at the top. The cylindrical shape was especially popular for the combined cigarette and vanity cases (see section 3, cat. 63–5), since the depth provided more space. Few Cartier designs retained the idea of the compartment held by a cord. One exception is a design for a cigarette case of *c.* 1925 in the Paris archive. The case appears to be of carved jade, but it was never executed. Sometimes Cartier added a tassel to the ring: cat. 190, a vanity with carved coral plaque, originally had a black silk tassel, as did cat. 64. But there were no tassels on Japanese *inro*: the idea came from Chinese pendants.

Perhaps the most notable influence of Japan is in the series of clocks designed to resemble a Shinto shrine gate (cat. 122–3), with columns of dark green jade or black onyx. Nevertheless, as was so often the case, different sources are mixed up in the same object: in cat. 123 the rock-crystal dial hangs from a secondary cross-bar inspired by the frame for a Chinese bell, gong or drum.

NOTES

1. For an illustration of a Chinese bronze chime of this form, see *Europa und die Kaiser von China*, exh. cat., Berlin, Martin-Gropius-Bau, 1985, no.11/9.

2. See Lausanne 1996, cat. 203, for a jade pendant of 1921 in the Cartier collection.

3. See Paris 1989, cat. 376, and Snowman (ed.) 1990, p. 199.

4. *The Sketch*, 24 March 1926, p. 536, and 3 June 1926, p. 517.

5. Undated press cutting, 1920s, Cartier archive, Paris.

6. The mandarin duck is now in the Lindemann collection: see New Orleans 1988, pl. LXIV. For the elephant, see Paris 1989, cat. 391. For Kuan Yin, see Paris 1989, cat. 395.

7. See Nadelhoffer 1984, col. pls 36 and 38.

8. See Nadelhoffer 1984, p. 203 and col. pl. 39, a vanity case of 1927 now in the Cartier collection (Lausanne 1996, cat. 195).

107 Jade screen clock

Made by Couet for Cartier Paris for stock, 1927

Jade, coral, onyx, emeralds, sapphires, enamelled gold, mother-of-pearl, diamonds. The dial formed of a Chinese carved jade screen in a frame of coral rods set with diamonds, mounted on an onyx stand, the vertical supports set with cabochon emeralds and ending in dragons' heads with emerald eyes. Plinth edged in mother-of-pearl; pearl plaques with diamonds at base of two arches. The front carved with a mountainous landscape and a donkey rider with a boy attendant; coral hands and diamond numerals. At top and bottom a gold foliate motif enamelled green and set with cabochon sapphires in a black frame. The reverse carved with a rocky landscape, set with an enamelled gold dragon and, at the top, an enamelled foliate motif as on front. Between base of screen and plinth a carved coral bead conceals the drive for the mechanism, contained within the jade.

Entered in stock book on 16 December 1927; sold 14 May 1928 to George Blumenthal.

MARKS Paris eagle's head assay mark for gold on frame below screen and pre-1919 third gold standard mark on base.

H. 33 cm

Musée des Arts Décoratifs, Paris, inv. no. 27898, given by George Blumenthal in 1931

EXHIBITIONS Paris 1966, no. 818; Paris 1976, cat. 304.

LITERATURE Nadelhoffer 1984, col. pl. 52; Barracca *et al.* 1989, p. 174.

The 'modèle écran', or screen model, was introduced in 1923 (Nadelhoffer 1984, p. 252). The shape was used both for mystery clocks with transparent rock-crystal dials (see cat. 124) and for genuine Chinese jade screens. The movement was in the base, and the motive power was carried by a central axle system through a hollow sphere between the base and the dial. The system was thus the same as that of the second mystery clock model (see cat. 69). The carved jade screen was either hollowed out to take the wheels and driving mechanism, or two screens were placed back to back with the wheels between them. Because the dial was not transparent,

107.1 Front of cat. 107.

ordinary brass wheels could be used instead of crystal or glass discs. The winding hole is visible in the base from the back. According to Barracca *et al.*, it activates not only the hands but also the dragon, which climbs up the panel.

Jade screens mounted on a stand in this way were traditionally used in China as ornaments for scholars' desks: see Rawson 1995, cat. 29:17, for an eighteenth-century example. They were also used in Japan to compartmentalise the desk. The present screen dates probably from the eighteenth century.

The dragon motif was taken either from a Chinese textile or possibly from a Japanese bronze.

For another closely similar jade screen clock of 1926, see Los Angeles 1982, cat. 59. A third example, dated 1928, much squatter in form, with sides and base of lapis lazuli, is in the Cartier collection: see Tokyo 1995, cat. 230.

For George Blumenthal, see cat. 90.

108 Carved jade brooch

Made by Renault for Cartier Paris as a special order, 1924

Jade, enamelled gold, sapphires and diamonds set in platinum. A carved jade Chinese belt hook, with a dragon's head forming the hook, its diamond eyes encircled with black enamel, facing a second dragon with diamond eyes whose body runs down the length of the carving. Mounted in gold with black enamel and pavé-set diamonds forming a crest on the larger dragon's head. Three sapphires set at base and a fourth beneath the larger dragon's head. The head of the second dragon is deeply undercut.

Completed in May 1924.

MARKS Reverse of gold mount engraved *CARTIER PARIS LONDRES*; Paris eagle's head assay mark for gold on mount and pin, together with workshop mark *R* with a crescent and flame (?).

L. 9.3 cm

Cartier collection, CL 80 A24

EXHIBITIONS Paris 1989, cat. 250; Lausanne 1996, cat. 204.

LITERATURE Cologni and Nussbaum 1995, p. 119.

The Chinese carved jade belt hook belonged to the client and dates from the eighteenth or nineteenth century. The illustrations 108.1–2 show a closely comparable example in the British Museum, dating from the late Ming or Qing period, in which the stud for attachment to the belt is clearly visible beneath the curve. This has been removed on the Cartier piece. The British Museum example also shows the upper dragon's horns, which on the Cartier piece are partly obscured by the setting. For another comparable example, see Rawson 1995, p. 346, fig. 2, dating from the fifteenth or sixteenth century.

108

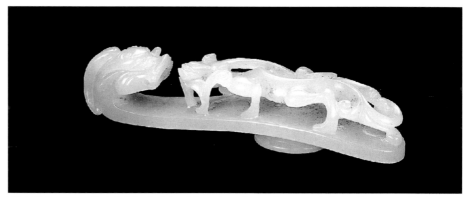

108.1 Chinese carved jade belt hook of the eighteenth or nineteenth century, similar to that mounted by Cartier as cat. 108. This example shows the stud for attachment to the belt which Cartier removed to make the brooch. L. 9 cm. British Museum, OA 1955.7–18.8.

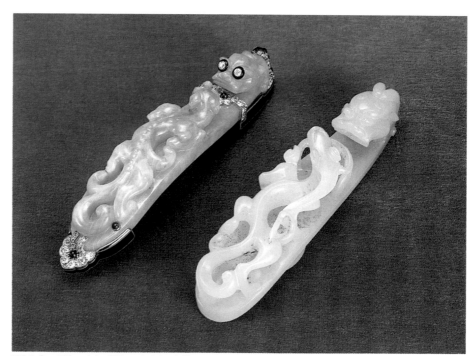

108.2 Cat. 108 and the Chinese belt hook illustrated in 108.1, showing undercutting of dragons.

109

110

109 Pendant watch

Made by Jaeger and Picq for Cartier Paris for stock, 1924 and 1929

Jade, rubies, onyx and diamonds set in platinum. A carved jade Buddhist seal in the form of a lion with watch set at its base, hung from a diamond brooch with ruby bead, diamond and onyx chains.

Seal-watch made in 1924, brooch-pendant entered in stock book on 1 February 1929; apparently unsold, still in stock in 1964.

MARKS French dog's head assay mark for platinum.

L. 10.8 cm

Private collection

EXHIBITIONS New York 1976, cat. 69; Los Angeles 1982, cat. 99; Paris 1989, cat. 432.

LITERATURE Snowman (ed.) 1990, p. 199.

The watch was set into the base of the nineteenth-century jade seal in 1924, originally mounted as a pendant within a carved onyx arch and hung from a black silk cord (see 95.1). The carved jade with the watch was removed in 1927 and re-entered for stock on its own. Then in 1929 the present brooch-pendant was added, with an additional ruby and diamond loop beneath the body of the lion. The incorporation of antiquities or oriental carvings into Cartier designs was not always successful with their clientele, and, despite various modifications, this piece did not sell.

Another closely similar jade seal with a lion on a rectangular plinth, also dated 1924 and set with a watch at the base, within an onyx ring suspended on a black silk cord, appears in the photograph albums (Barracca *et al.* 1989, p. 98).

110 Pair of jade earrings

Made by American Art Works for Cartier New York for stock, 1926

Jade, red enamel, diamonds set in platinum. Jade discs with red enamel Chinese character in the centre, hung from diamond and coral bead chains. Screw fittings with milled platinum wire wheels at each end of screw thread.

Entered in stock book on 11 August 1926; sold December 1932.

MARKS Engraved *CARTIER* on chain.

L. 5 cm

Private collection

EXHIBITIONS Los Angeles 1982, cat. 71.

The Chinese character is a corrupted form of the *shou* or long life character, often depicted within a roundel. The red enamel was no doubt intended to imitate Chinese lacquer.

111 *Lacque burgauté* powder box and lipstick tube

Designed in 1926 and made by Lavabre for Cartier Paris for stock, 1927

Enamelled gold, emeralds, lapis lazuli, *lacque burgauté*, diamonds set in platinum. The powder box set with two *lacque burgauté* roundels depicting figures in a landscape, on one side a gentleman and attendant boy on horseback and, on the other, a scholar holding a book, with attendant boy carrying a musical instrument. A compartment on each side, the mirrored lids with diamond push-pieces opening from the top; hinges at base. The sides with foliate scroll pattern in deep blue and green relief enamel, the green translucent enamel on an engine-turned ground. The chain formed of emerald cylinders and lapis lazuli discs attached to box with lapis and diamond loop. The lipstick tube decorated with matching blue and green relief enamel, the ends enamelled black and set with a cabochon emerald.

Entered in stock book on 18 January 1927; sold 19 August 1927 to Mrs Louis Cartier.

MARKS Box: inner rim of one lid engraved *Cartier Paris*; both lids with Paris eagle's head assay mark for gold and French third standard gold mark. Tube: inner tube with *MECAN* (for *Mécanisme*, indicating the use of base metal parts) and French third standard gold mark.

DIAM. of box 5.3 cm, L. of tube 5.5 cm. Total H. 11. 7 cm

Cartier collection, VC 55 A27

RELATED MATERIAL Original design in pencil, ink and watercolour on buff tracing paper, in Stock Design Record Book, 1926, p. 79, in Paris archive.

This is the first of a group of similar powder boxes and matching lipsticks, all executed within a few months of each other. The second was identical in design, but with different scenes on the lacquer plaques; the original design is in the Stock Design Record Book, 1927, p. 55b, also given to Lavabre and completed in early 1927. The third example was entered in the stock book on 10 December 1927. It did not sell. The box was separated from the tube in 1932 and dismantled in 1949. The lipstick tube was re-entered for stock on 3 June 1932 and sold on 24 November 1932. It was acquired for the Cartier collection in 1989 (see Christie's Geneva, 16 November 1989, lot 404, and Limoges 1992, cat. 115, pl. 48).

Unlike the enamelling on cat. 117, which is taken directly from Chinese sources, the enamel scroll pattern used here is a debased form of Chinese scroll found on the borders of blue and white porcelain and on textiles and carpets. For a similar pattern of relief enamelling, see cat. 144.

111

111

Lacque burgauté is the name generally given to lacquer with inlays of mother-of-pearl tinted pink, green, blue and purple to provide brilliant contrasts, often with additional gold and silver foil inlays, on a black ground (*burgau* = mother-of-pearl mussel). Although the technique is of Chinese origin, it spread to the Ryukyu islands between China and Japan in the Qing dynasty and thence to Japan, which became the centre of the industry in the nineteenth century. Most of the lacquer used by Cartier is likely to have been made in Ryukyu or in Japan.

Cartier incorporated similar *lacque burgauté* panels into a number of vanities, cigarette cases and clocks. For other examples, see Nadelhoffer 1984, col. pls 36 and 38; Los Angeles 1982, cat. 18, 57, 73 and 91.

112

112.1 Archive photographs of lacquer vases containing 'a magic barometer flower' ordered by James A. de Rothschild in 1926 as Christmas presents. He ordered thirty-four vases in all, being a mixture of the four designs.

112 *Lacque burgauté* vase

Made by Lavabre for Cartier Paris to the order of Baron James Armand de Rothschild, 1926

Lacque burgauté, red lacquer, mounted in gold. Four-sided vase, with lacquer panels on each side of body and neck, depicting landscapes with figures and buildings (fragments of mother-of-pearl inlay missing). Red lacquer inlay on angled shoulders and round edge of square rim.

Completed in December 1926. Sold Christie's Geneva, *The Robert Greene Collection of Art Deco*, 16 November 1982, lot 516.

MARKS Mount at base engraved *Cartier*; French third standard gold mark three times on gold mount.

H. 12.5 cm

Cartier collection, IV 01 A26

EXHIBITIONS London 1988, cat. 303.

This lacquer vase was one of thirty-four commissioned by James de Rothschild (1878–1957) of Waddesdon Manor, near Aylesbury, Buckinghamshire, at the beginning of November 1926 as Christmas presents. The order book lists a number of lacquer panels already in stock as well as panels purchased specially for this commission from L. Michon Frère and the Compagnie de la Chine et des Indes. The thirty-four vases comprised four different models, each containing a rose spray, with a card that read:

THE MAGIC BAROMETER FLOWER
This little flower you must grant
Is something of a sensitive plant.
Place it in the open air,
T'is pink when stormy, blue when fair,
And turns a lovely lilac hue,
When undecided which t'will do.

112.1 shows contemporary archive photographs of the four models. Different quantities were made of each model. From the prices quoted in the order book it appears that, reading the photographs from left to right, fourteen examples were made of model 1, three of model 2, ten of model 3 and seven of model 4. The Cartier collection vase is model 3 (these figures must be read as a possible interpretation only).

Another vase from this group is to be found in the Lindemann collection: see New Orleans 1988, pl. XXXVII. It is model 4 on the archive photograph and survives with its original red leather case. All thirty-four vases were supplied with leather cases. They were undoubtedly inspired by nineteenth- or early twentieth-century snuff bottles of *lacque burgauté* made in Japan for the Japanese market.

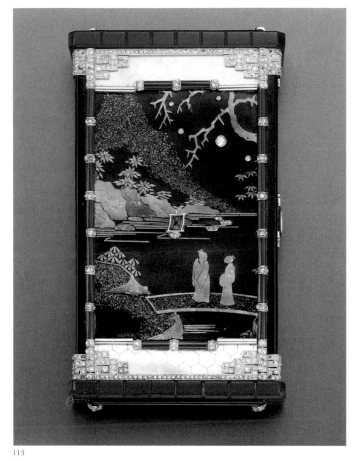

113

113

113 *Lacque burgauté* vanity case

Made by Lavabre for Cartier Paris for stock, 1929

Lacque burgauté, enamelled gold, carnelian, jade, mother-of-pearl, emeralds, sapphires and diamonds set in platinum. Two lacquer plaques depicting night scenes on each side, framed with rods of carnelian with diamond 'joints' imitating bamboo stems; plaques of mother-of-pearl honeycomb inlay top and bottom with geometric diamond motifs at the corners. Jade sides bordered with black enamel; diamond push-piece. The lacquer panels studded with diamond moon and stars, an emerald and a sapphire. Interior with mirrored lid,

two compartments (for powder and rouge), lipstick with holder and space for comb.

Entered in stock book on 7 February 1929; sold 11 September 1929.

MARKS Inside lid engraved *Cartier Paris Londres New York* and *MADE IN FRANCE*; Paris eagle's head assay mark for gold.

L. 9.2 cm, W. 5.2 cm

Lindemann collection. Sold Christie's Geneva, 17 November 1988, lot 469

RELATED MATERIAL Original design in pencil, ink, watercolour and bodycolour on grey-green tracing paper in Stock Design Record Book, 1928, p. 51c, in Paris archive.

114

114 Chinese dragon vanity case

Designed in 1926 and made by Renault for Cartier Paris for stock, 1927

Enamelled gold, emeralds, onyx, diamonds set in platinum. Red enamel ground, the front with black dragon with emerald horns and Chinese clouds in blue, the back with moon and cloud motifs and cabochon emeralds. The sides in fluted onyx and diamonds. Opened by pressing two of the diamond studs at top. Interior with two compartments and lipstick.

Entered in stock book on 6 April 1927; sold 30 April 1928.

MARKS *Cartier Paris Londres New York* inside lid; Paris eagle's head assay mark for gold.

H. 9.7 cm

Private collection

EXHIBITIONS Los Angeles 1982, cat. 12.

LITERATURE Nadelhoffer 1984, col. pl. 33; Cologni and Mocchetti 1992, p. 102 (with colour illustration of design).

RELATED MATERIAL Original design in ink, watercolour and bodycolour on ochre tracing paper from Stock Design Record Book, 1926, p. 58a, in Paris archive (exhibited Paris 1989, cat. 342).

The red ground was no doubt intended to imitate Chinese lacquer. The executed object thus differs significantly from the design, where the background is black, the dragon purple with emerald horns, claws and eyes, and the clouds black with gold outlines.

The dragon itself is probably taken from Chinese embroidered textiles of the eighteenth and nineteenth centuries: for an example, see V. Wilson, *Chinese Dress*, London 1986, pl. 30.

118 Evening bag

Made by Renault for Cartier Paris for stock, 1924

The mount of enamelled gold and diamonds set in platinum. The bag of black velvet, a modern replacement. The mount enamelled black and set with two plaques of oynx on each side, each plaque with diamond border comprising central geometric motif and ending in dragons' heads; the front with rectangular tag of onyx and diamonds. The catch pavé-set with diamonds on an enamelled base. Hung from two black silk cords with black enamel and diamond slides to alter the length as desired.

Entered in stock book on 31 January 1924, with bag of reindeer skin lined with cream watered silk; sold 16 October 1924.

MARKS Paris eagle's head assay mark for gold and workshop mark R with a crescent and flame (?) inside mount.

W. of mount 9.8 cm, L. of bag (without handles) 19.2 cm

Cartier collection, EB 24 A24

The dragons are loosely inspired by inlay patterns on ancient Chinese bronzes.

118 (greatly reduced)

118.1 Detail of cat. 118.

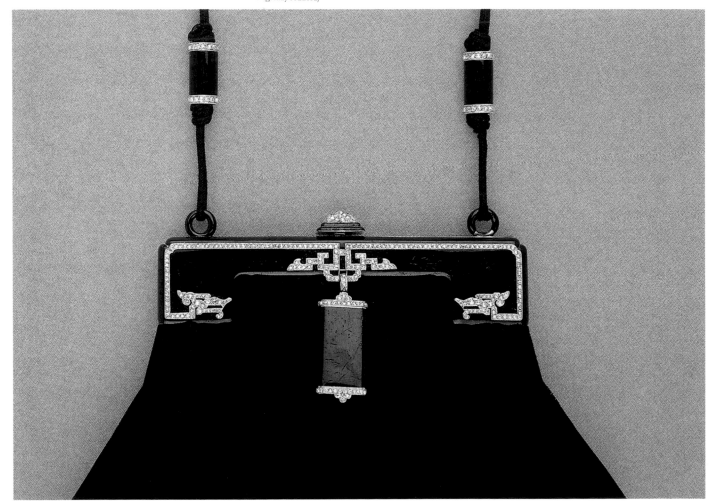

119 Diamond dragon brooch

Made by Renault for Cartier Paris for stock, 1925

Rock crystal, enamel, onyx and diamonds in open-back platinum setting. A barrel-shaped ring of polished rock crystal with faceted sides, the inside lined with black enamel; at each end a diamond motif forming the head and tail of a dragon looking left, with onyx eye. Cliquet fitting as on cat. 181: the dragon's head is hinged and turns forward to release the pin.

Entered in stock book on 12 June 1925; sold 28 September 1925 to Mrs R. Townsend. Sold Sotheby's New York, *Jewels from the Estate of Thora Ronalds McElroy*, 23 April 1991, lot 23.

MARKS On reverse of fitting *CARTIER BTE SGDG*; French dog's head assay mark for platinum.

W. 5.7 cm

Cartier collection, CL 135 A25

EXHIBITIONS St Petersburg 1992, cat. 143; Lausanne 1996, cat. 187.

LITERATURE Cologni and Nussbaum 1995, p. 125.

RELATED MATERIAL Original design in pencil, ink, watercolour and bodycolour on buff tracing paper in Stock Design Record Book, 1925, p. 12c, with initials R.R. for René Révillon, given to the Renault workshop on 29 April, for delivery on 30 May. The same page has a design for a larger version of this brooch (illustrated in Lausanne 1996, cat. 187).

Like those on the evening bag (cat. 118), the dragon here is loosely inspired by inlay patterns on ancient Chinese bronzes, which were often in the form of repeating patterns of square blocks, so that the motif was squashed into a square or rectangular format.

For other Cartier pieces owned by Mrs R. Townsend, see cat. 2 and 13.

120 Buddha earrings

Made by American Art Works for Cartier New York for stock, 1928

Carved jade Buddhas, onyx, enamel, diamonds in open-back platinum setting. The Buddhas surrounded by diamond flames against a black enamel ground. Floral motif at top and bottom and loop set with onyx. Original screw-fittings altered to hooks.

Entered in stock book on 19 July 1928; sold 13 September 1928.

MARKS On rim *CARTIER*.

L. 5.8 cm

Cartier collection, EG 11 A28

EXHIBITIONS Tokyo 1995, cat. 172.

LITERATURE Nadelhoffer 1984, col. pl. 31.

The source of inspiration for the flames sur-

119 (greatly enlarged)

120

rounding the Buddha is unclear. The flames could be intended to refer to the miracle of Śrāvastī, when the Buddha's supernatural power manifested itself in flames issuing from his shoulders, but the carved jade figures look much more like Budai, the fat, laughing Buddha, who would not be represented with flames.

121

121.1 Detail of cat. 121.

121 'Pagoda' vanity case

Made by Lavabre for Cartier Paris for stock, 1927

Enamelled gold; round, square and baguette diamonds set in platinum. Enamelled black all over with applied diamond-set pagoda on the lid, diamond borders with geometric motifs, diamond push-piece. Interior with mirrored lid, two compartments for rouge and powder with original gauze sifters and central lipstick holder.

Entered in stock book on 14 May 1927; sold 8 August 1927.

MARKS Inside lid engraved *Cartier Paris Londres New York*; Paris eagle's head assay mark for gold and workshop mark *HL* flanking a four-leaf clover on all three lids.

L. 8.5 cm, W. 5 cm

Cartier collection, VC 11 A27

EXHIBITIONS Paris 1989, cat. 349; Tokyo 1995, cat. 201.

LITERATURE Cologni and Nussbaum 1995, p. 150.

RELATED MATERIAL Original design in pencil, ink, watercolour and bodycolour on buff tracing paper in Stock Design Record Book, 1927, p. 69b, in Paris archive.

The black enamel circular motif in the centre of the pagoda is probably intended as the Chinese character for 'longevity', but it has been much simplified.

122 Gravity clock

Made by Couet for Cartier Paris for stock, 1927

Jade, coral, onyx, enamelled gold, diamonds set in platinum. In the form of a Japanese Shinto shrine gate with jade columns and cross-bar set with coral 'rivets'; coral bases to columns and onyx plinth. The gold clock set with carved Chinese jade plaques of birds in fruiting branches on both front and back, with diamond hands and numerals on a black enamel ground. Further jade plaques encrusted with rubies at each side and black enamel stylised beasts round the edge.

Entered in stock book on 9 December 1927, originally with two jade Dogs of Fo on top of the portico; sold 13 July 1943. Sold Sotheby's New York, 3 March 1994, lot 143 (collection of Barbra Streisand).

MARKS Paris eagle's head assay mark for gold and workshop mark inside clock case.

H. 24.5 cm, W. 12.5 cm

Cartier collection, CD 134 A27

EXHIBITIONS Tokyo 1995, cat. 226.

LITERATURE Nadelhoffer 1984, p. 148.

This gravity clock was the only example ever made by Cartier. It remained in stock unsold for sixteen years. Various later modifications were carried out and it was finally sold without the jade Dogs of Fo in 1942.

The gravity clock or pillar clock belongs to a group classified as semi-mystery clocks. The clock itself is the driving weight and slides down the pillar, controlled by a system of wheels. When it reaches the bottom it has to be moved to the top again by hand, and the process is repeated. The clock takes a week to reach the bottom. Although the principle goes back to the seventeenth century, gravity clocks were first widely produced c. 1900–10. English patents were taken out in 1919 and American patents followed in 1921 (see A. and R. Shenton, *The Price Guide to Collectable Clocks 1840–1940*, Woodbridge 1985, pp. 264–5).

The stylised beasts round the outside of the clock are inspired by inlay patterns on ancient Chinese Eastern Zhou bronzes of the seventh to eighth century BC, usually inlaid in gold in square or rectangular shapes. For an example of such decoration see D. Lion-Goldschmidt, *Chinese Art*, Oxford 1980, pl. 42.

The jade plaque is close in size and decoration to Chinese Qing dynasty examples.

123 Shinto shrine gate mystery clock

Made by Couet for Cartier Paris for stock, 1923

Rock crystal, onyx, enamelled gold, coral, diamonds set in platinum. In the form of a Japanese Shinto shrine gate with columns of rock crystal and enamelled gold, the bases of onyx and stepped rock crystal; onyx entablature set with coral cabochons and a carved rock-crystal seated figure with upturned feet. The twelve-sided rock-crystal dial hung from a rock-crystal cross-bar, the diamond-set numerals on a black enamel ground, diamond hands.

Entered in stock book on 29 January 1923; sold 31 January (?) 1923 to Mrs H. F. McCormick (Ganna Walska).

MARKS Gold base engraved at the front *Fait par Cartier Paris Londres New York*.

H. 35 cm, base 24 × 13 cm

Cartier collection, CM 09 A23

EXHIBITIONS Los Angeles 1982, cat. 4; London 1988, cat. 117, pl. XXII; Naples 1988, cat. 39; Paris 1989, cat. 383; Rome 1990, cat. 167; St Petersburg 1992, cat. 174; Hong Kong 1995, p. 39; Tokyo 1995, cat. 214; Lausanne 1996, cat. 108.

LITERATURE Nadelhoffer 1984, pp. 252–3; Barracca *et al.* 1989, p. 101; Cologni and Mocchetti 1992, p. 80.

This is one of six celebrated mystery clocks in the form of Japanese Shinto shrine gates produced by Cartier Paris between 1923 and 1925, as a result of a collaboration between Louis Cartier and Maurice Couet (1885–1963). For a full list of all six, described as 'portico clocks', see Nadelhoffer 1984, pp. 352–3 and col. pls 54 (crystal columns crowned with Buddha, 1924) and 56 (pink quartz columns, 1924). For other examples, see New York 1976, cat. 100 (rock crystal with Buddhist lion to left, 1925), and New Orleans 1988, pl. LXV (Linde-mann collection, 1924). Characteristically, they all combine Japanese and Chinese elements. The dials hang from a secondary cross-bar inspired by the frame for a Chinese gong. Van Cleef & Arpels produced a similar Japanese temple gate clock in 1926, probably copying Cartier models, in rock crystal, onyx and black enamel (Gabardi 1989, p. 12).

The Japanese temple gate clocks are a variant of Cartier's second mystery clock model (see cat. 69), with pendent dial and transmission to the hands via a central axle from the movement contained in the roof instead of the base. In this example the movement is beneath the rock-crystal figure.

The figure with upturned feet first appears in the Cartier records *c.* 1910, set on an ivory perch with hardstone plinth, like the carved hardstone birds (see Nadelhoffer 1984, col. pl. 74 and p. 95). The figure was described by Cartier as 'Billeken, the Anglo-Saxon god of happiness', and indeed the figure on this clock is described on the stock sheet as a 'Billeken'. But there is no such Anglo-Saxon or Norse deity. Nadelhoffer notes that this may have been based on pure invention (1984, ch. 6, n. 13).

Alternatively, the figure may have been inspired by Hotei, the Japanese fat-bellied god of happiness, but he is never depicted with upturned feet. Nevertheless, the figure does indeed appear to have a Japanese association and this would explain why Cartier placed it on a Shinto temple gate. An identical figure is to be found in the Tsutenkaku, a would-be Eiffel Tower in the centre of Osaka, destroyed by fire in 1943 and rebuilt in 1980. The figure, described as 'Piriken' or 'Piliken', has a box for money offerings in front of him; those who throw in a coin will have their wish granted if they tickle the soles of his feet (this information comes from a recent Japanese newspaper clipping shown to me by Victor Harris). The precise origin of 'Piriken' or 'Biliken' still remains a mystery.

The Polish soprano Ganna Walska was the second wife of Harold Fowler McCormick (1872–1941), president of the International Harvester Company of Chicago and son of Cyrus Hall McCormick, who invented the reaping machine that revolutionised farming. Harold Fowler McCormick's first wife was Edith Rockefeller, from 1895 to 1921. He married Ganna Walska in August 1922; his third wife was Adah Wilson, whom he married in 1938. He was also a client of Fabergé's London shop (see San Francisco 1996, pp. 29 and 349–50).

123 ▶

Fait par Cartier   Paris-Londres-New York

CARTIER COLOUR COMBINATIONS

Most original is the combination of carved coral, of the old-fashioned type, with large uncut emeralds,

diamonds and onyx. This daring color harmony is another Cartier invention, which is gradually growing

in popularity. It, however, requires very careful handling, the combination being rather dangerous.

(Baron de Meyer in *Harper's Bazaar*, New York, March 1926)

This comment was made with reference to Cartier jewellery at the 1925 Paris Exhibition and precisely defines the nature of Cartier's colour combinations. They were new, daring and dangerous. Some had been introduced before 1925, for example blue and green. But all of them were to be seen at that exhibition and must have created a sensation. The following groups are arranged purely by their colour combinations.

(a) Blue and green

The blue and green combination has already been discussed in the introduction to section 6 with reference to blue and green enamel. The dominant materials used, in addition to enamel, are jade, lapis lazuli and turquoise. An American newspaper of 9 August 1928 noted that 'Parisian women cast envious glances at Cartier's windows, with their new collections of bracelets that join jade with lapis, jade with sapphires, jade with topaz'.[1] The combination of jade and sapphires had been used since 1913, in the designs of Charles Jacqueau (see cat. 29 and 238). But by the 1920s, jade might be combined with black enamel (cat. 126–7), blue enamel (cat. 130 and 135) or lapis lazuli (cat. 134). Lapis lazuli in its turn was combined with turquoise, a combination derived from ancient Egypt (cat. 137–8) and discussed in the introduction to section 4. Kingfisher feathers, used only occasionally and mainly for clock dials, provided blue-green reflections that changed according to the light.

(b) Multigem jewellery

Lapis lazuli was also occasionally combined with coral (cat. 139–40), but, as Baron de Meyer noted, the most startling combination was coral with emeralds, often large cabochon emeralds or emerald beads (cat. 141–4, 287 and 289–91). This group contains a bracelet sold to Daisy Fellowes and the dragon-head bracelet with carved coral heads, melon-cut emerald beads and hoop enamelled in blue and green that was sold to Ganna Walska.

Jade, lapis lazuli and turquoise are all semi-precious stones. Cartier's celebrated multigem jewellery relied on the combination of three precious gemstones – emeralds, rubies and sapphires – in the form of carved leaves and beads (cat. 152–9). Although this has in recent years been described as 'tutti frutti' jewellery, the term 'tutti frutti' was not used by Cartier at the time.[2] Cartier's contemporary descriptions of these pieces simply say 'pierres de couleur' (coloured stones). An article in the London magazine *The Graphic* for 17 May 1930 describes Cartier's jewellery with clusters of gems as 'Christmas tree' jewellery, but this term does not seem to have been widely adopted. The term used in this catalogue is 'multigem' jewellery, a term used by the London firm of Garrard in their ledgers of the 1920s and 1930s.

The carving of the stones into leaves was almost certainly done for Cartier in India, and, although stones carved in this way were not used in Indian jewellery, Cartier often used them for their jewels in the Indian style. These are discussed in section 5. The most celebrated example is the 'collier hindou' made for Daisy Fellowes in 1936, which itself used stones from earlier multigem jewellery not in the Indian style made by Cartier in the 1920s (cat. 106). One of the pieces used to make the 'collier hindou' was a multigem bracelet similar to those made for Mrs Cole Porter (cat. 155–6) and to one shown at the Paris 1925 Exhibition (cat. 285).

(c) Emeralds, onyx and diamonds

In addition to carved gemstone leaves, Cartier also incorporated into their jewellery huge numbers of emeralds in all forms from at least 1913. Carved Indian emeralds are discussed in detail in the introduction to section 5 and also under cat. 269, the 'collier Bérénice' shown at the Paris 1925 Exhibition. The emeralds included in this section are in the form of carved, faceted and cabochon stones and beads. They are mixed only with diamonds or onyx or black enamel, creating another of Cartier's stunning colour combinations – black, white and green (cat. 160–66). An example of 1913, combined also with pearls, is included in section 1b (cat. 30). The examples that follow all date from the early 1920s and include carved Indian emeralds with diamonds and onyx discs (cat. 165) or with 'panther-skin' ornament (cat. 163), or black enamel (cat. 166). Black enamel or onyx were often used to create the effect of a shadow along one edge: this is done with particular success in cat. 160–61.

By the later 1920s, the fashion seems to have veered towards emeralds and diamonds alone. According to a press cutting of May 1928 in the Cartier New York archive, Cartier was asked by a fashion magazine, sadly unidentified, to select jewels to accompany an imported beige crepe and wool model by Vionnet:

> Keeping in mind, the fact that the jewel is always an integral part of the ensemble and that color harmony plays an important role in the matter, Cartier has selected the vivid grass green gem – the emerald – as a fitting complement to the soft pastel tones of the gray beige. A subtle note is sounded in the seemingly simple emerald, sapphire and pearl necklace, worth a king's ransom, fashioned of graduated beads, which forms the nucleus of the jewelry ensemble. A glittering oblong, diamond and platinum brooch of emeralds and diamonds is used to hold the blouse in place and two flexible, platinum slave bracelets, mounted with emeralds, baguette and round diamonds may be worn on either wrist.
>
> … An ingenious bit of designing is displayed in the ultra-smart cliquet hat pins. A rare carved emerald combined with baguette diamonds is embodied in one, and rich blue carved lapis lazuli mounted with small emeralds in the other… Emeralds are decidedly the smart stone of today.

The fashion for emeralds and diamonds continued into the 1930s and two later examples are included here (cat. 168–9). Cat. 68 is set with an unusually large uncut rectangular emerald. It was probably left uncut because of its flaws.

(d) Onyx and diamonds

The combination of onyx (or black enamel) and diamonds goes back to the first decade of the century. Louis Cartier's Notebooks of *c.* 1906–7 list a group of onyx and diamond mourning jewellery ordered by Pierre Cartier. By 1910 the Notebooks refer to onyx and diamonds surprisingly as daytime wear. Two examples dating from 1913 are included in other sections, a wrist watch (cat. 27) and an Egyptian-style pendant (cat. 76). In a stock analysis of September 1919, the Notebooks record the following among items then in production: 'two new necklaces in onyx and diamonds', 'cliquet brooches in onyx and diamonds' and 'ten pairs of fancy earrings in onyx and diamonds'. One of these may have been the flower-head earrings of carved onyx made in 1919 (cat. 177). The years immediately after the First World War saw the production of large numbers of black and white watches, whether wrist watches (cat. 175), pocket watches (cat. 176) or pendant watches, usually hung on a black silk ribbon (cat. 174).

These were also the peak years of one of Cartier's great inventions, the so-called 'panther-skin' ornament, consisting of pavé-set diamonds studded with onyx chips, cabochons or tiny pyramids (see p. 17). Four examples are included here (cat. 170–73) and one in section 7c (cat. 163). Further examples, sometimes covering large areas of the jewel, are to be found in the designs for the 1925 Paris Exhibition (cat. 271–2, 277, 287).

Onyx and black enamel were also combined with another colourless material, rock crystal, to create a more subtle black and white contrast. Before 1914 rock-crystal plaques engraved with foliate scrollwork formed the basis of a series of elaborate Renaissance-revival pieces (cat. 16–19). But in the 1920s rock crystal was given a completely different treatment. Carved into rings or rectangles, polished or matt, it formed the basis for large brooches (cat. 182–3), belt clasps and belt brooches (cat. 181). In the 1930s, with the taste for more three-dimensional jewellery, it was carved into chunky rigid bangles with removable brooch centrepieces (cat. 185) or protruding clip brooches (cat. 184).

By the 1930s onyx was synonymous with elegance. Chips Channon described in his diaries a ball given by the Rutlands at Belton House in January 1935 for their daughters, one of whom was 'already out and is chic and sleek and onyx-y'.[3]

(e) Coral with black lacquer or onyx

Another elegant contrast was that of onyx or black lacquer with coral. Whereas onyx with brilliant-cut diamonds was an evening combination, the rounded surface of carved coral was generally considered suitable for daytime wear, and although no contemporary references to coral and black jewellery or accessories have been found, it is likely that these pieces were intended for daytime use. The use of black lacquer on silver as a cheaper substitute for enamelled gold has been discussed in section 3. But there was another reason for using black lacquer: it was significantly more resistant to chipping than enamel and so was ideally suited to the vanity case. Several examples are included here, all with coral clasps and the occasional diamond.

NOTES
1. Cartier New York press clippings book (newspaper unidentified).
2. It appears to have been adopted for bakelite fruit jewellery in the 1940s, inspired by Carmen Miranda's famous number 'The Lady in the Tutti Frutti Hat', choreographed by Busby Berkeley in the 1943 Hollywood film *The Gang's All Here*. But this has nothing to do with Cartier's gemstone jewellery.
3. Rhodes James (ed.) 1967, p. 21.

124 Jade mystery clock

Made by Couet in Paris for stock, 1923

Enamelled gold, jade, onyx, rock crystal, diamonds set in platinum. The screen mounted on a plinth of jade and onyx with two semicircular onyx rings and an onyx sphere on the base; the dial of rock crystal, diamond hands, numerals reserved in gold on a white enamel chapter-ring, with a row of jade cylinders above and below.

Imported into America by the European Watch & Clock Company and recorded in Cartier New York stock in 1923.

MARKS On base *CARTIER.N.Y. No.786 European Watch & Clock Co. Inc. France, 13 Jewels*; Paris eagle's head assay mark for gold.

H. 13.7 cm, L. 11 cm, W. 7 cm

Cartier collection, CM 07 A23

EXHIBITIONS Naples 1988, cat. 112; London 1988, cat. 116, pl. XXI; Paris 1989, cat. 382; Rome 1990, cat. 166; St Petersburg 1992, cat 173.

LITERATURE Nadelhoffer 1984, col. pl. 58.

The system used here is that of the second mystery clock model (see cat. 69), that is, a central axle system with motive power carried through a hollow sphere at the base.

Most other examples of this type had coral cylinders framing the dial; this is the only one with jade. The jade cylinders imitate bamboo, a symbol of rectitude in ancient China and an appropriate ornament for a clock that was no doubt intended to recall the carved jade rectangular screens mounted on stands and traditionally used in China as ornaments on scholars' desks. But this is not a true screen clock because it has a transparent dial in the centre of the 'screen'. For a true screen clock incorporating a slab of carved jade, see cat. 107.

124

125 Cigarette holder

Made for Cartier Paris, *c.* 1925

Jade, onyx and diamonds set in platinum. Variegated jade with onyx mouthpiece and rings, two diamond rings at centre and tip of trumpet.

Similar pieces of *c.* 1925 recorded in Paris photograph volumes.

MARKS The wide end engraved *Cartier Paris, Londres, New York*.

L. 13.5 cm

Cartier collection, AG 25 C25

EXHIBITIONS Los Angeles 1982, cat. 54; Naples 1988, cat. 54; Paris 1989, cat. 334; Rome 1990, cat. 150; Tokyo 1995, cat. 192.

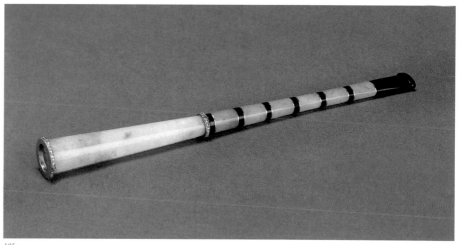

125

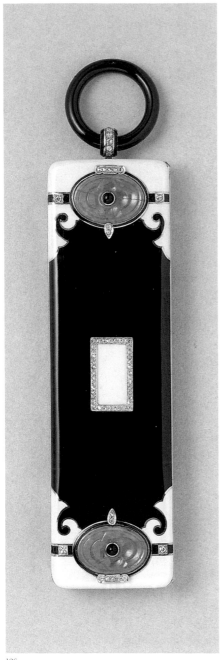

126 Vanity case

Made for Cartier New York, c. 1926

Enamelled gold, jade, onyx, sapphires, diamonds set in platinum. Oblong case enamelled in cream and black with central diamond-bordered rectangle, the front with two carved jade plaques set with diamonds and a central sapphire cabochon; onyx ring. Interior with mirrored lid and two compartments, the smaller one with separate clip-in lipstick inside the lid, both lids with sunken hinged handles, space in front for comb (see p. 118, fig. 63).

MARKS Engraved inside *Cartier N.Y.* and *18K*.

L. 11.4 cm, with loop 14.1 cm, W. 3.5 cm

Cartier collection, VC 25 C26

EXHIBITIONS London 1988, cat. 199; Paris 1989, cat. 344; Limoges 1992, cat. 101, pl. 47; Tokyo 1995, cat. 196.

There is no push-piece on this or cat. 135; they are both very flat and open with the fingernail. This long oblong shape is relatively rare, but occurs in examples made *c.* 1925–6 for Cartier London and Paris as well as New York. Most examples have a chain to which the ring is attached.

127 Cigarette case

Made by Renault for Cartier Paris for stock, 1928

Enamelled gold, jade, rubies, diamonds set in platinum. Oblong square-section box, reeded sides with bands of scale pattern in black enamel, each end set with a carved jade plaque encrusted with a ruby cabochon. Diamond push-piece.

Entered in stock book on 28 March 1928; sold 16 May 1928.

MARKS Engraved *CARTIER PARIS LONDRES NEW YORK MADE IN FRANCE*; Paris eagle's head assay mark for gold.

L. 8.6 cm, W. 2.7 cm

Cartier collection, CC 36 A28

EXHIBITIONS Naples 1988, cat. 116.

This square-section box is described in the Paris archive records as a 'ladies' cigarette case for 9 cigarettes'. The overlapping scale pattern is Chinese in origin. A matching lipstick case is recorded in the photograph albums.

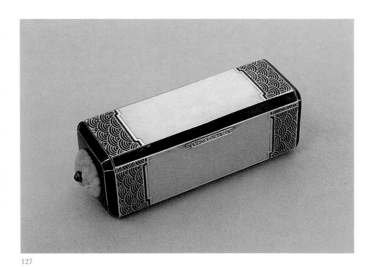

126

127

128 Desk clock

Made probably by Couet for Cartier Paris for stock, c. 1929

Rock crystal, enamelled gold, rubies, jade, diamonds set in platinum. Arched rock-crystal frame with rock-crystal support, dial of blue enamel with central jade roundel, diamond-set numerals and hands; six rubies round edge and on hour hand. At base, two stylised trees of carved jade in ruby pots, bordered with blue enamel.

A similar piece made by the Couet workshop entered in stock book on 6 November 1929.

MARKS Engraved on reverse of clock *Cartier*; movement with *E.W.C. Co. Inc.* for the European Watch & Clock Company.

H. 9.7 cm, W. 7.9 cm

Cartier collection, CD 30 C29

EXHIBITIONS Naples 1988, cat. 86; Tokyo 1995, cat. 236; Lausanne 1996, cat. 73.

LITERATURE Nadelhoffer 1981, col. pl.55; Barracca *et al.* 1989, p.179.

The central carved jade roundel is a Chinese button of the nineteenth century.

129

128

129 Cigarette case

Made by Lavabre for Cartier Paris for stock, 1929

Enamelled gold, agate, emerald, rubies, diamonds set in platinum. Formed of two agate plaques, the gold mounts enamelled with blue and white borders and two motifs top and bottom; a geometric pattern round the sides in blue and green enamel. In centre of lid a square diamond-bordered enamelled plaque with fruit bowl, cup and pavé-set diamond gourd-shaped vase on a tray, the fruit formed of a cabochon emerald and rubies and two diamonds, all on an engine-turned ground. Carved sapphire push-piece.

Entered in stock book on 29 October 1929; transferred to New York for sale on 28 August 1930.

MARKS Rim of base engraved *Cartier Paris Londres New York MADE IN FRANCE*; Paris eagle's head assay mark for gold and workshop mark on spring fitting for catch.

L. 8.2 cm, W. 5.5 cm

Cartier collection, CC 35 A29

EXHIBITIONS Naples 1988, cat. 49.

Several elements of this box are inspired by Chinese sources. The central Chinese style gem-set plaque shows a Chinese gourd-vase, bowl and cup (see half-title page), while the blue and green enamel pattern round the sides is derived from Chinese running border patterns. For a closely similar agate box, see New York 1976, cat. 62. The gem-set plaque has a similar still-life scene with enamelled and gem-set objects on a tray, set on a jade background. The push-piece is a carved ruby.

130   Vanity case

Made by Couet for Cartier Paris for stock, 1927

Enamelled gold, with jade ends, sapphire push-piece and border of diamonds in square-cut platinum settings. All-over enamel pattern of overlapping horizontal bands reserved in polished gold on a deep blue enamel ground. Interior with mirrored lid, lipstick complete with tube and powder compartment complete with puff; space at front for comb.

Entered in stock book on 20 May 1927; sold to Baron Edmond de Rothschild on 2 February 1928.

MARKS Engraved on rim of lid *CARTIER*; lipstick with Paris third standard gold mark.

L. 8.4 cm, W. 5.2 cm

Cartier collection, VC 18 A27

EXHIBITIONS Limoges 1992, cat. 113.

The pattern of overlapping horizontal bands of different lengths is inspired by cloud patterns in Japanese painted hand-scrolls. This example is somewhat stylised, but two other vanity cases recorded in the Paris photograph albums have comparable patterns with 'clouds' reserved in gold on a black enamel ground, where the inspiration is evident. Cat. 130.1 illustrates a seventeenth-century copy of an eleventh-century hand-scroll depicting the adventures of Prince Genji, with the cloud patterns in pale blue.

    The purchaser of this vanity case, Edmond de Rothschild (1845–1934), owned a distinguished collection of French eighteenth-century gold boxes which came to Waddesdon Manor through his son James (see cat. 43 and 112).

130

130.1 Seventeenth-century Japanese painted hand-scroll, with cloud patterns in pale blue. Such patterns are the ultimate source for the design on cat. 130. British Museum, Japanese Painting no. 183.

131   Powder box and lipstick

Made by Renault for Cartier Paris for stock, 1927

Enamelled gold, jade, sapphires. Both compact and lipstick with striped cream enamel (*émail pékin mille raies*), the compact with central carved jade flower basket with high handle, set with cabochon sapphires and a calibré-cut sapphire foot, dark blue enamel motifs at the corners, sapphire push-piece at top; the lipstick with jade ends set with sapphire cabochons and central band of calibré sapphires. Enamelled gold chain with jade and sapphire marquetry links. Interior of compact with mirrored lid and original powder puff (see p. 117, fig. 61).

Entered in stock book on 26 April 1927; sold 6 May 1927 to Mrs C. H. Sherill.

MARKS Paris eagle's head assay mark for gold and workshop mark *R* with a crescent and flame (?) inside lid of compact and on gold loop for puff and lipstick.

131

Compact: W. 5.2 cm. Lipstick: W. 5.4 cm. Total H. 10.2 cm

Cartier collection, AL 41 A27

EXHIBITIONS London 1988, cat. 339, pl. XLIII; Limoges 1992, cat. 114.

Jade plaques carved with flower baskets were made as pendants in the eighteenth and nineteenth centuries. The flower basket was also a popular decorative motif on Chinese blue and white porcelain: see also cat. 151.

Charles Hitchcock Sherill (1867–1936) was an American ambassador to Turkey. He married in 1906 Miss G. Baker, daughter of the late Edward N. Gibbs of New York.

132 Bracelet
(bracelet égyptien)

Designed by Charles Jacqueau and made by Lavabre for Cartier Paris for stock, 1921

Enamelled gold; emeralds, sapphires and diamonds set in platinum. Gold hoop with white enamel dashes and black enamel bands at terminals and at hinge. One terminal with faceted octagonal emerald surrounded by calibré-cut emeralds and diamonds, the other with faceted oval sapphire surrounded by calibré-cut sapphires and diamonds.

Entered in stock book on 17 February 1921; sold 23 June 1921. Sold Christie's Geneva, 27 May 1993, lot 813.

MARKS Rim of sapphire terminal engraved *Cartier Paris Londres New York*; Paris eagle's head assay mark for gold on terminals; French dog's head mark for platinum on rims of terminals.

W. 7 cm

Cartier collection, BT 65 A21

EXHIBITIONS Tokyo 1995, cat. 95.

RELATED MATERIAL Sheet of working sketches in pencil, pen and ink for closely similar bracelets amongst Jacqueau's working designs, no. 772.

One of the sketches by Jacqueau has exactly the same pattern of enamel dashes with black terminals, while another is coloured to indicate diamonds and black enamel, but there is no suggestion that the heads of the terminals were set with coloured stones.

Another bracelet from this group designed by Jacqueau was sold at Christie's Geneva, 15 May 1996, lot 21; it was decorated with black and cream enamel stripes, and the terminals had diamond-studded onyx discs. For a third example, see Nadelhoffer 1984, p. 193, fig. 114.

The name 'bracelet égyptien' does not relate to an ancient Egyptian prototype; what

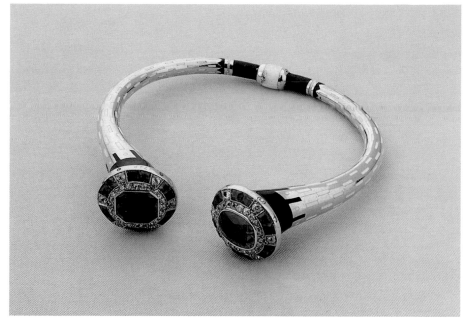

132

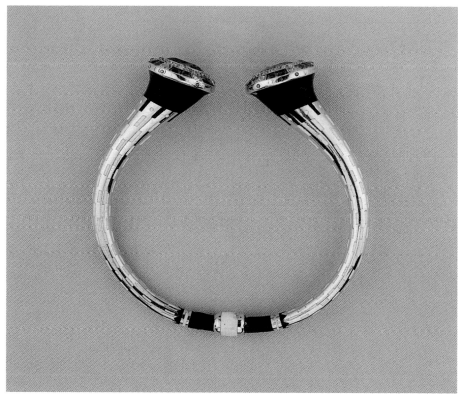

132

Jacqueau was probably looking at were the copper or brass trading bangles found in West Africa and known as manillas. These had the same form of hoop with expanding trumpet-shaped terminals as Bronze Age Irish bracelets. Cartier often gave exotic-sounding names to their pieces. Cat. 187 is described as a 'bracelet soudanais' in the archive records. Both bracelets are in fact loosely derived from African sources.

133 Vanity case and lipstick

Made for Cartier New York (workshop unknown), 1925

Enamelled gold, sapphires, turquoises and diamonds set in platinum. Enamelled white all over, with diamond-set hinges and corners; in centre of lid a motif in pavé-set diamonds, with a lozenge-shaped turquoise between two cabochon sapphires and a row of turquoises either side. Two further sapphires above and below. Interior with mirrored lid and two compartments, the lids engraved LILYAN LOVE JOSE 1932.

Dated to 1925 by the New York archive photograph.

MARKS *Cartier N.Y.* inside lid.

L. 7.7 cm

Lindemann collection. Given by Joseph S. Lindemann to his wife in 1932.

EXHIBITIONS New Orleans 1988, pl. XLV.

LITERATURE Cologni and Mocchetti 1992, p. 113.

The archive photograph shows the case as originally made, with matching lipstick tube attached with a white-enamelled chain (133.1).

134 Belt buckle

Made by Bellemans for Cartier Paris for stock, 1928

Carved jade plaque, enamelled gold mounts, turquoises and sapphires. Rectangular jade plaque set with four sapphires at each corner, two turquoise talismans engraved in Arabic and set with sapphires, one of which forms the clasp, deep blue enamelled mounts and two separate slides in deep blue enamel set with turquoises. Mounted by Cartier on modern fabric.

Entered in stock book on 30 June 1928; sold 10 December 1928 to Mr. R. Stuyvesant. Originally with deep blue watered silk belt, to which the slides were attached, to alter the length as desired.

MARKS Reverse engraved *CARTIER MADE IN FRANCE*; Paris eagle's head assay mark for gold and workshop mark JB flanking a bell.

L. 6.7 cm, W. 3.1 cm

Cartier collection, AL 40 A28

EXHIBITIONS London 1988, cat. 357; Paris 1989, cat. 362; Hong Kong 1995, cat. 45.

133

133.1 Archive photograph of cat. 133 as originally made by Cartier New York in 1925. At that time the lipstick was attached by an enamelled gold chain.

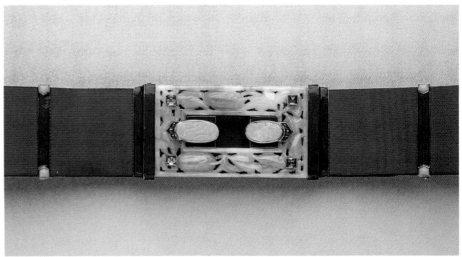

134

135 Vanity case

Made for Cartier New York (workshop unknown) for stock, *c.* 1925

Enamelled gold, jade, sapphires, diamonds set in platinum, with rock-crystal ring. The oblong case enamelled in royal blue and light blue; in the centre, a jade disc carved with flowers and fruit set with diamonds and cabochon sapphires. Further gem-set strap motifs at top and bottom on both sides. Interior with mirrored lid and two compartments, the smaller one with separate clip-in lipstick inside the case; space at front for comb.

MARKS Engraved inside *Cartier NY*.

L. 11.4 cm, with loop 14.6 cm, w. 3.5 cm

Cartier collection, VC 20 C25

EXHIBITIONS London 1988, cat. 198, p. 143.

The Chinese jade disc would not originally have had a hole in the middle and has been recarved to take the gem-set motif in its centre. It was probably made originally as a pendant in the eighteenth or nineteenth century. See cat. 126 for another vanity case of this shape.

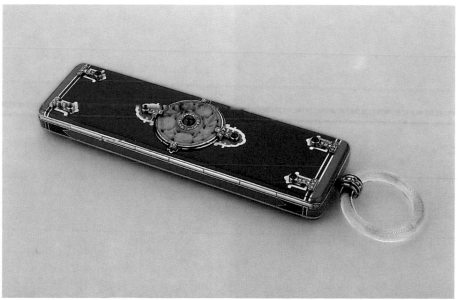

135

136 Belt buckle

Made by Droguet for Cartier Paris for stock in 1922, using the turquoise matrix from a sautoir made for stock in 1920

Two onyx rings, joined by large turquoise matrix with straps of diamonds, onyx and black lacquer and central onyx and diamond motif. The diamonds set in platinum, the turquoise and straps in gold, forming an ornamental openwork motif behind the turquoise. Straps at sides set with onyx and decorated with double row of black lacquer squares

Entered in stock book as belt buckle on 26 July 1922, with plaited black silk belt. Sold 5 August 1922.

MARKS Gold setting at back stamped *CARTIER PARIS*; Paris eagle's head assay mark for gold and workshop mark *HD* flanking a flower.

L. 11.4 cm, DIAM. of rings 5.1 cm

Cartier collection, AL 14 A22

EXHIBITIONS London 1988, cat. 169; Paris 1989, cat. 312; Rome 1990, cat. 140; Tokyo 1995, cat. 177.

LITERATURE Nadelhoffer 1984, col. pl. 43.

RELATED MATERIAL Original pencil and watercolour design in Stock Design Record Book for 1922, p. 95b, in Paris archive with black belt and the initials RP for René Prieur.

The sautoir which originally contained the turquoise matrix was entered for stock on 23

136

March 1920 and was made by Lavabre. It comprised turquoise and onyx beads and pearls strung on a long black silk cord, the large turquoise matrix at the base, with a pearl tassel hanging from its centre. It was sold in June 1920 but bought back into stock two days later and eventually dismantled. The remaining turquoise beads went to make two bracelets, the pearls to make a pearl tassel.

This is one of four belt buckles with onyx rings and turquoise matrix designed in 1922. Droguet made at least seven buckles of this type with turquoise matrix for Cartier; designs for three others are in the same Stock Design Record Book for 1922.

149 Ring

Made by Picq for Cartier Paris for stock, 1927

Emerald, rubies, sapphires and diamonds in platinum setting, with black enamel. A large carved emerald of 31.33 carats on a base of black enamel, the shoulders each set with rubies, a sapphire and diamonds, edged in black enamel.

Entered in stock book on 28 December 1927; sold 14 June 1928.

MARKS Engraved *CARTIER PARIS MADE IN FRANCE* inside hoop; French dog's head assay mark for platinum and workshop mark *HP* flaking an ace of spades.

H. 3.4 cm

Cartier collection, RG 21 A27

EXHIBITIONS New York 1976, cat. 7; Los Angeles 1982, cat. 81; Tokyo 1995, cat. 164.

LITERATURE Nadelhoffer 1984, col. pl. 26.

A number of rings of this type were made in London as well as in Paris. A closely similar one was made for Cartier London in 1928 with an emerald of 48.80 carats (English Art Works job record book, August 1928, with pencil working sketch).

The criss-cross pattern of cutting on the emerald is not found on Mughal emeralds and must have been done specially for Cartier, probably by an Indian lapidary.

150 Flower vase brooch

Made by English Art Works for Cartier London for stock, 1928

Emeralds, rubies, sapphires, pearls and diamonds in open-back platinum setting. The vase set with a large hexagonal carved emerald of 27.24 carats, carved on both sides; on the front a stylised lotus (?), on the back four triple-petal motifs. Four carved ruby leaves.

Job given to English Art Works on 11 June 1928, completed item entered in stock book on 7 August 1928. Sold 7 November 1928.

MARKS Lower edge engraved *Cartier Ld London*.

W. 4.7 cm, H. 3.7 cm. Carved emerald: 1.6 × 2 cm

Cartier collection, CL 98 A28

EXHIBITIONS Tokyo 1995, cat. 166.

RELATED MATERIAL (1) Pencil working sketch in English Art Works job record book, June 1928. (2) Original pencil, pen and ink and watercolour design in London Design Scrapbook.

149

150

151

151.1 Cat. 151 with terminals turned through 90 degrees to form an S-shape.

This brooch was made largely from stones in stock, described as follows:

1 emerald carved	27.14 carats
1 " "	0.50 "
4 ruby leaves	3.53 "
1 emerald boule	0.45 "
82 brilliants	2.38 "
6 button pearls	23.68 grams
1 pearl	6.24 "
2 pearls	2.48 "

English Art Works had to supply '2 cab. [cabochon] emeralds, 2 cab. rubies, 6 cab. sapphs, 8 roses. Mounting in platinum.'

The large double-sided carved emerald is a reused Indian stone of the late eighteenth or nineteenth century which has been drilled for suspension. The hole is just visible beneath the setting at the base, so originally it was worn the other way up. The smaller stones have cage settings typical of gem-set pieces of this period, with a central rib behind each stone or a cross in a circle for pearls or beads (see cat. 106.2).

A brooch of identical design but with different stones was illustrated in colour in a Cartier New York catalogue, *Gift Suggestions* of 1927.

151 Collapsible 'S'-type brooch

Made by Ploujavy in Paris and English Art Works in London for Cartier London for stock, 1930

Diamonds, rubies, sapphires and an emerald in open-back platinum setting. A bar with central carved emerald flanked by diamond-set terminals edged with a row of calibré-cut sapphires and set with three ruby beads, each with diamond stud. Each terminal mounted on expanding pivot to turn at right angles to the bar. Only one terminal can be moved at a time and only in one direction; the pin fitting slides out and back into place.

Entered in stock book on 27 October 1930; sold 21 February 1921. Sold Sotheby's Geneva, 15 May 1991, lot 376.

MARKS Rim engraved *CARTIER MADE IN FRANCE*; French dog's head assay mark for platinum and workshop mark comprising the letters *PL71* (or *PL71*) between a diagonal cross.

L. (straight) 3.3 cm

Cartier collection, CL 139 A30

EXHIBITIONS Tokyo 1995, cat. 254.

Brooches of this kind are described in the London archive records as 'collapsible S-type' or 'transformable' brooches. Only three others were produced, all for Cartier London stock, two set with diamonds and one with coloured

152

stones. The latter was entered in the stock book in September 1930 and was also made jointly by English Art Works in London and Ploujavy in Paris. It is not clear why these two brooches were partly made in Paris. According to the stock records for 1926, Ploujavy and English Art Works had previously worked jointly on other items, including buttons.

All four brooches were made between September 1930 and January 1931. The reason this type of brooch had such a short-lived vogue may have been that acquaintances of the first client were requesting similar items.

152 Bracelet with fruit bowl

Made by American Art Works for Cartier New York for stock, 1926

Diamonds, rubies, rock crystal, onyx, enamel, in open-back platinum setting. A central fruit bowl of carved rock crystal, the fruit of ruby beads studded with diamonds, set on a pavé-set diamond ground with black enamel border; clusters of four diamond-studded rubies on a square diamond plaque alternating with square rock-crystal links set with diamonds and onyx.

Entered in stock book on 11 August 1926; sold 30 December 1927. Sold Christie's Geneva, 21 May 1992, lot 746.

MARKS On rim *CARTIER*.

L. 18.7 cm

Cartier collection, BT 54 A26

EXHIBITIONS Tokyo 1995, cat. 155.

153 Chinese vase brooch

Made by American Art Works for Cartier New York for stock, 1927

Lapis lazuli, rubies, onyx, enamel and diamonds in open-back platinum setting. Carved lapis lazuli vase set with diamonds and a diamond handle, carved ruby leaves and berries of collet-set diamonds and onyx beads. The underside and right-hand side of the handle enamelled black to create the effect of a shadow.

Entered in stock book on 19 May 1927; sold 7 September 1927.

MARKS Base engraved *CARTIER*.

H. 4 cm

Cartier collection, CL 47 A27

EXHIBITIONS Los Angeles 1982, cat. 48; Paris 1989, cat. 284; Rome 1990, cat. 132; St Petersburg 1992, cat. 149; Tokyo 1995, cat. 160; Lausanne 1996, cat. 174.

LITERATURE Nadelhoffer 1984, col. pl. 47.

The design of this brooch is inspired directly by the flower vases with square handles depicted as central decorative motifs on Chinese blue and white porcelain plates of the Ming dynasty. The idea appears in the sixteenth century, but the designer of this brooch was probably looking at eighteenth-century examples.

153

154 (greatly enlarged)

154.1 Cat. 154 on its side, showing folding buckle.

154 Bracelet-watch

Made by Jaeger in Paris, c. 1930

Diamonds, emeralds, rubies, sapphires in open-back platinum setting, double black silk cord with gold *boucle déployante* (folding buckle) enamelled black. Baguette watch bordered with baguette-cut diamonds and two triangular-cut diamonds, the front part of the bracelet set with carved emerald, sapphire and ruby leaves, ruby beads and diamonds.

Not recorded in Paris archive.

MARKS On dial *CARTIER FRANCE*; Paris eagle's head assay mark for gold and workshop mark *EJ* flanking an hourglass on clasp; *E.W.C.Co.Inc.* on movement, for the European Watch & Clock Company.

W. of watch 0.6 cm

Cartier collection, WL 66 C30

EXHIBITIONS Milan 1988, p. 28; Paris 1989, cat. 436; Rome 1990, cat. 209; Tokyo 1995, cat. 278.

LITERATURE Cologni and Nussbaum 1995, p. 161.

This miniature piece of multigem jewellery combines one of Cartier's celebrated tiny watches with unusually small-scale multigem work. The term 'baguette watch' was used to describe the very narrow watches in which Cartier specialised. The name refers to the shape, which echoed the baguette-cut diamonds with which they were decorated. They were especially fashionable in the 1920s, but still made in the 1930s. The term was widely used: in 1931 the *Watchmaker's Weekly* noted, 'As articles that enjoy particular popularity today, the so-called Baguette wristwatches for women can be named' (quoted in H. Kahlert *et al.*, *Wristwatches*, Westchester, Pennsylvania, 1986, p. 49). For other baguette-form watches, see cat. 169 and 210–12.

155–7 Two bracelets and a pair of clip brooches

Bracelets made by Picq for Cartier Paris for stock in 1925 (cat. 155) and 1929 (cat. 156). Clip brooches (cat. 157) made by Dubois for Cartier Paris to the order of Mrs Cole Porter, July 1935

Sapphires, emeralds, rubies, onyx and diamonds in open-back platinum setting.

Bracelets: both in the form of undulating branches of leaves and berries. Cat. 155: central diamond branch ringed with onyx and emerald, carved ruby and sapphire leaves, onyx and emerald bead berries, the emerald beads encrusted with diamonds. Entered in stock book on 28 December 1925; sold to Mrs Cole Porter on 9 June 1926. Cat. 156: the diamond branch partly hidden; carved emerald, sapphire and ruby leaves, cabochon sapphires and emeralds; ruby bead berries encrusted with diamonds. Entered in stock book on 10 April 1929; sold to Mrs Cole Porter on 9 May 1930. Clip brooches: a cluster of carved sapphires, emeralds and rubies, in geometric diamond mount with round and baguette-cut diamonds. Separate fitting for wear as a brooch.

MARKS Bracelets: *Cartier Paris*; French dog's head assay mark for platinum.
Clip brooches: *Cartier Paris*; French dog's head assay mark for platinum and workshop mark *RD* flanking three chevrons.

Bracelets: (cat. 155) L. 18.5 cm, W. 3.5 cm; (cat. 156) L. 18.3 cm, W. 3.9 cm. Clip brooches: L. 5 cm each

Private collection

EXHIBITIONS New York 1976, cat. 31 (bracelet cat. 155 and brooches); Los Angeles 1982, cat. 2 (all three items).

LITERATURE Nadelhoffer 1984, col. pl. 46; Snowman (ed.) 1990, p. 197; Proddow *et al.* 1992, cover illustration (bracelet cat. 155 only).

RELATED MATERIAL Original ink, watercolour and bodycolour design for the clip brooches on grey paper in order book for 1935, p. 153, in Paris archive, both front and side view.

The first bracelet of this kind, in the form of an undulating branch of leaves and berries, incorporating carved stones and gemstone beads, was made for the Paris Exhibition of 1925; the design for it (cat. 285) is described '1 Bracelet large liane feuilles pierres de couleur' (1 wide bracelet, leafy branch, coloured gemstones). The 1925 Exhibition also included a brooch in the form a branch of berries, all formed of diamond-studded multigem beads (see cat. 286).

The clip brooches mostly used stones belonging to the client and the design had to incorporate four square carved emeralds of 22.72 carats. The order book describes them thus '2 Broches pince platine à 2 epingles et sûreté avec armature pour les porter en broche ordinaire, motif feuillage pierres de couleurs et brillants' (2 clip brooches in platinum with 2 prongs and safety catches, and frame for wear as ordinary brooch, leaf motifs in coloured stones and diamonds).

For a similar bracelet and matching handbag made for Cartier Paris *c.* 1930, said to have been given by the perfumier François Coty to his wife, see Christie's Geneva, 15 May 1996, lots 391–2.

The composer and lyricist Cole Porter (1893–1964) married Linda Lee Thomas in 1919.

From top 157, 155, 156 ▶

158

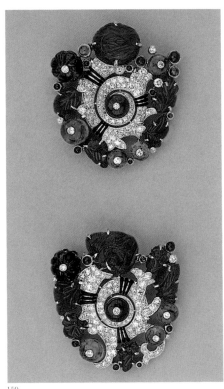

159

158 Bracelet

Made for Cartier New York (workshop unknown) for stock, 1928

Rubies, emeralds, sapphires and diamonds in open-back cagework platinum setting. A diamond-set sinuous branch with carved ruby leaves, with berries of diamond-studded carved emerald beads and small sapphire beads. The branch enamelled on lower-edge with a thin black line to create the effect of a shadow.

Entered in stock book on 4 December 1928; sold 31 December 1928.

MARKS Reverse of clasp stamped *CARTIER*.

L. 20.1 cm, W. 3.3 cm

Cartier collection, BT12 A28

EXHIBITIONS London 1988, cat. 403, pl. LXIV; Paris 1989, cat. 310; Rome 1990, cat. 139; St Petersburg 1992, cat. 159; Tokyo 1995, cat. 163; Lausanne 1996, cat. 223.

LITERATURE Nadelhoffer 1984, col. pl. 44; Cologni and Nussbaum 1995, p. 156.

For the shadow effect in black enamel or onyx, see also cat. 153 and 160. This bracelet and the following brooches use only two main colours, red and green, with a few sapphires on the bracelet.

159 Pair of brooches

Made for Cartier New York (workshop unknown), 1929

Rubies, emeralds, enamel and diamonds in open-back cagework platinum setting. Carved ruby leaves, ruby beads and emerald beads studded with diamonds, set round a pavé-set diamond dragon in the form of a tight scroll, with bands of black enamel.

MARKS Reverse stamped *CARTIER PLAT 14K*.

L. 4.4 cm, W. 3.9 cm

Cartier collection, CL 31 A29

EXHIBITIONS Venice 1986, cat. 119; London 1988, cat. 402, pl. LXIII; Paris 1989, cat. 308; Rome 1990, cat. 138; St Petersburg 1992, cat. 158; Tokyo 1995, cat. 174; Lausanne 1996, cat. 222.

LITERATURE Nadelhoffer 1984, col. pl. 44; Cologni and Nussbaum 1995, p. 156.

The scroll-shaped dragon is extremely stylised. The form is taken from ancient Chinese Eastern Zhou jades carved in the form of coiled dragons (see Rawson 1995, p. 212, fig. 2), but is somewhat misunderstood and could equally be read simply as a scrolling branch.

160 Shoulder brooch

Made by Renault for Cartier Paris for stock, 1922

Emeralds, onyx and diamonds in open-back platinum setting. A curved bar with angled ends set with a pear-shaped faceted emerald, from which hang two open links joined by onyx cabochons studded with emeralds, and below, two emerald bead strings with diamond tops and drops. The bar and two open links both set with diamonds and on the right-hand side a line of calibré-cut onyx to give the effect of a shadow. The upper part hinged in three places for flexibility. Two hinged loops at back for wear as a pendant.

Entered in stock book on 1 September 1922; sold 19 October 1922 to Mr Cowasji Jehangir. Sold Sotheby's Geneva, 15 May 1991, lot 373.

MARKS Rim engraved *CARTIER PARIS*; most other elements with French dog's head assay mark for 950 platinum and workshop mark *R* with a crescent and flame (?).

L. 15 cm

Cartier collection, CL 138 A22

EXHIBITIONS St Petersburg 1992, cat. 120; Tokyo 1995, cat. 122; Lausanne 1996, cat. 208.

LITERATURE Cologni and Nussbaum 1995, p. 123.

The history of the stones used in this brooch demonstrates the care and precision with which elements from an earlier piece bought back for stock were reused and recorded in minute detail. In this instance, stones from a brooch of 1920 provided the inspiration for not just one but four entirely new and successful creations, of which this shoulder brooch is one.

The 1920 brooch was a striking cliquet pin with a long dangling element formed of four open links, each with onyx shadow effect, and ending in two drops with pear-shaped emeralds (see 160.1). It was sold to Mrs W. K. Vanderbilt in April 1920, bought back for stock by Cartier in October that year and eventually dismantled in 1922. The bottom two open links with their emerald-studded onyx cabochons were reused for the present shoulder brooch. The *cache-pointe* or decorative catch to secure the end of the pin was used for a simple cliquet pin with an emerald head. The two pear-shaped emeralds were set into a necklace of diamonds and square-cut emeralds sold to King Peter of Serbia. The upper two open onyx and diamond links with one of the emerald-studded onyx cabochons and the

two rectangular emeralds from the pear-shaped drops were mounted as the centre of a belt buckle with two onyx rings and a plaited black cord belt.

The 1920 cliquet pin was among the earliest pieces with Cartier's new shadow effect in black enamel or onyx. Cliquet pins seem to have been popular for a few years only, from just before the First World War to just after it.

The purchaser of this piece, Sir Cowasji Jehangir, was one of two prominent Bombay citizens of the same name. The father (1858–1934) contributed to the funding of the Convocation Hall, Elphinstone College and the Cowasji Jehangir Ophthalmic Hospital in Bombay. His son (1879–1962) owned a distinguished collection of Indian miniatures and sculptures, and paid for the erection of the Jehangir Art Gallery in Bombay, where his collection was displayed. The latter's son (1911–44) married in 1938 the daughter of Sir Dhunjibhoy Bomanji, who commissioned the diamond upper-arm bracelet (cat. 99).

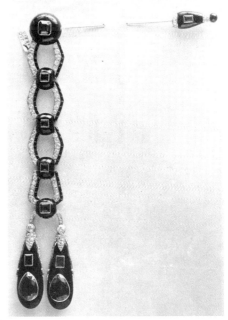

160.1 Cliquet pin of 1920 that was broken up and the stones reused in four new pieces, of which cat. 160 is one. The two open links at the bottom of the long pendant element appear in the centre of cat. 160.

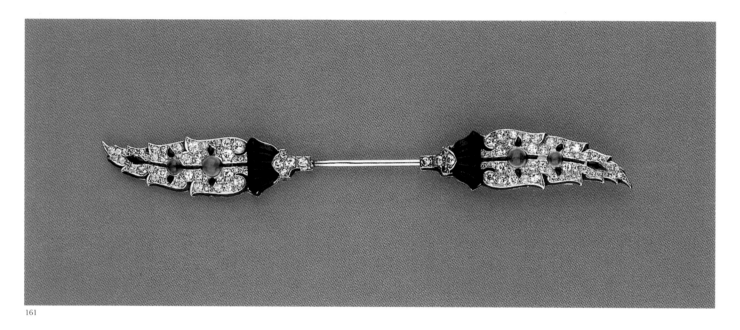

161

161 Double-headed cliquet pin

Made by Lavabre for Cartier Paris for stock, 1923

Diamonds, emeralds, onyx and black enamel in open-back platinum setting. Two leaves with serrated edges shadowed on one side with black enamel, pavé-set with diamonds, each leaf with onyx central vein set with emerald cabochons and a carved onyx calyx.

Entered in stock book on 30 October 1923, originally with coral calyces, changed to onyx in February 1925; sold 13 May 1925.

MARKS Reverse engraved CARTIER; French dog's head assay mark for platinum on gallery.

L. 10 cm

Cartier collection, CL 56 A23

EXHIBITIONS Paris 1989, cat. 239; Rome 1990, cat. 112.

RELATED MATERIAL (1) Original design in pencil, watercolour and bodycolour on buff tracing paper in Stock Design Record Book, 1923, p. 18b, with coral calyces and showing one leaf only. (2) Another loose design showing the whole brooch, with onyx calyces.

This is a particularly subtle use of black enamel to create the effect of a shadow. The enamel is used not only for the side in shadow but also to highlight the serrated edges on the other side of the leaf. The leaf with serrated edge is found in both Islamic and Indian ornament. In India it was a common form for the *sarpech* or turban ornament.

The loose design shows that the pin was originally considerably longer, and the contemporary archive photograph confirms that it was executed to this longer length of 12.4 cm. The date when it was shortened is not recorded. Most pins of this type had one main large element and a smaller decorative catch. The double-headed type seems to have been a Cartier speciality, and was often worn in the hat as well as elsewhere on the corsage. At a party held in London by Lady Cunliffe-Lister in March 1926, Mrs Wilfrid Ashley was 'smart in one of the new high-crowned hats, hers being of black corded silk, with a series of coloured vertical stripes at the side, through which glittered a Cartier double-headed pin of diamonds in a closely-set pattern, rather different from the ordinary favourites' (*The Sketch*, 24 March 1926, p. 537). Mrs Wilfred Ashley was the second wife of Wilfred William Ashley, Baron Mount Temple (1867–1938). His first wife, Amalia, who died in 1911, was the daughter of Sir Ernest Cassel (see cat. 1).

162

162 Onyx ring brooch

Made by Renault for Cartier Paris for stock,
c. 1925

Diamonds, emeralds, onyx, in open-back platinum
setting. An onyx ring, flanked by pierced pavé-set
diamond motifs with central cabochon emerald
bordered with calibré-cut onyx; further calibré onyx
motifs at the edges and two small emeralds at the tips.
One of the flanking motifs turns forward to release
the pin.

Entered in stock book on 5 September 1923;
sold 14 December 1923.

MARKS On reverse of fitting *CARTIER BTE SGDG*; French
dog's head assay mark for platinum and workshop mark
R with a crescent and flame (?) in a lozenge.

L. 9 cm

Lindemann collection. Sold Sotheby's London,
11 December 1986, lot 371.

EXHIBITIONS New Orleans 1988, pl. IV.

A number of designs for similar ring brooches
are to be found in the archives of all three
Cartier houses. They were introduced *c.* 1922
with infinite variations of shape and colour,
with rings of rock crystal (see cat. 181), onyx
or coral, or with rectangles instead of rings. A
page of designs from the London Design
Scrapbook gives some idea of the range of
possibilities (p. 56, fig. 42). They were designed
to be worn either as belt brooches – and are
described in the archive records as such – or
to decorate the fashionable cloche hats of the
1920s. Several were included in Cartier's display at the Paris Exhibition of 1925. For other
examples, see Gabardi 1989, p. 83 (with onyx
ring), p. 79 (rock-crystal ring) and p. 82 for a
page of photographs from the Cartier archive.

The patent mark refers to Cartier's special
cliquet fitting involving a turning pin-head
instead of a straightforward pull-out snap fitting (see cat. 119 and 181 for other examples).

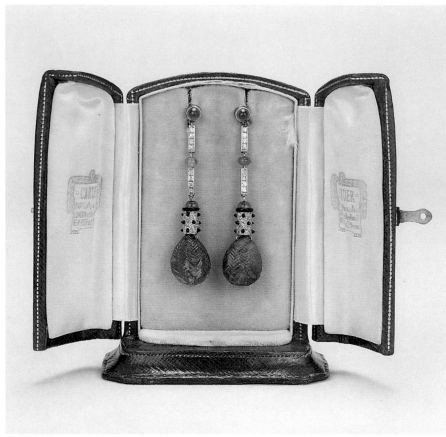

163 (in original case)

163.1 Cat. 163
showing original
screw fittings.

163 Pair of earrings

Made by Andrey for Cartier Paris for stock, 1922

Emeralds, onyx and diamonds mounted in platinum. The chains of square-cut diamonds and emerald beads, with pavé-set diamond cylinders studded with onyx; pear-drop emeralds drilled across the top and engraved with a chevron pattern and a flower-head at the base.

Screw fittings set with cabochon emeralds; milled platinum wire wheels at each end of the screw thread. Contained in the original green leather case with gold tooling, in the form of a standing triptych.

Entered in stock book on 8 December 1922; sold to Mme René Révillon 4 April 1923. Sold Sotheby's Geneva, 16 May 1990, lot 108.

MARKS Earrings: chain and screw fitting engraved

CARTIER, with French dog's head assay mark for platinum and workshop mark GA flanking a branch of mistletoe (?). Case: stamped in gold inside each wing CARTIER PARIS 13 RUE DE LA PAIX LONDON 175 NEW BOND STREET NEW YORK 712 5TH AVENUE, on the back CARTIER in gold, and on the base MADE IN FRANCE.

L. 6 cm, H. of case 9.4 cm

Cartier collection, EG 05 A22

EXHIBITIONS St Petersburg 1992, cat. 121; Hong Kong 1995, cat. 35; Tokyo 1995, cat. 128.

René Révillon was Louis Cartier's deputy and often gave approval for pieces to be made. He was also Louis Cartier's son-in-law, having married Anne-Marie, Louis' daughter by his first marriage, in 1921.

The finely carved large pear-drop emeralds are reused Indian stones dating probably from the nineteenth or early twentieth century.

164 Bracelet

Made by Picq for Cartier Paris for stock, 1922

Emeralds, onyx and diamonds mounted in platinum. Six flat-backed cylinders pavé-set with diamonds and studded with onyx, between small onyx cylinders and emerald beads. Rectangular clasp, one side of which is hinged and lifts up to open.

Entered in stock book on 29 August 1922; sold 28 September 1922.

MARKS Clasp engraved CARTIER with French dog's head assay mark for platinum on the cylinders.

L. 19 cm

Cartier collection, BT 55 A22

EXHIBITIONS New York 1976, cat. 26; Los Angeles 1982, cat. 36; Tokyo 1995, cat. 127.

LITERATURE Cologni and Nussbaum 1995, p. 122.

This is very close in design to the bracelet with coral cylinders (cat. 143).

165 Bracelet

Made by Lavabre for Cartier Paris for stock, 1923

Emeralds, onyx, enamel, diamonds, set in platinum. A large central rectangular emerald of 57.80 carats, carved on both sides, with hatched edges; on the front, a central four-petal flower surrounded by leaves, and on the back a flower vase containing a central blossom and two leafy stems. At each side diamond-set square links and two melon-cut emerald beads, the bracelet formed of a series of onyx discs and diamond-set links decreasing in size towards the back. Black enamel clasp and attachment loops for emerald.

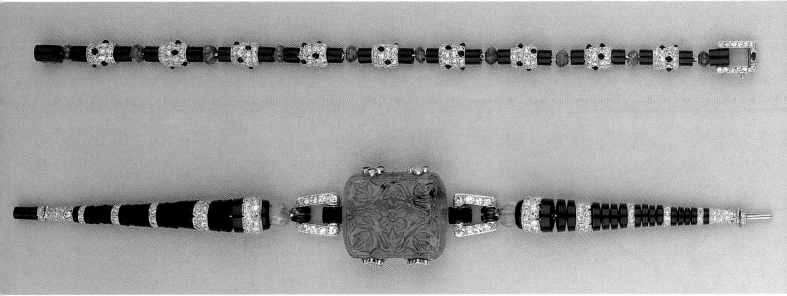

164, 165

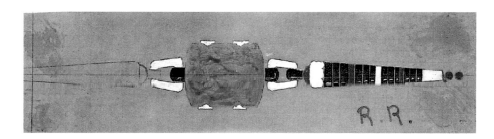

165.1 Original pencil, watercolour and bodycolour design of 1923 for cat. 165, showing the coral discs and beads before alteration in 1924.

Entered in stock book on 31 December 1923; sold, following modifications, in December 1924. Sold Christie's New York, 25 April 1990, lot 332.

MARKS On reverse French dog's head assay mark for platinum and workshop mark *III* flanking a four-leaf clover.

L. 19.7 cm, W. 2.5 cm. Carved emerald: 2.2 × 2.6 cm

Cartier collection, BT 10 A23

EXHIBITIONS St Petersburg 1992, cat. 125; Tokyo 1995, cat. 131; Lausanne 1996, cat. 184.

LITERATURE Cologni and Nussbaum 1995, p. 122.

RELATED MATERIAL Original design in pencil, watercolour and bodycolour on buff tracing paper in Stock Design Record Book, 1923, p. 40b, in Paris archive, with initials R.R. for René Révillon (see 165.1).

The design of this bracelet is loosely inspired by the Indian upper-arm bracelet (*bazuband*), formed usually of a central element with two smaller flanking elements attached to plaited cord strings which decrease towards the back. For examples in the Victoria and Albert Museum, acquired in 1855, see Stronge *et al.* 1988, cat. 83. The Cartier bracelet has a large emerald forming the central part, while

165.2 Reverse of large carved emerald.

decreasing onyx discs imitate the plaited cords.

The shape and carving of the large rectangular emerald are consistent with a reused Mughal emerald of the late seventeenth or eighteenth century. It has not been drilled for suspension, as one would expect with an emerald carved on both sides, but may have had a suspension loop which has been removed, leaving a ground-out patch in one of the hatched edges.

In its early years, the bracelet underwent a number of changes. The original bracelet of 1923 was made by the Picq workshop and had

two coral, instead of emerald, beads and four coral discs (see 165.1). In June 1924, the large emerald in its original setting of four diamond and onyx claws was mounted on a diamond bracelet made by the Lavabre workshop as a special order; in December 1924 the same client ordered the original design to be reconstituted but without the coral discs and with two emerald beads, as it is now. This reconstitution was done by Lavabre. The diamond bracelet was remounted without the large emerald.

166

166

166 Pendant watch

Made by Jaeger for Cartier Paris for stock, 1923

Enamelled gold, emeralds, pearls, diamonds set in platinum. In the form of a seal with swivel watch in enamelled gold, the white dial with two sets of numerals, the outer set of numerals reserved on black, the sides with a wavy line of diamonds and black enamel, the reverse with large 44.15-carat emerald carved as a lotus with scooped-out petals. Swivel setting in the form of a diamond-set scalloped arch with black enamel edge and a pearl at each side, a lotus motif on the loop and a diamond chain with melon-cut emerald bead and a pearl.

Entered in stock book on 30 June 1923, originally with a cord chain, the emerald bead acting as a slide; sold 4 August 1923.

MARKS On dial *CARTIER BTE SGDG*.

L. 9.3 cm. Carved emerald: DIAM. 2.9 cm

Cartier collection, WC 08 A23

EXHIBITIONS London 1988, cat. 182, pl. XXVII; Paris 1989, cat. 421; Rome 1990, cat. 195; Tokyo 1995, cat. 241; Lausanne 1996, cat. 94.

LITERATURE Barracca *et al.* 1989, p. 97.

The quality of cutting on the large emerald is markedly higher than on many of the emeralds catalogued here. It has been foiled with silver to enhance the colour and is probably a reused stone of the late seventeenth or eighteenth century. The melon-cut emerald is also a reused Indian stone, but is difficult to date, given that melon-cut stones are still produced in India today.

The double set of numerals has no apparent function and seems to be purely a design feature.

167 Penannular brooch

Made by English Art Works for Cartier
London for stock, 1924

Diamonds and emeralds in open-back platinum setting.
An open-ended diamond ring, a square-cut emerald in
each terminal; pin-head set with large emerald of 30.32
carats, carved on both sides with leafy stems and a
lozenge pattern round the edges. A square carved
emerald at join of pin and ring; pin-catch of calibré-cut
emeralds and diamonds.

Entered in stock book on 21 January 1924;
sold 4 November 1924.

MARKS Engraved *CARTIER LONDRES* on edge of ring.

L. 11.1 cm, W. 4 cm. Carved emerald: 3.2 × 1.7 cm

Cartier collection, CL 03 A24

EXHIBITIONS New York 1976, cat. 35; Los Angeles 1982,
cat. 83; Paris 1989, cat. 248; Rome 1990, cat. 117;
St Petersburg 1992, cat. 136; Tokyo 1995, cat. 138;
Lausanne 1996, cat. 183.

LITERATURE Nadelhoffer 1984, col. pl. 22.

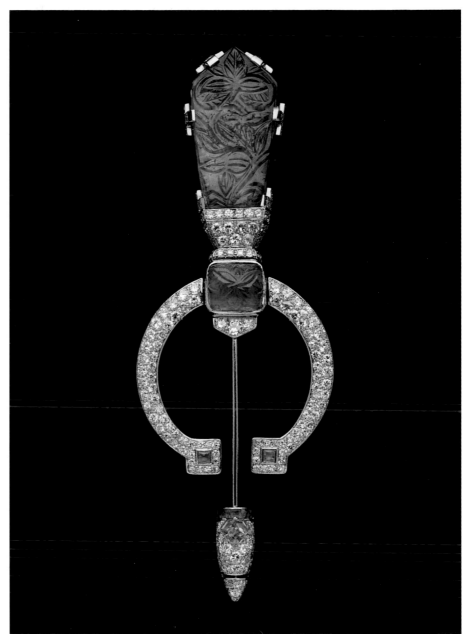

167

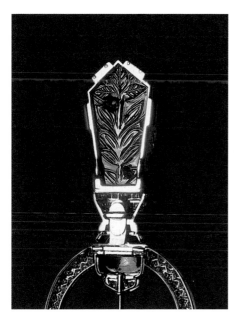

167.1 Reverse of large carved emerald.

This brooch is described in the London stock
sheets as an 'Agrafe sûreté. Circle two lines
brilliants square ends c/ [centre?] of each one
square emerald, point of pin bullet shape in
brilts [brilliants] and emeralds. Large carved
emerald (flat) 30.32. The other end set in a
base of three lines brilts with pyramids round
edge in brilts. 1 cab emerald at base 3.78.'

The smaller, square, carved stone is a typical
reused Indian stone. The large carved emerald,

however, is not a shape normally found in
Mughal emeralds and may have been specially
shaped and cut for this brooch in the 1920s.
Nevertheless, the engraved edges are a feature
of early emeralds and a date in the late seventeenth or eighteenth century should not be
ruled out.

The form of this brooch is derived either
from Celtic models of the eighth to ninth century AD, where the pin is movable and slides
round the open-ended ring to enable the
brooch to be fastened, or from Indian penan-

nular brooches of the nineteenth century, usually in steel with gold overlay. In this example,
the pin has only one position and has a standard cliquet or click fitting.

Only a handful of diamond-set penannular
brooches as large as this were made by Cartier.
But a number of miniature ones were produced, of which two are in the Cartier collection (see Paris 1989, cat. 304, for an example
with diamonds and sapphires). Others were
made in semi-precious materials such as onyx
and coral (see Gabardi 1989, p. 87).

168 Necklace

Made for Cartier London to the order of Lady Granard, 1932

Diamonds in open-back platinum settings; in the centre, a large rectangular emerald of 143.13 carats. The front part with graduated Persian-style fringe on a flexible collar with diamonds set in a crescent shape; the back part with graduated buckle-shaped links detaches at the sides.

Completed in January 1932. Sold Christie's St Moritz, 8 February 1995, lot 373.

MARKS None.

H. of central element with emerald 8.5 cm

Cartier collection, NE 25 A32

This is one of several elaborate diamond necklaces made for Cartier London between about 1931 and 1937. In addition to the huge emerald, there are four baton diamonds flanking the emerald and, on the lower element, fourteen square diamonds for each of the geometric fringe motifs, plus no fewer than 2,011 brilliant-cut diamonds. The stones were all supplied by the client.

The change from the long sautoir (see cat. 214) to a round collar-type necklace occurred around 1930–31. From about 1934 necklaces of this type all seem to have been made with a detachable central element wearable as a clip brooch. Others were also wearable as a tiara, usually of 'halo' type, and up to three elements could be worn as clips.

Beatrice, Lady Granard, OBE, was the daughter of Ogden Mills of Staatsburg, Duchess County, USA. She married the 8th Earl Granard in 1909. She was a regular client of Cartier London and was one of the last great buyers of *kokoshniks*; she ordered one in 1922, another in 1923 and a third in 1937, presumably for the coronation of George VI (Nadelhoffer 1984, p. 72). In his diaries, Chips Channon described a dinner party he gave in February 1938, attended by Winston and Mrs Churchill and the Granards among others. Channon wrote, 'Lady Granard could scarcely walk for jewels' (Rhodes James (ed.) 1967, p. 116).

169 Clip watch

Made by Jaeger for Cartier Paris for stock, 1938

Carved emerald, round and baguette-cut diamonds set in platinum. A polygonal emerald, engraved on the

169

169.1 Reverse of cat. 169, showing double-prong clip fitting and two secondary prongs behind watch.

front only with foliate decoration, forms the visible part of the clip brooch, with pointed side facing downwards when worn, the narrow baguette watch set at top. Hinged double-prong clip fitting at base point of emerald, with secondary prongs behind watch. The dial is set so that it is the right way up for the wearer.

Entered in stock book on 30 August 1938, originally mounted on an earlier bracelet set with carved coloured stones forming a leafy branch (see 169.2). Sold Christie's Geneva, 19 May 1994, lot 323.

MARKS On reverse of watch French dog's head assay mark for platinum and workshop mark *EJ* flanking an hour-glass. Watch movement with *E.W.C. CO. INC.* for the European Watch & Clock Company.

L. 2.8 cm, W. 2.1 cm. Carved emerald: 1.6 × 2.4 cm

Cartier collection, WB 26 A38

EXHIBITIONS Lausanne 1996, cat. 95 (with 1951 woven gold bracelet).

LITERATURE Barracca *et al.* 1989, p. 232; Cologni and Nussbaum 1995, p. 161.

The bracelet with carved gemstone leaves set in platinum on which this clip watch was originally mounted was made by the Dubois work-

shop in May 1935 (see 169.2). The bracelet did not sell and was re-entered for stock without the watch on 13 December 1938. The watch was re-entered for stock mounted on a woven gold bracelet. This bracelet was replaced with another plaited gold band in 1951; the piece finally sold on 27 September 1951.

The polygonal emerald is a reused Indian stone, possibly of the late seventeenth or eighteenth century, drilled for suspension across the top, with a chevron pattern round the edge.

169.2 Archive photograph of the bracelet with carved gemstone leaves made in 1935, on which cat. 169 was originally mounted. The clip watch formed a detachable centrepiece.

170 Diamond and onyx pendant watch

Based on a design by Charles Jacqueau and made by Jaeger for Cartier Paris, 1915

Diamonds and onyx in platinum setting. An oblong watch and circular link, watch-back and link both in pavé-set diamonds studded with onyx chips, hung from a bar brooch with upturned scrolled ends. Three diamond drops at base.

Entered in stock book on 2 December 1915, originally as a much longer brooch with black silk cord and diamond and onyx slide separating the watch from the brooch (see 170.1). Sold to Pierre Cartier on 1 July 1916.

MARKS On dial *CARTIER FRANCE*; on watch French dog's head assay mark for platinum and workshop mark *EJ* flanking an hour-glass.

L. 8.5 cm

Private collection

EXHIBITIONS New York 1976, cat. 73.

LITERATURE Nadelhoffer 1984, col. pl. 21, p. 229; Snowman (ed.) 1990, p. 193.

This is the earliest surviving piece to incorporate Cartier's celebrated 'peau de panthère' or 'panther-skin' decoration, achieved by setting pieces of onyx cut in different shapes to resemble spots into a ground of pavé-set diamonds (see p. 17).

Although 'panther-skin' decoration was first used in 1914, it was not described as such until 1917. The example catalogued here was described as having 'tiger-skin' decoration: 'montre pendant décor peau de tigre pavage brillants et onyx' (watch-pendant with tiger-skin decoration in pavé diamonds and onyx).

The Cartier collection includes a simplified version of this watch-pendant, with just the ring and the oblong watch: see London 1988, cat. 386; Paris 1989, cat. 419; Rome 1990, cat. 193; Tokyo 1995, cat. 237; Cologni and Nussbaum 1995, p. 131.

For the design by Charles Jacqueau, see cat. 245. It shows a watch-pendant on an identical bar brooch with a black watered silk strap and an oval or *baignoire* watch, with two pendant tassels. Jacqueau's working designs include several sketches for other jewels with 'panther-

170 (greatly enlarged)

skin' ornament, often mixed with coral. An example in the Cartier collection is the bracelet of 1930 with three rows of ribbed coral beads and panther-skin clasp (Paris 1989, cat. 437). For examples of 'panther-skin' ornament shown at the 1925 Paris Exhibition, see cat. 271–2 and 277.

171 Diamond and onyx brooch

Designed probably by Charles Jacqueau and made by Renault for Cartier Paris for stock, 1920

Diamonds and onyx set in platinum. 'Broche poigneé' or drawer-handle brooch, formed of two onyx half-rings each with two collet-set diamonds and diamond-set terminals bordered with calibré-cut onyx, joined by a pavé-set diamond cylinder studded with onyx cabochons. The pin slots into a hole in the opposite terminal.

Entered in stock book on 15 November 1920; sold 27 July 1921 to the Maharajah of Patiala.

MARKS Reverse stamped *CARTIER PARIS LONDRES NEW YORK BTE SGDG*; French dog's head assay mark for platinum and workshop mark *R* with a crescent and flame (?) on pin.

L. 5.5 cm

Cartier collection, CL 181 A20

EXHIBITIONS Hong Kong 1995, cat. 32; Lausanne 1996, cat. 213.

LITERATURE Cologni and Nussbaum 1995, p. 131.

Jacqueau's working designs include a number of brooches of this form (private collection, e.g. nos 771 and 774).

For a pair of earrings commissioned by the Maharajah of Patiala, see cat. 102.

171

170.1 Archive photograph of cat. 170 as originally made in 1915, with a black silk cord separating the brooch and the watch.

172.1 Archive photograph of cat. 172 as originally made in 1924, with pouch-shaped velvet bag. The fabric was replaced as fashions changed in the late 1920s or early 1930s.

172

172 Evening bag

Designed and made in Paris for Cartier New York as a special order, 1924

Black satin bag. Mount of diamonds and onyx in platinum setting; on one side a strip of pavé-set diamonds studded with onyx cabochons and flecks, the other side with plain strip of onyx cut in one angled piece to form the top of the mount as well as the side, set with two onyx cabochons. Two further onyx cabochons at base of opening. Push-button catch set with cabochon onyx. Silk cord. Interior fittings in brass.

Dated by original design of 1924 in New York client file.

MARKS Inside of mount engraved *Cartier Paris PT 950*; French dog's head assay mark for platinum and workshop mark *C* between two crescents with the letters *S* and *A* above and below, and the initials *M. D.* for 'Métaux Divers' (mixed metals).

W. (approx.) 20.5 cm, H. with catch 19.5 cm, with handle 32.5 cm

Cartier collection, EB 03 A24

EXHIBITIONS Paris 1989, cat. 338.

LITERATURE Cologni and Mocchetti 1992, p. 79; Cologni and Nussbaum 1995, p. 131.

RELATED MATERIAL Original design dated 25 June 1924, with annotations in French and stamped NEW YORK in New York client file, showing a pouch-shaped bag, also in black fabric, with long double black cord handle.

The New York client file also contains a contemporary photograph dated 1924 indicating that the bag was made according to the design (172.1). The date when the present bag was fitted is not recorded, but the fabric and shape are consistent with a date in the late 1920s or early 1930s. The alteration may have been made in Paris, which would explain the appearance of the Cartier workshop mark, in use from 1929.

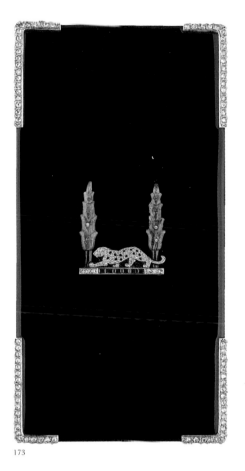

173

173.1 Enlarged detail of cat. 173

173 Vanity case

Made by Lavabre for Cartier Paris to the order of Leopold Marx, 1928

Black lacquer on gold; emeralds, rubies, diamonds set in platinum. On the lid a panther in pavé-set rose-cut diamonds with spots of black lacquer, between two cypress trees, each formed of a carved emerald and a baguette ruby; a line of diamonds and calibré-cut rubies forms the ground. The push-piece set with a diamond baton between two square-cut emeralds. Interior with mirrored lid and compartments for cigarettes (with hinged bracket to keep them in place), powder and a lipstick (the tube is missing). The original red leather case survives: see p. 44, fig. 34.

Completed in October 1928.

MARKS Inside rim engraved *Cartier Paris Londres New York MADE IN FRANCE*; Paris eagle's head assay mark for gold.

L. 10.9 cm, W. 5.6 cm

Cartier collection, VC 08 A28

EXHIBITIONS London 1988, cat. 388; Paris 1989, cat. 360; Rome 1990, cat. 158.

LITERATURE Nadelhoffer 1984, col. pl. 21.

RELATED MATERIAL For a design for a similar, but not identical vanity case, see London 1988, p. 88, with the same central motif of panther and trees, but a diamond border across the top and bottom instead of round the corners.

This is one of a series of vanity cases based on designs by Georges Barbier, with panthers, dogs or gazelles between cypress trees (see Nadelhoffer 1984, p. 230). Another, with greyhounds, was owned by Elma Rumsey, Pierre Cartier's wife: see St Louis 1995, no. 9, ill. p. 27, originally with a green bead tassel.

174 Diamond and onyx pendant watch (*montre régence*)

Made by Jaeger for Cartier Paris for stock, 1919

Diamonds and onyx, in closed-back platinum setting, black watered silk strap. Oval watch (*baignoire*) with diamond border surmounted by a lotus motif in diamonds. The clasp in the form of a Celtic brooch set with square-cut onyx, long vertical pin with tubular sliding catch. An onyx and diamond slide enables the length of the strap to be altered.

Entered in stock book on 15 May 1919; sold 23 July 1919.

MARKS On dial: *CARTIER PARIS*.

L. 19.4 cm

Cartier collection, WB 12 A19

EXHIBITIONS Milan 1988, p. 25.

LITERATURE Cologni and Nussbaum 1995, p. 115.

Oval watches of this type were known as *baignoires* (bath tubs) because of their shape. Clasps of this design were known as 'broches romaines' in the Paris archive records. The watch hangs upside down, so that it is correct for the wearer. The term 'montre régence' was used by Cartier to describe a watch hanging from a ribbon band; its derivation is unclear.

175 Diamond and onyx bracelet watch

Made by Jaeger for Cartier Paris for stock, 1921

Diamonds and onyx in closed-back platinum setting, with five-strand pearl bracelet. Square watch with diamond border, onyx and diamond attachment links; the bracelet of white and grey pearls in alternate rows set with five onyx and diamond plaques and ending in diamond and onyx loops.

Entered in stock book on 21 December 1921; sold 5 January 1922. Sold Sotheby's London, 9 October 1986, lot 329.

MARKS On dial *CARTIER*; on reverse of watch French dog's head assay mark for platinum and workshop mark *EJ* flanking an hour-glass; gold tongue with Paris eagle's head assay mark for gold and workshop mark.

w. of watch 1.8 cm

Cartier collection, WL 25 A21

EXHIBITIONS London 1988, cat. 184; Paris 1989, cat. 216; Rome 1990, cat. 106.

LITERATURE Barracca *et al.* 1989, p. 115.

175, 174

176 Pocket watch

Made by Jaeger for Cartier Paris for stock, 1928

Diamonds, black enamel, gold and platinum. Black enamel case with triangular platinum loop, the outer edge bordered with diamonds; the dial in white enamel on engine-turned ground with vertical lines, diamond-set Roman numerals on a black enamel chapter-ring with gold rim, blued steel hands.

Imported into America by the European Watch & Clock Company and sold by Cartier New York in 1928.

MARKS On loop French dog's head assay mark for platinum and workshop mark *EJ* flanking an hour-glass; on movement *E.W.C.*

DIAM. 4.5 cm

Lindemann collection

EXHIBITIONS New Orleans 1988 p. 176, pl. LIV

For a similar watch made in 1925, see Barracca *et al.* 1989, p. 86. For another similar model with diamond edge, dated 1921, on a pearl and onyx chain, see New York 1976, cat. 64.

The use of strongly contrasting black and white for watches dates from *c.* 1912. The flat gentleman's pocket watch was introduced *c.* 1908; early examples were generally in gold with coloured gems. Although wrist watches had become acceptable for everyday wear during the First World War, pocket watches continued to be the acceptable timepiece for formal occasions. This elegant and restrained model was produced with variations over several years.

In Edith Wharton's *Certain People* (1930), Mr Warley wears 'onyx studs and a thin evening watch in his pocket, a dust of lavender on his handkerchief' (quoted in Scarisbrick 1995, p. 270).

176

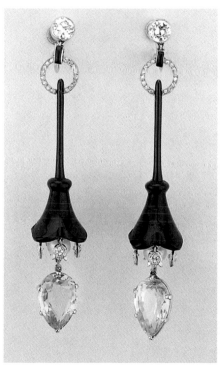

177

177 Pair of earrings

Made by Renault for Cartier Paris for stock, *c.* 1919

Onyx, diamonds and yellow sapphires set in platinum. In the form of flower-heads, the stem and bell-shaped head carved out of a single piece of onyx, with four diamond drops in lily of the valley settings, a central pearl and pear-shaped yellow sapphire drops. Diamond-set pendant rings and screw fittings, with milled platinum wheels at each end of the screw thread.

A similar pair of earrings made by the Picq workshop entered in stock book on 28 November 1919.

MARKS Fittings engraved *CARTIER*; French dog's head assay mark for platinum and workshop mark *R* with a crescent and flame (?).

L. 7.4 cm

Cartier collection, EG 01 A19

EXHIBITIONS New York 1976, cat. 24; London 1988, cat. 55, pl. VIII; Paris 1989, cat. 178; Rome 1990, cat. 81

The Renault workshop would have been responsible for the setting only; the carving of the onyx flowers would have been given to one of the specialist lapidaries. The settings of the four small diamonds are described as 'muguets' (lilies of the valley) because of their shape. For discussion of lily of the valley settings, see cat. 3.

Earrings with the same onyx flower-head are illustrated in a four-page Cartier advertisement in London *Vogue* for January 1925, p. 42, with the following caption: 'The Earrings are cut from one piece of onyx with diamonds coming out like drops of water and pear-shaped diamond pendants.'

178

178 Diamond and black enamel domino brooch

Made for Cartier New York (workshop unknown) for stock, c. 1925

Diamonds and black enamel in open-back platinum setting. A rectangular ring with tear-drop motif at each side, the left half black enamel with pear-shaped diamond in black enamel border, the right half pavé-set diamonds, with black enamel drop in diamond border.

MARKS Reverse engraved *Cartier*.

L. 7.7 cm

Cartier collection, CL 50 C25

EXHIBITIONS New York 1976, cat. 29; Los Angeles 1982, cat. 34; Naples 1988, cat. 123; Paris 1989, cat. 259; Rome 1990, cat. 123; St Petersburg 1992, cat. 144; Tokyo 1995, cat. 148; Lausanne 1996, cat. 215.

LITERATURE Cologni and Nussbaum 1995, p. 125.

Cartier made a range of designs with alternating elements in black enamel and open-back diamonds. In this piece, the balance of opaque and translucent elements is particularly successful. Also noteworthy is the setting of the diamonds with their tables in exactly the same orientation, emphasising the individual rows of diamonds within the pavé-set area.

179 Onyx and diamond strap bracelet *(bracelet lanière)*

Made by Lavabre for Cartier Paris for stock, 1925

Diamonds and onyx in platinum setting. Formed of onyx plaques each with two diamond-set palmettes, joined by diamond-set links giving the effect of a row of buckle-and-strap motifs. Each palmette set with a fan-shape diamond, behind which the onyx is cut away so that they are open at back; links also set open-back.

Entered in stock book on 24 October 1925; sold 26 April 1926. Sold Christie's New York, 11 April 1989, lot 297.

MARKS Clasp engraved *Cartier Paris*; French dog's head assay mark for platinum.

L. 18.5 cm

Cartier collection, BT 29 A25

EXHIBITIONS Tokyo 1995, cat. 135; Lausanne 1996, cat. 217.

RELATED MATERIAL Original design in pencil, ink and bodycolour on buff tracing paper in Stock Design Record Book, 1925, p. 32c, in Paris archive, given to the Lavabre workshop on 18 July for delivery on 14 August 1925.

The fan-shape cuts in this bracelet demonstrate Cartier's reputation for incorporating stones cut to fit the design. This was normally done with sapphires or rubies, and is unusual with diamonds because the wastage is so great. A fan-shape diamond could mean that as little as 20–25 per cent of the original stone was left. Possibly the stones were already in stock from a previous purchase or dismantled piece, and the designer was asked to incorporate them.

179

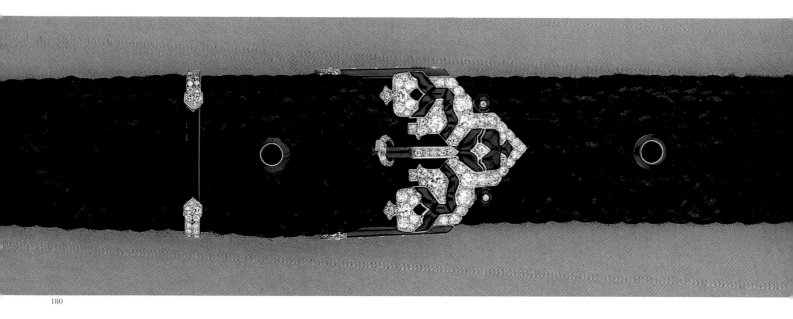

180

180 Onyx and diamond belt buckle and belt

Made by Renault (the buckle) and Mayeras (the belt) for Cartier Paris for stock, 1928. The buckle made from the lower part of the long *broche de décolleté* made for the 1925 Paris Exhibition

Original plaited black satin belt with buckle of enamelled gold, with diamond and onyx Persian-style motif in open-back platinum setting; loop and eyeholes in black enamel and diamonds. Side bars enamelled black and set with a row of tiny diamonds.

Entered in stock book on 29 May 1928; sold 8 November 1928 to Count Széchényi. Later owned by Mrs Gertrude Vanderbilt Whitney.

MARKS Paris eagle's head assay mark for gold and workshop mark R with a crescent and flame (?) on tongue; dog's head assay mark for platinum on reverse of buckle.

W. 4.5 cm, L. of belt (doubled) 37.2 cm

Cartier collection, AL 100 A28

The Persian-style motif on the buckle is all that remains of a 15-inch-long (38 cm) *broche de décolleté* designed for the 1925 Paris Exhibition. This did not sell and was eventually dismantled. Two pairs of stylised blossoms from the *broche de décolleté* were made into brooches in 1927, and apart from these the lower pointed motif was the only element that survived to be reused for this buckle (180.1). For a detailed account of the *broche de décolleté* see pp. 17–18.

Only a few original belts survive. This one appears to be unaltered; if so, the total length before the belt was fastened, 29 inches (73.6 cm), suggests that it was intended not as a hip belt but as a waist belt, which must have been newly fashionable at this time.

Count Széchényi (d. 1938) married Gladys Moore Vanderbilt, daughter of Cornelius Vanderbilt II, in 1908. Her sister, who later owned the belt, was the sculptor and art patron Gertrude Vanderbilt Whitney (1875–1942), who married Henry Payne Whitney in 1896 and founded the Whitney Museum of American Art.

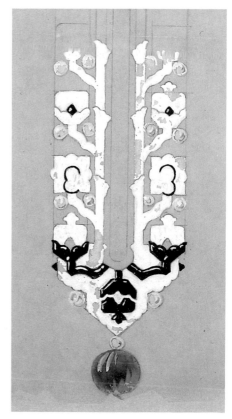

180.1 Detail of original design in pencil, watercolour and bodycolour for a 15-inch (38 cm) long *broche de décolleté* made for the Paris Exhibition of 1925. The bottom part, without the emerald, was reused for cat. 180.

181 Rock-crystal and onyx belt brooch *(broche de ceinture)*

Made by Renault for Cartier Paris for stock, 1923

A rock-crystal ring with onyx and diamonds set in platinum. The inner edge of the ring with a row of diamonds and onyx. At each side a strap motif with leafy branch in carved onyx on a ground of pavé-set diamonds; two cabochon emeralds at the base and top of each branch. The right end is hinged and turns forward to release the pin.

Entered in stock book on 30 May 1923; sold 6 June 1923. Sold Christie's Geneva, 27 April 1978, lot 307.

MARKS Reverse engraved *CARTIER*; French dog's head mark for platinum and workshop mark *R* with a crescent and flame (?). The cliquet fitting is engraved *Cartier*, with *Bte SGDG*.

W. 8.5 cm, DIAM. of ring 4.9 cm

Cartier collection, CL 66 A23

EXHIBITIONS Milan 1988, p. 43; Paris 1989, cat. 236; Rome 1990, cat. 111; St Petersburg 1992, cat. 134; Lausanne 1996, cat. 214.

LITERATURE Cologni and Nussbaum 1995, p. 125.

RELATED MATERIAL Original design in pencil, ink and bodycolour on tracing paper in Stock Design Record Book 1923, p. 4b, Paris archive. The design is initialled R.P. for the salesman René Prieur.

Rock-crystal brooches of this kind, first introduced *c.* 1922, became especially fashionable following the Paris Exhibition of 1925, where they were shown as belt brooches, with or without long pearl tassels (see cat. 273). They could also be worn as hat ornaments. For another example with an onyx ring, see cat. 162.

The patent for the cliquet or click fitting (described on the stock sheet as 'système cliquet no. 3') refers to the method of opening, which differs from the standard cliquet. The end is turned forward at right angles to the

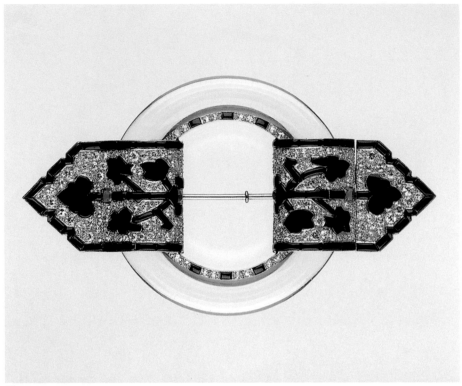

181

ring; it then slides out to release the pin, which is also hinged, enabling the pin to be pushed through the fabric (see also cat. 119 and 162). The pin has a small ring to stop it sliding out completely, which means that it can only be used on a coarse fabric that passes over the ring, otherwise part of the pin remains visible.

The carving and setting of the onyx leafy branch is technically superb, while the stark black and white contrast of the diamonds, onyx and crystal is lightened by the four tiny cabochon emeralds.

181.1 Cat 181 showing the pin-head turned through 90 degrees to release the pin.

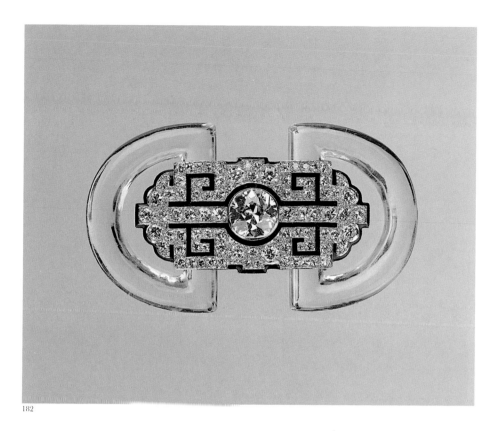

182

182 Rock-crystal and black enamel brooch

Made by American Art Works for Cartier New York for stock, 1926

Rock crystal, diamonds and black enamel in open-back platinum setting. Two hemispherical rock-crystal rings joined by a pavé-set diamond plaque with large central brilliant-cut diamond, black enamel geometric motifs and outlines.

Entered in stock book on 30 September 1926; sold 9 November 1926. Sold Sotheby's St Moritz, 24/26 February 1983, lot 622.

MARKS Reverse engraved *CARTIER*.

L. 6.3 cm, W. 3.5 cm

Cartier collection, CL 15 A26

EXHIBITIONS Venice 1986, cat. 115; Milan 1988, p. 45; Paris 1989, cat. 258; Rome 1990, cat. 122; Lausanne 1996, cat. 142.

LITERATURE Gabardi 1989, p. 83.

The black enamel outlines are loosely derived from the inlay patterns on ancient Chinese bronze vessels, or from later Chinese furniture or lacquer.

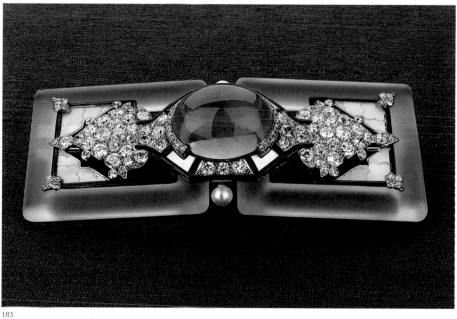

183

183 Rock-crystal brooch

Made by Renault for Cartier Paris for stock, 1924

Rock crystal, diamonds, mother-of-pearl, pearls, black enamel and cabochon sapphire of 57.63 carats in open-back platinum setting. Two matt-polished rock-crystal rectangles with superimposed pavé-set diamond motif outlined in black enamel, a pearl above and below between the two rectangles. In the centre, the large sapphire; at each side a Persian-style diamond leaf surrounded by mother-of-pearl inlay work with black enamel outlines.

Entered in stock book on 21 March 1924, originally set with a large carved emerald in the centre instead of the sapphire; sold 14 June 1924.

MARKS Reverse engraved *Cartier Paris*; workshop mark *R* with a crescent and flame (?).

L. 9.3 cm, W. 3.7 cm

Cartier collection, CL 02 A24

EXHIBITIONS London 1988, cat. 190, pl. XXX; Naples 1988, cat. 91; Paris 1989, cat. 247; Rome 1990, cat. 116; St Petersburg 1992, cat. 135; Hong Kong 1995, p. 40; Tokyo 1995, cat. 137.

LITERATURE Nadelhoffer 1984, col. pl. 11; Cologni and Nussbaum 1995, p. 128.

The date when the present sapphire was inserted instead of the original emerald is not recorded. The combination of rock crystal and mother-of-pearl is unusual.

184

184 Rock-crystal and onyx clip brooch (broche pince)

Made by the Cartier workshop for Cartier Paris for stock, 1931

Rock crystal, onyx, black enamel, diamonds in platinum setting. A flat disc of rock crystal with faceted edge is set into an onyx cylinder ornamented with pavé-set and baguette diamonds. Both disc and cylinder bordered with black enamel. Contained in the original red leather case with gilt tooling. The pad at the base lifts out and folds backwards to enable the clip fitting to be inserted.

Entered in stock book on 22 July 1931; sold 16 September 1931. Sold Christie's London, 20 June 1990, lot 169.

MARKS Clip: edge of clip fitting engraved *Cartier Paris Londres New York*, MADE IN FRANCE and DEPOSE, with MECAN (for 'Mécanisme', indicating the use of base metal parts) inside the clip fitting; French dog's head assay mark for platinum and workshop mark c between two crescents with the letters s and A above and below. Case: base stamped CARTIER in gold; kid leather lining to lid printed with standard Cartier label.

L. 3 cm, L. of case 6.5 cm

Cartier collection, CL 111 A31

EXHIBITIONS Lausanne 1996, cat. 191.

LITERATURE Cologni and Nussbaum 1995, p. 155.

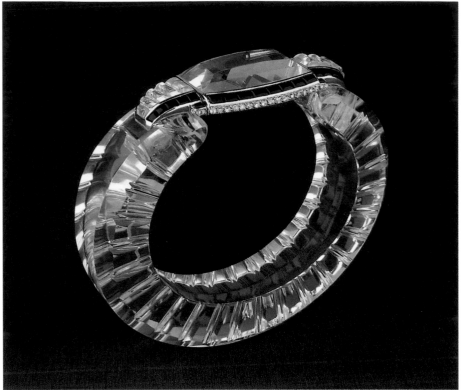

185

186

185 Rock-crystal and onyx bracelet

Made by English Art Works for Cartier London as a special order, 1936

Carved rock crystal, onyx and diamonds set in open-back platinum. Rigid rock-crystal bracelet with an opening at the top and a square hole at each end to take the clasp, a large rectangular rock crystal edged with calibré-cut onyx and a row of diamonds. The two side elements of the clasp slide outwards to enable it to be removed.

Job given to Roots on 30 January 1936; sold 27 April 1936.

MARKS Reverse of clasp engraved *Cartier London*.

Max. W. 8.5 cm, H. 7.7 cm

Cartier collection, BT 66 A36

EXHIBITIONS Tokyo 1995, cat. 268; Lausanne 1996, cat. 247.

RELATED MATERIAL Pencil working drawing in English Art Works job record book for 1936 in London archive.

Described in the English Arts Works job record book as a 'spring motif bracelet', this is one of a handful of bracelets with removable clasps that could also be worn separately as a brooch (see also cat. 219).

187

186 Carved agate bangle

Made by American Art Works for Cartier New York for stock, 1923

Agate hoop, the edge with diamonds, onyx and sapphires in platinum setting. The onyx and sapphire motifs – a central onyx flanked by two sapphires with diamonds in between – are repeated four times round the hoop.

Date of entry in stock book unknown; sold 26 March 1923.

MARKS Rim engraved *CARTIER*.

DIAM. 8.5 cm

Cartier collection, BT 43 A23

Two similar bracelets, both made for Cartier New York, are illustrated in the London archive photograph albums. One appears to be of a dark stone, perhaps onyx, and has a line of diamonds round the outer edge; the other dates from 1924 and is described in the New York archive records as 'one agate bangle with a row of sapphires and brilliants alternating set in center at flush angle'.

As in cat. 178, the diamonds on this bracelet are set with their tables in exactly the same orientation. This kind of attention to detail enhances the design and makes a huge difference to the overall finish of a piece.

187 Bracelet (bracelet soudanais)

Made by Lavabre for Cartier Paris for stock, 1919

Ivory, enamelled gold, coral, diamonds set in platinum. Carved ivory bangle with engraved decoration coloured black, gold terminals enamelled with black chequerboard pattern on outside edge and black enamel sides. Diamonds at the joints and diamond arrowhead on outside edge. One of the terminals twists outwards to open. Two carved coral beads at each end.

Entered in stock book on 20 September 1919, originally with onyx beads studded with a diamond at the end, instead of coral beads; sold 1 December 1919. Bought back for stock 30 December 1919 and sold for the second time on 29 June 1920.

MARKS Inside of gold terminal engraved *Cartier Paris Londres New York*; Paris eagle's head assay mark for gold and workshop mark *IIL* flanking a four-leaf clover.

Max. W. 7.5 cm

Cartier collection, BT 15 A19

EXHIBITIONS Paris 1989, cat. 179; Tokyo 1995, cat. 93.

Eight further versions of this model are recorded in 1919, of which one was a special order.

Cartier often gave exotic-sounding names to their jewels. They used the term 'bracelet soudanais' for a series of similar bracelets with ivory hoops and ball terminals. Although there is nothing specifically Sudanese about this design, the name and the use of ivory were no doubt intended to suggest an African origin. The shape recalls that of silver bracelets from Nubia, while incised black ring-and-dot decoration is found on Sudanese ivory bracelets, but these are in the form of complete thick rings.

188 Tassel pendant

Made by Picq for Cartier Paris for stock, 1922

Pearls, onyx, coral, enamel, diamonds set in platinum. Pendant formed of onyx ring encrusted with diamonds, a coral cylinder with applied diamond-set dragon joined by diamond-set loops outlined in black enamel, and a tassel of pearl strings ending in onyx beads. Pearl strings attach pendant to a black silk cord.

Entered in stock book on 15 June 1922; transferred to Cartier London for sale on 3 August 1922. Sold 8 August 1922 to Countess Curzon.

MARKS Diamond loops engraved *CARTIER*; French dog's head assay mark for platinum.

L. of pendant (including pearl strings at top) 17.5 cm. Total L. (with cord) 46.5 cm

Cartier collection, NE 03 A22

EXHIBITIONS Paris 1989, cat. 220; Rome 1990, cat. 108; St Petersburg 1992, cat. 119; Tokyo 1995, cat. 121.

The design of this piece, with its pendant ring on a knotted cord, from which hangs a coral rod and a tassel, is inspired directly by Chinese amuletic jade discs worn in pendant form in the eighteenth and nineteenth centuries, with a toggle, usually of carved wood or stone, and a textile tassel. For illustrations of Chinese Qing dynasty pendants of this kind in the National Palace Museum in Taipei, see Taipei 1986, cat. 208 and 213–27.

Grace Duggan, widow of Alfred Duggan of Buenos Aires and daughter of Joseph Monroe Hinds, United States Minister in Brazil, became in 1917 the second wife of George Nathaniel, Marquess Curzon of Kedleston (1859–1925), Viceroy of India 1898–1905 and Earl Curzon of Kedleston from 1911.

189 Belt brooch

Made by American Art Works for Cartier New York for stock, 1925

Onyx, coral, diamonds set in platinum. An onyx ring flanked by two hexagonal motifs in coral set with diamonds. The right-hand motif turns forward to release the pin.

Entered in stock book on 9 January 1925; sold 24 December 1925.

MARKS On reverse *CARTIER*.

W. 6.5 cm

Cartier collection, CL 81 A25

EXHIBITIONS Paris 1989, cat. 257; Rome 1990, cat. 124; Tokyo 1995, cat. 149.

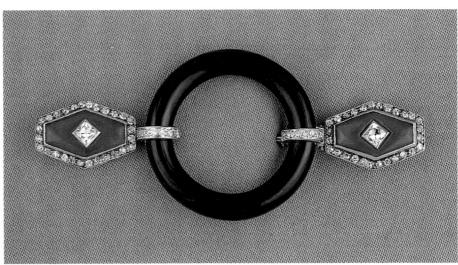

189 (greatly enlarged)

190

190 Vanity case

Made by Lavabre for Cartier Paris for stock, 1923

Enamelled gold, onyx, coral, emeralds, diamonds set in platinum. The case with black enamel stripes all over and black enamel ends; in the centre a flower basket in carved coral, cabochon emeralds, diamonds and black enamel; suspension chains of enamelled gold, coral beads and onyx batons with diamond loops; onyx suspension ring. Interior with mirrored lid, powder compartment and lipstick holder.

Entered in stock book on 29 March 1923, originally with a black silk tassel attached to the onyx ring; sold 5 June 1923 to Mrs W. K. Vanderbilt.

MARKS Inside rim engraved *Cartier Paris Londres New York*; Paris eagle's head assay mark for gold, workshop mark *HL* flanking a four-leaf clover.

L. (with ring) 14.6 cm, (case only) 6 cm, W. 4.2 cm

Cartier collection, VC 01 A23

EXHIBITIONS Hong Kong 1995, cat. 29

This vanity case was originally made with a black silk tassel. Many vanities of this type were made with tassels, which gave them a much more obviously Chinese look, but few of the original tassels survive. The small size of this vanity case is unusual. The model was introduced in 1922 and is described in the archive as a 'nécessaire grandeur Espagne' or a 'petit nécessaire modèle Espagne'. It seems that the term 'modèle Espagne' originated in the Lavabre workshop, where these small vanity cases were made.

For Mrs W. K. Vanderbilt, see cat. 91.

191 Bracelet

Made by Picq for Cartier Paris for stock, 1925. Included in the Cartier display at the 1925 Paris Exhibition

Coral, onyx and diamonds in open-back platinum setting. A flat band of inlaid alternating coral and diamond pennants, with border of cabochon onyx, the clasp in the form of two square pavé-set diamond motifs with central baton diamond. Each vertical element fully articulated.

Entered in stock book on 6 May 1925; sold 14 January 1929.

MARKS On reverse *CARTIER PARIS* and *MADE IN FRANCE*; on tongue French dog's head assay mark for platinum and workshop mark *IP* flanking an ace of spades.

L. (including tongue) 19 cm

Cartier collection, BT 05 A25

EXHIBITIONS Paris 1925; Venice 1986, cat. 114; Naples 1988, cat. 34; Paris 1989, cat. 260; Rome 1990, cat. 125; Tokyo 1995, cat. 150.

RELATED MATERIAL Original design in pencil, watercolour and bodycolour on buff tracing paper in the Stock Design Record Book, 1925, p. 29a, in Paris archive.

A design for a similar bracelet, with central diamond-set elements, appears in the Stock Design Record Book, 1922, p. 29b (see Tokyo 1995, cat. 125, with colour illustration, p. 338).

The construction of this bracelet is remarkable. Each element is hinged so that the bracelet bends evenly round the arm but remains solid when the bracelet is curved, due to the use of very narrow vertical elements, corresponding to each pennant-shaped piece of coral and forming a box at the back.

191

192

193

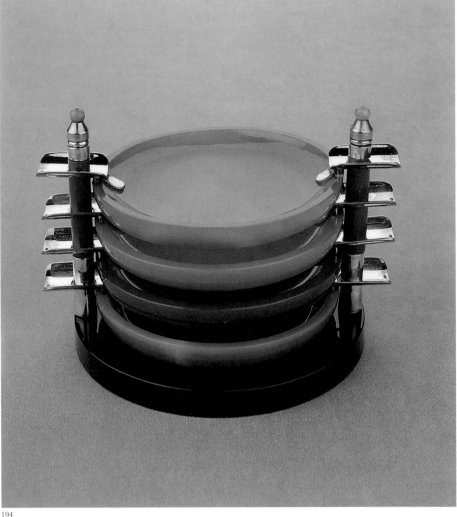

194

192 Ring

Made for Cartier New York to the order of
Mrs E. F. Hutton (Marjorie Merriweather
Post), 1933.

Coral, onyx, diamonds and platinum. Bezel formed of
three alternating onyx and coral rods joined by
diamond-set bands, two semicircular motifs in coral and
diamonds on the shoulders, platinum hoop.

Sold 2 December 1933.

MARKS Hoop engraved *Cartier* with the date 12.2.33
(2 December 1933).

L. of bezel 2.6 cm, DIAM. of hoop 1.9 cm

Cartier collection, RG 01 A33

EXHIBITIONS Los Angeles 1982, cat. 68; Naples 1988.
cat. 36; Paris 1989, cat. 447; Rome 1990, cat. 220.

The motif of graduated rods was probably
derived from French models; a very similar
ring in silver, the bezel formed of a row of
rods increasing in size toward the middle,
was exhibited by Jean Deprès at the XXI
Salon des Artists Décorateurs (*Art et Décoration*, 1931, p. 21).

For another piece owned by Marjorie
Merriweather Post, see cat. 100.

193 Scent bottle

Made by Couet for Cartier Paris for stock,
1924

Rock crystal, enamelled gold, coral and a pearl. The
bottle of carved rock crystal, with gold mount round the
neck enamelled in black with geometric pattern. The
screw stopper of coral set with a pearl, with black
enamel handle and original gold spatula.

Entered in stock book on 22 April 1924; sold 16 June
1924. Bought back for stock on 8 August 1924 and sold
for the second time on 21 October 1924.

MARKS Mount engraved *Cartier*; Paris eagle's head assay
mark for gold on stopper.

H. 5.6 cm

Cartier collection, AL 30 A24

EXHIBITIONS Paris 1989, cat. 322; Rome 1990, cat. 144;
Tokyo 1995, cat. 183.

LITERATURE Cologni and Mocchetti 1992, p. 79.

194 Set of four stacking
ash-trays

Made possibly by Couet for Cartier Paris
for stock, *c.* 1923

Gold, silver, agate, onyx, coral, jade. Four grey agate
ash-trays each with two silver-gilt cigarette rests, pierced
to slot over two vertical rods in coral and silver with jade
bead finials; onyx plinth.

Similar pieces both made by the Couet workshop entered in stock book on 29 March 1923 (sold to Louis Cartier) and on 3 December 1923 (sold 6 December 1923 to Mrs G. Blumenthal).

MARKS On reverse of cigarette rests *CARTIER*; Paris boar's head assay mark for silver and assay mark for mixed metals.

H. 6.7 cm, DIAM. of base 7.9 cm

Cartier collection, IV 07 C23

LITERATURE Cologni and Mocchetti 1992, p. 92.

A design for a similar set of four stacking ash-trays in rock crystal, with gold rods and an onyx plinth, is illustrated in Cologni and Mocchetti 1992, p. 98. These sets of ash-trays may have been intended for a bridge foursome.

195 Ash-tray

Made by Fourrier (jade lily) and Pillard for Cartier Paris for stock (Department S) in 1936, the jade lily initially mounted as a table bell in 1927

Carved pale jade lily on obsidian plinth; two diamond-studded carved coral motifs either side.

The table bell entered in stock book (Department S) on 6 December 1927; modified in 1931, still as table bell. Transferred to smokers' articles as an ash-tray in 1935; altered to present state on 20 October 1936; sold 21 November 1936.

MARKS Base engraved *Cartier*

L. 9.1 cm, W. 5.8 cm, H. 5 cm

Cartier collection, IV 08 A36

This object has been included as an example of a relatively inexpensive item, made for Department S, undergoing multiple modifications and indeed changing its function altogether. The carved jade lily remained the only constant feature and the element round which each modification was constructed. The four modifications made between 1927 and 1936 are as follows:

(1) 1927: table bell entered in stock book on 6 December 1927, incorporating the jade lily carved by the Fourrier workshop. The lily mounted by the Couet workshop on square base of fluorite and enamel, with eleven cabochon topazes in enamelled gold settings in the centre. Unsold.

(2) 1931: fluorite base replaced by pink mirror-glass framed in black-lacquered silver; object re-entered in stock book, still as table bell, on 3 December 1931. Unsold.

(3) 1935: table bell changed to ash-tray by removing the topazes from the centre (modifi-cation executed by the Cartier workshop); transferred to smokers' articles on 5 October 1935. Unsold.

(4) 1936: ash-tray modified by replacing pink mirror-glass base with obsidian plinth (modifi-cation by the Pillard workshop); re-entered in stock book for the fourth time on 20 October; finally sold 21 November 1936.

While high jewellery was automatically unset and redesigned if it did not sell, it is unusual for a Department S piece to have been changed so many times and to have remained in stock for so long. If there were no customers for what must have been a rather garish object in jade, topaz and fluorite, the pink mirror-glass did not help, and it was only when a restrained black base was substituted that the piece finally sold. For Department S, see p. 120.

196 Cigarette holder

Made by Pillard for Cartier Paris for stock, 1928

Jet, coral, diamonds and emeralds set in platinum. The tube of jet and coral, with diamond-set rings at the joins, the ring nearest the trumpet with three square-set emeralds. The original cigar-shaped case in brown leather survives.

Entered in stock book on 9 July 1928; sold 11 August 1928.

MARKS Platinum mount at end of trumpet engraved *CARTIER MADE IN FRANCE*; Paris eagle's head assay mark for gold and partly legible workshop mark, second letter *P*.

L. 8.9 cm

Cartier collection, AG 20 A28

EXHIBITIONS Venice 1986, cat. 153; Naples 1988, cat. 38.

This model is described as a 'fume cigarette trompette' in the archive record.

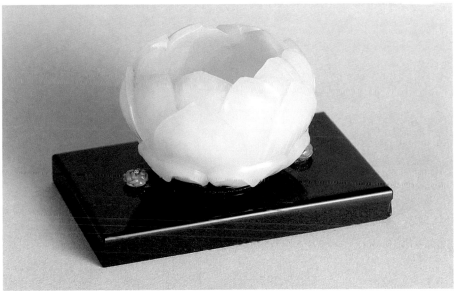

195

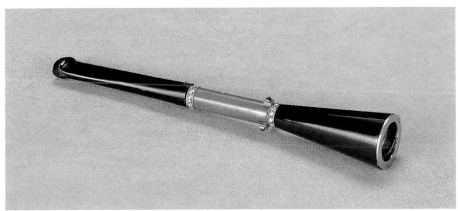

196

197, 198

They no doubt all contained compacted powder, permitting the use of such a flat shape. Powder boxes with loose powder were usually quite deep, with a gauze cover so that the powder did not spill.

199 Lipstick case

Made by the Cartier workshop for Cartier Paris for stock (Department S), 1935

Black lacquer on silver, square-section, with coral disc set with a single diamond; hinged lid turns sideways to form a right angle behind the coral disc.

An identical piece made by the Cartier workshop entered in stock book on 10 October 1935; sold 13 December 1935 to Comte Luzarche d'Azay.

MARKS Inside rim engraved *Cartier Paris Bte SGDG*; Paris boar's head assay mark for silver and workshop mark *C* between two crescents with the letters *S* and *A* above and below.

L. 6 cm, W. 1.4 cm

Cartier collection, AL 10 A35

LITERATURE Cologni and Mocchetti 1992, p. 155.

This model was designed to hold a Guerlain lipstick.

Charles Antoine Roger Luzarche d'Azay (1872–1961), who purchased an identical lipstick case, served in the French cavalry in the First World War. His collection of Fabergé and Cartier cigarette cases was left to the Musée des Arts Décoratifs, Paris (see St Petersburg/London 1993, pp. 376–87).

197 Powder box

Made in Paris by Pillard for Cartier London for stock, 1930

Black lacquer on silver, gold rims and hinges, coral, diamonds set in platinum. At top and base of lid three graduated coral rods joined by diamond bands. Interior silver-gilt with mirrored lid, lipstick, and powder compartment that opens from the right-hand side.

Dated by Cartier London photograph to October 1930. Sold Christie's Geneva, 16 November 1989, lot 401.

MARKS On mirror frame *CARTIER MADE IN FRANCE*; Paris boar's head assay mark for silver and workshop mark *AP* flanking a tripod (?) on lipstick and lid; London import marks and date letter for 1930 with importer's mark *JC* for Jacques Cartier on base.

L. 5.1 cm, W. (with coral rods) 5.1 cm, H. 1.4 cm

Cartier collection, AL 31 A30

EXHIBITIONS Paris 1989, cat. 473; Rome 1990, cat. 231.

LITERATURE Cologni and Mocchetti 1992, p. 155.

This is one of six powder boxes of the same design, all made in Paris for Cartier London; the first was photographed on 6 May 1930, the next on 18 May 1930, and three more on 20 May 1931.

An identical box, also made by the Pillard workshop, was entered in the Cartier Paris stock book for Department S on 21 July 1930 and sold on 11 December 1939.

198 'Flap-jack' powder box

Made in Paris by Pillard for Cartier London for stock, 1934

Black lacquer on silver, coral, diamonds. Flat circular shape, elliptical section, all in black lacquer, the rims reserved in silver-gilt; hinge pin in the form of a coral rod set with diamonds; friction-twist clasp set with coral, square-set diamond at hinge and on upper push-piece. Interior gilded with mirrored lid, the base filled with compacted powder.

Dated by Cartier London photograph to April 1935; sold 20 January 1936.

MARKS Engraved inside lid *Cartier Paris MADE IN FRANCE*; Paris boar's head assay mark for silver and workshop mark *PP* flanking a playing card (?); on base London import marks and date-letter for 1934 with importer's mark *JC* for Jacques Cartier.

DIAM. 8.5 cm

Cartier collection, AL 98 A35

Described in the London archive records as a 'flap-jack', presumably referring to the method of opening, whereby the two push-pieces, one on the lid and one on the base, are twisted against each other so that the lid flips up.

This model was popular for some time. A similar version, with lapis instead of coral and with two compartments for powder and lipstick, was received from Paris on 29 May 1931 and sold on 9 June 1931. An identical piece, also made by Pillard, was entered in the Paris stock book on 29 June 1934 and sold on 30 December 1934.

199

200 (greatly reduced)

200 Dressing-table vanity case

Made by Frontin (the setting), Maréchal (the coral) and Pillard (the comb) for Cartier Paris for stock (Department S), 1938

Black lacquer on aluminium, silver-gilt, coral, diamonds set in platinum. Black lacquer case with roll-down bar to release lid, the bar set with a coral rod bordered with diamonds, two diamonds on the pivots at each side. Interior silver-gilt with mirrored lid and five compartments, two of them lidded, for powder and a smaller one for rouge, the lids lacquered black; silver-gilt lipstick holder and a slot at the back containing the original blonde tortoiseshell comb. The powder and rouge compartments contain the original gauze sifters and kid leather puffs.

Entered in stock book on 11 January 1938; sold 4 February 1938.

MARKS Engraved inside lid *CARTIER PARIS*; Paris boar's head assay mark for silver and workshop mark *FRONTIN* with a star above and below, *Cartier* printed in gold on puffs.

L. 16 cm, W. 11 cm

Cartier collection, VC 47 A38

LITERATURE Cologni and Mocchetti 1992, p. 155.

A Cartier New York catalogue of 1937 included a vanity case of the same design in engine-turned gold, the bar decorated with jade tubes. See also p. 119, fig. 64.

200.1 Cat. 200 shown open, with the original tortoiseshell comb and the gauze sifters and kid leather puffs for powder and rouge compartments.

DIAMOND
JEWELLERY
BETWEEN THE
WARS

Of all Cartier's many areas of production, the design of jewellery in diamonds and precious stones is most closely bound up with fashions in *haute couture*. The links with high fashion houses, begun with Cartier's move to the Rue de la Paix, were further strengthened with Louis Cartier's marriage in 1898 to Jean-Philippe Worth's daughter Andrée.[1] In the early 1900s Cartier purchased watered silk for their dog-collar necklaces (see p. 00), which were displayed at Worths. In the following decade, Cartier's aigrettes (diamond brooches holding a tuft of feathers, worn in the hair or attached to a jewelled band) were an essential part of Worth's evening wear.

For the 1920s and 1930s there is a wealth of documentary evidence from contemporary fashion magazines, and numerous fashion photographs show Cartier jewels on designer outfits. The accompanying texts suggest that in many cases a close collaboration existed between jeweller and couturier. No detailed study of Cartier's relationship with the couturiers has been carried out, and it is impossible to say whether Cartier designed jewels for specific costumes or whether the couturiers requested designs from Cartier. Since such a study is beyond the scope of this catalogue, the following remarks can only draw attention to how the jewels catalogued here were worn and to the influence of high fashion on their design.

The short, cropped hair of the 1920s could not support an elaborate tiara, hence the development of the flat, flexible, lightweight bandeau worn low on the forehead and tied at the back (cat. 203–5). In 1925 Cartier London advertised their flexible bandeaux as ideal for the shingled or very closely cropped sleek head (p. 22, fig. 16). The neo-classical wide combs, hinged or straight (see cat. 8–9), and Cartier's *fourches* or two-pronged combs (see p. 47, fig. 35, and p. 49), all ornaments for piled-up hair, gave way to the comb bandeau. This appears to have been an innovation of Cartier's. Unlike the bandeau, which went right round the head, the comb bandeau encirled the back of the head, reaching to the ears, and so was visible from the back and the side only. It was held by the natural spring of the tortoiseshell, and the comb was hidden beneath short curls at the back. The elegant and restrained example included here (cat. 202) may be contrasted with the *outré* comb bandeau shown at the 1925 Paris Exhibition (cat. 271): on each side was a pair of

FIG. 77. Archive photograph of a mannequin designed by Pierre Imans with Cartier diamond sautoir, bandeau and earrings, 1929. Cartier archive, Paris.

orchids in diamonds and onyx. In March 1928 Cartier London created an emerald and diamond back-of-the-head bandeau formed of a narrow line of square-cut emeralds with a diamond oriental palm leaf at each end. According to the archive description it was 'mounted on a cable or watchmaker spring'; there were special clips at each end and a small comb in the middle.

With the waistless or low-waisted dresses of the 1920s, a long necklace was *de rigueur*, whether a tasselled necklace (cat. 188), a seal-watch on a long black cord (cat. 95–6), a long chain of beads or a diamond sautoir. Cartier diamond sautoirs of the 1920s generally had a detachable pendant element at the base that could be worn as a brooch, while the chain itself divided into a number of bracelets (cat. 214). Fig. 77 illustrates a

La robe que nous reproduisons en couverture est portée par la comtesse A. de Castéja, née princesse Emeline de Broglie. C'est une création de Chanel. Les bijoux sont de Cartier.

FIG. 78. The Comtesse de Castéja (née Emeline de Broglie), daughter of Daisy Fellowes by her first husband, Prince Jean-Anatole de Broglie, photographed for Paris *Vogue* in 1934 wearing a Cartier halo head ornament in the form of a diamond-set spiral, with matching bracelet, and a Cartier necklace of square-cut diamonds.

Cartier diamond sautoir, with bandeau and earrings, on a mannequin created for Cartier by Pierre Imans in 1929. It should also be noted that many flat bandeaux of the 1920s could also be taken apart to form strap bracelets, usually two (cat. 205). Sometimes the centrepiece of the bandeau formed a brooch. The sleeveless, loose-fitting evening dresses of this period meant that brooches had to be secured to the undergarments. Cartier designed a range of long shoulder brooches (cat. 100, 213 and 261–5) and belt brooches to fasten the low-slung belts (cat. 181 and 273).

The softer, wavier hairstyles of the 1930s demanded head ornaments of a different kind from those worn in the 1920s. Cartier's most original contribution here was the halo head ornament. It was worn at a steep angle so that it framed the head like a halo, and was attached with elastic at the back. Unlike the flat bandeau, it was often three-dimensional, like the halos in the form of open spirals that blended with the curls of the hair. Two such spirals were made by Cartier Paris for the Comtesse de Castéja in 1934 (fig. 78) and for Elsie de Wolfe in 1935 (see below). A halo head ornament made by Cartier London in 1934 with diamond lotus blossoms is included with other Egyptian-style pieces in section 4 (cat. 80). The halo head ornament was often designed so that it could also be removed from its frame and worn as a necklace. One example designed in 1937 and advertised in London *Vogue* for March of that year (see fig. 80) could be worn in this way (fig. 79). The design comprised a series of scrolls, decreasing in size towards the back. The central, larger scrolls were detachable for wear as three clip brooches, similar to cat. 222. This example was one of twenty-seven tiaras and head ornaments made by Cartier London in 1937. This was an astonishing number compared with seven in 1936 and fifteen in 1938. The coronation of George VI in May 1937 and its associated events led to a flurry of activity in April and early May. Fifteen of the twenty-seven were produced in that period, nine of them for stock and six for special orders. Most were of aquamarines and diamonds or topaz and diamonds.

Sautoirs and long shoulder brooches disappeared with the new shapelier profile of the 1930s. The return of the waist meant that necklaces were reduced to a short collar. With necklines that were wider or cut away on the shoulders, the long pendant shoulder brooches were replaced by clip brooches. Introduced in the late 1920s, the clip brooch became the most versatile and essential piece of jewellery of the 1930s, to

FIG. 80. Advertisement in London *Vogue* for March 1937 for a halo head ornament made by Cartier London. The crown in the background symbolised the coronation of George VI, which was to take place in May that year. Cartier made an extra large number of tiaras for stock in 1937 with this event in mind.

FIG. 79. Archive photograph of the halo head ornament of 1937 shown in fig. 80 converted for wear as a necklace. The central, larger scrolls were detachable for wear as three clip brooches. Alternatively, the long central scroll could be retained and the flanking ones removed, making a shorter necklace. Cartier London.

secure the dress at the front, back or on the shoulder line, or to decorate the hat. Most Cartier clip brooches have a double-prong sprung fitting at the back, often with a smaller series of subsidiary prongs protruding from the reverse of the jewel to ensure maximum security (see cat. 169.1). They are therefore true clip brooches, as opposed to the kind of clip that has one sprung solid arm and which can only be worn on the edge of a garment. The Cartier double-prong fitting acts like a double brooch pin so that the brooch can be worn anywhere on the costume. Cartier took out patents for clip brooch fittings in 1927 and 1934. Illustrations of clip brooches worn as buttons and at the base of a low-backed dress are shown on p. 22, fig. 15, and p. 24, fig. 20.

The double clip brooch was supplied with a frame fitted with an ordinary brooch-pin, so that both could be worn together as a single brooch or separately as clip brooches (cat. 220–23). From 1931 Cartier produced clip brooches that separated into as many as seven graduated elements. And from 1934 Cartier Paris introduced what turned out to be a best-selling line in all three houses – the double clip brooch with black lacquer bracelet as well as brooch fitting. Each clip could be attached to the bracelet, creating three separate jewels in one (cat. 292–4). The introduction of three-dimensional forms with curving rather than rigidly geometrical, flatter elements dates from the mid-1930s. The two styles ran in parallel until the end of the 1930s.

The problem of designing a double clip brooch in which each element stood on its own, but without an obvious dividing line when both parts were worn together, was considered a challenge for the designer.[2] The early geometric examples tended to be symmetrical mirror-images of each other. With the introduction of a more fluid style, the effect was of a right-hand and a left-hand image, with the angles reversed, although the two parts were the same: cat. 223 is formed of two identical scroll clips, both curving to the left if worn side by side, but when joined together they form an S-scroll. A completely different effect was achieved by joining the two brooches along the long side instead of the shorter side (cat. 222). Some of the Cartier clips could be joined along either side, giving three possibilities.

The inter-war years saw a number of Cartier novelties that were independent of changes in dress. Among the most notable were the diamond bracelet-watches of the 1920s, specially designed to conceal one of Cartier's tiny *baguette* watches for evening wear (cat. 210–12). The hinged lids were adapted from earlier hunter-cased watches and could be lifted with the flick of a nail to reveal the dial. The black lacquer bracelets to take clip brooches of the mid-1930s have already been mentioned. Another ingenious invention was the bracelet of carved rock crystal with detachable centrepiece that could be worn as a brooch (cat. 185 and 219).

Finally, many pieces of this period use old-cut diamonds. While this is to be expected in the case of special orders which reused stones belonging to the client, it is perhaps surprising in the case of modern designs made for stock. The most successful pieces were those in which the cutting of the stones complemented the design, for example the ruby and diamond bracelet (cat. 216), the pyramid clip brooch (cat. 220), or the bracelet-watch (cat. 211).

Topaz

Topaz and aquamarine (see below) play a particularly important role in Cartier's work of the 1930s. The confusion between topaz and yellow quartz has a long history: all yellow stones have traditionally been described as topaz, although many of them are in fact yellow quartz or citrine, a much less expensive stone. The highly prized sherry-yellow topaz crystals are found only in Brazil. The Cartier ledgers refer frequently to 'dark and light topaz', much of which was probably yellow and brownish-yellow quartz or topaz and citrine combined.

Topaz, set in gold, is generally regarded as one of the most fashionable gemstones of the late 1930s, but it was already being used by Cartier during the 1920s both for multigem jewellery and in combination with diamonds. For example, in November 1928 English Art Works made a flower vase brooch with nephrite vase, lapis lazuli birds and topaz leaves. In the same month, they made a diamond and topaz head ornament comprising a diamond motif with 19 topazes, 65 baton topazes and 121 bead topazes. It was one of a series of extraordinary head ornaments with elaborate side-pieces that fitted tight over the brow of the head and was held with a continuous band round the back. It was sold in October 1929 (fig. 81). The diamonds were set in platinum while the baton topazes, a novelty in 1928, were set in gold and formed a thin band of parallel stones, as in the head ornament catalogued here (cat. 226). In June 1929 English Art Works made

FIG. 81. Archive photograph of a wax model wearing a topaz and diamond head ornament made by Cartier London in November 1928. The band of baton-cut topazes continued right round the back of the head to keep the ornament in place.

an 'all baton topaz ring' with gold mount, the topazes set parallel to one another in the same way. In 1930 Cartier London made a topaz and diamond head ornament, set in gold and platinum, in the manner of an Indian turban ornament, with a raised central jewel. Cat. 226, although made seven years later, is virtually the same design.

The number of topaz pieces increases dramatically from 1934. In January 1935, Lady Elizabeth Paget, second daughter of Lord and Lady Anglesey and a 1934 débutante, was photographed for *Harper's Bazaar* (p 59) wearing 'Cartier's magnificent parure… of light and dark topaz', comprising necklace, earrings, bracelet and huge shoulder clip (fig. 82). In October 1938 Cartier London advertised a set of topaz jewellery in *Vogue* (p. 52), comprising what appears to be the identical necklace with a different bracelet, ring and clip (worn in the hair). The accompanying text demonstrates the emphasis given to topaz by Paris houses such as Mauboussin, as well as by Cartier themselves, for whom

> Topaz and gold are a famous old team revived in this season of revivals. If you have any of those big, old, and pale topazes languishing in a forgotten corner, bring them out and have them reset. With diamonds, if you feel that way about it. Or with *massy gold*. The

only requirement is that topaz jewellery must look as important as if it were emeralds or rubies. That is the way Cartier has treated it in the rather sensational pieces above, combining light and dark topaz and yellow gold in a bracelet, clip, and ring. The topaz-and-diamond necklace can become a tiara … the bracelet can become one of those magnificent 'clumpy' clips that make any costume important.

Aquamarines

Aquamarines are pale blue stones cut from large crystals of flawless clarity. Indeed, cut aquamarines need to be of some size for the colour to be sufficiently intense. Most of the sky-blue stones seen in jewellery are the result of the heat-treatment of greenish-yellow stones. The problems of obtaining stones of a good colour are apparent from documents in the Cartier archive, quoted below. The aquamarine tiara included here (cat. 227) is of traditional crown-like form, but with stones cut in the modern style.

Much of Cartier's aquamarine jewellery seems to have been made by the London branch, where it appears in the records from 1932. Aquamarines were popular not only with the London clientele but also with the American clients of both the London and Paris branches. There are a number of instances of American clients ordering aquamarine jewellery in London. One of these is documented by correspondence in the Cartier New York archive. In October 1934 Cartier London wrote to Cartier New York enclosing photographs of a bracelet and clip brooch in aquamarines and diamonds recently sold to the client, together with estimates for similar pieces in 'two-coloured topazes' (again a reference to dark and light topaz, almost certainly topaz and citrine). A month later, at New York's request, Cartier London sent designs and details of stones for a proposed aquamarine and diamond necklace. Either the price or the design was rejected by the client, for in December 1936 Cartier London sent photographs of two further necklaces. One was 'as near as possible like the photo she saw in London. However, owing to the rise in platinum, wages and prices of aquamarines since that date, we find ourselves unable to supply this necklace at the same price as quoted for the necklace the customer so insistently demands.' The second example was similar but smaller, 'in order to meet our client as regards price', and would still match her own jewellery. The letter continues: 'We would mention that owing to the difficulty of obtaining quickly a supply of good colour aquamarines, we are unable to fix a definite date for completion of the order, but we hope to deliver in America in 2 months from receipt of order. As a matter of fact, we have for our own stock, a number of partly completed necklaces, which we are unable to finish owing to lack of the necessary aquamarines.' The order was finally confirmed on 19 January 1937.

Another American client, Elsie de Wolfe, commmissioned an aquamarine tiara from Cartier Paris and, true to form, had her hair tinted to match it. In the autumn of 1935, then aged 70, she had been named the Best Dressed Woman in the World by the Parisian couturiers. This was a new title, created to single her out from the twenty women who had been picked each year since 1933, and who had to spend anything from $10,000 to $40,000 to acquire the accolade. On her return to New York in November 1935, she posed for photographers, pointing out that 'her hair was tinted aquamarine to match her latest acquisition, a curling spiral tiara of diamonds and aquamarines that she had commissioned from Cartier of Paris, her favourite jewelers'.[3] The design of the tiara was almost identical to the diamond spiral tiara worn by the Comtesse de Castéja in 1934 (see p. 258, fig. 78)

NOTES
1. The marriage lasted only until 1910.
2. It is discussed at length in Selwyn 1945, pp. 68–71.
3. Smith 1982, p. 269.

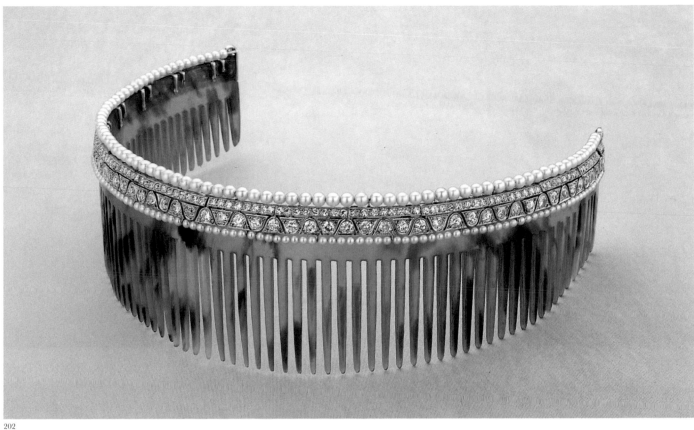

202

201 Serpent necklace

Made by Lavabre for Cartier Paris for stock, 1919

Diamonds in open-back millegrain platinum setting. A band of openwork scale pattern with curved surface, the head with diamond-set eyes. The tail twists round the neck, with stud fastening at front.

Entered in stock book on 22 September 1919; sold 11 June 1921. Sold Sotheby's St Moritz, 19 February 1993, lot 319.

MARKS Rim engraved *Cartier Paris Londres New York*; French dog's head assay mark for platinum and workshop mark *HL* flanking a four-leaf clover.

L. 22.5 cm, W. 12.2 cm

Cartier collection, NE 20 A19

EXHIBITIONS Tokyo 1995, cat. 91.

LITERATURE Cologni and Nussbaum 1995, p. 110.

The band is articulated enough to open and close, but forms a rigid collar when worn. The scale pattern was repeated several times on flat bandeaux (see cat. 204), but this is an exceptional use on a curved surface.

202 Comb bandeau for the back of the head

Made by Picq for Cartier Paris for stock, 1923

Tortoiseshell comb with diamonds and pearls in platinum setting. The sprung comb fits right round the back of the head and is bordered with openwork alternating diamond flower-heads forming a wave motif, with a row of seed pearls at top and bottom. The gem-set band is fitted to the comb with pairs of tiny rivets along the back.

Entered in stock book on 24 May 1923; sold 4 June 1926 to the Duchesse de Talleyrand. Sold Christie's St Moritz, 22 February 1990, lot 391.

MARKS None.

DIAM. (max.) 13.8 cm, H. at centre 4.1 cm

Cartier collection, AL 74 A23

LITERATURE Cologni and Nussbaum 1995, p. 144.

This bandeau still has its original case of semicircular form, with standard Cartier stamp inside the lid.

Comb bandeaux of this type were intro-duced by Cartier shortly after the First World War, in about 1922. They were intended for bobbed hair, worn smooth on top with short curls hiding the comb below the gem-set band. Two comb bandeaux were shown at the Paris Exhibition of 1925, one set with pairs of diamond and onyx orchids on each side (see cat. 271), the other with coral, diamonds and onyx. The idea was taken up by Cartier London in the late 1920s with a series of back-of-the-head bandeaux mounted on a sprung wire instead of a comb.

The Duchesse de Talleyrand ordered two further comb bandeaux for the back of the head in January 1936; one had a line of flat-cut diamonds round the top designed to be worn alternatively as a necklace.

Anna Gould, daughter of the American financier Jay Gould, married the 5th Duc de Talleyrand in London in 1908. She was previously married to Comte Boniface de Castellane (marriage dissolved in 1906), a regular Cartier client of the early 1900s.

◀ 201

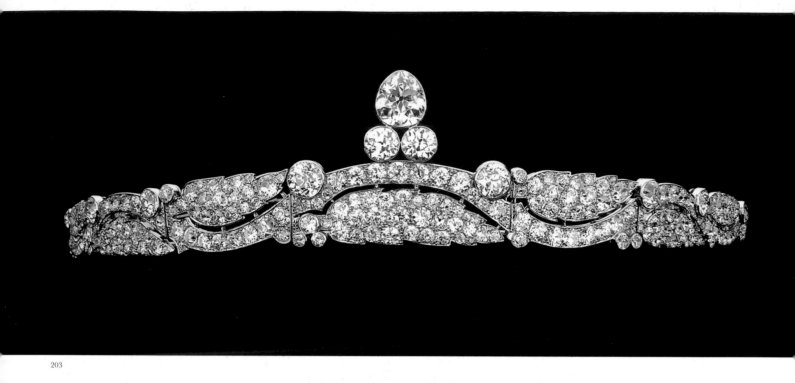

203

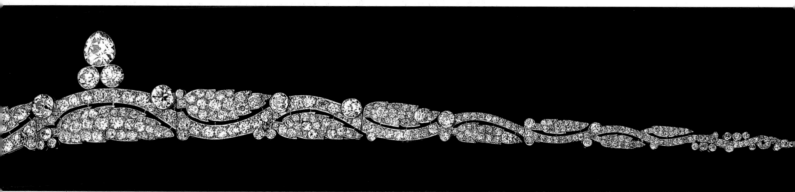

203

203 Bandeau

Made by Renault for Cartier Paris as a special order, 1919

Diamonds in open-back platinum setting. A sinuous flexible hinged branch of leaves and berries tapering to scrolling tendrils at the ends; the centre with a pear-shaped diamond above two brilliant-cut diamonds in collet settings. The reverse fitted with screw holes to take a frame. The present frame is modern.

Completed in December 1919. Sold Christie's Geneva, *Jewellery by Cartier*, 21 May 1992, lot 745. Previously sold Christie's London 20 June 1990, lot 178.

MARKS Lower rim engraved *CARTIER PARIS LONDRES*; French dog's head assay mark for platinum on gallery and workshop mark *R* with a crescent and flame (?) on central diamond.

DIAM. (max.) 16.3 cm, H. 3.1 cm

Cartier collection, JV 22 A19

EXHIBITIONS Tokyo 1995, cat. 90.

LITERATURE Cologni and Nussbaum 1995, p. 111.

From 1913 two varieties of bandeaux worn low on the forehead were introduced by Cartier. One was a thin line of diamonds with a central diamond aigrette (see Nadelhoffer 1984, pp. 84–5). The other took the form of a wider band, the diamond aigrette replaced by a smaller central element which held a plume of ostrich feathers (see Nadelhoffer 1984, p. 81). This bandeau is of the second type and possibly once held feathers.

204 Bandeau

Made by Lavabre for Cartier Paris, 1923

Diamonds in open-back millegrain platinum setting.
A tapering articulated band with openwork scale
pattern and three hexagonal elements removable for
wear as brooches.

This piece is dated by the archive photograph.

MARKS Rim engraved *Cartier Paris Londres New York*;
French dog's head assay mark for platinum and
workshop mark *HL* flanking a four-leaf clover on
attachment loops.

L. (with loops) 40.5 cm, (without loops) 39.7 cm

Cartier collection, JV 27 A23

This model was repeated several times with
variations in design and in size. These flat,
flexible bandeaux were extremely fashionable
from *c.* 1913 (see Nadelhoffer 1984, fig. 71) to
the mid-1920s; they were attached at the back
with ribbons.

According to a four-page Cartier advertisement for 'The New Jewellery' in London *Vogue*
(January 1925, p. 44), these narrow, flexible
bandeaux were specially designed for the
newly fashionable closely cropped hair (see
p. 22, fig. 16).

At a ball given in London by Lady Headfort
in June 1926, the hostess wore a 'becoming
Cartier bandeau of closely set diamonds, and
a white dress embroidered with jade green'
(*The Sketch*, 30 June 1926).

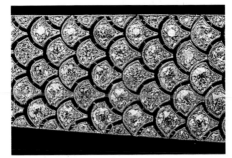

204.1 Detail of cat. 204.

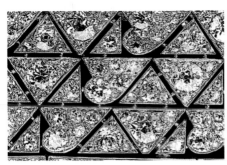

205.1 Detail of cat. 205.

205 Bandeau

Made by Lavabre for Cartier Paris as a special order, 1923

Diamonds in open-back millegrain platinum setting. An
articulated band of geometric openwork design rising to
a peak in the centre. The band comes apart to form two
bracelets by detaching the central Persian-style
palmette, the upper row of diamonds on each side
(in closed-back setting) and the central raised part.
A modern fitting fastens the diadem at the back.

Completed in November 1923, originally with sloping
ends formed of two triangular pieces. Sold Christie's
New York, 24 October 1989, lot 412.

MARKS French dog's head assay mark for platinum and
workshop mark *HL* flanking a four-leaf clover on tongues
of both bracelets; workshop mark also on lower edge of
central palmette.

L. (excluding modern fitting) 42.5 cm, H. 7.5 cm; L. of
bracelets 18.2 cm

Cartier collection, JV 11 A23

EXHIBITIONS St Petersburg 1992, cat. 129; Hong Kong
1995, cat. 31; Tokyo 1995, cat. 130.

LITERATURE Cologni and Nussbaum 1995, p. 141.

This bandeau was made using the client's own
stones, taken from a *rivière* (a necklace formed
of a row of large individually set diamonds), a
finger-ring and a pendant loop.

205.2 Exploded view showing bracelets detached
from cat. 205 and three brooches detached from
cat. 204 .

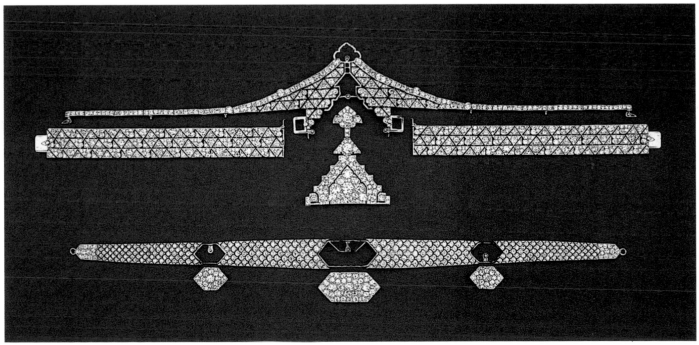

(overleaf) 205, 204 ▶

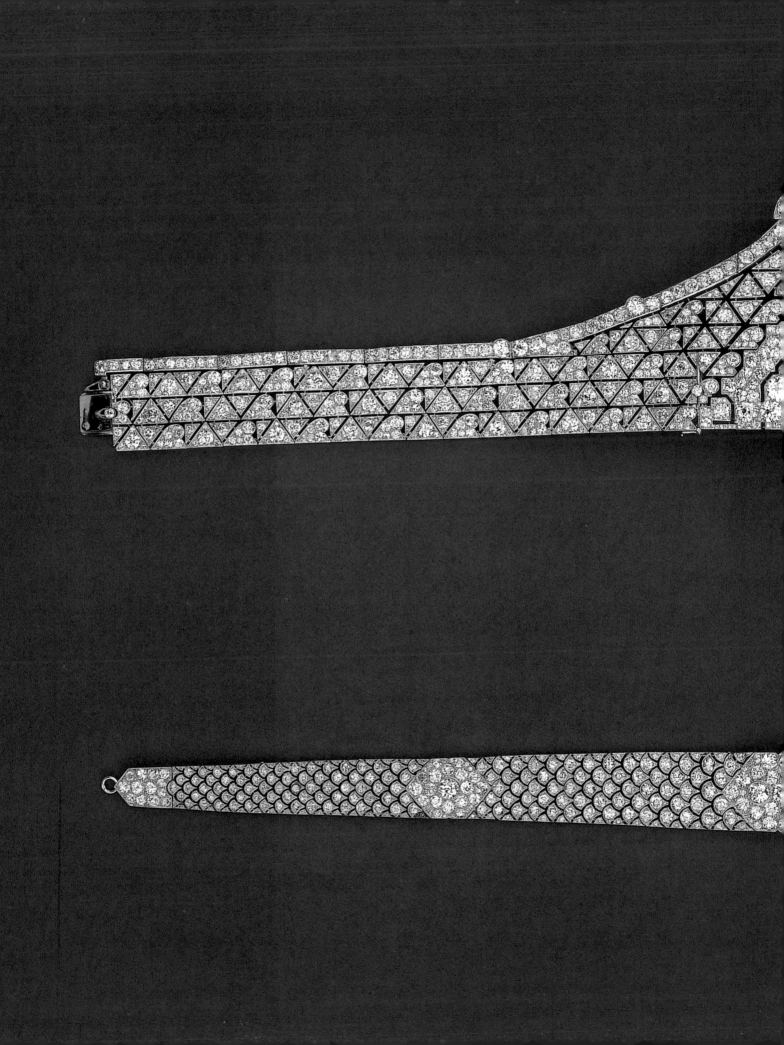

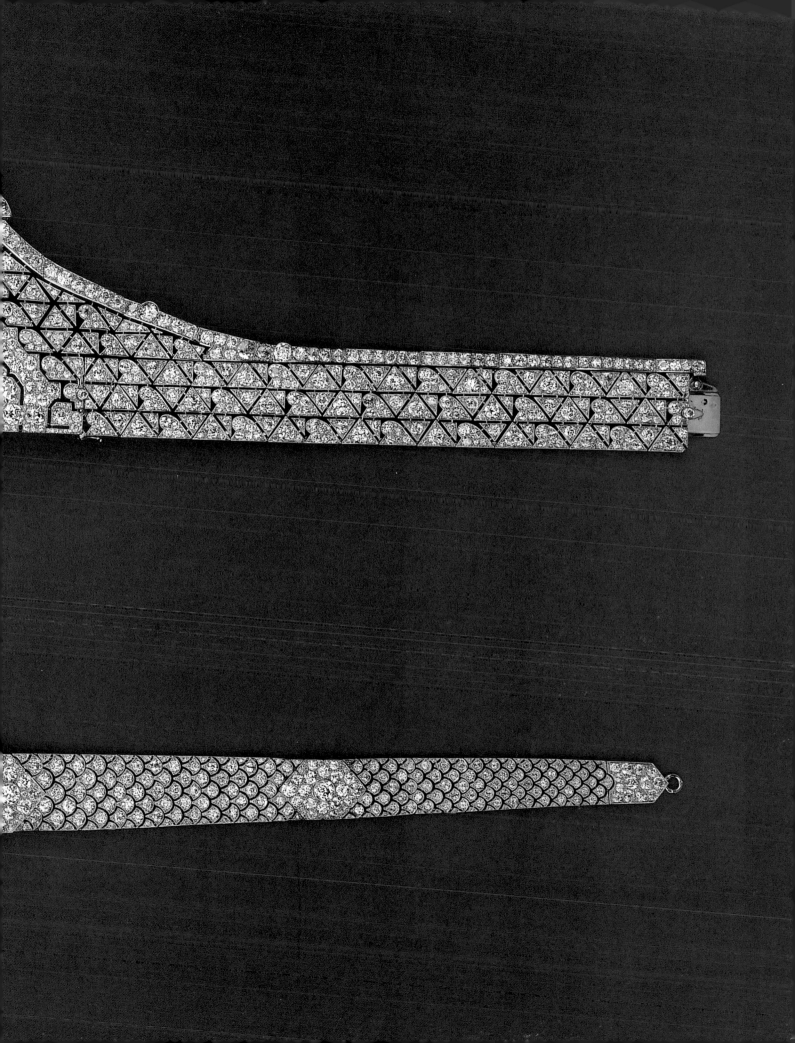

206 Pair of earrings

Made for Cartier London to the order of
Viscountess Harcourt, 1924

Diamonds in open-back platinum setting. Of Persian-
style design with stylised palmettes at top, another
palmette at base and three marquise-cut diamond drops
in spectacle settings. Screw fittings with milled wheels.

Completed in November 1924. Sold Christie's London,
12 December 1990, lot 238.

MARKS Edges engraved CARTIER on one earring and
LONDRES on the other.

L. 6.1 cm

Cartier collection, EG 06 A24

EXHIBITIONS Tokyo 1995, cat. 140.

These earrings were made from the client's
own stones: 96 diamonds totalling 5.43 carats
and 6 navette diamonds totalling 3.43 carats.
When sold by Christie's in 1990, the earrings
had been shortened by removing the upper
sections of diamonds between the shaped
motif at the top and the central round diamond. Cartier inserted a modern replacement
in 1991.

Mary, Viscountess Harcourt was the daughter of American parents, Walter Hayes Burns
(d. 1897) of New York and Mary Lyman
Morgan (1844–1919), sister of J. Pierpont
Morgan Sr (1837–1913) (San Francisco 1996,
p. 342). She married Lewis, 1st Viscount Harcourt (1863–1922) in 1899.

207 Strap bracelet
(bracelet lanière)

Made by Sauvan for Cartier Paris as a
special order, 1923

Diamonds in open-back platinum setting. An openwork
band, divided by two rings, with calibré-cut diamonds in
graduated square and trapezoid settings expanding
towards the centre of each half. The end ring hinged at

206

centre to form clasp. Original curved red leather case
with gilt tooling.

Completed in July 1923.

MARKS Bracelet: on rim CARTIER; French dog's head
assay mark for platinum on gallery. Case: standard
Cartier label in gold inside lid.

Bracelet: L. 18.7 cm. Case: L. 23 cm, W. 4.7 cm

Cartier collection, BT 71 A23

LITERATURE Cologni and Nussbaum 1995, p. 111.

These flexible flat bracelets are always
described in the Paris archive records as
'bracelets lanière' or 'strap bracelets', but the
English term generally used was 'slave
bracelet'. They remained fashionable right
through the 1930s, and are almost always
shown both in Cartier advertisements and in
contemporary fashion plates worn in twos
and threes on the same wrist (see p. 37, fig. 29,
a fashion photograph from American Vogue,
1 October 1934).

208 Strap bracelet
(bracelet lanière)

Made by Renault for Cartier Paris as a
special order, 1926

Pavé-set diamonds in open-back platinum setting;
openwork design of lotus flowers, with central 'buckle
and strap' motif repeated in the design of the clasp, so
that when bracelet is closed, back and front are identical
and each strap has a pear-shaped diamond 'button'.

Completed in September 1926.

MARKS Rim engraved CARTIER; French dog's head assay
mark for platinum on gallery and clasp.

Bracelet: L. 20.7 cm, W. 3 cm. Case: L. 23.7 cm

Cartier collection, BT 14 A26

EXHIBITIONS Paris 1989, cat. 274; Rome 1990, cat. 131;
St Petersburg 1992, cat. 147; Tokyo 1995, cat. 156.

The repetition of the clasp motif as a central
element is a characteristic feature of flat
bracelets of this kind.

This bracelet has its original red leather
case with gold tooling, printed inside the lid
in gold with standard Cartier label (see
cat. 163). It was designed to incorporate the
client's stones from eight different bracelets
and two fragments of jewels. The bracelet used
479 brilliant-cut diamonds, 2 pear-shaped
diamonds and 61 rose-cut diamonds, leaving
10 brilliant-cut and 83 rose-cut diamonds to
be returned to the client.

The pattern of alternating flower-heads is a
standard feature in Islamic art, occurring in
architecture, painting, textiles, etc. In this
instance it may have been taken from a
famous Persian miniature in Louis Cartier's
collection, a folio from Shah Tahmasp's
Quintet of Nizami of c. 1540, where the motif
occurs as an architectural element. This folio
is now in the Fogg Art Museum, Harvard
(illustrated in S. C. Welch, Wonders of the Age.
Masterpieces of Early Safavid Painting 1501–1576,
Harvard 1979, no. 68).

209, 207, 208

209 Strap bracelet
(bracelet lanière)

Made by Lavabre for Cartier Paris as a special order, 1926

Pavé-set diamonds in open-back platinum setting; a geometric pattern with brilliant-cut diamond motifs, the clasp in the form of a rectangular open link with 'buckle and strap' motif. The inner motifs have millegrain settings.

Completed in February 1926.

MARKS Stamped *CARTIER PARIS LONDRES* on the clasp, together with French dog's head assay mark for platinum.

L. 18.7 cm, W. 2 cm

Cartier collection, BT 10 A26

EXHIBITIONS Naples 1988, cat. 124; Paris 1989, cat. 273; Rome 1990, cat. 130.

This bracelet was designed to incorporate the client's stones from a sautoir and a bracelet. With Cartier's customary care and precision, the few tiny stones left over were returned to the client.

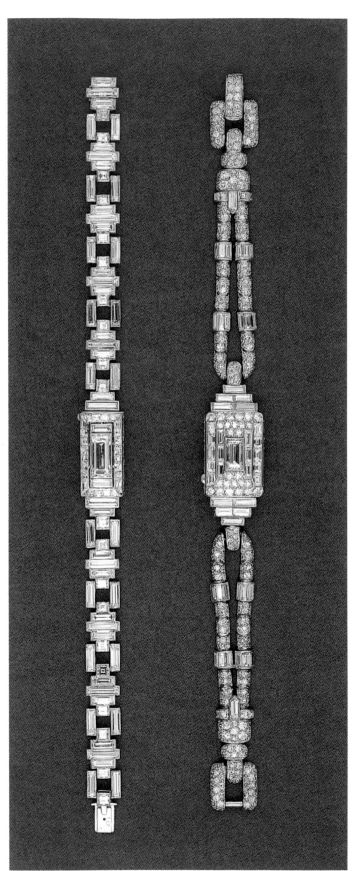

210 Bracelet-watch

Made by Jaeger and Renault for Cartier Paris, *c.* **1927**

Round, baguette and specially shaped diamonds in open-back platinum setting. Rectangular baguette watch with pavé-set cover, bracelet formed of a double diamond-set cord with cylindrical links, a shaped diamond at each end. Watch-lid hinged at side, catch at top right; the narrow dial has upright arabic numerals down each side.

A similar piece made by Jaeger and Renault entered in stock book in June 1927.

MARKS Dial marked CARTIER; rim of watch-lid engraved CARTIER; French dog's head assay mark for platinum and workshop mark *EJ* flanking an hour-glass on reverse of watch and watch-lid.

L. 17.5 cm, W. of watch 1.4 cm

Cartier collection, WL 03 C27

EXHIBITIONS Milan 1988, p. 29 (left); Naples 1988, cat. 20; Paris 1989, cat. 487; Rome 1990, cat. 238.

LITERATURE Barracca *et al.* 1989, p. 155; Cologni and Nussbaum 1995, p. 161.

The comparable model recorded in the Paris archive is described as a 'montre savonette' or hunter-cased wrist watch, that is, a watch with an outer hinged cover to protect the glass. The idea originated in the late eighteenth century to give extra protection when the wearer was on horseback, hence the term 'hunter'. The term 'hunter-cased' is not normally associated with wrist watches, and the adaptation of earlier hunter casing to diamond wrist watches was a speciality of Cartier. For baguette-form watches, see cat. 154.

In this example, intended for evening wear (see also cat. 211–12), the black silk cords fashionable for daytime wear (see cat. 154) are executed entirely in diamonds. In a four-page advertisement in London *Vogue* (January 1925, p. 45), Cartier illustrated a similar bracelet-watch, described as a 'diamond and emerald bracelet especially designed to conceal a wrist watch for evening wear. The tiny timepiece is set under a great oblong emerald framed by pearls and diamonds.'

Another similar model recorded in the London photograph albums was sold in August 1929.

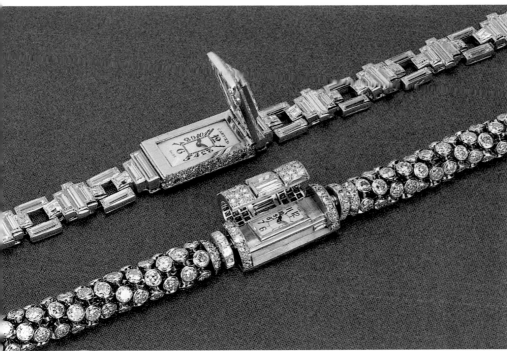

211, 212

212

211 Bracelet-watch

Made by Jaeger and Lavabre for Cartier Paris for stock, 1929

Round, square and baguette-cut diamonds in open-back platinum setting. Baguette-form watch, the lid with baguette-cut diamonds and specially shaped diamonds, the bracelet of baguette and square-cut diamonds forming alternate openwork and solid geometric motifs. Lid hinges at top. Dial with radial arabic numerals, i.e. angled at the corners and placed horizontally down the sides.

Entered in stock book on 17 April 1929; sold 12 July 1929. Sold Christie's Geneva, 17 November 1994, lot 276.

MARKS The dial with *CARTIER SWISS*; bracelet engraved *Cartier Paris MADE IN FRANCE*; French dog's head assay mark for platinum and workshop mark *EJ* flanking an hour-glass on bracelet tongue and watch.

L. 18 cm, W. of watch 1.1 cm

Cartier collection, WL 121 A29

This is one of Cartier's most successful designs for a baguette-form wrist watch. The baguette-cut diamonds in the bracelet complement the shape of the watch. The quirky placing of the radial numerals with constant changes of direction is less successful. On the right-hand side, they even change direction in midstream: 1–3 face inwards, while 4 and 5 face outwards.

212 Bracelet-watch

Made by Jaeger for Cartier Paris for stock, 1928

Diamonds set in platinum. Flexible cylindrical-section bracelet, each link comprising five collet-set diamonds. Cylindrical baguette watch with flat base, pavé-set lid opening at side, with two shield-shaped diamonds at the ends and a central band of baguette diamonds.

Entered in stock book on 3 September 1928 and sold 14 September 1928.

MARKS On dial *CARTIER*; French dog's head assay mark for platinum and workshop mark *EJ* flanking an hour-glass.

L. of bracelet 18 cm, L. of watch barrel 2.2 cm

Cartier collection, WL 97 A28

EXHIBITIONS Lausanne 1996, cat. 102.

There are no other bracelet-watches of this unusual cylindrical form; it was used once or twice more for a bracelet without a watch and for a bracelet set with an Egyptian faience bead (see p. 15, fig. 6).

Jaeger were primarily watch manufacturers; although many of the Cartier watch bracelets bear the Jaeger maker's mark, they were in fact sub-contracted by Jaeger to other workshops.

213 Shoulder brooch

Made for Cartier New York as a special order, 1928

Diamonds in open-back white gold setting. Geometric motifs and 'S' shapes increasing in size towards the base, from which hang three pendant drops.

Dated by the archive photograph. Sold Sotheby's London, 14 December 1993, lot 92, from the collection of Elton John.

MARKS Rim engraved *CARTIER*.

L. 14.7 cm, W. 4.2 cm

Cartier collection, CL 178 A28

EXHIBITIONS Hong Kong 1995, cat. 51; Tokyo 1995, cat. 169; Lausanne 1996, cat. 245.

RELATED MATERIAL Original design for this piece in pencil and bodycolour on buff tracing paper, in New York archive client file.

214 Sautoir

Made by Holl for Cartier Paris for stock, 1929

Diamonds in open-back millegrain platinum setting. A long chain of geometric design formed of alternate twisted and rectangular links; shield-shaped pendant with five diamond drops. The chain separates into four identical bracelets.

Entered in stock book on 24 April 1929, sold 21 December 1929.

MARKS On the chain *CARTIER MADE IN FRANCE*; French dog's head assay mark for platinum and workshop mark *CH* flanking a set square.

L. of pendant 5 cm, L. of each bracelet 19.5 cm. Total L. of full chain and pendant 46.5 cm

Cartier collection, NE 14 A29

EXHIBITIONS St Petersburg 1992, cat. 215; Tokyo 1995, cat. 173.

This sautoir has previously been illustrated with two of the bracelets forming a short necklace, but short necklaces were not the fashion until the early 1930s, and the original design, described as a 'necklace forming four bracelets', is shown in the Paris archive photograph albums as a long chain, or sautoir, with and without the pendant.

Transformable long chains and pendants of this kind seem to have been a speciality of

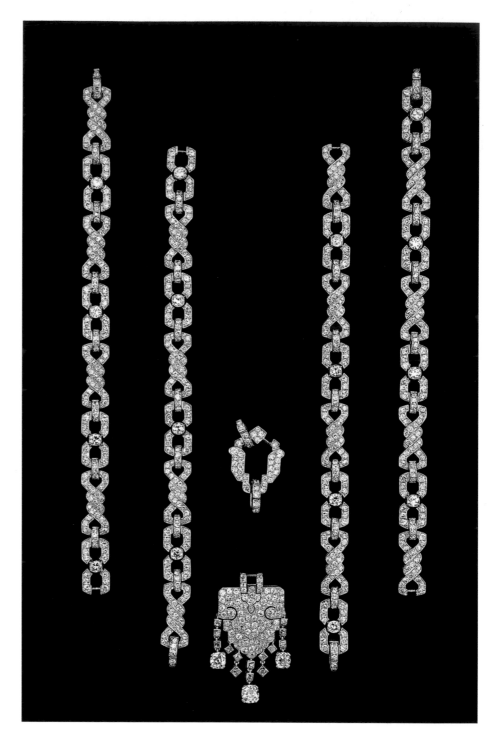

Cartier London at this period, to judge by the number that appear in the ledgers of the late 1920s. The English Art Works job record books for 1928–9 contain one such example, made between 21 December 1928 and 24 April 1929. It contained 1,141 diamonds and comprised 'a chain forming four bracelets and one brooch', which could also be worn as

214.1 Cat. 214 taken apart to show the four bracelets.

'a head band and one bracelet and one brooch', 'two shoulder straps, one bracelet and one brooch', 'a large shoulder strap, one bracelet and one brooch', or 'a shoulder strap and three bracelets' (see p. 21).

215

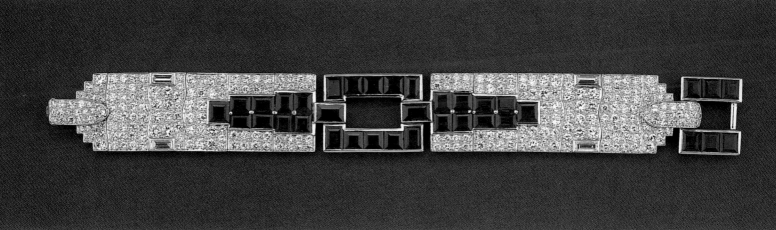

216

215 Bracelet

Made by American Art Works for Cartier
New York as a special order, 1929

Diamonds and sapphires in open-back platinum setting.
Three large and very high cabochon sapphires flanked
by sapphire ziggurat motifs on a pavé-set diamond
ground, the links with curved outlines. The clasp in the
form of two rectangles.

Completed in July 1929. Sold Christie's New York,
19 September 1994, lot 241.

MARKS Rim engraved CARTIER.

L. 18.3 cm, W. 1.3 cm

Cartier collection, BT 72 A29

EXHIBITIONS Lausanne 1996, cat. 201.

The links with curved outlines also occur on
the ruby and diamond bracelet (cat. 216),
another New York piece. The three cabochon
sapphires belonged to the client and are
unusually high for a strap bracelet of this
kind.

216 Bracelet

Made for Cartier New York as a special
order, 1929

Diamonds and rubies in open-back platinum setting.
Pavé-set diamond links with wavy edges, two baguette-
cut diamonds either side of central motif, formed of a
square open link of calibré-cut rubies with two flanking
ruby motifs. Square-link clasp also of rubies, with two
diamond 'strap' motifs either side.

Completed in August 1929. Sold Christie's New York,
24 October 1995, lot 452.

MARKS Rim engraved CARTIER.

L. 17.4 cm, W. 1.9 cm

Cartier collection, BT 79 A29

RELATED MATERIAL Original design in pencil, pen,
watercolour and bodycolour on buff tracing paper in
New York archive client file.

The New York client files contain a number
of designs for flat strap bracelets of this kind
with bold geometric two-colour designs in
diamonds with rubies, sapphires or emeralds.

217–18 Two bracelets

Made by the Cartier workshop for Cartier
Paris for stock, 1930

Rock crystal and diamonds in platinum setting.
Cat. 217: flexible expanding bracelet; thirty
hemispherical discs of rock crystal strung on coiled
sprung wire, a line of diamonds down the outer edge
of each disc, with a baguette diamond in the centre of
each line. Between each disc, a row of rock-crystal
beads at top and bottom. Cat.218: flexible bracelet;
forty-seven hemispherical discs of rock crystal strung
on coiled wire, a row of diamonds at top and bottom,
and a row of three graduated diamonds along outer
edge of each disc. Platinum bars at regular intervals
across the back for strength.

Entered in stock book on 12 May 1930 (cat. 217) and
12 August 1930 (cat. 218); both sold 10 November 1932
to Mrs Michael Farmer (Gloria Swanson). Both sold
Christie's Geneva, 12 May 1988, lot 576.

MARKS On both bracelets, CARTIER MADE IN FRANCE on
platinum mount; French dog's head assay mark for
platinum.

218, 217

Cat. 217: H. 2.7 cm, DIAM. (approx.) 7.8 cm.

Cat. 218: H. 2.8 cm, DIAM. (approx.) 7.4 cm

Cartier collection, BT 27 A30 (cat. 217) and BT 28 A30 (cat. 218)

EXHIBITIONS Paris 1989, cat. 440–41; Rome 1990, cat. 213–14; St Petersburg 1992, cat. 216–17; Hong Kong 1995, cat. 58–9; Tokyo 1995, cat. 253 (A only); Lausanne 1996, cat. 267–8.

LITERATURE Proddow *et al.* 1992, pp. 160–61; Cologni and Nussbaum 1995, p. 152.

Both bracelets were sold in 1932 to the film star Gloria Swanson (1897–1983), then Mrs Michael Farmer (married August 1931). She was married six times, first to Wallace Berry, later to the Marquis de la Falaise and in 1945 to William Davey. Cat. 217.1 shows a contemporary photograph of her wearing both bracelets, one on each wrist. For a later photograph in which she wears both bracelets on the same wrist, see Hong Kong 1995, p. 59. Further photographs of her wearing both bracelets on one wrist, in the 1950 film *Sunset Boulevard* and at a New York party in 1951, are illustrated in Proddow *et al.* 1992, p. 160.

Cat. 218 is much heavier than cat. 217, owing to the increased number of crystal discs. A model similar to cat. 218, made for Cartier Paris and sold to Mrs Harold McCormick, the Polish singer Ganna Walska, in 1929, was the first of its kind to appear, and marked a radical

departure from the predominant taste for flat strap bracelets (see Sotheby Parke Bernet, New York, 1 April 1970, lot 54, from the collection of Ganna Walska). A third example of this type was sold to Madame Coty.

217.1 Contemporary photograph of Gloria Swanson wearing the bracelets of rock crystal and diamonds which she purchased from Cartier Paris in 1932 (cat. 217–18), in a still from the 1933 film *Perfect Understanding*.

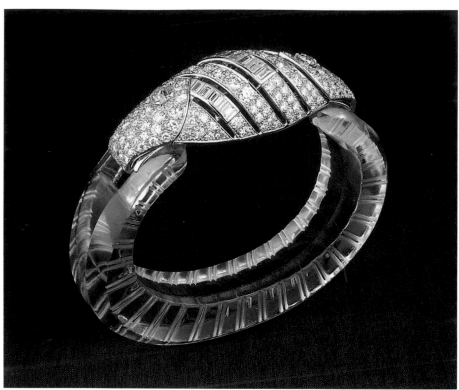

219

219 Bracelet

Made by Levoyer (centrepiece) and Fourrier (carved crystal) for Cartier Paris for stock, 1934. Exhibited by Cartier at the Brussels Exhibition of 1935

Rock crystal and diamonds in open-back platinum setting. A rigid carved rock-crystal bracelet, with opening at top to take a detachable clasp formed of scrolling lines of round and baguette diamonds. The clasp has expanding ends so that it can be removed completely and worn as a brooch.

Entered in stock book on 14 December 1934, sold 5 June 1935. Sold Christie's Geneva, 19 May 1994, lot 122.

MARKS Centrepiece engraved *Cartier Paris*; French dog's head assay mark for platinum.

Max. w. 7.7 cm, max. w. of centrepiece 2.2 cm

Cartier collection, BT 70 A34

EXHIBITIONS Lausanne 1996, cat. 246.

LITERATURE Cologni and Nussbaum 1995, p. 155.

For a contemporary illustration of this bracelet, see American *Vogue*, 15 February 1935, p. 38, in an article on 'Ingenuity in jewels', and *Art et la Mode*, Paris, 20 May 1935, p. 64, in an article on jewellery at the Brussels Exhibition of 1935 entitled 'Le splendeur retrouvé des gemmes et de l'or'. The centrepiece is also shown detached for wear as a brooch (219.1).

Two other rock-crystal bracelets of this type with removable clasp are recorded; one, with diamond clasp, is illustrated in a Cartier London advertisement in *Harper's Bazaar*, June 1935, and again in January 1936, p. 71, together with a rock-crystal ring, worn by a model, in an advertisement for Cartier notepaper. Another, with onyx and diamond clasp, was made by Cartier London (cat. 185).

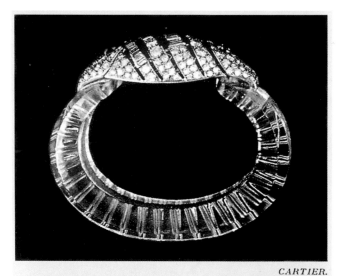

CARTIER.

Bracelet démontable en cristal taillé et diamants.

CARTIER.

Le motif du bracelet se détache pour former broche.

219.1 Illustration of jewellery from the Brussels Exhibition of 1935, showing cat. 219 with centre detached for wear as a brooch. *Art et la Mode*, 20 May 1935.

220 Clip brooch

Made by the Cartier workshop for Cartier Paris as a special order for an American client, as one of a pair of clip brooches, 1935

Diamonds in open-back platinum setting. A projecting pavé-set pyramid of trapezoid shape, with a line of graduated baguettes set horizontally down each side and down the middle, and a large central brilliant-cut diamond. At the top a cylindrical hinge with double-pronged fitting. Two further pairs of prongs on the reverse of the front.

Completed in May 1935. In December 1935 the same client commissioned a black lacquer bracelet from Cartier Paris to take one of the clips. At a later,

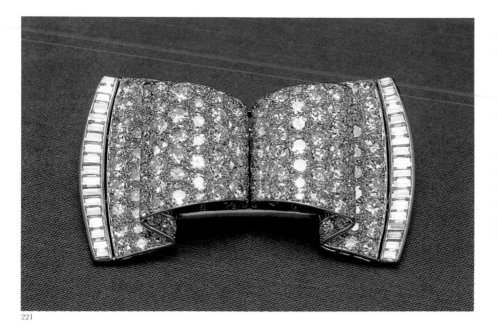

221

The large double clip brooch made by Cartier Paris in 1935 could be worn as a single brooch or as two clip brooches, of which this is one. The newly fashionable black lacquer bracelet commissioned later that year to take one of the clips was in white gold.

Two examples of closely similar double clip brooches made by Cartier London are recorded in the London photograph albums. One is identical in design but slightly smaller, the other lacks the row of baguette diamonds down the centre. For a Cartier New York design for a pair of pyramid-shaped clips on a black lacquer bracelet, see cat. 293.

Illustrated on p. 59, fig. 45.

221.2 Cat. 221 with one clip removed to show brooch fitting.

221 Ribbon bow clip brooches

Made by the Cartier workshop for Cartier Paris for stock, 1936; originally wearable also on a white gold bangle as a bracelet

Pavé-set and baguette diamonds in open-back platinum setting; the ribbon bow formed of two identical clip brooches mounted on a detachable brooch frame. The frame has four tiny projections at each end which slot into loops on the reverse of each clip brooch.

Entered in stock book on 29 February 1936, sold 14 November 1936. Sold Sotheby's Geneva, 16 April 1994, lot 37.

MARKS *Cartier Paris* on each clip; French dog's head assay mark for platinum and workshop mark *c* between two crescents with the letters *s* and *a* above and below.

L. 5.3 cm, W. 3.2 cm

Cartier collection, CL 192 A36

A virtually identical pair of clip brooches was made in Paris as a special order in September 1936, while a number of closely similar clip brooches were made in London. A design for one of them, given to Sutton & Straker to execute, appears in the job record books for 5 May 1937. It is annotated '40 Batons Diamonds 2.58 ct on wax, Brilliants to be supplied', 'Make a Pair of Diamond Clips Brooch to photo as before', and '20th May certain for NY', indicating that it was ordered by Cartier New York from an existing model. Many of the London designs bear annotations referring to the practice of arranging the stones on wax (see pp. 39–40).

White gold without black lacquer became the favoured material for bracelets to take a pair of clip brooches in the second half of the 1930s.

---

unrecorded date, she asked Cartier New York to make designs for a gold necklace to take both clips as pendants. Single clip brooch sold Christie's Geneva, 12 May 1988, lot 625.

MARKS Reverse engraved *Cartier Paris*; French dog's head assay mark for platinum and workshop mark *c* between two crescents, with the letters *s* and *a* below.

H. 4 cm

Cartier collection, CL 63 A35

EXHIBITIONS Milan 1988, p.40 (bottom); Paris 1989, cat. 457; Rome 1990, cat. 224.

LITERATURE Cologni and Nussbaum 1995, p. 160.

RELATED MATERIAL (1) Original bodycolour design for double clip brooch in white on buff tracing paper in Paris order book for 15 May 1935. (2) Original pencil, pen and ink design for black lacquer bracelet in Paris

order book for 23 December 1935, showing two views, top with clip and side. (3) Two original designs, in pencil and bodycolour on white paper in Cartier New York client file, for a gold chain necklace to take both clips, either separately or together as a bow pendant in the front. See pp. 60–61, figs 46–8.

The complex history of this piece demonstrates how the Cartier archive records can be used not only to document the changes and additions made to a single piece over a period of time, but also to show how clients patronised different Cartier houses. American clients, in particular, often had dealings with all three branches. Thus, information about one piece can be found in more than one of the three archives. This is discussed more fully on pp. 58–62.

222 Vertical scroll clip brooches

Made by English Art Works for Cartier London as a special order, 1936

Diamonds in open-back platinum setting; a double scroll motif which splits into two single scroll clips, joined at the centre with a removable snap clasp. Each clip formed of an inner line of baguettes and an outer line of alternate baguette and brilliant-cut diamonds.

Completed in September 1936.

MARKS Rim engraved *Cartier London*.

H. 4.3 cm

Cartier collection, CL 146 A36

LITERATURE Cologni and Nussbaum 1995, p. 160.

RELATED MATERIAL Pencil working sketch in English Art Works job record books for 1 September 1936, delivered on 18 September.

A number of variants of this popular model, made in all three houses, appear in the photograph albums, some thin and elongated, others comprising triple or quadruple scrolls. Three other London examples were made in June and December 1936 and June 1937.

The vertical arrangement of the two scrolls meant that the standard brooch frame could be dispensed with, requiring only a supremely simple double snap clasp and a tiny projecting pin at the top of one half, which slots into a hole in the other half to ensure that the tops are aligned.

222 (greatly enlarged)

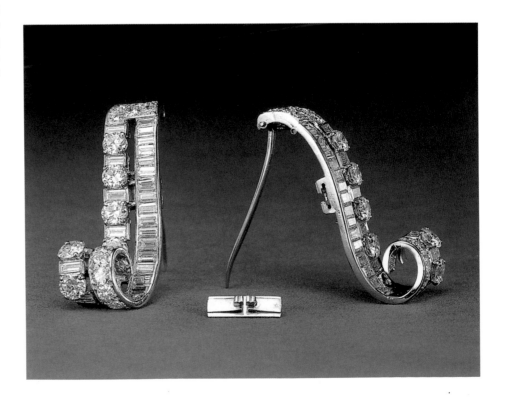

222.1 Cat. 222 taken apart to show double snap clasp and tiny projecting pin for alignment at top.

223 Diamond and ruby S-scroll clip brooches

Made for Cartier New York (?), *c.* 1935

Diamonds and rubies in open-back platinum setting. Two clip brooches in the form of three-dimensional scrolls ending in curling tendrils, the scrolls set with baguette and triangular diamonds; the tendrils bordered with calibré-cut rubies. A detachable frame enables the clips to be joined as a brooch forming a continuous S-scroll.

MARKS Reverse stamped *CARTIER*.

L. of each brooch 2.8 cm

Lindemann collection. Sold Christie's New York, 12 April 1983, lot 291.

EXHIBITIONS New Orleans 1988, pl. XIII.

These S-scroll clip brooches are a good example of curving three-dimensional forms introduced in the mid-1930s. The problem of designing a double clip brooch in which each element stood on its own, but without an obvious dividing line when both parts were worn together, was considered a challenge to the designer. It is discussed at length in Selwyn 1945, pp. 68–71. Instead of a symmetrical mirror-image (e.g. cat. 221), the two clips form a right-hand and left-hand image, with the angles reversed, although the two parts are the same.

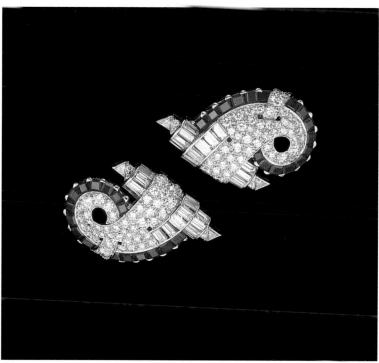

223

224 Oval brooch

Made for Cartier London for stock, 1935

Diamonds in open-back platinum setting; an asymmetrical oval scroll with graduated baguette-cut diamonds, square-cut and pavé-set diamonds, and one trapeze-cut diamond.

Entered in stock book on 16 July 1935; sold 27 June 1936.

MARKS Rim engraved *Cartier Made in London*.

W. 5 cm

Cartier collection, CL 186 A35

LITERATURE Cologni and Nussbaum 1995, p. 160.

This is an unusual design and there are only a handful of other pieces of this type, based on an asymmetrical scroll.

224

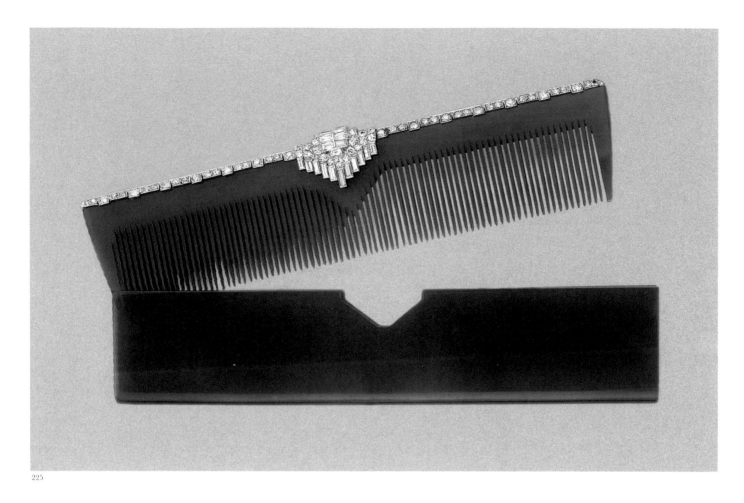

225

225 Comb

Made by English Art Works for Cartier
London to the order of Barbara Hutton,
then Countess von Reventlow, 1937

Blonde tortoiseshell, with diamonds set in platinum.
A row of baguette diamonds along the top edge and a
row of diamonds at the top of each side. In the centre
a geometric motif bordered with baguette diamonds.
With original blonde tortoiseshell slip-case, open at the
ends and cut out in the centre to accommodate the
diamond motif.

Completed in July 1937.

MARKS None.

Comb: L. 17.7 cm, W. 4.4 cm. Case: L. 17.7 cm,
W. 3.7 cm

Cartier collection, IV 115 A37

LITERATURE Cologni and Nussbaum 1995, p. 145.

RELATED MATERIAL Pencil working sketch in the English
Art Works job record book for 26 June 1937.

Diamond-set handbag combs seem to have
been much in favour from about 1928, when
they appear in both the Paris and London
records, throughout the 1930s. But this is an
unusually large example at 7 inches long
(17.7 cm) and the only one of this length in
the London records. Several others are
described in the English Art Works job record
books. They are all about 4 inches (10.2 cm)
in length, and the colour of the tortoiseshell is
always indicated, either 'blonde' or 'dark'. For
a typical smaller example made by Cartier
London and now in the Lindemann collection, see New Orleans 1988, pl. XIX.

Barbara Hutton (1912–79) was the granddaughter of F. W. Woolworth. She married
the Russian Prince Alexis Mdivani in the
Russian church in Paris in June 1933 and
divorced him in May 1935 to marry the
Danish Count Court von Haugwitz-Reventlow,
from whom she separated in 1938 (for a
recent biography of Barbara Hutton see
Heymann 1983). She was a client of all three
Cartier houses. Her wedding headdress for
her marriage to Mdivani was commissioned
from Cartier Paris and was also made of
tortoiseshell studded with diamonds (see p. 29,
fig. 24).

226 Head ornament
with clip brooch

Made by English Art Works for Cartier
London for stock, 1937

Clip brooch: topazes and diamonds in open-back
setting, the topazes set in gold, the diamonds in
platinum. Described in the stock records as 'large clip
brooch in dark topaz, round and baton diamonds with
large rectangular light topaz in centre (62.35 cts) clip
with double prong back'. Five additional spikes on
reverse of jewel. Head ornament: baton-cut topazes set
in gold. A circlet of 143 vertically set topazes rising at
the centre, with frame to take the clip brooch, attached
with prongs pointing upwards, with hexagonal topaz at
top and wider part of brooch towards the base. When
worn as a clip brooch, it is turned the other way up.

Clip brooch given to English Art Works on
10 September and returned from setting 25 September.
Complete head ornament entered in stock book on
26 November 1937 and sold 27 June 1938.

MARKS None.

Clip brooch: H. 5.7 cm, W. 4.6 cm. Head ornament:
DIAM. 17 cm

Cartier collection, JV 23 A37

THE
DESIGN
DRAWINGS

E ach of the three Cartier archives, in Paris, London and New York, holds designs relating to its own products, and designs from all three houses are illustrated in this section. The different kinds are discussed on pp. 57–8. They comprise both preliminary sketches and finished designs. The latter were kept either in scrapbooks or with the records for stock and special orders.

The role of the design drawings in the production of Cartier's jewels is explained on pp. 39–41. Many of the designs included here are annotated with initials and 'à ex' for *à exécuter* (to be produced) indicating that the design had been approved and was to be made up. In Paris the initials were ususally 'LC' for Louis Cartier, 'RR' for his deputy (René Révillon) or 'RP' for the senior salesman René Prieur. In most cases the initials 'LC' are not in Louis Cartier's hand, an exception being the earring, cat. 283. The Paris order books contain the approved design only. The New York client files retain all the designs made, including the rejected ones. In some cases up to seven different alternatives were made before one was finally approved by both the client and Cartier (cat. 265 and 299). Dennis Gardner, who joined Cartier London as a designer immediately after the Second World War, recalls making three designs for each special order, one as the customer required, one interpreting the customer's requirements in the Cartier style, and one representing the designer's interpretation.

Charles Jacqueau archive

In addition to the material held in each of the three Cartier archives, a group of working designs made by Charles Jacqueau for Cartier Paris from 1909 until the 1930s has survived in private hands (cat. 235–46). They descend from Jacqueau himself and have enabled many of the objects included in this catalogue to be attributed to him; they have also made it possible to attribute to him many designs in the Cartier archive, some of which are included here (cat. 233–4). This group comprises sketches made in museums or from books together with many sketches of ideas for jewels and unfinished designs. Some of these were later worked up into finished designs, now in the Cartier archive, for pieces that were actually made. Many of these designs were later pasted together onto larger sheets, and the sheets catalogued here often include designs of different date.

The designers

It is almost impossible to identify the hands of individual designers because of the insistence on their anonymity, traditional in the trade at this time. Their names were never given in contemporary publicity or exhibition catalogues. Few of the Paris or London designs bear any designer's signature. An exception is cat. 252, signed 'Deringer', but little is known about him. The New York client designs, on the other hand, are frequently signed with the designer's initials, neatly added in pen or pencil, often as a monogram, in the top or bottom right-hand corner (see cat. 288 and 292–3, 296–7). But, tantalisingly, the records do not enable these initials to be identified. There is only one exception. The initials 'G.G.' and the full signature 'Genaille' occur in some instances on alternative designs for the same special order, leaving no doubt that they are those of Georges Genaille. Georges Genaille and his brother Alexandre both worked for Cartier Paris before transferring to New York. However, there seems to be some confusion over the identity of the Genaille brothers. According to his daughter, Alexandre joined Cartier Paris in 1907, transferring to New York in 1908 and remaining there until 1929 or 1930. Georges was apparently born only in 1904.[1] Nadelhoffer states that it was Georges who transferred to New York in 1909.[2] The designs signed 'Genaille' are all disappointingly conventional (see fig. 83), but this may have had much to do with the taste of the clients. Nadelhoffer notes the names of two other New York designers recruited from Paris – Maurice Duvallet, who left with Genaille in 1910, and Emile Faure, who joined New York in 1912.[3] However, their drawings cannot be identified.

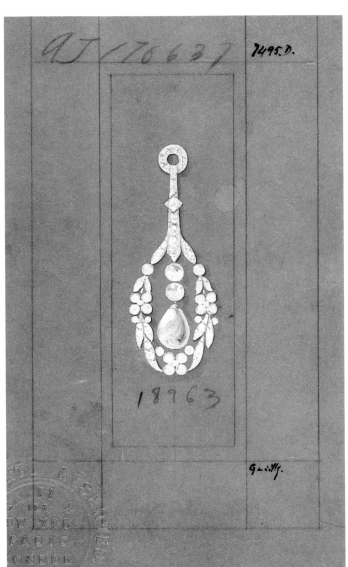

FIG. 83. Original design for an earring in pencil and bodycolour on brown tracing paper, signed 'Genaille' in the lower right corner. Client file, New York archive, 1923.

Charles Jacqueau (1885–1968) is the one designer whose contribution to the Cartier style can be assessed. He trained first at the Ecole Bernard Palissy, where he studied ceramic painting as well as drawing and where a number of other Cartier designers also trained. In 1902–3 he transferred to the Ecole des Arts Décoratifs and then worked for the firm of Raingo Frères, which dealt in bronze sculptures. He joined Cartier in 1909 as a replacement for one or other of the Genaille brothers and was responsible for some of the most imaginative and unexpected designs of the 1910s and 1920s.

Nadelhoffer credits Jacqueau, together with Louis Cartier, with the creation of the Egyptian-style range of the 1920s incorporating ancient fragments. However, Jacqueau's surviving working drawings do not include any designs for this range. What they do show is his contribution to many of the avant-garde designs of the 1910s (see cat. 29–32), including the earliest examples of one of Cartier's great inventions, the 'panther-skin' ornament in diamonds studded with onyx (see cat. 245 and 170). His designs for 'panther-skin' ornament continued into the 1920s in a series of bracelets or chains with alternating coral and 'panther-skin' links, some of which were shown at the 1925 Exhibition (cat. 287). Other actual objects included in this catalogue that can definitely be attributed to him on the basis of surviving working designs or sketches are the so-called 'bracelet égyptien' with flared terminals (cat. 132) and the dragon-head bracelet with its eclectic mixture of Chinese and Indian sources (cat. 144).

Jacqueau's papers include many sketches of Islamic ornament as well as photographs of Islamic tiled interiors. Some of his designs with stylised trees or flower vases within banner-shaped pendants may have been inspired by Islamic tiled panels (see cat. 234). Other photographs pasted onto sheets with the designs provide much information about his sources. For example, one photograph depicts a fragment of embossed Spanish leather of the sixteenth century with a dense pattern of flowers and leaves. This was copied unaltered as the engraved pattern on a gold vanity case of 1925.[4]

Nadelhoffer lists some of the other Paris designers and describes certain features of their work.[5] He also mentions some of the London designers of the 1930s, in particular Frederick A. Mew, who worked closely with Jacques Cartier and was reponsible, with Ernest C. Frowde, for many of the geometric pieces produced by Cartier London in the 1930s. Although the design studio was directed by a Frenchman, G. Massabieaux, Jacques Cartier was careful to employ English designers where possible. James Gardner, who joined the design studio in 1923, recalled that he was given preference over a young French designer offered by Paris.[6] According to the London trade magazine *Watchmaker, Jeweller and Silversmith* for 3 July 1930, Frowde won first prize in a competition for jewellery design with a combined clip and brooch, a corsage ornament and six other ornaments.

The selection

The following selection of designs has been made primarily to illustrate items that do not survive or whose whereabouts are unknown, in order to complement the selection of objects. There are two instances only where both the object and its related designs have been included. In both cases the designs add considerably to the understanding of the object and are therefore reproduced with the object (cat. 253 and 255).

Among types of object that have rarely survived are the black lacquer bracelets with detachable clip brooches introduced by Cartier Paris in 1934 and enormously popular in all three houses over the next two or three years. A pair of clip brooches could be worn in three ways: clipped to each end of a flat lacquered band, worn individually, or combined on a separate fitting as a single brooch. Three designs are included here, all special orders by Cartier New York (cat. 292–4). One of them varies in having a single large clip brooch instead of a pair. The bracelets themselves were usually in white gold, a softer metal than platinum, to give flexibility. Possibly they bent out of shape with frequent use, or the lacquer chipped, which may explain why so few survive. Although the three examples here were intended to be lacquered in black, other surviving designs provide evidence of lacquer in several different colours. One New York special order of 1935 was lacquered deep blue to match the sapphire and diamond clip brooches designed to incorporate two carved sapphire leaves. One London client wanted to maximise the possibilities and ordered no fewer than four lacquered bands of different colours. The commission was described in the English Art Works job record book for July 1935 as follows: 'Make 2 Diamond motifs as clips, interchangeable with 4 lacquer bangles: Green, Red, Blue, Deep Yellow.'

The designs are divided into the following categories, some of which relate directly to previous sections:

(a) Designs *c.* 1907–14 (see section 1)
(b) Designs by Charles Jacqueau
(c) Designs in the Egyptian style (see section 4)
(d) Designs in the Indian style (see section 5)
(e) Designs of the 1920s
(f) Designs for objects shown at the Paris Exhibition of 1925
(g) Designs of the 1930s

Most of these groups are self-explanatory. Only (f) needs further comment.

The Paris Exhibition of 1925

The Exposition des Arts Décoratifs et Industriels Modernes held in Paris in 1925 was intended as a showcase for the best of French work in the field. Initially planned to take place in 1915, it was postponed on the outbreak of war, and when it finally took place in 1925 it was a matter of immense national pride.[7] Other countries were naturally invited to participate, and the pressure on French exhibitors to excel was enormous. Against this background, Cartier's fantastic creations, some of which verged on the bizarre, can be more easily understood. Their display was full of extraordinary pieces, such as the shoulder ornament (cat. 269) and the orchid comb bandeau (cat. 271), created specially for the exhibition. Very few of them were ever sold – perhaps Cartier never expected them to sell – and most pieces were later broken up and the stones reused. As a result, none of what seem to have been among Cartier's grandest creations survive intact. To compensate for this, a large group of twenty-four designs has been selected for this section.

All the other jewellery houses exhibited in the jewellery section, which was housed in the Grand Palais. Cartier did have a stand in the Grand Palais, but no record survives in the archive of what it contained and it was clearly a subsidiary display.[8] Cartier's primary display was in the Pavillon de l'Elégance, or fashion pavillion, together with the *grands couturiers*, and Cartier was the only jeweller to exhibit there.[9] How this came about is not yet clear. Fortunately, enough documentation survives to put together a very clear picture of the Pavillon de l'Elégance display. Firstly, there is in the Cartier archive an insurance document compiled in August 1925 which lists some 150 pieces. It gives a brief description and stock number for every object and a thumbnail sketch for most of them. With this information it is possible to locate either the original design or the contemporary archive photograph for every item. Secondly, surviving photographs of the display record Cartier's clever use of mannequins, placed in front of mirrors to show the jewels to best advantage, as worn. This was especially important for the head ornaments, such as the back-of-the-head comb bandeau (cat. 271.1), and for the shoulder ornament (cat. 269.2).

Owing to the long delay in organising the exhibition after the end of the war, some items on the list had been sold before it opened and were borrowed back from the purchasers (for example, cat. 287). This also explains why the exhibition included pieces made two or three years earlier. Some were even designed before the war, as, for example, a pendant and brooch very similar to designs by Charles Jacqueau of *c.* 1913. Other pre-1925 pieces included a number of ring-and-tassel brooches of 1922–3, a Persian-style diamond bandeau and another bandeau consisting of a thin diamond band with a tuft of black feathers at each end, both made in 1923. The emerald diadem shown on one of the mannequins was also made in 1923.

But the outstanding pieces of the show were specially created in 1925. They stood out in many ways, for their novelty of design, their technical virtuosity, or, in the case of the enormous carved Mughal emeralds, their intrinsic and historic value. The 'panther-skin' pieces were remarkable for the size of the area that was pavé-set with diamonds and studded with onyx cabochons, chips or cones to catch the light at different angles and create a different effect. Many of these surfaces were curved, requiring exceptional skill on the part of the setter. The *tour de force* of this work is the comb bandeau (cat. 271) with its two pairs of three-dimensional orchid blossoms. A variant of this technique, unparalleled in Cartier's *oeuvre*, appears in the shoulder ornament, where pavé-set diamond bosses are encrusted with pointed diamonds instead of onyx (cat. 269.5).

Even more than technical supremacy, it was Cartier's bold use of colour, combined with new ways of wearing jewels, that struck contemporary critics. Baron de Meyer has already been quoted on Cartier's revolutionary combination of coral and emerald (see p. 208). According to one eye-witness account, the Cartier display was contained in a circular vitrine made up of several smaller cases, each dedicated to a different stone: diamonds, jade, sapphires etc.[10] For novelty of design, contemporary critics singled out the 15-inch (38-cm) long *broche de décolleté* or *fermeture de corsage*, to be pinned down the front of the dress as a fastener (see pp. 17–18, fig. 10). They also praised Cartier's inventiveness in bracelet design, in particular the bracelet of graduated carved coral 'tulips' separated by a ring of pearls and terminating in a large emerald (cat. 288), and the upper- and lower-arm bracelets with carved emerald centrepieces and coral links (cat. 287).

Little now survives of this stunning display. Of the less spectacular items, three are included in their relevant sections: a Chinese-style lipstick and vanity case (cat. 116), a coral, onyx and diamond bracelet (cat. 191) and a coral and emerald bracelet, which is identical in design to one shown at the exhibition (cat. 143). The coral bracelet from Cartier's smaller display in the Grand Palais has already been mentioned (see note 8). A few pieces comparable with ones shown in the exhibition are now in the Cartier collection, for example the two pendant seal-watches (cat. 95–6). Doubtless, other pieces surviving in private collections will in due course come to light.

Perhaps the final word should rest with the report on the Cartier display given by their rival Georges Fouquet in his 1934 publication on twentieth-century jewellery:

> The reputation of this house does not need to be made – they are universally known. Messrs Cartier are without doubt among the *bijoutiers-joailliers* who have done most to revive the techniques of jewellery and introduce colour by using materials such as coral, onyx, jade and carved emeralds. All the products of this firm shown in the Exhibition reveal the subtle taste of Mr Louis Cartier and his leaning towards the orient, especially India. Mother-of-pearl and onyx, or coral and emeralds, are mixed to make ornaments that are both colourful and harmonious. Is that what is nowadays called modern? Among the outstanding pieces were a beautiful ensemble comprising a diadem of emeralds, diamonds and pearls [cat. 269.1 and 269.2], and a large brooch with a carved emerald [cat. 270], necklaces of engraved emeralds or carved coral [cat. 289], a ravishing coral comb and a bracelet made of little barrels of diamonds and black enamel.

It is unfortunate that the Maison Cartier thought it unnecessary to mention their designers or the ateliers who work for them, as they might well have earned prizes.[11]

NOTES

1. Information supplied by M. T. Genaille to Eric Nussbaum, 26 July 1996.
2. Nadelhoffer 1984, p.141.
3. Ibid., p. 43.
4. Stock Design Record Book, 1925, p. 60b.
5. He gives no sources for his information (1984, pp. 141 and 188–9).
6. Nadelhoffer 1984, p. 241, and Gardner 1993, p. 25.
7. The exhibition was organised by the Société des Artistes Décorateurs, a group founded in 1901 with the aim of organising regular exhibitions on the decorative arts.
8. One of the few pieces illustrated at the time as being in the Grand Palais was a bracelet of coral links with diamond and mother-of-pearl plaques: see Gabrielle Rosenthal, 'Le bijou moderne' in *L'Art Vivant*, 15 October 1925, p. 30. The bracelet was sold by Antiquorum/Tajan, Geneva, 19 November 1996, lot 120, and is now in the Cartier collection.
9. For a detailed description of the exhibition buildings and their contents, with further bibliography, see V. Arwas, *Art Deco*, London 1992, pp. 27–50.
10. *L'Art Vivant*, 1 August 1925, p. 30.
11. Fouquet 1934, pp. 189–90. Louis Cartier was a member of the jury and so Cartier as a firm could not compete, but the individual designers and workshops would still have been eligible for prizes, had they been acknowledged.

70

228

(a) DESIGNS *c*. 1907–14

228 Page with nine geometric-style brooches

Design Scrapbook, I, f. 70. Cartier archive, Paris, 1907–8

Pencil, ink, watercolour and bodycolour on buff tracing paper

27.2 × 20.5 cm

These delicate openwork designs with geometric motifs began to appear *c*. 1907. Closely similar pieces were made by Andrey and Lavabre in 1907 and 1908. The pale blue indicates diamonds, while the other colours were used to emphasise the openwork effect and do not necessarily conform to the stones with which the piece was made. For instance, the brooch top left is annotated 'saphirs' for the white stones, and 'émeraudes' for the red strips. Two geometric-style brooches of this period are included as cat. 24 and 25.

229 Page with two devants de corsage

Above: an Egyptian-style pendant with lotus flowers. Below: a semicircle with Renaissance-style foliate scrollwork.

Design Scrapbook, I, f. 10. Cartier archive, Paris, *c*. 1913

Pen and ink with watercolour on buff tracing paper

27.2 × 20.5 cm

In both designs, pale blue is used to indicate diamonds. This was standard practice during the first two decades of the century and continued into the early 1920s in both London and Paris. The dark green in the Egyptian-style piece with lotus flowers (top) probably indicates onyx (see cat. 76). Neither of these two designs was executed.

229

230

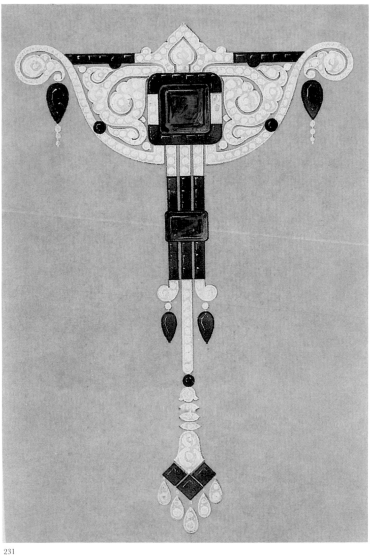

231

232

230 Devant de corsage

Loose design. Cartier archive, Paris, c. 1912

Pencil, watercolour and bodycolour on brown tracing paper

19.7 × 7 cm

EXHIBITIONS Rome 1990, cat. 40.

Opaque white bodycolour, thickly applied to indicate diamonds, was introduced c. 1910. The colours suggest that this large piece was intended to be made in diamonds with sapphires, emeralds and rubies, but it was never executed.

Both this and cat. 229 (bottom) appear to have been inspired by Renaissance architectural ornament. The archive contains sketches of similar architectural motifs. One of them,

with acanthus scroll ornament, is annotated 'commencement du XVIe siècle'. In the present design the acanthus has been replaced by a classical palmette.

231 Persian-style brooch-pendant

Garland Style Design Scrapbook, III, f. 13. Cartier archive, Paris, c. 1913

Pencil, watercolour and bodycolour on buff tracing paper

14.2 × 10 cm

Similar brooch-pendants were designed to be worn alternatively with the point facing upwards, as aigrettes on thin bandeaux (see Nadelhoffer 1984, p. 84, fig. 75). This one was not executed.

232 Greek column pendant

Workshop Estimate Book, 1913. Cartier archive, Paris

Pen and ink on buff tracing paper

15 × 6 cm

EXHIBITIONS Rome 1990, cat. 77.

This pendant was made in opals, onyx and diamonds; it was sold to Mrs W. B. Leeds. The column in onyx and diamonds with ivy-leaf wreath represents an altar, with the flame in carved Mexican fire opal. It was hung on a black silk cord with tubular slide that repeated the ivy-leaf motif in onyx and diamonds.

Another similar Ionic column pendant is illustrated by Nadelhoffer (1984, p. 188, fig. 103) and a plaster cast from it survives.

(b) DESIGNS BY CHARLES JACQUEAU

All the Jacqueau designs described as 'private collection' are from a single collection and have a direct provenance from Jacqueau himself. The attribution is therefore certain. They comprise working sketches and unfinished designs that he was allowed to keep. Many of these designs were never produced. In the case of pieces that were actually made, a finished design also remains in the Cartier archive. These finished designs are always unsigned, but have now been attributed to Jacqueau on the basis of working designs for the same pieces in the private collection.

233

233 Page of ornament sketches annotated 'Décoration Arabe'

Sketchbooks, f. 88. Cartier archive, Paris, c. 1910

Pencil, pen and ink, dark blue watercolour on buff tracing paper

16.5 × 24.8 cm

These arabesque and geometric patterns are taken from a variety of Islamic sources. The annotation is not in Jacqueau's hand, but the sketches are attributed to him by comparison with a page of ornament sketches containing identical motifs amongst the group of working designs kept by Jacqueau (private collection, no. 739). The page is headed 'Caractéristiques arabes' and contains detailed drawings of foliate ornament.

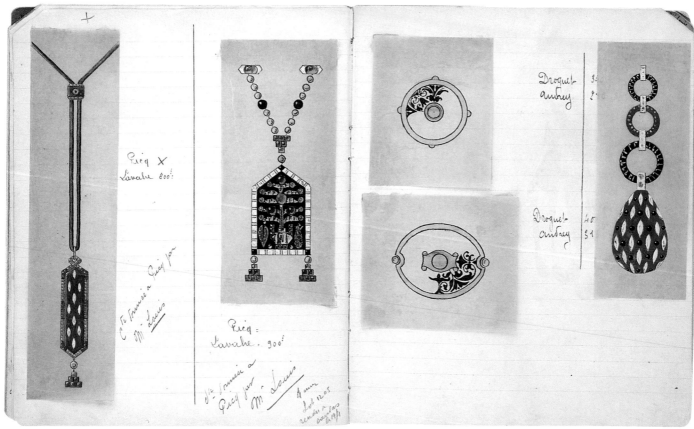

234 (greatly reduced)

234 Workshop Estimate Book, 1913–14

Left: a pendant and brooch, with estimates of 600F and 900F from Lavabre, both annotated 'Commande donnée à Picq par Mr Louis'. Right: two brooches and a pear-shaped coral pendant, with estimates from Droguet and Andrey for the brooches. There is a cross by Andrey's lower estimate in both instances. Both estimates refer to the brooches only and not to the coral pendant.

Cartier archive, Paris (pp. 32–3)

Pencil, ink, watercolour and bodycolour on buff tracing paper

22 × 36 cm (width of open book)

LITERATURE Nadelhoffer 1984, col. pl. 17 (coral pendant only)

This book contains estimates for production costs from the different workshops. Unfinished designs for the five pieces shown here are to be found in Jacqueau's working designs (private collection, no. 771, recto and verso). All of them were executed. The two coral pendants were made for stock in October 1913 and sold to the Duc d'Orléans in 1914. The brooch with tree motif was also made for stock in 1913.

The annotations on Jacqueau's unfinished designs indicate the materials in which the pieces were to be executed. For example, the small pyramid at the base of the long, thin coral pendant was to be set with an emerald, amethysts and coral, with a pearl above. The brooch with gem-set tree motif is annotated 'plaque du fond onyx noir' (background plaque of black onyx). The unfinished design for the large pear-shaped coral pendant is annotated 'onyx, corail, onyx' for the three rings and 'bt' (brillant) for the diamond-set loops. The pear-drop is annotated 'points onyx noir' (black onyx spots) and appears to be a unique use of coral encrusted both with diamonds and onyx, as well as one of the earliest recorded uses of onyx encrustation.

The two sketches for brooches among Jacqueau's working designs are annotated 'to be executed in diamonds and engraved rock crystal'. From the design in the Workshop Estimate Book alone, it would not have been obvious that the black pattern was to be engraved in rock crystal rather than enamelled. Although there is a cross by Andrey's lower estimate, the Droguet workshop seems to have set most of the rock-crystal pieces made between 1911 and 1913.

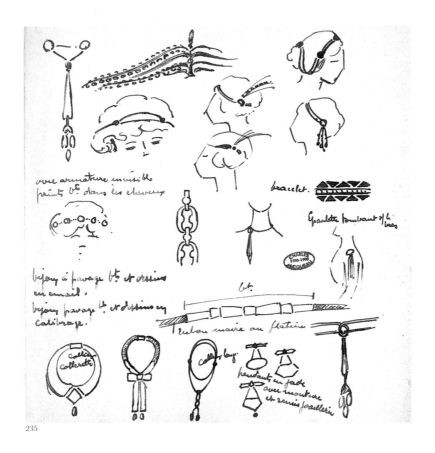

235

236

235 Page with sketches of head ornaments and pendants

Private collection, no. 45 (recto), c. 1913–23

Pen and ink on buff tracing paper

19.5 × 19 cm

This page contains sketches which may have been done over several years. The heads with cropped hair are unlikely to date from before about 1920. At the top right is an undulating head ornament similar to the Indian-style head ornament of 1928 (cat. 256). The other head ornaments comprise bandeaux with aigrettes, and a line of diamonds annotated 'avec armature invisible, points brillants dans les cheveux' (diamond dots in the hair, with invisible frame).

The oval bracelet links drawn vertically in the centre are characteristic of Cartier bracelets of the early to mid-1920s. At the right-hand side is a female bust with shoulder brooch, annotated 'épaulette tombant sur le bras', suggesting that it was intended to be worn falling down the outside of the arm.

At the bottom are necklaces in pavé-set diamonds, one with a diamond bow on a black watered silk ribbon, and a group of jade pendants mounted in diamonds. Pendants of this form, with polygonal elements hung from a horizontal bar brooch, were at their most popular around 1913, but the hanging elements were generally gem-set or carved in rock crystal. The use of jade suggests a date nearer 1920.

236 Page with sketches of classical and other head ornaments

Private collection, no. 125, c. 1910–20

Pencil on buff paper

20.6 × 26.5 cm

These sketches taken from classical, medieval and later models illustrate some of the source material that provided the inspiration for the many and varied head ornaments produced by Cartier. The sketches on the upper half of the page are taken mostly from Greek and Roman sources. Below are two heads with close-fitting caps edged with jewels copied from late fifteenth-century sources, possibly from paintings in the Louvre, such as the Maître de Moulins' portrait of Madeleine de Bourgogne (1490). There is also an Empire-style head with a broad diadem and a comb in a high chignon.

Few of these sketches were translated directly, but the two medieval heads may have inspired the undulating ruby and pearl head ornament made by Cartier London (cat. 256). The Greek female head top centre may have inspired the tortoiseshell bandeau for the back of the head, which is exactly this shape and was also produced by Cartier London in 1928 (p. 23, fig. 17).

At the far right is a sketch of the tortoiseshell and diamond wedding headdress made for Barbara Hutton's marriage to Prince Mdivani in 1933 (p. 29, fig. 24). As it is the only piece of Cartier jewellery on the page, it may have been added later.

237 Pendant with rock-crystal ring

Private collection, no. 781 (recto), c. 1913

Pencil, watercolour and bodycolour on buff tracing paper

18.5 × 6.4 cm

238 Necklace centrepiece in jade, turquoises and sapphires

Private collection, no. 59, c. 1913

Pencil, ink, watercolour and bodycolour on buff tracing paper

5 × 14 cm

Turquoise with sapphires and jade appears to have been a favourite colour combination of Jacqueau's. This necklace centrepiece relates closely to the brooch-pendant in the Cartier collection (cat. 29).

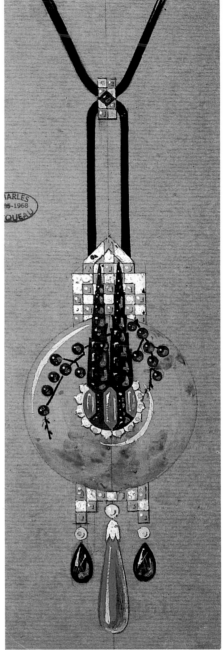

237

238

239 Flower vase
with drooping spray

Private collection, no. 291, *c.* 1910–13

Pencil, watercolour and bodycolour on buff tracing paper

23 × 4.8 cm

Cartier made a series of brooches in the form of vases with drooping flower sprays. A plaster cast of one of them, dated 1911, is illustrated on p. 47, fig. 35.

240–41 Two vases
with garlands

Private collection, no. 752 (recto), *c.* 1913

Pencil, watercolour and bodycolour on pale grey paper

11.6 × 4.5 cm and 4.8 × 5.8 cm

The design for the classical vase draped with garlands is inspired directly by a series of ornament prints published in Paris in 1771, entitled *Ouvrages de Bijouterie et Gravures de Théodore Bertren* (see 240.1). Bertren's designs were reissued in book form by A. Guérinet in the late nineteenth century, and Louis Cartier had them in his library. A plaster cast from a similar brooch is illustrated on p. 47.

Jacqueau's working designs also contain flower pots with drooping sprays placed on diamond and onyx plinths, perhaps interpreting Louis Cartier's 'vase sur socle' described in 1915 in his Notebooks, 1910–25.

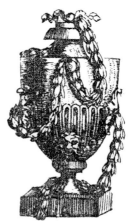

240.1 Design for vases with garlands from T. Bertren, *Ouvrages de Bijouterie et Gravures*, Paris 1771. Bertren's pattern book of ornament prints provided the inspiration for the brooches in the form of garlanded classical vases designed by Jacqueau (cat. 240–41).

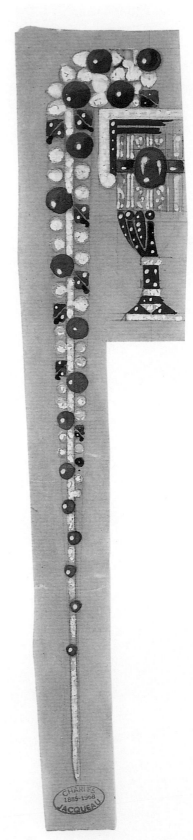

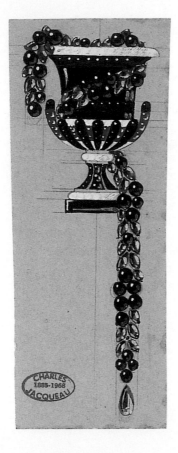

242 Page of designs with flower bowl brooches

Private collection, no. 451, *c*. 1913

Pencil, watercolour and bodycolour on buff tracing paper

25.5 × 18.5 cm

EXHIBITIONS Paris 1989, cat. 177.

The wide, flat bowls with drooping fruit or flowers are among Jacqueau's most original designs. Several variations were executed, the bowls gem-set or cut in onyx and the fruit in a variety of coloured stones. A plaster cast from one of these brooches, dated 1914, is shown in fig. 35 on p. 47. Although designed *c*. 1913, these brooches remained popular after the war. An example made by Cartier London is described in the Stock Record Book for 19 March 1920. 'Brooch, basket in onyx & bts [brilliants], line of cab. [cabochon] sapphires c/ [centre] cab emerald running along top & hanging over the ends finishing with one cut emerald, one brt. round & 2 small cab. onyx each side.' It was sold five days later, on 24 March 1920.

The amphora with falling water recurs repeatedly in Jacqueau's working designs.

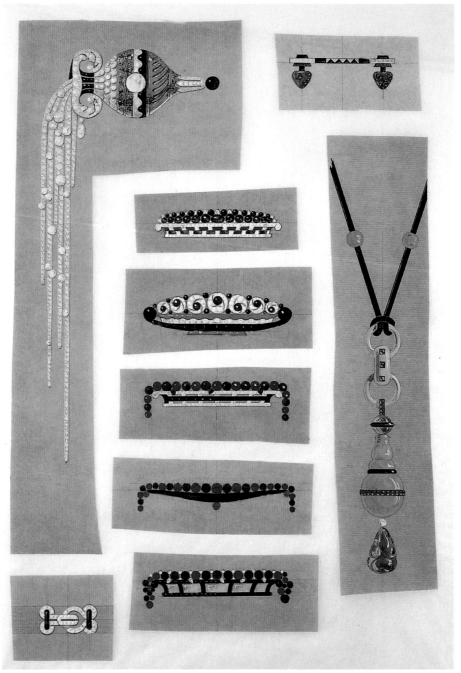

242 The bar brooch with a tree in a pot at each end, shown top right, is mounted upside down.

243

243 Page of designs, including brooch-pendant with vase

Private collection, no. 754 (verso), *c.* 1913

Pencil and bodycolour on buff tracing paper, eight designs and a photograph stuck separately onto buff paper

26.5 × 19 cm

The brooch-pendant in diamonds and onyx with a vase hanging from ivy-leaf garlands was repeated with several variations. One example, with the vase in coral, is included here as cat. 32. For a design for another version, see Rome 1990, cat. 79.

This page also contains designs for two stirrup brooches (for an example, see cat. 141), two pendants on black cord, two brooches and a brooch-pendant with long central drop, and a bar brooch ending in two trees in ruby pots (see cat. 242 for a variant of this design with the trees in emeralds, onyx and diamonds on a bar of zigzag pattern).

The photograph shows a *fourche*, or twopronged hair-pin. Jacqueau's working designs include a page of designs for *fourches* (no. 822, recto). Plaster casts taken from two executed examples are shown in fig. 35 on p. 47.

244 Page of designs for pendants

Private collection, no. 753 (recto), *c.* 1913

Pencil, ink, watercolour and bodycolour on buff tracing paper, each design stuck onto buff paper

26.5 × 19 cm

LITERATURE Nadelhoffer 1984, col. pl. 48.

The top pendant on the left is derived from traditional North African ornaments and was almost certainly taken from M. Gerlach's *Primitive and Folk Jewellery*, published in Vienna in 1906, pl. 6, but Jacqueau has turned the brooch into a pendant by placing the ring at the point of the triangle instead of below it. For a more recent publication of simlar North African ornaments, see M. Jenkins and M. Keene, *Islamic Jewelry in the Metropolitan Museum of Art*, New York 1982, nos 80–81.

On the lower left of the page is a design for a *sarpech*, or turban ornament, in the form of a curved oriental palm leaf.

244

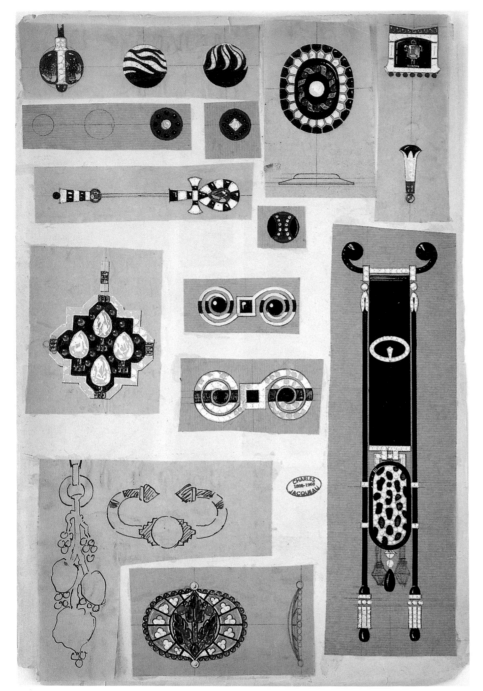

245

245 Page of designs including 'panther-skin' brooch-pendant

Private collection, no. 774 (recto), *c.* 1913

Pencil, ink, watercolour and bodycolour on buff tracing paper, each design stuck onto buff paper

28.5 × 19.2 cm

LITERATURE Nadelhoffer 1984, col. pl. 17 (panther-skin brooch-pendant only).

A variant of Jacqueau's design for the 'panther-skin' brooch-pendant was executed in 1915 and is included in this catalogue (cat. 170). This page also contains designs for spherical hat-pin heads, two Egyptian-style cliquet pins, one with an *ankh* or good luck symbol, the other in the form of a stylised fan, and a 'handle' brooch similar to cat. 171.

246 Page of designs for necklaces and cliquet pins

Private collection, no. 775 (recto), *c.* 1913–20

Pencil, ink, watercolour and bodycolour on buff tracing paper, each design stuck onto buff paper

28 × 19 cm

The jade, turquoise and sapphire pendant on the left belongs with the group of designs of *c.* 1913 that use these materials. The necklaces with central elements mounted on black silk or attached with black cord loops also date from just before the First World War. But the two chains on the left and the cliquet pins, all in black and white and incorporating cubes, discs and cylinders, do not appear to relate to any objects actually executed and are therefore impossible to date. Even if one assumes that they post-date the First World War, they are still exceptional for their modernist approach, and may never have been put into production for this reason.

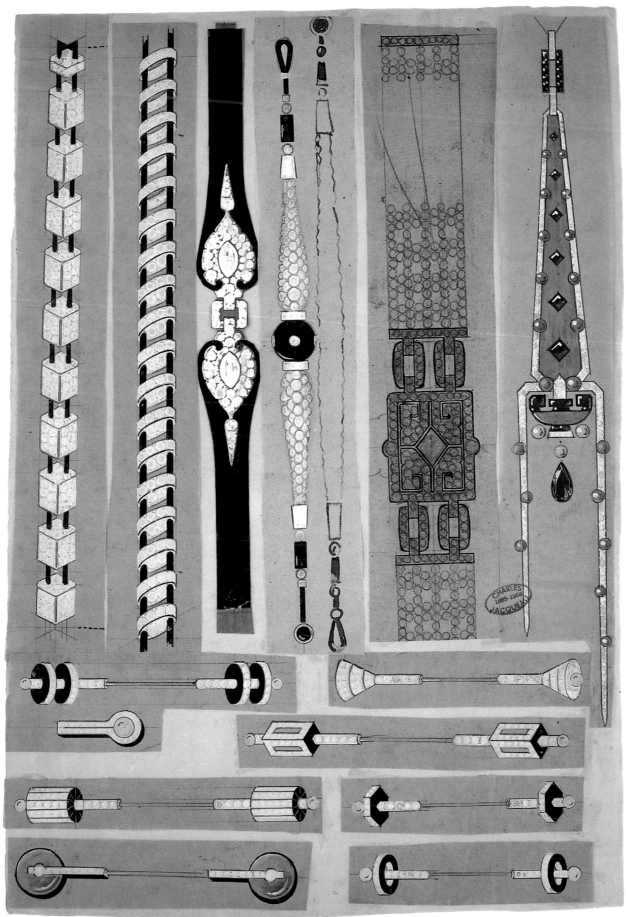

(c) DESIGNS IN THE EGYPTIAN STYLE

247

248

247 Page of studies of Egyptian motifs

Sketchbooks, f. 25. Cartier archive, Paris, *c.* 1910

Pen and ink with watercolour on buff tracing paper

24.5 × 17.5 cm

EXHIBITIONS Rome 1990, cat. 59.

LITERATURE Cologni and Nussbaum 1995, p. 103.

These studies are all copied directly from Owen Jones's *Grammar of Ornament*, published in London in 1856. Illustrated with colour lithographs, it presented a survey of decorative styles from Ancient Egypt to nineteenth-century Europe and remained a classic source book for decades. The knotted lotus bunch, the papyrus, the fans and the oars are copied from plates IV and V, while the patterns are copied from plates VIII–XI. Some of the patterns were transferred directly to objects, for example the sarcophagus vanity case (cat. 87).

Other pages of Egyptian studies from the Sketchbooks include further designs copied from Owen Jones as well as sketches of Egyptian jewellery (see Paris 1989, cat. 144)

248 Pendant with cobras

Garland Style Design Scrapbook, III, f. 19. Cartier archive, Paris, *c.* 1912

Pencil, ink and watercolour on buff tracing paper

21.8 × 5.6 cm

EXHIBITIONS Rome 1990, cat. 72.

This pendant was never executed.

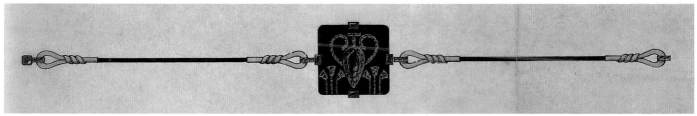

250 (reduced)

249–50 Two choker necklaces

Design Scrapbook, II. Cartier archive, Paris, *c.* 1912

Pencil, ink, watercolour and bodycolour on buff tracing paper

(249) Stylised lotus in emeralds and sapphires on a pavé diamond ground, long pendant in centre, attached with black silk cords

16.9 × 23.2 cm

(250) Square black onyx plaque with amphora and papyrus in emeralds and rubies, on black silk cord with diamond loops

16.4 × 33.9 cm

EXHIBITIONS (249) Paris 1989, cat. 164.

Delicate choker necklaces with a central element or pendant were introduced by Cartier in the 1910s. They were very different from the much wider dog-collar necklaces of the early 1900s. Louis Cartier's Notebooks for September 1919 contain a detailed analysis of current stock, in which he notes a lack of 'colliers pour le haut du cou supportant une pierre ou un ornement' (choker necklaces with pendant stones or ornament), indicating that they were still in fashion after the war. Neither of these two was executed.

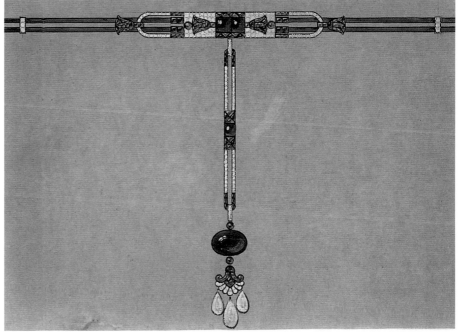

249 (detail, greatly reduced)

251 Scarab belt buckle

Stock Design Record Book, 1926, p. 53. Cartier archive, Paris

Pencil, watercolour and bodycolour on buff tracing paper

12.5 × 14.7 cm

EXHIBITIONS Paris 1994, cat. 364.

LITERATURE Nadelhoffer 1984, col. pl. 16; London 1988, p. 88.

This buckle was sold to Mrs Cole Porter. It incorporated ancient Egyptian faience scarab wings set in platinum, gold, enamel, sapphires and diamonds.

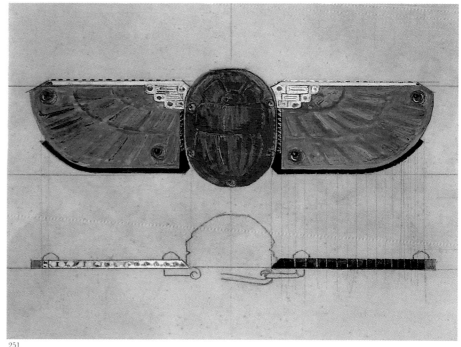

251

252 (greatly reduced)

252 Evening bag

Loose design, done in Paris for Cartier London, *c.* 1925. Cartier archive, Paris

Watercolour and bodycolour on black-painted card, signed Deringer (?).

31.5 × 20.5 cm

EXHIBITIONS Paris 1989, cat. 336; Paris 1994, cat. 373.

LITERATURE Nadelhoffer 1984, col. pl. 16.

This bag, designed as a special order, was never made. The scene depicts two female figures amongst papyri growing in water, with pintailed ducks above. Its interpretation is not immediately clear, but it may represent the shaking of papyri to summon the goddess Hathor. This is a rarely depicted ceremony and there is no obvious direct source of inspiration.

According to annotations on the back of the design, the bag itself was to be of woven coloured gold and platinum, with diamonds set in platinum (one of them supplied by the client). The mounts on each side were to be in pierced and engraved coloured gold, with gems on one side only.

Deringer worked in the Paris design studio between the wars. His first name is not known.

253 Designs for the sarcophagus vanity case (cat. 87)

Stock Design Record Book, 1923, p. 95. Cartier archive, Paris

Pencil, watercolour and bodycolour on buff tracing paper

19.6 × 15 cm

EXHIBITIONS Paris 1989, cat. 314; Paris 1994, cat. 371.

LITERATURE Snowman (ed.) 1990, p. 200.

For illustrations of these designs and full discussion of the vanity case itself, see cat. 87.

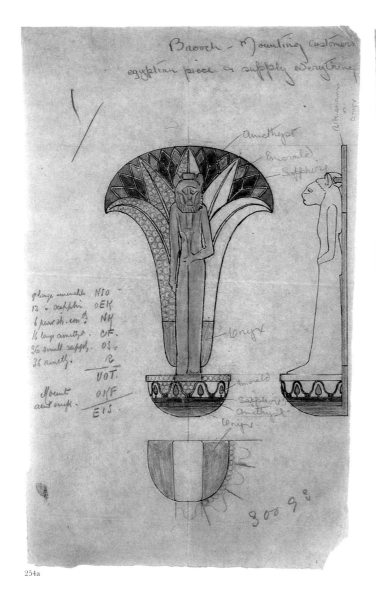

254a

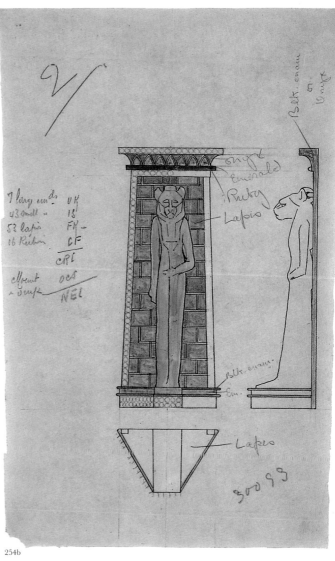

254b

254 Two alternative designs for a brooch with lion-headed goddess

London Design Scrapbook. Cartier archive, London, c. 1925

(a) Lion-headed goddess against a lotus
(b) Lion-headed goddess in a shrine

Pencil, ink and watercolour on buff tracing paper

23 × 14 cm each

EXHIBITIONS Paris 1989, cat. 275–6; Paris 1994, cat. 360–61.

LITERATURE (a) Nadelhoffer 1984, col. pl. 16.

These two alternative designs were done for a special order, to incorporate the client's ancient Egyptian faience figure holding a papyrus sceptre. The figure dates from the second half of the first millennium BC. The Egyptian pantheon included several lion-headed goddesses: Sekhmet, Bastet, Tefnut, and others. Most comparable figures of this kind wear either a uraeus (an upreared cobra) or a sun-disc on their heads. The figure shown in the design has lost its emblem, though the pendant loop behind the head can be seen in the side views. For a brooch made by Cartier Paris in 1925 with a lion-headed goddess in faience with sun-disc on her head, see Paris 1994, cat. 360–61.

The annotations indicate that the lotus and the semicircular base were to be set with diamonds, amethysts, emeralds, sapphires and onyx. The base has lotus buds and an undulating wave motif. The lotus petals have become curved; ancient Egyptian models invariably have straight petals. The shrine, in the form of a temple gate, was to be predominantly of lapis, with an entablature of onyx, emeralds and rubies, and a border of diamonds. The stones are all listed and costed at the left-hand side, but there is no record that the brooch was ever made.

(d) DESIGNS IN THE INDIAN STYLE

255 Designs for an upper-arm bracelet (cat. 99)

Loose designs, executed as a special order for Cartier London, 1922. Cartier archive, Paris

(a) Pencil, pen and ink on buff tracing paper. Small sketches lower left indicate how the bracelet transforms to a *devant de corsage*, a brooch and a pendant

23 × 37 cm

(b) Pencil, ink and watercolour on buff tracing paper. Detail of the front part of the bracelet with central plaque and two horizontal leaves

26.2 × 31 cm

For illustrations and discussion of these designs. see cat. 99.

256 Ruby, pearl and diamond head ornament

London Design Scrapbook. Cartier archive, London, 1928

Pen and ink with bodycolour on buff tracing paper

21 × 21.5 cm

A continuous undulating diamond band, decreasing towards the back, with a row of ruby beads along the upper edge, punctuated by ruby rosettes with pearl centres. Diamond and ruby motif at the front, with ruby pendant and pear-shaped pearl at top.

This head ornament was made by English Art Works for Cartier London for stock in November 1928, but was not sold until June 1930. The London archive contains photographs of a contemporary wax mannequin wearing the head ornament (256.1) over bobbed hair. Certain aspects of this design, such as the use of rubies, pearls and diamonds, and the large central jewel, are clearly inspired by Indian turban ornaments. The undulating shape of this head ornament, however, has no Indian precedent. It is taken directly from late fifteenth-century Northern European women's headdresses, often in the form of a continuous band of pearls securing a bonnet that hides the hair completely. Charles Jacqueau's sketches of head ornaments (cat. 236) include two headdresses of this kind.

256

256.1 Archive photograph of cat. 256 displayed on a contemporary wax model. The ornament continued unbroken round the back of the head. Cartier London.

257 (greatly reduced)

257 Headdress with tassel

Designed by Charles Jacqueau. Private collection,
no. 411, mid-1930s (?)

Pen and ink, watercolour and bodycolour on grey paper

54.2 × 47.1 cm

This is one of two alternative designs for an elaborate headdress incorporating a deep red fabric cap with a wide diamond and emerald band across the forehead, a tall *sarpech* with huge pear-drop diamond, a diamond and emerald band across the top of the head with another pear-drop diamond and a diamond and emerald tassel at the back. Strings of pearls and emeralds decorate the cap. For the alternative design, viewed from the front, see 257.1 (also illustated in Nadelhoffer 1984, col. pl. 17).

There is no record in the Cartier Paris archive that this headdress was ever made. A precise date is therefore impossible, but it may have been designed as part of one of the large commissions received by Cartier Paris from Indian maharajahs, among them the Maharajah of Patiala, who ordered several grand pieces in 1935 (see cat. 258 below). Most of the designs for special orders in the mid-1930s seem to have been done on the same grey paper, which appears frequently in the Paris order books in these years.

257.1 Alternative design by Charles Jacqueau in watercolour and bodycolour on grey paper for an Indian-style headdress, *c.* 1930 (greatly reduced). Private collection.

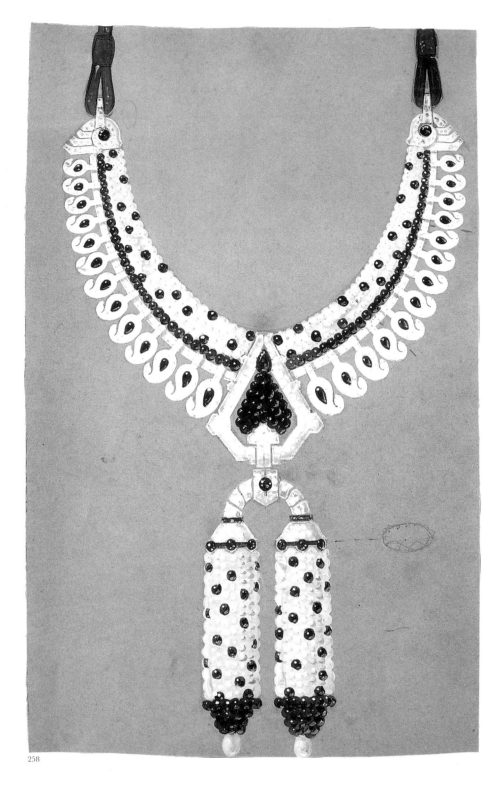

258

258 Ruby, pearl and diamond tassel necklace

Order Book, 26 June 1935. Cartier archive, Paris
Pencil, watercolour and bodycolour on grey paper
29.8 × 18.6 cm

Designed as part of a large commission from the Maharajah of Patiala (see pp. 32–3 and 159). The front has an inner frieze of closely set pearls and rubies above a row of curving diamond-set oriental palm leaves, each set with a ruby; at the centre is a polygonal diamond link containing a ruby cluster, with two pendant tassels of ruby beads and pearls. The necklace is tied round the back with woven silk cords.

This necklace was made by the Lavabre workshop, entirely from the client's stones: 1,159 pearls, 283 ruby beads, 13 pear-shaped rubies, 59 other rubies and 834 diamonds. While the Maharajah's earlier commission of 1925–8 comprised mainly state jewels to be worn by himself, this second group included a number of pieces made for the Maharani, for example a pair of ruby bead and pearl bracelets with diamond mounts.

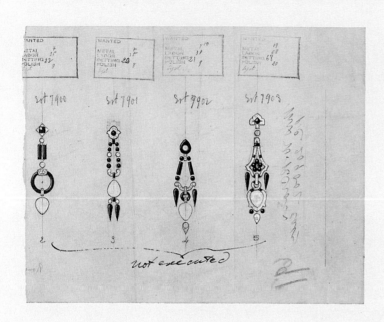

260 (greatly reduced)

259 Stock Design Record Book, 1922

Cartier archive, Paris (pp. 40–41)

Pencil, ink, watercolour and bodycolour on buff tracing paper

26 × 41 cm (width of open book)

Designs for six bracelets in diamonds, onyx and coral, each with initials L. C. or R. P., for Louis Cartier or the senior salesman, René Prieur. To the right of each is the name of the workshop to whom the design was given to be made up (Lavabre, Picq, Renault and Droguet), with the prices in code. Most also have the date when the design was given to the workshop and the expected date of delivery of the finished jewel. For example, the bracelet top left is annotated 'Donné le 26–10' and 'à livrer le 30–11'.

When the piece was delivered the design was stamped 'LIVRÉ'. The bracelet lower right is annotated 'nul' in blue pencil, indicating that it was not in the end produced – sadly, as it is the most striking design on the page. The annotations on the bracelet centre right indicate that two buttons from stock were incorporated (presumably the two lozenges).

Illustrated on p. 58, fig. 44.

260 Six alternative designs for earrings

Client file, Cartier archive, New York, 1925. Designed as a special order

Pencil, ink, watercolour and bodycolour on buff and brown tracing paper

From left to right: 16.8 × 20.8 cm (sheet with four designs); 13.5 × 5.9 cm (single design on buff paper); 12.5 × 9.9 cm (single design on brown paper)

Initially the earrings were made according to the single design on buff paper, annotated 'this one accepted', with onyx cylindrical batons and a heart-shaped diamond, from which hang onyx beads. Later in the same year the onyx beads were changed at the client's request to ten diamond drops, as in the single design on brown paper. The designs as executed are very much more conventional than the four designs with the annotation 'not executed'.

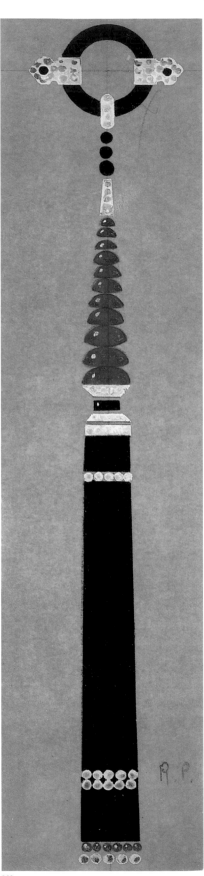

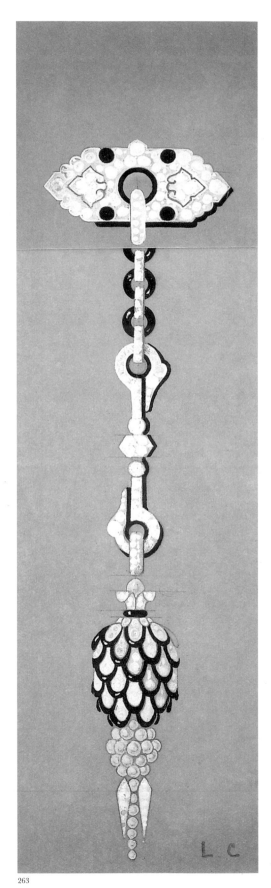

261

262

263

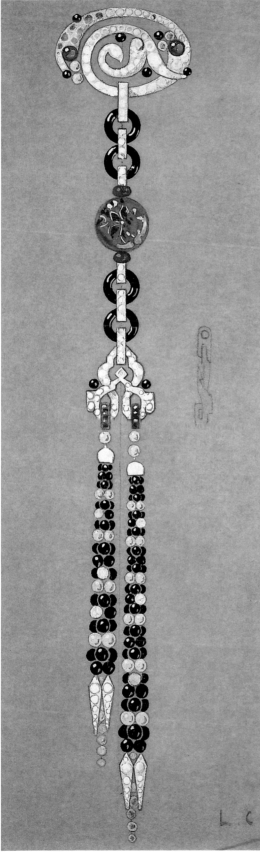

264

265

261–65 Pendant and four shoulder brooches (broches d'épaule)

Pencil, ink, watercolour and bodycolour on buff tracing paper

(261) Black and white tassel pendant

Stock Design Record Book, 1922, p. 43a. Cartier archive, Paris

20 × 5.8 cm

LITERATURE Nadelhoffer 1984, col. pl. 17

There is no record that this piece was ever made.

(262) Long shoulder brooch with tassel

Stock Design Record Book, 1922, p. 2. Cartier archive, Paris

22.7 × 5.5 cm

EXHIBITIONS Paris 1989, cat. 219; Tokyo 1995, cat. 119.

Executed in onyx and diamonds, with hemispherical ruby beads, in platinum setting.

(263) Brooch with pine-cone pendant and S-shaped motif on stem

Stock Design Record Book, 1922, p. 9. Cartier archive, Paris

22.8 × 7 cm

Executed in onyx, pearls and diamonds in platinum setting

(264) Shoulder brooch with stylised coiled dragon and double tassel

Stock Design Record Book, 1922, p. 6. Cartier archive, Paris

22.7 × 10.2 cm

EXHIBITIONS Paris 1989, cat. 218, pl. 41; Tokyo 1995, cat. 118.

LITERATURE Nadelhoffer 1984, col. pl. 17.

Executed in onyx, pearls, emeralds, rubies and diamonds in platinum setting, with a large carved emerald bead. With its coiled Chinese-style dragon, this brooch is loosely inspired by Chinese Han dynasty carved jade pendants: see Rawson 1995, p. 212, fig. 2.

(265) Shoulder brooch with ring and drooping tendril

Stock Design Record Book, 1923, p. 24. Cartier archive, Paris

19.3 × 6 cm

Executed in rock crystal, onyx and diamonds, with emerald drops, in platinum setting. For the contemporary archive photograph, see Gabardi 1989, p. 80.

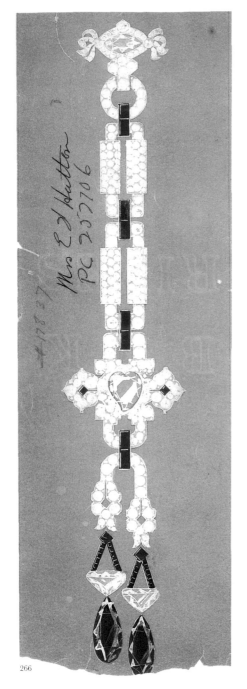

266

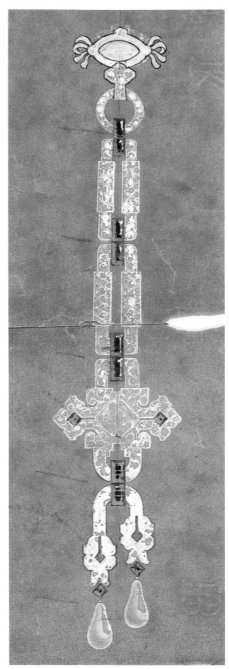

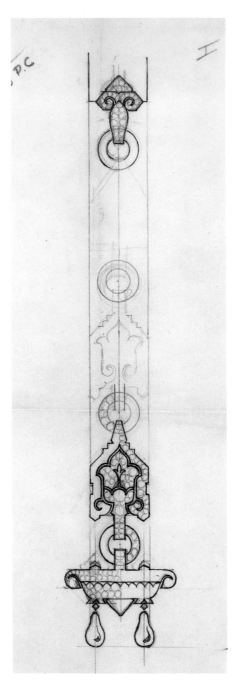

266 Design for a shoulder brooch

Client file, Cartier archive, New York, 1929.
Commissioned by Mrs E. F. Hutton (Marjorie
Merriweather Post).

Pencil, watercolour and bodycolour on buff tracing
paper

24.8 × 7.9 cm

This is one of a number of alternative designs
incorporating a heart-shaped diamond, a
navette diamond, two triangular diamonds
and two briolette sapphires. The brooch was
initially made up according to this design, but
it appears not to have been approved by the
client. The piece as finally executed was
shorter, with the navette diamond at the top,
set vertically.

The alternative designs show the difficulties
faced by the designers in having to incorporate a disparate group of client stones. In one
instance, the two triangular diamonds appear

266.1 and 2 Two alternative designs for the shoulder
brooch commissioned by Marjorie Merriweather
Post from Cartier New York in 1929. In each case
some of the stones are the same while others are
different. Client file, Cartier New York.

in place of the heart-shaped diamond, with
two pear-drop pearls at the bottom, instead of
the briolette sapphires (266.1).

In addition to the above designs, which are

all coloured, there are three pen and ink sketches. One of these is so different in conception that one would not associate it with the same commission, were it not annotated with the same estimate number as the other sketches. It takes the form of a Persian-style flower vase with stylised tree motifs, the two pear-drop pearls at the bottom (266.2). No doubt in 1929 it was considered too old-fashioned.

267 Vanity case with panther

Stock Design Record Book, 1925, p. 61a. Cartier archive, Paris

Pencil, ink, watercolour and bodycolour on buff tracing paper

14.5 × 6.4 cm (front) and 13.8 × 2.9 cm (side)

EXHIBITIONS Paris 1989, cat. 327.

This piece was to be made in enamelled gold, with borders of onyx cylinders, inlaid mother-of-pearl panels studded with rubies and turquoises, the panther in black-enamelled gold. With its mixture of materials and snake handle, this vanity case was more elaborate than the others from this series with panthers amongst cypress trees, most of which comprised a gem-set motif on a plain black ground (see cat. 173).

267

268 Vanity case with floral ends

Stock Design Record Book, 1925, p. 60a. Cartier archive, Paris

Pencil, ink, watercolour and bodycolour on grey-green tracing paper

12 × 16.5 cm

This piece was to be executed in red gold enamelled in cream, the sides enamelled black and bordered with a mosaic of purple and green tinted mother-of-pearl; the flower-heads at each end in carved coral with pearl centres, diamonds and cabochon emeralds on a black ground. Below the coloured design, showing side and end view, is a pencil sketch indicating that there was a central compartment with a lipstick inside the lid, as well as compartments at both ends. For an example of a vanity case of similar construction, see cat. 63.

268

269 Necklace or shoulder ornament (*'collier Bérénice'*)

Stock Design Record Book, 1925, p. 44. Cartier archive, Paris

Pencil, ink, watercolour and bodycolour on green tracing paper

59 × 18.5 cm

EXHIBITIONS Paris 1989, cat. 253.

This unprecedented and outlandish ornament was designed as the central showpiece for the 1925 Exhibition. It is remarkable not only as a highly original design, but also for its technical virtuosity and, most importantly, its use of three exceptional carved Mughal emeralds. The ornament was unsold and broken up into many different elements, all now lost without trace except for the central carved emerald, which has recently been rediscovered (see below).

Executed in emeralds, pearls, black enamel and diamonds in a platinum setting, this piece comprised a long band of several hinged sections which was draped over the shoulders with no fastening. The design shows only half of it and is therefore difficult to understand without the aid of the archive photograph of the complete ornament (269.3). The band was formed of lozenge-shaped and triangular links of black enamel, each set with a central pearl and studded with diamonds. In the centre was a large hexagonal emerald with hinged diamond motifs of stylised leaves on each side (seen at bottom of design). At each shoulder was a large square emerald with similar hinged diamond motifs (the one for the right shoulder is seen at the centre of the design). The lozenge-pattern band continued over the shoulder and down the back, ending in two long tassels of pearls, emeralds and diamonds. The archive records describe it as a 'necklace–shoulder ornament'. The term 'shoulder ornament' is used here to reflect the way in which it was worn.

At the 1925 Exhibition, this shoulder ornament was displayed by Cartier on a specially designed mannequin, with a mirror to show the back (269.2). The mannequin also wore a diadem and large brooch, both set with diamonds and emeralds. The brooch had an enormous button pearl in the centre to match the pearls on the shoulder ornament (see cat. 270). This eye-catching display inspired a coloured illustration in a special number of the *Gazette du Bon Ton* on the Pavillon de l'Elégance at the exhibition (269.1). The illustration was

BÉRÉNICE

DIADÉME ET COLLIER, DE CARTIER

Modèle déposé. Reproduction interdite.

given the name 'Bérénice' and this name, invented by the *Gazette du Bon Ton*, has since been applied to both necklace and diadem. A drawing of the whole necklace was used as a frame for the page of text opposite the coloured illustration.

All the three pieces on the Cartier mannequin are remarkable for their use of carved Indian emeralds, some of which were outstanding pieces in their own right. The diadem was set with vertical rows of reused Indian melon-cut emeralds of irregular size, with an Egyptian lotus motif at each end. According to Nadelhoffer (1984, p. 193), it was designed by

269.1 Coloured illustration from the *Gazette du Bon Ton* special issue on the Pavillon de l'Elégance, 1925, with the shoulder ornament and diadem on a model named 'Bérénice'. Cartier Paris.

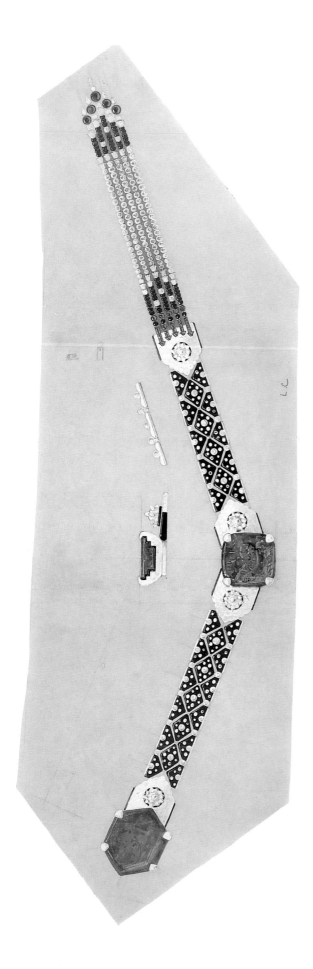

269.2 Archive photograph of a Cartier display mannequin at the 1925 Exhibition with shoulder ornament, diadem and brooch (cat. 269–70), all incorporating carved Indian emeralds. Cartier Paris.

269 Half the ornament is shown. At the bottom is the central or 'Taj Mahal' emerald. In the middle is one of the emeralds for the shoulder; the tassel at the top hung down the back (greatly reduced).

Henri Chenaud, who had joined the firm in 1908 and specialised in tiaras. However, it is not known whether he also designed the shoulder ornament.

The three large carved emeralds are exceptionally fine examples of Mughal flower decoration. (For Cartier's use of Indian emeralds see pp. 161–2.) The left- and right-hand emeralds were of 88.60 and 153.40 carats respectively. The central hexagonal emerald was of 141.22 carats. It was removed from the shoulder ornament in April 1926 and eventually remounted in September 1927 as a clip brooch, with a bizarre diamond mount which encased the stone at the back but was barely visible from the front. It was sold in this form to Mr Montague Stanley Napier. Its later history is not recorded by Cartier, and its rediscovery came about during the preparation of this catalogue as part of the attempt to date and properly describe the carved emeralds used in Cartier jewels. Michael Spink

269.3 Archive photograph of cat. 269. Cartier Paris.

269.4 The central carved Indian emerald of
c. 1630–50 from the shoulder ornament (cat. 269), shown
actual size. The emerald has recently been recognised as
the only surviving element of Cartier's exhibition centrepiece.

269.5 Archive photograph of the brooch containing
the right-hand emerald from the shoulder ornament (cat. 269),
made after the ornament was broken up in 1928. It is shown
in profile so that the 'chestnut motifs' with pointed diamonds
can be seen. Cartier Paris.

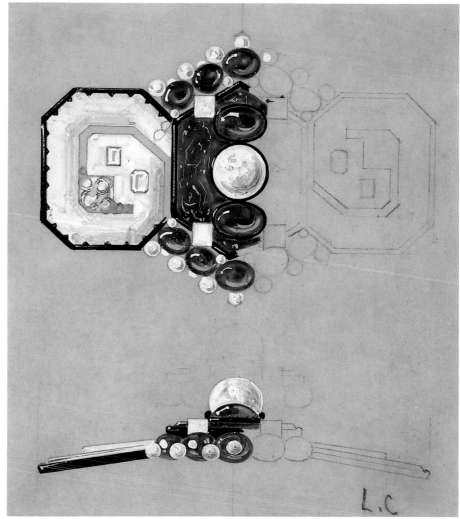

270

recognised the central emerald from the archive photograph of the shoulder ornament as the so-called 'Taj Mahal' emerald, published by P. Pal *et al.* in *The Romance of the Taj Mahal* (London 1989, p. 141, fig. 143), where it is dated to *c.* 1630–50. It resurfaced in the mid-1980s when it was acquired unmounted by Precious Stones Inc. of New York with the information that it had reputedly come from a Maharajah's collection. Its association with Cartier had by then been lost. It has been called the 'Taj Mahal' emerald in recent years by its present owners because the stylised lotus and poppies with which it is carved occur in the decoration of the Taj Mahal (269.4). For two comparable carved emeralds, both over 200 carats, see New York 1985, cat. 99 and 180.

Finally, a few words are needed to explain how the shoulder ornament was broken up and the various elements reused. The central emerald we already know was removed from the shoulder ornament in April 1926, but the brooch sold to Mr Napier was not its first reincarnation. Initially, it was removed together with its flanking diamond leaves; in May 1926 one of the tassels with its respective diamond leaf was attached to it to make a large *devant de corsage*. This did not sell, and in September 1927 the brooch sold to Mr Napier was made. In November 1928 the left-hand emerald of 88.60 carats was taken out and given a simple diamond setting. This had not sold by May 1929, when it was made as a special order into a pendant (also wearable as a brooch) for a necklace of carved emerald leaves and ruby beads. The right-hand emerald of 153.40 carats was also taken out in November 1928 and made into a brooch with its flanking diamond leaves. In March 1930 it was remounted again, in a diamond setting that encased the back, like the setting for the central emerald. It did not sell and was unmounted in January 1938, after which there is no further record in the archive. Meanwhile, in April 1930, the two 'chestnut motifs' of pavé-set diamonds studded with pointed diamonds were made into a brooch, which sold in August 1930. The original ornament had eight of these bosses with pointed diamonds, surely designed to demonstrate the consummate skill of the Cartier diamond setters (269.5).

As for the rest of the shoulder ornament, the lozenge-pattern band, part of the tassels and most of the remaining diamonds were made into a belt in November 1928 to the order of H. E. Thami Ben Mohamed El Glaoui, Pasha of Marrakesh. The diamonds were reset in a completely different style, with the addition of several baton diamonds that were not in the original ornament. Nadelhoffer's note (1984, p. 300, n. 29) that one of the three carved emeralds was purchased by the Glaoui of Marrakesh is incorrect. In February 1929 a belt buckle was made from the diamond leaf motifs at the top of each tassel with a row of five arrowhead motifs in calibré-cut emeralds; by November 1929 this had been altered to two separate brooches. Finally two of the 'chestnut' motifs with pointed diamonds were made into two brooches, sold in 1930.

270 Brooch with carved emerald and central pearl

Stock Design Record Book, 1925, p. 5b. Cartier archive, Paris

Pencil, ink, watercolour and bodycolour on buff tracing paper

14.8 × 12.8 cm

EXHIBITIONS Paris 1989, cat. 255; Tokyo 1995, cat. 144.

LITERATURE Cologni and Nussbaum 1995, p. 30.

This piece was executed in emeralds, pearls, enamel and diamonds set in platinum, with a hexagonal carved emerald of 88 carats and a large, round pearl at the centre. The profile view shows the astonishing size of the central pearl.

It was displayed at the exhibition on a mannequin together with the shoulder ornament (cat. 269) and a diadem, all with carved emeralds (269.2).

271

271 Comb bandeau with orchids

Stock Design Record Book, 1925, p. 39. Cartier archive, Paris

Pencil, watercolour and bodycolour on buff tracing paper

14 × 19 cm

EXHIBITIONS St Petersburg 1992, cat. 140, pl. 34.

LITERATURE Gabardi 1989, p. 21.

This piece was executed in onyx and diamonds set in platinum and mounted on a tortoiseshell comb. The three-dimensional orchid petals were pavé-set with diamonds and studded with onyx cones. It was one of the most ambitious pieces of Cartier's 'panther-skin' work actually made: surviving examples of this technique are generally much smaller.

In an article on jewels in *Harper's Bazaar* for 1 March 1926, Baron de Meyer described several pieces at the recent Paris Exhibition: 'Lovely too, at the Exposition, was a circular comb for a short-haired coiffure, worn across the back of the head, which had two large bunches of orchids in diamonds speckled with onyx placed on each side, the flowers nestling in the hair above the ears.' It was displayed on a mannequin (see 271.1) together with a stirrup brooch (cat. 272).

271.1 Archive photograph of a Cartier display mannequin at the 1925 Exhibition with the orchid comb bandeau (cat. 271), the stirrup brooch (cat. 272), and a rock-crystal belt with pearl and onyx tassels. The belt comprised five square rock-crystal links with diamond clasps. It was attached to a silk band and worn on the hips, the ornament to the side. From one of the rock-crystal links, off-centre, hung two onyx and pearl tassels, identical in design to those on a separate rock-crystal brooch (cat. 273). The mannequin also wore a bead necklace and a long shoulder brooch. To the left of the mannequin can be seen the coral and emerald tassel brooch (cat. 274). Cartier Paris.

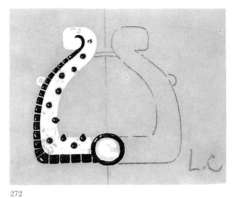

272

272 Stirrup brooch
(broche étrier)

Stock Design Record Book, 1925, p. 2b. Cartier archive, Paris

Pencil, ink, watercolour and bodycolour on buff tracing paper

6.3 × 7.4 cm

This piece, executed in onyx and diamonds set in platinum, is another example of Cartier's favoured 'panther-skin' ornament.

This brooch and the comb bandeau (cat. 271) were displayed by Cartier on the same mannequin, together with a rock-crystal and diamond belt (271.1).

273 Rock-crystal tassel brooch

Loose design. Cartier archive, Paris, 1924

Pencil, ink, watercolour and bodycolour on buff tracing paper

18.4 × 9.6 cm

LITERATURE Gabardi 1981, p. 79.

The tassels are of the same design as those on the rock-crystal belt displayed on one of the two Cartier mannequins (see 271.1). The tassels were reused from a pendant bought back from a client in 1923. They were removed from this brooch in 1927 and the rock-crystal brooch without the tassels was sold in 1928.

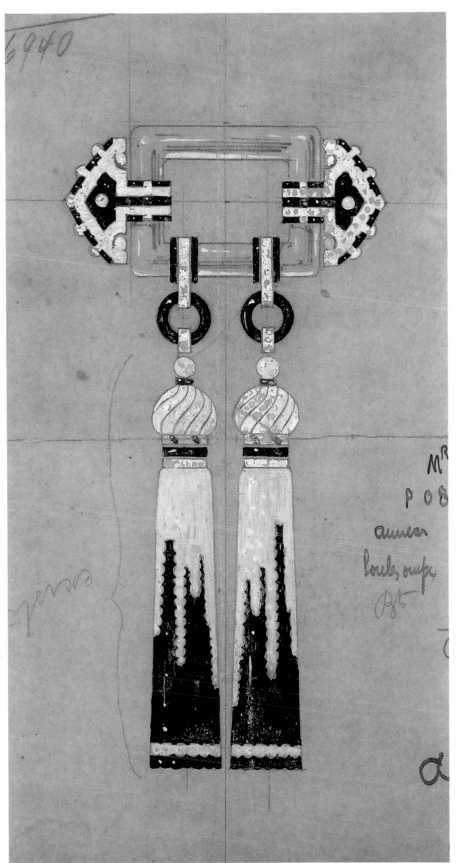

273

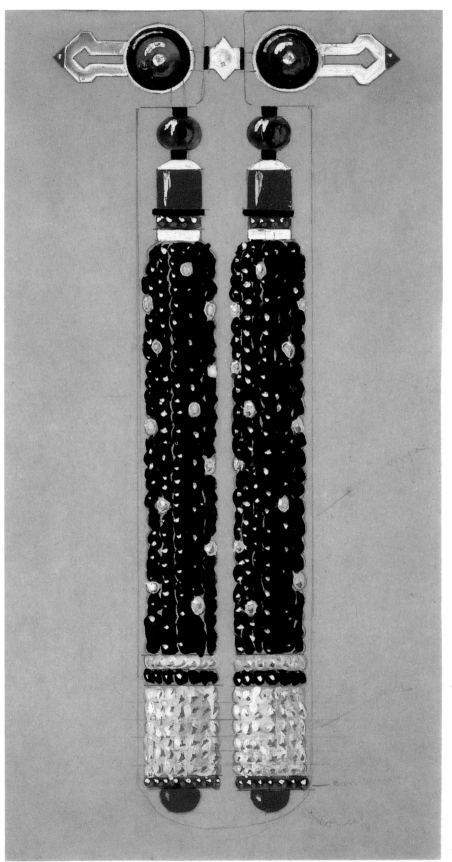

274 (enlarged)

274 Coral and emerald tassel brooch

Stock Design Record Book, 1925, p. 48. Cartier archive, Paris

Pencil, ink, watercolour and bodycolour on buff tracing paper

17.5 × 9 cm

EXHIBITIONS Paris 1989, cat. 254; Tokyo 1995, cat. 143.

This piece was executed in coral, emeralds, onyx, pearls and diamonds set in platinum. It was described in the records as a 'broche de décolleté'. There were two large emerald beads at the top; the tassels were of onyx and pearls with coral and emeralds at top and bottom. Coral and emerald was one of Cartier's favourite colour combinations at this time (see cat. 143–6). This brooch can be seen to the left of the mannequin in the contemporary photograph of Cartier's display (269.2).

275 Brooch with carved emerald

Stock Design Record Book, 1925, p. 7b. Cartier archive, Paris

Pencil, ink, watercolour and bodycolour on buff tracing paper

11 × 11.4 cm

EXHIBITIONS St Petersburg 1992, cat. 141.

This piece was executed with emerald beads, sapphires and diamonds set in platinum, with a large polygonal carved emerald of 74 carats in the centre.

276 Brooch with cabochon sapphire

Stock Design Record Book, 1924, p. 25b. Cartier archive, Paris

Pencil, watercolour and bodycolour on buff tracing paper

5.5 × 8 cm

This piece was executed in emeralds, sapphires, diamonds and onyx set in platinum.

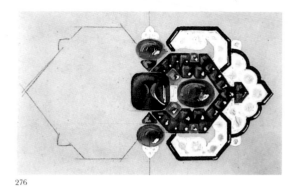

276

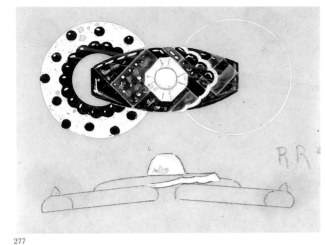

277

275

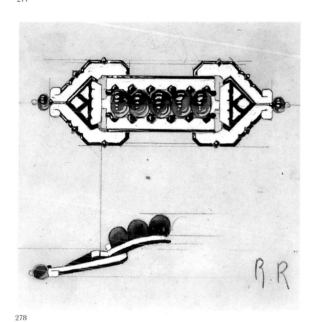

278

277 Brooch with diamond and onyx rings

Stock Design Record Book, 1925, p. 3c. Cartier archive, Paris

Pencil, ink, watercolour and bodycolour on buff tracing paper

7.5 × 9.8 cm

This piece was executed in sapphires, emeralds, onyx and diamonds set in platinum, the rings in pavé-set diamonds studded with onyx beads. The design shows two alternative patterns for the central motif and bears the initials of René Révillon.

278 Brooch with five emerald beads

Stock Design Record Book, 1925, p. 4a. Cartier archive, Paris

Pencil, ink, watercolour and bodycolour on buff tracing paper

10.5 × 11 cm

EXHIBITIONS Tokyo 1995, cat. 145.

This piece was executed in emeralds, diamonds and onyx set in platinum.

279

280

281

279 Vase pendant
(pendant vase)

Stock Design Record Book, 1925, p. 37. Cartier archive, Paris

Pencil, ink, watercolour and bodycolour on buff tracing paper

12.7 × 9.6 cm

EXHIBITIONS St Petersburg 1992, cat. 142.

This piece was executed in emeralds, sapphires and diamonds set in platinum with black enamel, on a black silk cord. It did not sell and was taken apart in 1927. The central element with the vase was reused as a belt buckle on a plaited black silk belt.

280 Shoulder brooch

Design Scrapbook, III, p. 18. Cartier archive, Paris, 1924

Pencil, ink, watercolour and bodycolour on buff tracing paper

16.8 × 5 cm

This piece was executed in emeralds, onyx and diamonds set in platinum.

281 Strap bracelet
(bracelet lanière)

Stock Design Record Book, 1924, p. 37b. Cartier archive, Paris

Pencil, watercolour and bodycolour on buff tracing paper

13.4 × 4.6 cm

This piece was executed in sapphires, emeralds, pearls and diamonds set in platinum.

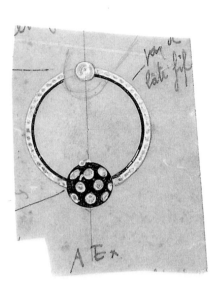
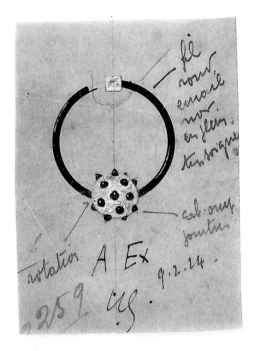
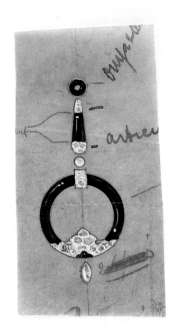

282–4

282–4 Three earrings

Pencil, ink, watercolour and bodycolour on buff
tracing paper

(282) Earring with diamond-studded
onyx ball

Design Scrapbook, II, p. 194. Cartier archive, Paris,
1924

6.7 × 5 cm

These earrings were executed in onyx, enamel
and diamonds set in platinum. The onyx ball
was studded with diamonds. Earrings in the
form of a hoop and ball, like this and the following design, were described in the archive
records as 'pendants d'oreille créole'. Nadelhoffer notes that the idea of a hoop and ball

recalls Merovingian earrings set with faceted
polyhedra (1984, p. 192) and refers to illustrations in E. Fontenay, *Les Bijoux Anciens et Modernes*, Paris 1887, p. 120, which remained an
important source book for decades.

(283) Earring with onyx-studded
diamond ball

Loose design, 1924. Cartier archive, Paris

8.7 × 6.3 cm

These earrings were executed in enamelled
gold for the hoop, with a ball of pavé-set
diamonds studded with onyx, in a platinum
setting. This is the reverse of the previous
design, with a black hoop and white ball with

black spots. The annotations indicate that the
hoop was to be very carefully enamelled all
round in black; the central ball was to be studded with onyx drops, and rotated on the hoop.
The signature below, with the date 9.2.24 and
'A EX' (to be executed) is thought to be that of
Louis Cartier.

(284) Earring with pendant hoop

Loose design, 1924. Cartier archive, Paris

8 × 4 cm

These earrings were executed in onyx and
diamonds set in platinum.

285

285 Leafy branch bracelet

Stock Design Record Book, 1924, p. 38c. Cartier archive, Paris

Pencil, ink, watercolour and bodycolour on buff tracing paper

5.9 × 18.1 cm

EXHIBITIONS St Petersburg 1992, cat. 134.

This bracelet was executed in rubies, sapphires, emeralds, diamonds and onyx set in platinum. It is one of the first of the group of jewels with carved mixed gems and diamond-studded beads that were later called 'tutti frutti' jewels (see section 7, pp. 208–9 and cat. 150–59). It is described in the Cartier records of the time as 'bracelet large liane feuilles pierres de couleur' (wide bracelet, creeping branch with leaves of coloured stones).

286 Palm-branch bouquet brooch

Stock Design Record Book, 1925, p. 9a. Cartier archive, Paris

Pencil, ink, watercolour and bodycolour on buff tracing paper

15.7 × 10.3 cm

EXHIBITIONS Paris 1989, cat. 261; Tokyo 1995, cat. 151.

This brooch was executed in emeralds, rubies, onyx and diamonds set in platinum. The emerald beads were encrusted with diamonds, while the stem was of pavé-set diamonds studded with onyx.

286

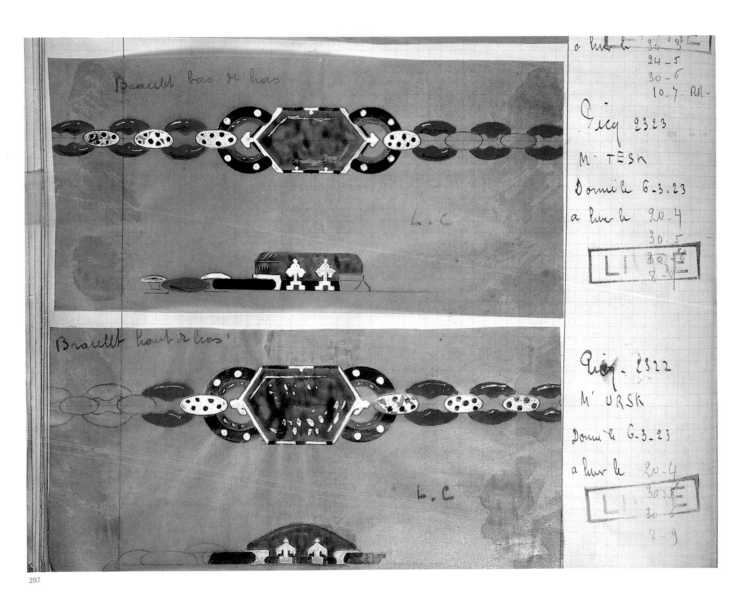

287

287 Pair of bracelets for the upper and lower arm *(bracelets haut de bras et bas de bras)*

Stock Design Record Book, 1923, pp. 34b and c. Cartier archive, Paris

Pencil, watercolour and bodycolour on ochre tracing paper

8.5 × 17.9 cm and 8.8 × 17.9 cm

These two bracelets were executed by Picq in emeralds, onyx and diamonds set in platinum, with carved coral links. In the centre of each were hexagonal carved Mughal emeralds of 104.45 and 93.28 carats. The profile views show the different shapes of the emeralds. Each emerald was flanked by onyx rings encrusted with diamonds, while the smaller elements between the coral links were of pavé-set diamonds studded with onyx.

This appears to be the only recorded set of upper- and lower-arm bracelets made by Cartier as a pair. They were sold before the exhibition opened and were lent back to Cartier by the client.

288 Coral snake bracelet

Client file, Cartier archive, New York, 1926

Pencil, watercolour and bodycolour on brown tracing paper, signed 'G.G.' in lower right corner

27 × 17.5 cm

This bracelet, designed as a special order, is an almost identical copy of one made for stock by Cartier Paris in 1923 and shown at the 1925 Exhibition. The initials 'G.G.' are very different in style to those used by Georges Genaille (see p. 286) and may be those of a different designer. The design for the Paris version shows the clasp and the first few links only. The bracelet is therefore difficult to understand (see St Petersburg 1992, cat. 124, pl. 30). For this reason, the New York design, which shows the whole bracelet, is included here instead. It was executed in diamonds, onyx and pearls set in platinum, with carved coral tulip links.

The Paris version had a large emerald forming the snake's head.

289 Fuchsia necklace (collier fuchsia)

Stock Design Record Book, 1925, p. 45. Cartier archive, Paris

Pencil, ink, watercolour and bodycolour on buff tracing paper

45 × 14.5 cm

EXHIBITIONS St Petersburg 1992, cat. 139.

This piece was executed in coral, emeralds, onyx and diamonds set in platinum. The coral fuchsia heads were based on the natural shape of the coral branches from which they were carved.

290 Coral and emerald pendant

Stock Design Record Book, 1923, p. 49b. Cartier archive, Paris

Pencil, ink, watercolour and bodycolour on buff tracing paper

28.7 × 5.2 cm

This piece was executed in emeralds, diamonds, enamel, onyx and coral set in platinum, with a chain of onyx beads. Also in the 1925 Exhibition was a bracelet with a double row of identical coral links interspersed with plaques of mother-of-pearl, diamonds and onyx (see *The Magical Art Of Cartier*, sale catalogue, Antiquorum/Tajan, Geneva, 19 November 1996, lot 120, illustrated together with original design of 1924). This bracelet is now in the Cartier collection.

288

291 Coral and emerald tassel pendant

Stock Design Record Book, 1923, p. 48b. Cartier archive, Paris

Pencil, ink, watercolour and bodycolour on buff tracing paper

17.4 × 5.2 cm

This piece was executed in emeralds, diamonds, coral, onyx and pearls set in platinum. The idea of a chandelier-shaped tassel at the end of a long pendant is derived from Indian head ornaments of the kind illustrated by T. H. Hendley in his *Jeypore Enamels*, London 1886, pl. 23, a copy of which would almost certainly have been in Louis Cartier's library.

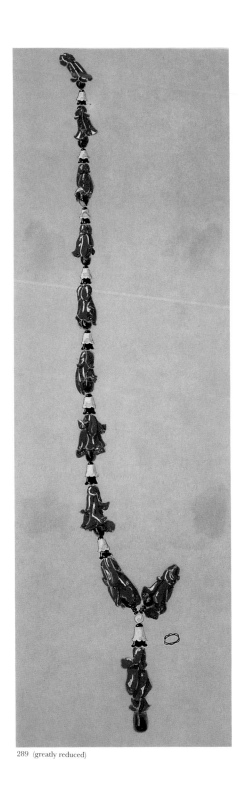

289 (greatly reduced)

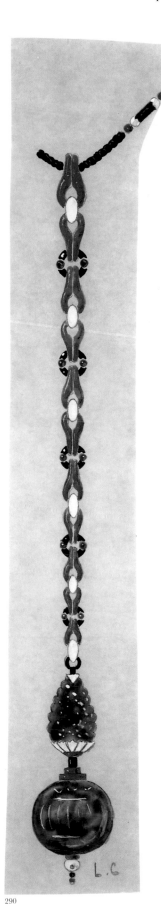

290

291

292–4 Three black lacquer bracelets

Client files, Cartier archive, New York, *c.* 1935. All designed as special orders, (292) and (293) for the same client, (294) for Mrs H. F. McCormick (Ganna Walska)

(292) With circular diamond clip brooch

Pencil, ink, watercolour and bodycolour on buff tracing paper mounted on grey paper, signed with monogram MD in lower right corner

14.8 × 8.2 cm

A black lacquer band with circular diamond clip brooch incorporating a large polygonal diamond in the centre. The profile sketch shows the huge proportions of the clip, covering the entire front of the wrist. There is also a sketch of the wrist size. The frontal view bears annotations indicating that the six diamonds round the ring stick up above the surface and were to be attached with four claws, allowing the light to pass underneath.

This design was done in Paris and was based on a bracelet of similar design, but all in gold, with a gold ring forming the clasp. The design was then sent to New York, where the bracelet was made, accompanied by the following letter dated 14 September 1935:

> This client will hand you some jewels for the purpose of executing in New York, a bracelet on flexible white gold band, black enamel lacquer, with brilliant clip motif, to be worn also on corsage, double stem system, and not full back or open work.
>
> Herewith design approved by client. For more security, please take the customer's wrist size again. We are enclosing photograph of an all gold bracelet, by which we were inspired to execute the project of the bracelet in brilliant.

(293) With two pyramid clip brooches

Pencil, watercolour and bodycolour on buff tracing paper, signed with monogram GGM bottom centre

12.5 × 10 cm

A black lacquer open band with flared terminals to which are attached a pair of pyramidal diamond clip brooches. The clips were made from the client's stones, except for the 'stick brilliants' supplied by Cartier. But the design is undated and there is no record of whether the piece was ever made. Like the previous bracelet, the design is based on Cartier Paris models (see cat. 220).

292

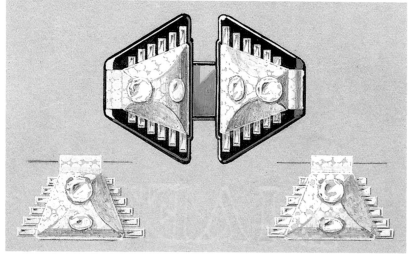

293

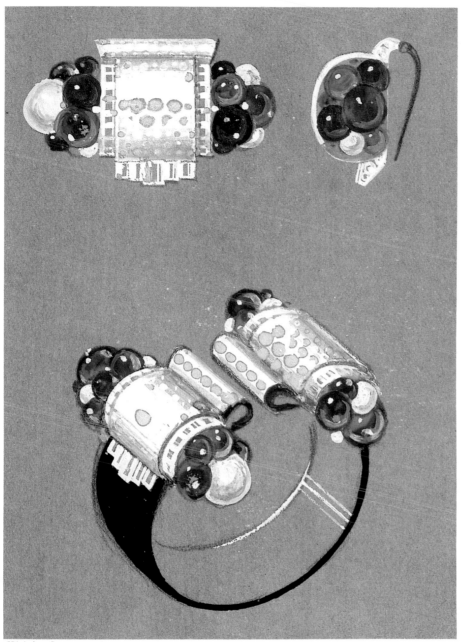

294 (enlarged)

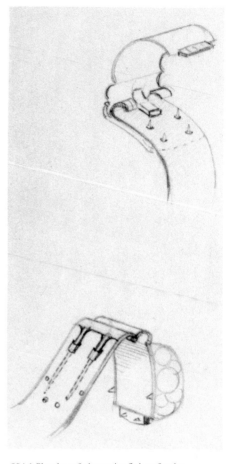

294.1 Sketches of alternative fittings for the multigem clip brooches designed for Mrs H. F. McCormick in 1935 to be worn on a black lacquer bracelet (cat. 294). The alternatives were a double prong fitting or a solid back. Cartier New York.

(294) With two multigem clip brooches

Pencil, ink, watercolour and bodycolour on grey paper
12.5 × 9.5 cm

A black lacquer bracelet with a pair of clip brooches set with diamonds and ruby, emerald and sapphire beads. There is no record that the bracelet and clips were ever made.

The design is undated, but is accompanied by a letter from Cartier Paris to Cartier New York of April 1935. The letter informed Cartier New York that Mr and Mrs H. F. McCormick were to leave the following day for New York and enclosed detailed instructions and sketches for the remounting of her brooch as two clip brooches or bracelet terminals. The bracelet itself was to be a supple band of grey gold, lacquered black on the exterior. The two clip brooches were to be in the form of a half-cylinder with coloured stones and pearls, set either with double-prong fitting or with a solid back and claws. If the latter, the bracelet would be gripped between the gem-set part and the solid back by means of holes in the bracelet corresponding to the claws in both front and back of the clip. If the clips were made with two prongs, the interior of the bracelet would have to have two small tubes into which the two prongs would slide before closing the clip onto the bracelet (294.1).

Most of the clip brooches designed for black lacquer bracelets were of diamonds alone, or perhaps with one other coloured stone. In this instance the client wanted the stones from her existing large multigem brooch to be reused.

295–8 Five designs for rings

Client files, Cartier archive, New York, 1928–36. All designed as special orders.

Pencil, ink, watercolour and bodycolour on buff tracing paper

(295) With oval cabochon emerald, 1928

19.5 × 10 cm. Salesman's initials and estimate number down right-hand side

(296) A cabochon emerald on a wide black hoop, 1936

12.5 × 10 cm. Signed with monogram GM in lower right corner

(297) A brilliant-cut diamond in a modernist platinum setting, 1929

12.3 × 8.7 cm

This design has the initials PL (or JL) at the top right. It is one of three alternative designs sent with the following letter dated 9 August 1929 from Cartier Paris:

> This client is in Paris for a very short stay, has brought us a stone of which you will find the exact size on our design No. 1.
>
> He has asked us to make designs for a mounting of gentleman's ring in a new style and we are enclosing herewith the designs.
>
> We have made sketches in which you will see the size of the stone is considerably increased. This in order to enable to judge the shape of the mounting. You would have to naturally reduce them to the dimensions of the stone of the client and according to the finger size he will give you.
>
> The client is to call on you. We have quoted no price not knowing if the mounting must be made in platinum or in grey gold.

A platinum setting would have been significantly more expensive. There is no record in the New York archive that any of the three designs was ever made. Significantly, Cartier described this simple, bold design as a 'new style', and it is indeed exceptional given that Cartier paid almost no attention to the modern movement or the idea of form without ornament.

(298) Two alternative designs for an open ring with black hoop and diamond cylinders, 1935

12.5 × 10 cm each. Monogram HG (?) in lower right corner

The designs indicate that the band was to be in gold, with black enamel or lacquer. One

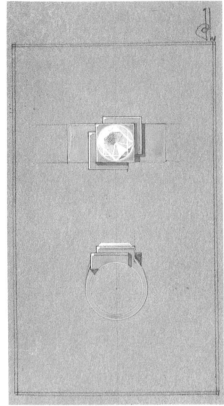

297

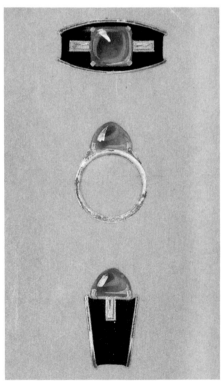

296

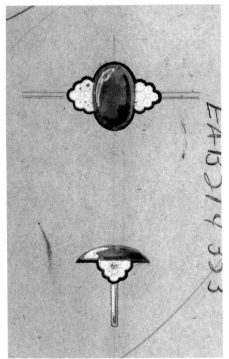

295

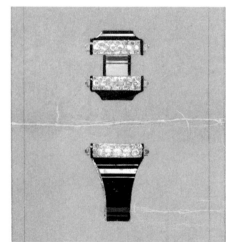

298

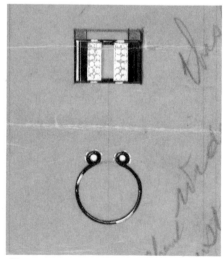

298

version, (a), had the band decreasing towards the back. The version as executed, (b), had a broad band of constant width. There was also a third design with a narrower band of constant width.

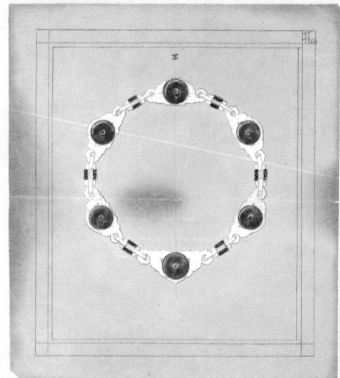
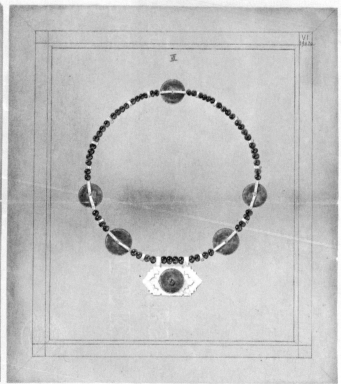

299

299 Two alternative designs for a necklace with emeralds

Client file, Cartier archive, New York. Designed for
Mrs H. F. McCormick (Ganna Walska), 1932

Pencil, ink, watercolour and bodycolour on buff tracing
paper

25.5 × 21.5 cm each

These are two of seven alternative designs
for a necklace incorporating six emerald
roundels. The client file refers to a letter of
30 September 1932 discussing these designs
and also to the proposal to make a pair of earrings and a ring to match, with two emeralds
and one emerald respectively. But the letter
does not survive, and there is no indication
whether any of the seven designs for the necklace were ever made.

300a

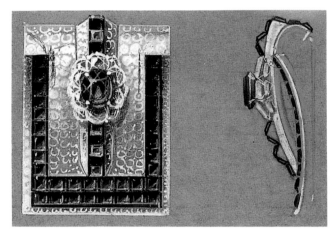
300b

300 Sapphire and diamond clip brooch

Order Book, 4 January 1937, p. 144. Cartier archive, Paris

(a) Watercolour and bodycolour on buff tracing paper

6.3 × 4.3 cm

(b) Ink, watercolour and bodycolour on grey card

5.7 × 8.3 cm

EXHIBITIONS Paris 1989, cat. 464.

This brooch was to be made with sapphires and diamonds set in platinum. It incorporated an oval sapphire and various other stones belonging to the client. The other sapphires were calibré-cut; the three-quarter design shows them set in a raised zigzag pattern down the centre.

This design has the bold, three-dimensional quality characteristic of many designs of the late 1930s. The combination of simple curved shapes with contrasting areas of colour is equally characteristic of the work of Cartier's contemporaries in the Rue de la Paix and the Place Vendôme, such as Boucheron or Van Cleef & Arpels. This marks a turning-point in Cartier design which sets the period after 1939 apart from the previous two or three decades.

GLOSSARY

Aigrette
(French = a tuft of feathers.) A hat or hair ornament in the form of jewelled feathers or a brooch to hold a tuft of real feathers.

Baton-cut
See **baguette-cut**.

Baguette-cut
A gemstone cut in the shape of a long narrow rectangle with a flat top. According to Selwyn 1945, 'baton' is used for a larger stone (such as those on the band of the topaz head ornament, cat. 226) and 'baguette' for a smaller one of the same size, but in many cases the two terms are used interchangeably. The Cartier London records from between the wars use the term 'baton', while the New York records refer to 'stick' brilliants. The shape of the cut gave its name to the baguette watch (see cat. 210-12).

Bandeau
A flexible, flat, gem-set band worn low on the forehead, tied at the back with cords.

Bezel
The salient or characteristic part of a ring, such as the setting including the stone.

Boucle déployante
Folding buckle for wrist watches and bracelets, formed of three hinged curved elements that open out and snap shut (see cat. 27.1). They were introduced by Cartier in 1910 and were easier to use than a traditional buckle and strap.

Bought in
Trade term used in the UK for finished pieces purchased from other firms.

Brevet
Patent. Many of the Paris-made pieces are marked *Breveté SGDG* (often abbreviated *BTE*). The letters *SGDG* stand for *sans garantie du gouvernement*.

Brilliant (*brillant*)
English and French terms for a brilliant-cut diamond. The standard brilliant-cut has 58 facets, 33 on the top part of the stone and 25 on the lower part. Most modern brilliant-cuts are circular in outline, but older stones were often 'cushion-shaped', i.e. squarish with rounded corners.

Briolette
A drop-shaped stone cut with facets all over.

Broche draperie
Term used in the Cartier records to describe a brooch in the form of a swag or garland with a central element hanging from it; the brooch pin is hidden when worn, to give the effect of gem-set drapery.

Broche étrier
Literally 'stirrup brooch'. Term used in the Cartier records initially to describe a brooch formed of a bar with upturned ends joined by the brooch-pin and thus resembling an upside-down stirrup in shape. Later, the brooches were actually designed in the form of upended stirrups (see cat. 141).

Broche de décolleté
Term used in the Cartier records to describe a new type of brooch introduced *c*. 1925 and designed to outline the central fastening of a dress. Attached with a brooch-pin at the top, it could be long enough to reach the waist with further pins as necessary (see cat. 274 and p. 18, figs 10-11).

Cabochon
A stone with a polished rounded surface that has not been cut into facets.

Calibré-cut
A stone cut in a specific shape to fit the setting exactly.

Cartouche
An area defined by a frame of fanciful design.

Cavetto
A hollow moulding, about a quarter of a circle in section, seen for example on the cornice or projecting moulding on the Egyptian temple gate clock (cat. 88).

Chasing
The art of working metal from the front with punches and a hammer to coax it into the right place to form the pattern. In engraving the metal is taken away, whereas in chasing it is simply moved.

Cliquet pin
A brooch formed of two elements joined by a long pin attached to one element and with a snap or click fitting at the other end. Cartier examples date from shortly before the First World War. Sometimes the two elements were identical (see cat. 97), but more usually the top element was larger with a small decorative element or *cache-pointe* at the base to hide the end of the pin and secure the brooch (see cat. 78). A nick in the end of the pin was caught in a sprung fitting on the reverse of the *cache-pointe*. Described as 'broches cliquet' in the archive records, these brooches have traditionally been called jabot pins. But as they were worn on a lapel or in the fashionable cloche hats of the 1920s (see cat. 95.1) rather than used to secure a jabot or cravat, the term cliquet pin has been used here.

According to Pierre Cartier, quoted in a newspaper article on 'Jewelry forecasts for 1925', 'One of the novelties for the smart woman to wear, especially since the small hat has appeared, is the cliquet brooch. The pin frequently contains extremely valuable pearls, and in fact this ornament has become so fashionable that it is worn in the morning, made of coral and semi-precious stones, and in the afternoon it is made of pearls and precious stones, especially large pearls.'

Closed-back setting
A method of setting a gemstone whereby the lower part of the gemstone is entirely encased

in the setting, leaving only the upper part of the stone visible.

Collet-set

A simple box setting with straight sides enclosing the gem.

Devant de corsage

A large brooch that covers the central part of the bodice in the manner of the eighteenth-century stomacher, which filled the area from the bust to the waist and was often formed of jewelled elements sewn to the corsage.

Email pékin mille raies

See **enamel**.

Emerald-cut

A rectangular stone with mitred corners, producing an octagonal outline, with a large central facet or table and a series of sloping rectangular facets (step-cut). Mainly used for emeralds, but large diamonds are sometimes cut in this way.

Enamel

Coloured glass, or a combination of vitreous glazes, fused onto a metallic surface.

Most of the enamel decoration on the objects catalogued here is **champlevé** enamel. In this technique the metal surface is gouged out to create troughs and channels, each separated by a thin ridge of metal. The coloured enamels, in powdered form, are laid in the troughs and fused onto the metal, with the ridges forming the outline of the pattern. A variant of this method is **basse-taille** enamel, in which translucent, as opposed to opaque, enamels are thinly applied over the metal so that the patterns engraved in it can be seen through the enamel. This method was perfected in eighteenth-century Paris for use on gold boxes with engine-turned or *guilloché* decoration forming delicate patterns resembling sun-rays or watered silk beneath the enamel (see cat. 40-43). Another variant was **ombré** or shaded enamelling, in which the thicknesses of successive layers of enamel were varied as they were applied. This gave an iridescent or opalescent surface effect (see cat. 41).

A different technique altogether and one rarely used by Cartier is **cloisonné** enamel, in which thin strips of metal are soldered to the surface forming the outline of the pattern or picture and creating cells or *cloisons* into which the powdered enamel is laid and fused. The sarcophagus vanity case (cat. 87) was originally designed to have cloisonné enamel on the base; the enamel was never applied but the *cloisons* remain. A variant of cloisonné enamel was **plique-à-jour** enamel, in which translucent enamel was held within a metal cellwork but without a backing, to give the effect of a stained-glass window. During firing the cells were attached to a temporary metal sheet, removed after firing. The technique was widely fashionable *c*. 1900 and appears in pieces in the Art Nouveau style purchased from other suppliers and stocked by Cartier.

During the 1920s boxes and vanity cases were frequently decorated with ***émail pékin mille raies***, a term used in the Cartier records to describe thin parallel stripes of enamel against a gold ground (see cat. 63, 65 and 131).

Engine-turning

Engraving metal with a lathe to produce a multiplicity of symmetrical linear patterns executed with precision. The French term for engine-turned is *guilloché*.

Engraving

Cutting metal away with a burin or V-shaped tool.

Faience

The name traditionally given to the glazed composition used in ancient Egypt for scarabs and other amulets.

Fourche

Arch-shaped tortoiseshell comb with double prong, introduced *c*. 1900.

Gallery

A raised platinum frame at the back of a jewel that lifts the piece off the body and allows light to pass through the stones.

Grosgrain ribbon

A silk ribbon with wide ribbing.

Inro

Japanese term for a small case to carry personal effects, comprising a series of compartments which slot together and are held in place by a cord.

Integral hinge

The invisible hinge found on many of Cartier's cigarette boxes and vanity cases. A finely rolled, hinged cylinder with a traverse pin was attached so as to be flush with the walls of the box and thus invisible when the box was closed. Integral hinges were a feature of eighteenth-century French gold boxes.

Kokoshnik

(Russian = cockscomb.) A head ornament in the form of a broad band that flared outwards.

Lacque burgauté

See **lacquer**.

Lacquer

A natural resin made from the sap of the lacquer tree, which is native to China. It is applied in numerous layers, each of which is allowed to dry before the next is added. Once dry, it is impervious to water and can be carved, inlaid or painted. The technique was perfected in China and later transmitted to Japan. Natural lacquer dries black, but with the addition of cinnabar it turns a rich red.

Much of the lacquer used by Cartier was in the form of small plaques imported from the Far East. These were of black lacquer inlaid with mother-of-pearl, a method known as ***lacque burgauté***, and were made in the nineteenth century either on the Ryukyu islands between China and Japan, or in Nagasaki, the main centre of production in Japan itself. The mother-of-pearl was partly tinted in purple and green. After the lacquer had been brought level with the mother-of-pearl inlay, a final layer of lacquer was applied to the whole object, thus concealing the mother-of-pearl. The surface was then rubbed with pumice stone until the inlay was once more exposed. In this way a perfectly smooth surface was obtained.

Cartier also used lacquer as a substitute for enamel that did not chip or crack so easily. This was particularly important for cigarette cases and also for the lacquer bracelets decorated with double clip brooches. Although black was the dominant colour, several other colours were used, and it may be that some of

these are what is commonly known as shellac rather than true lacquer. Shellac is made from the secretion of the lac insect, indigenous to India.

Lorgnette
A folding pair of eye-glasses, usually hung from a chain.

Marquise-cut
See **navette-cut**.

Melon-cut
A traditional Indian method of cutting emeralds into oblate beads (i.e. flattened top and bottom like a melon) with longitudinal grooves.

Milled wire
Wire marked with fluting or parallel indentations.

Millegrain setting
A setting in which the metal is pushed around the stone to form tiny beads or grains instead of claws to keep the stone in place. This is done with a small hardened wheel with depressions corresponding to the beads round the outside. The wheel is pressed down hard onto the metal edge formed by the setter's tooling until the bead shapes begin to appear. The technique seems to have been introduced in the nineteenth century, and became the favoured method for Cartier's diamond and platinum jewellery since it required a minimum amount of metal and was therefore ideal for Cartier's **open-back** settings. Millegrain setting also occurs along the outer edge of the jewel to give a decorative effect. The inner stones would then be set in straight-line settings (called 'thread settings' in the archive records).

Navette-cut
A boat-shaped faceted stone, alternatively called marquise-cut.

Nécessaire
Alternative term for a vanity case, sometimes used by Cartier. The term has been in use since the eighteenth century to describe a container for household implements.

Netsuke
Japanese term for a carved belt toggle to attach an **inro**.

Old-cut
This term refers to brilliant-cut diamonds with a flat top or table, unlike a modern brilliant-cut (see **brilliant**).

Open-back setting
A method of setting a gemstone in which the stone is held by a closely fitting cell with no back, allowing light into the stone and used especially for translucent faceted stones. The Paris archive records use the term 'diamant portrait', while the London records refer to 'glass-set' stones.

Pavé setting
A method of setting in which a whole area of metal is covered or paved with stones placed close together, with minimal settings between them.

Plaque-de-cou
The central element of a dog-collar necklace, fashionable around 1900.

Reeded
A surface pattern formed of parallel grooves.

Rock crystal
Colourless water-clear quartz of little intrinsic value. It occurs in large crystals which can be carved and engraved.

Rose-cut
A stone cut with 24 triangular facets on a flat base.

Sautoir
A long necklace or chain. To wear something *en sautoir* means to wear it diagonally or crosswise, such as a sash worn over the shoulder. The term was then applied to the long necklaces worn in this way, i.e. over one shoulder and under the other, in the late eighteenth and early nineteenth centuries. They were said to have been inspired by French military costume (see Bury 1991, vol. 1, col. pl. 6, p. 24, and pl. 95, p. 43). During the early nineteenth century long sautoirs were worn wide over the shoulders. From the late

nineteenth century they were worn round the neck and were often of pearls with tassels at the bottom. Diamond sautoirs or chains were especially fashionable in the 1920s. At a London dance in 1926, Mrs Walter Burns wore 'her attractive Cartier chain of long diamond links' (*The Sketch*, 24 March 1926, p. 536).

Spanner-head screw
Screw with two holes, requiring a double-armed or spanner-head screwdriver.

Spectacle setting
A stone set by means of a simple narrow loop round the girdle (the dividing line between the top and bottom parts of a stone).

Table
The large central facet at the top of a cut gemstone.

Trapeze-cut
A stone cut in the form of an equilateral triangle with the top chopped off.

Vanity case
A term introduced in the mid-1920s, initially for a powder box with a mirror inside the lid, loose powder and a puff. To prevent the powder spilling, improvements were made. The gauze sifter, laid upon the loose powder, kept it in place and furnished just the small quantity needed for application. An inner lid kept the powder from clinging to the mirror. The need for a close-fitting lid was paramount. Compressed powder in block form, with a firmer velour pad, was in use by *c.* 1930 and led to the term 'powder compact'. When thin, round, 4-inch wide powder boxes became fashionable in the early 1930s, they were called 'flap-jacks' (see cat. 198 and Selwyn 1945, p. 109).

Most of the Cartier vanity cases contain lipstick and rouge as well as powder, while dual-purpose vanity cases contained an upper compartment for cigarettes.

BIBLIOGRAPHY

The publications that follow are referred to in abbreviated form in the catalogue text. Publications on source material for a particular object that are referred to once only are listed in full in the relevant entry and are not repeated here. A number of publications are devoted solely to Cartier and these are listed in section A. Almost all the exhibition catalogues listed under the heading 'Exhibitions' in the catalogue entries will also be found in this section.

A. PUBLICATIONS DEVOTED SOLELY TO CARTIER

Monographs

BARRACCA, J., NEGRETTI, G., and NENCINI, F., 1989. *Le Temps de Cartier*, Milan, with English text (French edition with same title, Paris 1990).

COLOGNI, F., and MOCCHETTI, E., 1992. *Made by Cartier, 150 Years of Tradition and Innovation*, Milan (French edition, *L'Objet Cartier, 150 ans de tradition et d'innovation*, Paris).

COLOGNI, F., and NUSSBAUM, E., 1995. *Cartier, Le Joaillier du Platine*, Paris and Lausanne (English edition, *Platinum by Cartier. Triumphs of the Jewelers' Art*, New York 1996).

NADELHOFFER, H., 1984. *Cartier. Jewelers Extraordinary*, London (reprinted 1994).

TRETIACK, P., 1996. *Cartier*, Paris.

Exhibition catalogues

HONG KONG 1995. *Cartier 'King of Jewellers - Jewellers of Kings'*.

LAUSANNE 1996. *Cartier, splendeurs de la joaillerie*. Fondation de l'Hermitage.

LONDON 1988. *The Cartier Museum*. Goldsmiths' Hall.

LOS ANGELES 1982. *Retrospective Louis Cartier, Masterworks of Art Deco*. Los Angeles County Museum of Art.

MILAN 1988. Raffaele De Grada (ed.), *Platinum Rhinoceros, Sogni, segni e fantasie dei gioielli Cartier*. Museo Civico di Storia Naturale di Milano.

NAPLES 1988. *Capolavori di Cartier*. Castel Sant'Elmo.

NEW ORLEANS 1988. *Reflections of Elegance. Cartier Jewels from the Lindemann Collection*. New Orleans Museum of Art (exhibition also held at Birmingham Museum of Art, Birmingham, Alabama; The Walters Art Gallery, Baltimore; San Diego Museum of Art, San Diego).

NEW YORK 1976. *Retrospective - Louis Cartier, One Hundred and One Years of the Jeweler's Art*. Cartier New York.

PARIS 1989. G. Chazal, *L'Art de Cartier*. Musée du Petit Palais.

ROME 1990. G. Chazal, *L'Art de Cartier*. Accademia Valentino.

ST LOUIS 1995. S. Neely and D. Cassens, *The Legacy of Elma Rumsey Cartier*, Saint Louis University.

ST PETERSBURG 1992. *L'Art de Cartier*. State Hermitage Museum.

TOKYO 1995. *The World of French Jewelry Art - The Art of Cartier*. Tokyo Metropolitan Teien Art Museum.

VENICE 1986. *I gioielli degli anni '20-40. Cartier e i grandi del Déco*. Palazzo Fortuny.

B. GENERAL BIBLIOGRAPHY

Books and articles

ANDREWS, C., 1994. *Amulets of Ancient Egypt*, London.

ANDREWS, C., 1996. *Ancient Egyptian Jewellery* (2nd edn), London.

ARWAS, V., 1992. *Art Deco*, London.

BEEBE, L., 1967. *The Big Spenders*, London.

BALFOUR, I., 1987. *Famous Diamonds*, London.

BURY, S., 1991. *Jewellery 1789-1910. The International Era*, 2 vols, Woodbridge.

CAILLES F., 1994. *René Boivin. Jeweller*, London.

CERVAL, M. de, 1992. *Mauboussin*, Paris.

FIELD, L., 1992. *The Jewels of Queen Elizabeth II, Her Personal Collection* (2nd edn), London (first published New York, 1987).

FLANNER, J., 1972. *Paris was Yesterday 1925-1939*, London.

FORBES, R., 1939. *India of the Princes*, London.

FOUQUET, G., 1934. *La Bijouterie, la Joaillerie, la Bijouterie de Fantaisie au XXe Siècle*, Paris.

GABARDI, M., 1989. *Art Deco Jewellery 1920-1949*, Woodbridge (French edition: *Bijoux de l'art déco aux années 40*, Paris 1989).

GARDNER, J., 1993. *James Gardner, the Artful Designer*, London.

GERE, C., TAIT, H., RUDOE, J., and WILSON, T., 1984. *The Art of the Jeweller. A Catalogue of the Hull Grundy Gift to the British Museum*, 2 vols, London.

GERE, C., and CULME, J., 1993. *Garrard. The Crown Jewellers for 150 Years*, London.

HABSBURG, G. von, 1979. *Fabergé*, London.

HEYMANN, C. D., 1983. *Poor Little Rich Girl. The Life and Legend of Barbara Hutton*, London.

JONES, Owen, 1856. *The Grammar of Ornament*, London.

MARKEVITCH, E., 1987. *Bijoux Indiens*, London.

McLEAN, E. Walsh, 1936. *Father Struck it Rich*, London.

MENKES, S., 1985. *The Royal Jewels*, London.

MESNARD, J., 1887. *Les Merveilles de L'Exposition de 1867*, Paris.

MUNN, G., 1993. *The Triumph of Love. Jewelry 1530-1930*, London.

NERET, G., 1988. *Boucheron. Four Generations of a World-Renowned Jeweler*, Fribourg and New York.

GLOSSARY

Aigrette

(French = a tuft of feathers.) A hat or hair ornament in the form of jewelled feathers or a brooch to hold a tuft of real feathers.

Baton-cut

See **baguette-cut**.

Baguette-cut

A gemstone cut in the shape of a long narrow rectangle with a flat top. According to Selwyn 1945, 'baton' is used for a larger stone (such as those on the band of the topaz head ornament, cat. 226) and 'baguette' for a smaller one of the same size, but in many cases the two terms are used interchangeably. The Cartier London records from between the wars use the term 'baton', while the New York records refer to 'stick' brilliants. The shape of the cut gave its name to the baguette watch (see cat. 210-12).

Bandeau

A flexible, flat, gem-set band worn low on the forehead, tied at the back with cords.

Bezel

The salient or characteristic part of a ring, such as the setting including the stone.

Boucle déployante

Folding buckle for wrist watches and bracelets, formed of three hinged curved elements that open out and snap shut (see cat. 27.1). They were introduced by Cartier in 1910 and were easier to use than a traditional buckle and strap.

Bought in

Trade term used in the UK for finished pieces purchased from other firms.

Brevet

Patent. Many of the Paris-made pieces are marked *Breveté SGDG* (often abbreviated *BTE*). The letters *SGDG* stand for *sans garantie du gouvernement*.

Brilliant (*brillant*)

English and French terms for a brilliant-cut diamond. The standard brilliant-cut has 58 facets, 33 on the top part of the stone and 25 on the lower part. Most modern brilliant-cuts are circular in outline, but older stones were often 'cushion-shaped', i.e. squarish with rounded corners.

Briolette

A drop-shaped stone cut with facets all over.

Broche draperie

Term used in the Cartier records to describe a brooch in the form of a swag or garland with a central element hanging from it; the brooch pin is hidden when worn, to give the effect of gem-set drapery.

Broche étrier

Literally 'stirrup brooch'. Term used in the Cartier records initially to describe a brooch formed of a bar with upturned ends joined by the brooch pin and thus resembling an upside-down stirrup in shape. Later, the brooches were actually designed in the form of upended stirrups (see cat. 141).

Broche de décolleté

Term used in the Cartier records to describe a new type of brooch introduced *c.* 1925 and designed to outline the central fastening of a dress. Attached with a brooch-pin at the top, it could be long enough to reach the waist with further pins as necessary (see cat. 274 and p. 18, figs 10-11).

Cabochon

A stone with a polished rounded surface that has not been cut into facets.

Calibré-cut

A stone cut in a specific shape to fit the setting exactly.

Cartouche

An area defined by a frame of fanciful design.

Cavetto

A hollow moulding, about a quarter of a circle in section, seen for example on the cornice or projecting moulding on the Egyptian temple gate clock (cat. 88).

Chasing

The art of working metal from the front with punches and a hammer to coax it into the right place to form the pattern. In engraving the metal is taken away, whereas in chasing it is simply moved.

Cliquet pin

A brooch formed of two elements joined by a long pin attached to one element and with a snap or click fitting at the other end. Cartier examples date from shortly before the First World War. Sometimes the two elements were identical (see cat. 97), but more usually the top element was larger with a small decorative element or *cache-pointe* at the base to hide the end of the pin and secure the brooch (see cat. 78). A nick in the end of the pin was caught in a sprung fitting on the reverse of the *cache-pointe*. Described as 'broches cliquet' in the archive records, these brooches have traditionally been called jabot pins. But as they were worn on a lapel or in the fashionable cloche hats of the 1920s (see cat. 95.1) rather than used to secure a jabot or cravat, the term cliquet pin has been used here.

According to Pierre Cartier, quoted in a newspaper article on 'Jewelry forecasts for 1925', 'One of the novelties for the smart woman to wear, especially since the small hat has appeared, is the cliquet brooch. The pin frequently contains extremely valuable pearls, and in fact this ornament has become so fashionable that it is worn in the morning, made of coral and semi-precious stones, and in the afternoon it is made of pearls and precious stones, especially large pearls.'

Closed-back setting

A method of setting a gemstone whereby the lower part of the gemstone is entirely encased in the setting, leaving only the upper part of the stone visible.

Collet-set

A simple box setting with straight sides enclosing the gem.

Devant de corsage

A large brooch that covers the central part of the bodice in the manner of the eighteenth-century stomacher, which filled the area from the bust to the waist and was often formed of jewelled elements sewn to the corsage.

Email pékin mille raies

See **enamel**.

Emerald-cut

A rectangular stone with mitred corners, producing an octagonal outline, with a large central facet or table and a series of sloping rectangular facets (step-cut). Mainly used for emeralds, but large diamonds are sometimes cut in this way.

Enamel

Coloured glass, or a combination of vitreous glazes, fused onto a metallic surface.

Most of the enamel decoration on the objects catalogued here is **champlevé** enamel. In this technique the metal surface is gouged out to create troughs and channels, each separated by a thin ridge of metal. The coloured enamels, in powdered form, are laid in the troughs and fused onto the metal, with the ridges forming the outline of the pattern. A variant of this method is **basse-taille** enamel, in which translucent, as opposed to opaque, enamels are thinly applied over the metal so that the patterns engraved in it can be seen through the enamel. This method was perfected in eighteenth-century Paris for use on gold boxes with engine-turned or *guilloché* decoration forming delicate patterns resembling sun-rays or watered silk beneath the enamel (see cat. 40-43). Another variant was **ombré** or shaded enamelling, in which the thicknesses of successive layers of enamel were varied as they were applied. This gave an iridescent or opalescent surface effect (see cat. 41).

A different technique altogether and one rarely used by Cartier is **cloisonné** enamel, in which thin strips of metal are soldered to the surface forming the outline of the pattern or picture and creating cells or *cloisons* into which the powdered enamel is laid and fused. The sarcophagus vanity case (cat. 87) was originally designed to have cloisonné enamel on the base; the enamel was never applied but the *cloisons* remain. A variant of cloisonné enamel was **plique-à-jour** enamel, in which translucent enamel was held within a metal cellwork but without a backing, to give the effect of a stained-glass window. During firing the cells were attached to a temporary metal sheet, removed after firing. The technique was widely fashionable *c.* 1900 and appears in pieces in the Art Nouveau style purchased from other suppliers and stocked by Cartier.

During the 1920s boxes and vanity cases were frequently decorated with **émail pékin mille raies**, a term used in the Cartier records to describe thin parallel stripes of enamel against a gold ground (see cat. 63, 65 and 131).

Engine-turning

Engraving metal with a lathe to produce a multiplicity of symmetrical linear patterns executed with precision. The French term for engine-turned is *guilloché*.

Engraving

Cutting metal away with a burin or V-shaped tool.

Faience

The name traditionally given to the glazed composition used in ancient Egypt for scarabs and other amulets.

Fourche

Arch-shaped tortoiseshell comb with double prong, introduced *c.* 1900.

Gallery

A raised platinum frame at the back of a jewel that lifts the piece off the body and allows light to pass through the stones.

Grosgrain ribbon

A silk ribbon with wide ribbing.

Inro

Japanese term for a small case to carry personal effects, comprising a series of compartments which slot together and are held in place by a cord.

Integral hinge

The invisible hinge found on many of Cartier's cigarette boxes and vanity cases. A finely rolled, hinged cylinder with a traverse pin was attached so as to be flush with the walls of the box and thus invisible when the box was closed. Integral hinges were a feature of eighteenth-century French gold boxes.

Kokoshnik

(Russian = cockscomb.) A head ornament in the form of a broad band that flared outwards.

Lacque burgauté

See **lacquer**.

Lacquer

A natural resin made from the sap of the lacquer tree, which is native to China. It is applied in numerous layers, each of which is allowed to dry before the next is added. Once dry, it is impervious to water and can be carved, inlaid or painted. The technique was perfected in China and later transmitted to Japan. Natural lacquer dries black, but with the addition of cinnabar it turns a rich red.

Much of the lacquer used by Cartier was in the form of small plaques imported from the Far East. These were of black lacquer inlaid with mother-of-pearl, a method known as **lacque burgauté**, and were made in the nineteenth century either on the Ryukyu islands between China and Japan, or in Nagasaki, the main centre of production in Japan itself. The mother-of-pearl was partly tinted in purple and green. After the lacquer had been brought level with the mother-of-pearl inlay, a final layer of lacquer was applied to the whole object, thus concealing the mother-of-pearl. The surface was then rubbed with pumice stone until the inlay was once more exposed. In this way a perfectly smooth surface was obtained.

Cartier also used lacquer as a substitute for enamel that did not chip or crack so easily. This was particularly important for cigarette cases and also for the lacquer bracelets decorated with double clip brooches. Although black was the dominant colour, several other colours were used, and it may be that some of

PAL, P., *et al.* 1989. *The Romance of the Taj Mahal*, London.

PLIMPTON, G., and HEMPHILL, C. (eds), 1984. *D. V. Diana Vreeland*, New York.

POSSÉMÉ, E., 1993. 'L'influence d'un maître' in *Fabergé*, Connaissance des Arts Special Issue, no. 45.

PRINGUÉ, G.-L., 1950. *Trente ans de dîners en ville*, Paris.

PRODDOW, P., and HEALY, D., 1987. *American Jewelry. Glamour and Tradition*, Fribourg and New York.

PRODDOW, P., HEALY, D., and FASEL, M., 1992. *Hollywood Jewels, Movies, Jewelry, Stars*, New York.

PRODDOW, P., and FASAL, M., 1996. *Diamonds. A Century of Spectacular Jewels*, New York.

RAULET, S., 1986. *Van Cleef & Arpels*, Paris.

RAWSON, J., 1995. *Chinese Jade. From the Neolithic to the Qing*, London.

RHODES JAMES, R. (ed.), 1967. *Chips: The Diaries of Sir Henry Channon*, London.

RUBIN, N., 1995. *American Empress. The Life and Times of Marjorie Merriweather Post*, New York.

SCARISBRICK, D., 1989. *Ancestral Jewels*, London.

SCARISBRICK, D., 1995. *Chaumet. Master Jewellers since 1780*, Paris.

SELWYN, A., 1945. *The Retail Jeweller's Handbook*, London.

SMITH, J. S., 1982. *Elsie de Wolfe: A Life in the High Style*, New York.

SNOWMAN, K., 1952. *Carl Fabergé. Goldsmith to the Imperial Court of Russia*, London.

SNOWMAN, K., 1990. *Eighteenth Century Gold Boxes of Europe* (2nd edn), Woodbridge.

SNOWMAN, K. (ed.), 1990. *The Master Jewelers*, London.

STRONGE, S., *et al.* 1988. *A Golden Treasury. Jewellery from the Indian Subcontinent*, London.

VANDERBILT BALSAN, C., 1953. *The Glitter and the Gold*, London.

VEVER, H., 1904–8. *La Bijouterie Française au XIXe Siècle*, 3 vols, Paris.

WESTMINSTER, Loelia, Duchess of, 1961. *Grace and Favour*, London.

Exhibition catalogues

BRUSSELS 1982. M. Latif, *Mughal Jewels*. Musées Royaux d'Art et d'Histoire.

LIMOGES 1992. M. C. Kiener, *Emaux Art Déco*. Musée Municipal de L'Evêché.

MINNEAPOLIS 1971. B. Hillier, *The World of Art Deco*. Minneapolis Institute of Arts.

MUNICH 1986. G. von Habsburg, *Fabergé. Hofjuwelier der Zaren*. Kunsthalle der Hypo-Kulturstiftung.

MUNICH 1989. *Pariser Schmuck vom Zweiten Kaiserreich zur Belle Epoque*. Bayerisches Nationalmuseum (English translation: *The Belle Epoque of French Jewellery 1850-1910*, London 1991).

NEW YORK 1985. S. Cary Welch, *India: Art and Culture 1300-1900*. Metropolitan Museum of Art.

PARIS 1966. *Les Années 25*. Musée des Arts Décoratifs.

PARIS 1976. *Cinquantenaire de l'Exposition de 1925*. Musée des Arts Décoratifs.

PARIS 1983. M.-N. de Gary, *Les Fouquet. Bijoutiers et joailliers à Paris 1860-1960*. Musée des Arts Décoratifs.

PARIS 1992. *Van Cleef & Arpels*. Palais Galliéra.

PARIS 1994. *Egyptomania. L'Egypte dans l'art occidental 1730-1930*. Musée du Louvre.

SAN FRANCSICO 1996. G. von Habsburg, *Fabergé in America* (first shown New York 1996, organised by the Fine Arts Museums of San Francisco).

ST PETERSBURG/LONDON 1993. G. von Habsburg and M. Lopato, *Fabergé: Imperial Jeweller*. State Hermitage Museum; Victoria and Albert Museum.

TAIPEI 1986. *Catalogue of the Exhibition of Ch'ing Dynasty Costume Accessories*. National Palace Museum.

LIST OF LENDERS

Hillwood Museum, Washington cat. 100

Kurt König cat. 26

Mr and Mrs George L. Lindemann
cat. 113, 133, 137, 162, 176, 223

Metropolitan Museum of Art,
New York cat. 39

Musée des Arts Décoratifs, Paris
cat. 47, 107

Eric Nussbaum cat. 94

Private collections cat. 23, 32, 40, 83,
85-8, 91, 104, 109–10, 114–15, 117, 141,
144, 147, 155–7, 170, 235–46

PHOTOGRAPHIC ACKNOWLEDGEMENTS

David Behl: cat. 113, 133, 137, 162, 176, 223

Peter Clayton: cat. 83.1

Corbis Bettman: cat. 217.1

Edward Owen: fig. 23 and cat. 100

Precious Stones Inc., New York: cat. 269.4

INDEX